Expectations and Demands in Online Teaching:
Practical Experiences

Sorin Gudea
Claremont Graduate University, USA

 Information Science Publishing

Hershey • New York

Acquisition Editor:	Kristin Klinger
Senior Managing Editor:	Jennifer Neidig
Managing Editor:	Jamie Snavely
Assistant Managing Editor:	Carole Coulson
Development Editor:	Kristin Roth
Copy Editor:	Becky Shore
Typesetter:	Christopher Hrobak
Cover Design:	Lisa Tosheff
Printed at:	Yurchak Printing Inc.

Published in the United States of America by
Information Science Publishing (an imprint of IGI Global)
701 E. Chocolate Avenue
Hershey PA 17033
Tel: 717-533-8845
Fax: 717-533-8661
E-mail: cust@igi-global.com
Web site: http://www.igi-global.com

and in the United Kingdom by
Information Science Publishing (an imprint of IGI Global)
3 Henrietta Street
Covent Garden
London WC2E 8LU
Tel: 44 20 7240 0856
Fax: 44 20 7379 3313
Web site: http://www.eurospanbookstore.com

Library of Congress Cataloging-in-Publication Data

Expectations and demands in online teaching : practical experiences / Sorin Walker Gudea, editor.
    p. cm.
  Includes bibliographical references and index.
  Summary: "This book offers a better understanding of how teachers experience the online environment by exploring various dimensions of online teaching"--Provided by publisher.
  ISBN 978-1-59904-747-8 (hardcover) -- ISBN 978-1-59904-749-2 (ebook)
  1. Teaching--Computer network resources. 2. Computer-assisted instruction. 3. Distance education. 4. Internet in education. I. Gudea, Sorin Walker.
  LB1044.87.E97 2008
  371.33'4--dc22
                          2008008464

British Cataloguing in Publication Data
A Cataloguing in Publication record for this book is available from the British Library.

Expectations and Demands in Online Teaching:

Practical Experiences

Table of Contents

Foreword

One way in which I make a personal judgment of a manuscript's worthiness is by the number of margin notes I make. Judging from the amount of ink I went through when reading the manuscript for this book, the text is worthy indeed. As both a researcher and practitioner of online teaching, I found many interesting and provocative insights in Dr. Gudea's book. My copy of the manuscript is littered with margin notes such as "Interesting!" "Research idea?" and the like.

Regardless of the context, effective teaching requires both motivated teachers and motivated learners; one without the other borders on the useless. Despite the considerable, growing interest in online education, there are few in-depth studies of teachers' attitudes and perceptions of online teaching. This book is a refreshing exception. Through his ambitious research project, Dr. Gudea provides those interested in online teaching with two significant gifts. First, he offers a comprehensive, well-supported theory of online teaching. Such a theory is a clear contribution to researchers interested in this area by providing a ready means for developing testable hypotheses. Second, the insights offered throughout the text hold significant value for teachers and administrators. Teachers and administrators interested in online learning can use this text as a handbook full of valuable insights. The author carefully crafted the book so the reader can "skip around," reading chapters of particular interest in whatever order strikes one's fancy.

In addition to the focus on teachers' perceptions and attitudes, several other features set this book apart. First, it is based on extensive and rigorous research. Dr. Gudea followed a well-established, rigorous methodology while conducting his research. (In fact, this book can serve as a roadmap for others interested in qualitative research.) He interviewed literally dozens of educators engaged in online teaching, yielding a rich set of data, which he analyzes using well-established methods. Throughout the book he also compares his findings to previous research, pointing out areas of agreement and divergence. This technique has the dual benefit of solidifying earlier research and pointing out areas that need further investigation.

Second, Dr. Gudea took pains to interview a wide variety of online teachers. This yields a great diversity of opinions, which I found quite fascinating. Of particular interest is his inclusion of part-time, adjunct faculty. These individuals, who may teach for multiple universities, make up an increasing portion of college faculty. However, few researchers bother to tap this resource. Part-time faculty face a number of unique challenges and pressures; by interviewing these individuals, Dr. Gudea is able to bring many of these challenges to light.

Another feature of the text that I found particularly useful is the inclusion of a great many direct quotes, which adds considerable value. Including these quotes enables readers to gain a deeper understanding of the teachers' thoughts. In addition, the quotes allow readers to draw their own conclusions, rather than solely relying on the author's interpretation. Many of these quotes make for fascinating reading and provide interesting glances into the minds of the instructors.

Like it or not, online teaching and learning is here to stay. According to the Sloan Consortium, over 2.5 million people are currently taking online courses, and over 100,000 teachers are involved in online teaching. These numbers are only going to increase. Therefore, it is imperative that teachers, researchers and administrators understand what it takes to effectively deliver and manage online learning. Dr. Gudea's timely and insightful text goes a long way towards helping build this understanding. Anyone interested in the teaching side of online education is well advised to read this book; it is an investment that will be rewarded many times over.

Craig Van Slyke

Craig Van Slyke is an associate professor of management information systems and chair of the Decision Science/Management Information Systems department at Saint Louis University. Prior to joining SLU, he was on the faculties of University of Central Florida and Ohio University. He teaches a variety of courses at both the undergraduate and graduate levels. He holds a PhD in information systems from the University of South Florida. Dr. Van Slyke also spent many years in the information technology industry in a number of capacities. His current research interests focus on issues related to the adoption of information and communication technologies. Dr. Van Slyke has published in a number of journals, including Information Resource Management Journal, Communications of the ACM, Journal of the AIS, European Journal of Information Systems, Decision Sciences, and Database for Advances in Information Systems, among other journals. He serves on the editorial board of Information Resource Management Journal and the Journal of Information Systems Education. In addition, he has coauthored three information systems textbooks. Dr. Van Slyke holds leadership positions in AIS SIG:ED and the Southern Association for Information Systems.

Preface

Introduction

Educational researchers have conducted many studies to investigate individual and group learning, as well as the impact of technology on the learning process. A great deal of literature is available to the researcher, a clear indication of the degree of interest around online learning and distance education in general. However, the great majority of the studies focus on the students' perspectives (H.-L. Yang & Tang, 2003). A review of the literature finds only a handful of studies that attempt to address the teachers' point of view. Little has been published on the online teaching experience itself. Furthermore, the literature review reveals tremendous inconsistency in findings.

My interest in the online learning environment started in early 2000, as I began teaching technology courses for the University of Phoenix.[1] It was there that, for the first time, I got acquainted with the field of distance education and the use of the Internet to teach courses. Over time, based on my own observations and discussions with other online teachers at different universities, it occurred to me that the teachers describe their online experiences as either satisfying or frustrating to various degrees. Yet, none of them are left untouched by their online teaching experiences. As I later discovered, these stances were not unique to one teacher, or to one university. Rather, online teachers from different educational institutions and universities, responsible for teaching different subject matters, report similar experiences.

If teachers are using information technology (IT) to teach online, what does that mean to them? What variations in meaning exist? What do online teachers experience? How do teachers in an online setting view teaching? How do they view it otherwise? What do they think the expectations are? What are the demands? Teachers seem to adjust to the teaching environment and to embrace change. Yet, as they adjust, what do they give up? What do they feel they are gaining? These are some of the questions I try to answer in this book.

The material presented in this book is based on numerous hours of personal interviews, and the answers to the previous questions came from the online teachers themselves. For this, I am immensely grateful and would like to once again give thanks to all the teachers who had accepted to be interviewed. They gave even more of their time so that this study could be completed for the benefit of the entire profession, for students and teachers alike, and for the society as a whole as it marches into the uncharted territories of teaching online.

What gives value to this book is the light it sheds on the lesser known territory of teaching online from the teachers' perspectives, and, even more so, the invaluable quotes coming from the interviewed participants; the honesty, sincerity, and courage with which they opened their hearts and looked into the good and bad of their work and profession as it goes through this transitional process of developing a new way of guiding thoughts and disseminating information. Teachers that tackle online teaching are pioneers, ground breaking new territories as this new way of education develops into its own. The integration of cutting-edge technology into one of the oldest professions known to human kind is no simple thing.

The book, intended to be a handbook, is written in such a way that each chapter can stand on its own and can be read individually. Hence, some repetitions occur, and I hope you will accept them. This is particularly the case in Chapters III through VIII, which attempt to paint a picture that is as complete as possible. The many quotes sprinkled throughout the book pass on the passion of the respondents and help frame the research questions mentioned previously. Furthermore, these quotes are paramount to presenting teachers' thoughts, perceptions, and beliefs; their lived experiences in online teaching.

Several categories of people stand to benefit from the information relayed by this study. Some of them are the teachers themselves; others are the course developers; the educational technology specialists; the school administrators; and last, but not least, the students or anyone else interested and questioning this new area of development in the field of education. The teachers who are teaching online, or those considering doing it, would benefit from reading this book because it is based on information shared by other teachers who have experienced online teaching. In a similar manner, course developers could benefit from the insight provided by the teachers who teach online in order to produce courses that take into account the shortcomings of the technology used for delivery. Educational technology specialists stand to learn from the teachers' experience teaching online through better being able to identify new potential directions for research and technology development, as well as for educational systems that are more user friendly, easier to use and to support rich media interfaces.

Table 1. Perspectives on online learning

Study	Findings	Topic
Brewer (2001)	Organizational context affects faculty decisions.	Technology/pedagogy connection
Chu (2002)	Perceived technology importance; prior experience with technology; specialty; age; communication behavior; disbelief in the quality of learning.	Faculty adoption of technology
Esch (2003)	Compare effectiveness of training delivered online and in the classroom.	Training effectiveness
Chandler (1999)	Materials prepared for on-campus use can be applied to distance learners.	Effectiveness
Morse (2003)	Growing dependence on ALN for learning and training in a multicultural context. Increased flexibility, quantity, and quality of participation. Technology-related frustration, coordination issues, skill deficits.	Asynchronous learning networks
Dutton et al. (2002)	Significant doubts about an online medium that does not provide face-to-face. Flexibility and synchronicity of online is appreciated.	Benefits
Maxwell (2001)	Faculty uses a constructivist approach.	Teaching style
Guidera (2000)	Online improves promptness of feedback; promotes time to task; communicates higher expectations; promotes respect for diverse learning styles. The degree of interaction is perceived as a weakness. Increase in workload.	Effectiveness
Huang (2001)	Moderately easy to learn and use.	Technology
Varvel (2003)	Faculty performance increases with training.	Faculty development
Koory (2003)	Course design is more important than the learning modality employed.	Learning outcomes
Rovai (2002)	Active learning enhances online learning.	Effectiveness
Iken (2000)	Dissatisfaction.	Effectiveness
Kinuthia (2003)	Positive faculty attitudes. Drivers: personal motivation and facilitation of student learning. Perceived barriers: lack of time, skills, administrative support; funding; equipment; lack of training.	Web-based instruction
Kumari (1999)	Online education requires significant time.	Effectiveness
Lewis (2002)	Faculty development; institutional support; educational practices; collaboration.	Online education
McDonald Lucas (2002)	Positive faculty perceptions.	Online education
Hill Martin (2003)	Technical; professional objections; job security; copyrights; and course control.	Online education adoption barriers
Mendenhall (2003)	Individualized learning; modular; interactive.	Success factors
Monson (2003)	Interaction is important.	Online dynamics
Myers (2003)	Positive experience.	Student online experience
Perry (2003)	Faculty expertise is required; clear course organization; timely feedback to students.	Online teaching
Scott (2003)	Economic interests; little administrative support; and lack of technology skills.	Online education
Yang (2003)	Compared four distance education modalities.	Efficiency

Background

Current research points to various aspects of online education, yet a complete picture cannot be drawn. Several recurring themes underline the perceptions of faculty members in relation to online education. Instructors and students alike when asked to assess their online teaching or learning experience either love it or hate it, with few reactions in between. A great deal of research has been published about the online learning environment. The dimensions explored in the published studies include various psychological, social, pedagogical, and technological factors that affect teachers' attitudes. Among them are the organizational context (Brewer, 2001); personal interests (Scott, 2003); technology availability, skills, and ease of use (Chu, 2002); academic subject (Kinuthia, 2003); interaction (Guidera, 2000; Huang, 2001; Monson, 2003); faculty development (Hill Martin, 2003; Lewis, 2002); experience (McDonald Lucas, 2002); expertise (Perry, 2003); pedagogical skills (Angelo & Cross, 1993); lack of resources (Myers, 2003); disbelief in the quality of learning (Chu, 2002); the role of the teacher in the online environment (Kisner, 2001; Oliver, 2004); and increased time demands (Guidera, 2000; Iken, 2000; Kumari, 1999; University of North Carolina, 2004). Some of the studies are summarized in Table 1.

A review of the studies indicates that there are obvious differences in terms of the issues reported by faculty members and their ranking. Despite this growing body of work, anecdotal evidence indicates that we still do not know what the true issues are, or at least not all of them and how important they are. A clear understanding of the online teaching experience is still lacking.

This book brings value through its exploration of the online teaching experience, as lived by teachers.

Online Education and Teaching

The quality of the online education experience has been the subject of ongoing debate among researchers and lay people alike. Among other factors, user satisfaction, student performance, and ease of use are discussed in the literature. However, despite a growing body of research and published studies in the field, some users—teachers and students alike—do not believe the approach is working (Cyrs, 1997; Schell, 2004). There are many conflicting views related to the use of technology to teach online. The variety of the issues revealed in research papers indicates that a good understanding of what online teaching entails is still lacking. The literature stops short of giving educational leaders a theory of how teachers experience and adjust to the online environment (Hatterius, 2004).

Faculty members often report opposite views of the online environment. Many instructors question their ability to utilize technology in order to provide an effective, user-friendly learning environment for the students (Chu, 2002; Kumari, 1999). Stated differently, teachers report frustration with a variety of aspects of online education. Frustration and satisfaction can be construed as indicators summarizing many diverse experiences. That being said, it seems that there are matters not well explained in relation to teaching online. Teachers' attitudes, whether positive (Esch, 2003; Kinuthia, 2003) or negative (Chu, 2002; Kumari, 1999), seem to depend on many factors. Some teachers, when faced with the online environment, react not only in attitudinal terms but also in behavioral and other terms. For some, the change results in favorable reactions and attitudes, while for others, it is quite the opposite. Some teachers are successful and others are not. Why is that? There is ample evidence that some teachers have experiences that lead to frustration and dissatisfaction. Research is needed to address educators' experiences with online teaching and to help achieve the full potential of online education while ensuring access to adequate content, learning tools, and technologies.

Online education continues to expand (Bianchi, 2000; Chambers, 1999; Irvine, 2001). Mendenhall (2007) cited an Eduventures report stating that 7% of U.S. postsecondary students were taking courses solely online. By 2008, every tenth student will be enrolled in an online degree plan (Golden, 2006). However, online education has not reached yet its full potential. A recent report found that only 4.6% of chief academic officers saw no significant barriers to the widespread adoption of online learning (Sloan-C-Resources, 2006).

Teachers are an important component of online education, and their beliefs can affect the way they teach (Cuban, 1993). They are a key factor to educational change (Tyack & Cuban, 1995). As online education continues to expand, teachers and educational administrators must consider a variety of factors related to technology (administration, expectations, curriculum, course design and delivery, social interaction, learning, teaching) that may result in changes affecting education as a whole. Changes that involve deep understanding cannot begin with the whole system; rather, they have to begin with the individual and spread through the system (Senge et al., 2000). A better understanding of the changes teachers experience in relation to online education has the potential to help teachers and educational administrators plan more effectively and be better positioned to address changes stemming from online education. It follows that increasing the teachers' and schools' capacity for managing change and bringing about continuous improvement is imperative (Inos & Quigley, 1995).

A good image is important if any industry or profession wishes to attract the best people (Lim, Teo, & See, 2000). As higher education institutions strive to find new ways to serve a changing society, the faculty members' acceptance of the medium used for teaching is of significant importance (Goetzinger & Valentine, 1963; Jensen, 1995). If teachers are using IT to teach online, what does that mean to them? What variations in meaning exist? What do online teachers experience?

In general, faculty members recognize that the use of Internet resources in education cannot be avoided. Technologies that can help distance education offer a number of benefits to students and teachers alike (Chandler et al., 1999). Yet, faculty members' disbelief in the quality of learning is a major obstacle in their adoption of Internet resources for their courses (Chu, 2002).

Some faculty members express general dissatisfaction with the technologies available for teaching and assert that the demands for teaching are also greater than in the recent past (Oravec, 2003). Many teachers are unhappy about their lack of control over the situation (Altbach & Lewis, 1995). If it is true that teachers adjust to the teaching environment, they embrace change. Yet, as they adjust, what do they give up, and what do they feel they are gaining?

Models of learning can influence the design of the online teaching environment and, ultimately, its effectiveness (Alavi, 1994; Piccoli, Ahmad, & Ives, 2001). The online environment may help the teacher with class preparation issues, assist shy students, and help deal with sensitive issues (Horton, 2000). Yet, faculty members' perceptions of the effectiveness of the online learning environment vary (Esch, 2003; Guidera, 2000; Huang, 2001; Morse, 2003). What can make the online teaching process effective? The answer comes, at least in part, from the teachers themselves.

It is important to help teachers prepare for the online environment, not only by providing technical training and curriculum development support, but also for allowing them to learn from other teachers' experiences. For this reason, it is important to find out how teachers in an online setting view teaching and to learn more about what they think the expectations and the demands are online. In short, to learn how teachers experience the online environment.

Education is situated at the intersection of teaching efforts and learning efforts by different people—teachers and students. Dreeben (1970) found that prospective teachers would tend to be caring people who are not as much concerned with monetary gains as they are with doing creative work. In other words, teachers care: They are concerned about student learning, and about education itself.

Yet, much of the published literature focuses exclusively on the learners. While clearly the student body plays a significant part in education, one cannot discount the teachers. Questions concerning the circumstances of online teaching effectiveness can be asked. Some teachers may find themselves to be more effective in the on-ground classroom, while others will find themselves to be more effective online. From talking to teachers who have been involved in online teaching, it often seems like they are doing very different things. The meaning associated with online teaching may be different, yet the reasons behind it are not clear.

People often use the label *online teaching* like they know what they are talking about. They use the phrase like it has the same meaning for everyone involved in online education. Teaching is (at least to some extent) about "awakening the enthusiasm involved in the learning process" (Dreeben, 1970, p. 82). And, if it is true that teaching activities consist of an amalgam of spontaneous, diffuse, and ill-defined elements that together make teaching successful, do teachers believe that tradeoffs to teaching online affect their teaching? If so, in what ways? We must look at this from the perspective of the people who are doing it, and we must try to understand, based on their experiences, what makes sense with respect to the online teaching activities they engage in.

What follows are the results of a study predicated upon a particular stance for inquiry that is very flexible. The teachers that participated in the study shared their experiences with the author, whose task was to simply let them tell their story to the readers.

How the Answers Were Developed

In seeking to describe and analyze teacher attitudes in relation to the online teaching environment, the focus of the inquiry centered on how teachers view online teaching.

This book presents the results of a study that consists of a grounded-theory approach, which relies on in-depth interviews with faculty members who teach online courses. The intent was to sample professionals working at different colleges and universities that offer online classes, and to interview them to develop a theory highlighting issues they can identify in relation to their online teaching experiences. This qualitative study builds a theory providing a grounded understanding of the experience of teaching online, as viewed by the teachers.

Grounded theory relies on theoretical sampling and constant comparative analysis. Coding—open, axial, and selective—is used to create a theory. The unit of analysis is the individual teacher. Systematic coding and analysis, in an inductive manner, enables the researcher to develop a theory that is consistent with the data. The theory that gradually emerges through the research represents an attempt to develop an explanation about reality. It classifies and organizes concepts and may help predict

Table 2. Respondent age groups

Age group	Respondents	Percentage
< 30	0	0%
30–40	8	18%
40–50	16	36%
50–60	11	25%
> 60	8	18%
Declined to state	1	2%

future occurrences of events. A more detailed discussion of grounded theory as a research method is offered in Appendix A.

In this study, the developed grounded theory shows how teachers experience online teaching. This theory fills a gap in the research literature and may assist teachers and educational administrators in better understanding how the online environment affects teachers. By research design, the grounded-theory study was limited in terms of the sample size and scope of inquiry. The use of a theoretical sample and its relatively small size *does* decrease the generalizability (transferability) of the findings of this study. The interview participants were selected purposefully, further reducing the generalizability of the study. All of the participants are involved in postsecondary education and are teaching, have taught, or have considered teaching online courses. Theoretical saturation was reached with 44 participants interviewed.

Participant Demographics

The operationalization of the study involved interviews. As the primary data-collection instrument, the interviews allowed the researcher to explore the research questions in collaboration with the participants and arrive at thick descriptions of the participants' experiences in teaching online. As the interviews unfolded, it became evident that teachers have strong feelings about their teaching experiences. While all the participants had interesting accounts to tell, several of the participants stood out in terms of their teaching and online experience.

The interviews were conducted from October 2004 through May 2005. After the first round of interviews, follow-up interviews were used to seek clarification and explore the topic in greater depth. The demographic information reported by the participants in the study suggests a possible grouping of the participants, based on their teaching modality experience: classroom, online, or hybrid. The participants were selected in a manner to allow for as wide a representation as possible, balancing gender, primary teaching modality (classroom, online, or hybrid), and affiliation.

In terms of gender, of the 44 respondents in the sample, 29 were male and 15 were female. The sample has an almost 2:1 ratio of males to females. Six age groups were identified, as detailed in Table 2. Most of the respondents in the sample were between 40 and 50 years of age. Notably, all respondents were at least 30 years old.

Consistent with the academic requirements in effect at their respective universities, all of the respondents held at least a master's degree. Approximately one third of the participants held doctoral degrees, and two thirds of them held master's degrees.

The participants described their teaching experience in great detail. Their current teaching environment ranged from classroom only to online and included a variety of hybrid, or blended, environments. Some teachers taught in only one modality, while others taught in multiple modalities. The positions held by respondents were assigned different titles. The participants fall into two broad categories: academic faculty and part-time or adjunct faculty. There are 21 academics (e.g., professor, assistant professor, adjunct professor, associate professor) and 23 adjunct faculty (e.g., faculty, adjunct faculty, practitioner faculty, instructor, lecturer, facilitator).

While the subject matters taught by the respondents covered a wide range, there appears to be a higher occurrence of Management and Business courses. Yet overall, courses representations are fairly balanced among Business (Business: 20, Accounting/Finance: 5); Soft Sciences (Social Sciences: 14, Humanities: 2, Communications: 10); and Hard Sciences (Mathematics: 7, Computer Science/Information Technology/Engineering: 15).

Some of the teachers interviewed taught at multiple institutions concurrently: two participants taught at four universities, and two participants taught at three universities. More than one quarter of the participants (i.e., 12 teachers) taught at two universities. Yet the majority of the participants (i.e., 28 teachers) taught at only one institution. The mean of these data is 1.5, with a standard deviation of 0.8. Overall, respondents came from a total of 32 colleges and universities, thus their experiences are not limited to a unique institution.

The Goal of the Study

A good theory that explains online teaching will help modify the way teachers are placed in the online classroom. It helps predict, control, and understand online teachers' reactions. By helping the teacher selection process, it reduces turnover and assists professional development processes. A theory of the online teaching experiences provides an improved understanding of how teachers might use online tools to enhance their teaching. It may provide an explanation of why some teachers do not teach online, and how the technology used in education affects their teaching. In addition, it may help predict teachers' reactions relative to online teaching.

In order to increase the validity of the findings, I reviewed the concepts derived from analysis with fellow researchers and academics. Throughout the course of the study, I reflected on the concepts and their meaning. The process of reflection was evident in the careful consideration of my interpretation and understanding of what the respondents reported. In an attempt to look at the data from the respondents' perspective, I carefully weighed in on what seemed to be the participants' understanding of the phenomena. Convergence of the two positions was sought. Cognizant of my limitations and biases, I focused on dialogue as a means to generate knowledge about the phenomena, through collaboration with the participants (Jankowski, Clark, & Ivey, 2000). The theory presented in Chapter XI was validated by the teachers who participated in the study: They concluded that it made sense and was a good fit to their experiences.

Organization of the Book

The book is organized into XII chapters. A brief description of each of the chapters follows:

Chapter I identifies some of the various perspectives on online teaching. Specifically, its objective is to review what has been published in the academic literature about the online teaching environment and the various aspects reported by online teachers.

For Chapter II, four study participants were selected for in-depth profiling, because they were identified as representative, interesting subjects. Two of them, Jeremy and Deborah, are practicing only on-ground teaching. The other two, Derek and Sarah, teach mainly online or hybrid, but with experience on-ground as well. Each interview revealed extraordinary personalities, driven in their profession by passion and love towards the act of education.

Chapter III discusses how teachers view online teaching and what they experience when teaching online. It focuses on the accounts the respondents shared during the interviews taken for this book. A brief perusal through the literature finds reports of increased time demands, more preparation and hard work, as well as a need for improved technical skills—these being just some of the issues online education was reported to bring upon teachers. Yet, as a result of this research, new issues were found to exist, enhancing the knowledge on this subject of online teaching. To name just a few, are the extent of the adjustments made by teachers (discussed in greater detail in Chapter VII), the skill gap in technology among teachers and students (covered in Chapter V), and the kind of adjustments that are made by the teachers when moving to an online educational environment.

In Chapter IV, teachers share their thoughts regarding the determinants for success in online teaching (i.e., what makes online teachers successful). A brief discussion of the relevant published literature is followed by a discussion of the determinants of online teaching success, substantiated by copious citations from the interviews conducted for this book. Emotional involvement, teacher effectiveness, student quality, and technology reliability are only some of the issues identified as affecting online teaching success.

In Chapter V, the interviewees describe how they use IT for their online courses, discuss possible variations in the meaning they derive from their online teaching experiences, and offer several interesting suggestions. Teachers use technology in their daily activity. They are definitely not afraid to use technology in support of their teaching and are not avoiding it. However, the online educational environment poses specific challenges. The contents of this chapter should help increase teachers' awareness of what awaits them in the online classroom.

Chapter VI discusses online teaching demands. Teachers are aware of, and reflect on, a variety of issues related to teaching online. There are certain things they would like to change—things they feel would improve their online teaching. Their use of technology in the classroom affects their teaching. As technology continues to improve, its usability, availability, and actual use are ongoing concerns. The same can be said for curriculum development, course design, and faculty training. As the teaching profession is changing, different challenges are posed to teachers and universities.

Chapter VII reviews the gains and losses experienced by teachers who teach online courses. As they teach online, they learn from the experience and increase their awareness of what works well online. They adjust to the online environment in an attempt to maximize the gains and mitigate the losses. Some of the adjustments they make are for the better, while others are for the worse. Based on these adjustments, the teachers make choices whether they continue to teach one modality vs. another, or leave the profession altogether.

Chapter VIII explores possible tradeoffs teachers identify in relation to online teaching. When they are teaching, teachers have to constantly interact with their students, with their peers, with academic departments, with school administrators, course developers, and many others. Furthermore, the environment in which they function (i.e., where they teach) poses specific challenges they need to recognize and manage in order to maintain their effectiveness as teachers. The teachers who were interviewed as part of the study that was the basis of this book share their perceptions and experiences regarding the potential and actual tradeoffs they find themselves making as well as the adjustments they make in response to the challenges presented to them by the online environment.

In the earlier chapters, teachers shared their experiences and feelings about online teaching. They talked about how the online environment affects them and their teaching style; about the tradeoffs they find; the issues associated with technology and teaching online; about the adjustments they feel they have to make; and about the benefits and the losses they notice as a result of their teaching online. Having this in background, Chapter IX tries to put things in perspective and discover how, if at all, these stories intersect. The chapter focuses on the central ideas that are related to online teaching—ideas that have been derived from the interview data. The chapter discusses the first four main categories that center on teaching: *teaching, teaching demands, teacher needs,* and *teaching dimensions.*

Chapter X continues in the direction chalked out in the Chapter IX and focuses on the central ideas that are related to technology and its use in the online classroom. It continues the discussion of the core categories identified in Chapter IX and presents in detail the remaining categories: *teaching with technology, technology, differences among modalities, issues, adjustments,* and *choice.*

Chapter XI presents a theory of the online teaching experience, as viewed by the teachers who teach online courses. It draws on the core categories presented in Chapters IX and X and proceeds by validating the core categories by means of triangulation with other published research, by identifying relationships and interplay among the ten core categories, and by formulating the theory in narrative form.

Chapter XII concludes the discussion of the online teaching experience. A few suggestions are made and advice is offered to educational administrators, online teachers, online curriculum and course developers, and educational technology professionals.

Appendix A presents the research methodology of the study that forms the basis of this book. The detailed discussion of grounded-theory research offers valuable information to those interested in this form of qualitative research. It discusses grounded-theory research in detail and includes the research design and the operationalization of the study: sampling, data-collecting methods and procedures, analysis, and validity issues.

Appendix B presents in tabular format the demographical information of the respondent sample. Each respondent is assigned a two-digit number that helps identify quote authorship. Each of the quotes used in the book ends with a two-digit number (within square brackets [ ]); these numbers cross-reference to the respondents list.

References

Alavi, M. (1994). Computer-mediated collaborative learning: An empirical evaluation. *MIS Quarterly*, 159-174.

Altbach, P. G., & Lewis, L. S. (1995). Professorial attitudes—An international survey. *Change, 27*(6), 50-57.

Angelo, T. A., & Cross, P. K. (1993). *Classroom assessment techniques* (2nd ed.). San Francisco: Jossey-Bass.

Bianchi, A. (2000, July 1). E is for e-school: Dot-com start-ups go to the head of the class. *Inc.*

Brewer, L. (2001). *The development of online learning: An understanding of faculty and student experiences in an organizational context.* Unpublished doctoral dissertation, Arizona State University.

Chambers, J. (1999, November 17). Next, it's e-ducation. *New York Times,* A29.

Chandler, J. R., Fontenot, A. D., Hagler, M. O., & Marcy, W. M. (1999, November 10-13). *Why the distinction between on-campus and distance learning is blurring.* Paper presented at the 29th ASEE/IEEE Frontiers in Education Conference, San Juan, Puerto Rico.

Chu, Y.-H. (2002). *Factors related to adoption of Internet resources in instruction by faculty at the Pennsylvania State University.* Unpublished doctoral dissertation, Pennsylvania State University.

Cuban, L. (1993). *How teachers taught: Constancy and change in American classrooms: 1890-1990* (2nd ed.). New York: Teachers College Press.

Cyrs, T. E. (1997). *Teaching at a distance with the merging technologies: An instructional systems approach.* Las Cruces: New Mexico State University, Center for Educational Development.

Dreeben, R. (1970). *The nature of teaching: Schools and the work of teachers.* Glenview, IL: Scott Foresman.

Dutton, J., Dutton, M., & Perry, J. (2002). How do online students differ from lecture students? *Journal of Asynchronous Learning Networks, 6*(2), 1-20.

Esch, T. J. (2003). *E-learning effectiveness: An examination of online training methods for training end-users of new technology systems.* Unpublished doctoral dissertation, Touro International University.

Goetzinger, C., & Valentine, M. (1963). Faculty attitudes toward educational television: A survey report and preliminary analysis. *Speech Teacher, 12*(2), 127-130.

Golden, D. (2006). Degrees @ stateu.edu. *The Wall Street Journal, CCXLVII*(108), B1.

Guidera, S. G. (2000). *College teaching in the virtual classroom: Faculty perceptions of the effectiveness of online instruction.* Unpublished doctoral dissertation, Bowling Green State University.

Hatterius, G. G. (2004). *A study of cognitive changes made to teach a state mandated curriculum.* Unpublished doctoral dissertation, Texas Tech University, Lubbock, TX.

Hill Martin, M. (2003). *Factors influencing faculty adoption of Web-based courses in teacher education programs within the State University of New York.* Unpublished doctoral dissertation, Virginia Polytechnic Institute and State University.

Horton, S. (2000). *Taking discussions online.* Retrieved February 14, 2004, from http://www.dartmouth.edu/~webteach/articles/discussion.html

Huang, P.-W. N. (2001). *University faculty perceptions of WebCT for delivering courses.* Unpublished doctoral dissertation, University of South Dakota.

Iken, M. B. T. (2000). *Faculty attitudes toward computer-mediated distance education.* Unpublished doctoral dissertation, University of South Dakota.

Inos, R. H., & Quigley, M. A. (1995). *Synthesis of the research on educational change: Part IV, the teacher's role.* Honolulu, HI: Pacific Regional Education Laboratory.

Irvine, M. (2001). Net knowledge: The coming revolution in higher education. *Gnovis, 1*(1).

Jankowski, P. J., Clark, W. M., & Ivey, D. C. (2000). Fusing horizons: exploring qualitative research and psychotheraupetic applications of social constructionism. *Contemporary Family Therapy, 22*(2), 241-250.

Jensen, E. J. (1995). The Bitter Groves of Academe. *Change, 27*(1), 8-11.

Kinuthia, W. (2003). *An exploratory study of faculty participation in Web-based instruction at historically black colleges and universities.* Unpublished doctoral dissertation, University of South Alabama.

Kisner, C. G. (2001). *The virtual professor: teaching on the electronic frontier, 1995-1999.* College Park: The Graduate School of the University of Maryland.

Koory, M. A. (2003). Differences in learning outcomes for the online and F2F versions of "An Introduction to Shakespeare". *Journal of Asynchronous Learning Networks, 7*(2), 18-35.

Kumari, D. S. (1999). *A study of higher education faculty implementing Web-based teaching.* Unpublished doctoral dissertation, University of Houston, Houston, TX.

Lewis, J. E. (2002). *Perceived learning needs of post secondary faculty of institutions moving towards online course delivery.* Unpublished doctoral dissertation, University of Toronto, Canada.

Lim, V. K. G., Teo, T. S. H., & See, S. K. B. (2000). Perceived job image among police officers in Singapore: Factorial dimensions and differential effects. *The Journal of Social Psychology, 140*(6), 740-750.

Maxwell, J. L. (2001). *Faculty perceptions of community in online and traditional courses at catholic colleges.* Unpublished doctoral dissertation, University of San Francisco, CA.

McDonald Lucas, G. (2002). *Policy implications concerning distance education as perceived by faculty at two-year colleges in Georgia.* Unpublished doctoral dissertation, Georgia Southern University.

Mendenhall, R. (2007). Challenging the myths about distance learning. *Distance Learning Today, 1*(1), 1.

Mendenhall, R. W. (2003). *A model and principles for effective Internet-based distance education.* Unpublished doctoral dissertation, Brigham Young University.

Monson, J. A. (2003). *The Importance of human interaction in online learning: Learner and instructor perceptions and expectations.* Unpublished doctoral dissertation, Indiana University.

Morse, K. (2003). Does one size fit all? Exploring asynchronous learning in a multicultural environment. *Journal of Asynchronous Learning Networks, 7*(1), 37-55.

Myers, C. B. (2003). *The influence of goals, technology and structural characteristics on faculty teaching practices: Implications for higher education policy and administration.* Unpublished doctoral dissertation, Washington State University.

Oliver, C. (2004). *Teaching at a distance: The online faculty work environment.* Unpublished doctoral dissertation, the City University of New York, New York.

Oravec, J. A. (2003). Some Influences of on-line distance learning on U.S. higher education. *Journal of Further and Higher Education, 27*(1), 89-103.

Perry, D. R. (2003). *Faculty beliefs and faculty perceptions of student beliefs about quality distance education.* Unpublished doctoral dissertation, Gonzaga University.

Piccoli, G., Ahmad, R., & Ives, B. (2001). Web-based virtual learning environments: A research framework and a preliminary assessment of effectiveness in basic IT skills training. *MIS Quarterly, 25*(4), 201-226.

Rovai, A. A. P. (2002). *A preliminary look at the structural differences of higher education classroom communities in traditional and ALN courses.* Retrieved February 14, 2004, from http://www.aln.org/publications/jaln/v6n1/pdf/v6n1_rovai.pdf

Schell, G. P. (2004). Universities marginalize online courses. *Communications of the ACM, 47*(11), 107-112.

Scott, B. G. (2003). *Faculty attitudes toward residential and distance learning: A case study in instructional mode preferences among theological seminary faculty.* Unpublished doctoral dissertation, University of North Texas, Denton, TX.

Senge, P., Cambron-McCabe, N., Luca, T., Smith, B., Dutton, J., & Kleiner, A. (2000). *Schools that learn.* New York: Doubleday.

Sloan-C-Resources. (2006). *Making the grade: Online education in the United States, 2006.* Retrieved August 10, 2007, from http://www.sloan-c.org/resources/survey.asp

Tyack, D., & Cuban, L. (1995). *Tinkering toward utopia: A century of public school reform.* Cambridge, MA: Harvard University Press.

University of North Carolina. (2004, March 1). Gauging faculty attitudes about teaching online. *Distance Education Report,* 5-6.

Varvel, V. E., Lindeman, M., & Stovall, I. K. (2003). The Illinois online network is making the virtual classroom a reality: Study of an exemplary faculty development program. *Journal of Asynchronous Learning Networks, 7*(2), 81-95.

Yang, H.-L., & Tang, J.-H. (2003). *Effects of social network on students' performance: A Web-based forum study in Taiwan.* Retrieved February 14, 2004, from http://www.aln.org/publications/jaln/v7n3/pdf/v7n3_yang.pdf

Yang, J. F. (2003). *Distance education delivery modes and learning objectives: Experiences of South Dakota public university system faculty.* Unpublished doctoral dissertation, University of South Dakota.

Endnote

[1] University of Phoenix offers online college education with complete degree programs via the Internet. More information is available at http://online.phoenix.edu.

Acknowledgment

I dedicate this to my family. Your love and patience made this possible.

Sorin Gudea

None of this would have been possible without the help of many, many people. It is only natural to extend my heartfelt gratitude and appreciation to all those who were at my side during the long journey that got me where I am today.

I would like to acknowledge the help of all involved in the review process of the book, without whose support the project could not have been satisfactorily completed.

Thanks go to all those who provided constructive and comprehensive reviews. Some of the reviewers must be mentioned as their reviews were instrumental in improving the manuscript submitted for publication. Reviewers who provided the most comprehensive, critical, and constructive comments include: Craig Van Slyke, of University of Central Florida; Terry Ryan, of Claremont Graduate University; and professor Anthony Tebelskis. Support of the School of Information Systems and Technology at Claremont Graduate University is acknowledged.

Special thanks also go to the publishing team at IGI Global whose contributions throughout the whole process from inception of the initial idea to final publication have been invaluable. In particular to Kristin Roth, who continuously prodded via e-mail for keeping the project on schedule and to Jan Travers, whose enthusiasm motivated me to take on this project. The assistance of Deborah Yahnke is acknowledged.

The teachers who shared their experiences deserve credit. Although you must remain anonymous, I am very grateful for the time you spent answering questions and helping this research unfold.

I would also like to thank Dr. Lorne Olfman and Dr. Tom Horan, of Claremont Graduate University, who read an early draft of the manuscript and provided helpful suggestions for enhancing its content. And last but not least, my family, for your unfailing support and encouragement during the months it took to give birth to this book. Special thanks to Rodica Gudea for her tireless editing of the manuscript.

My mentor, Professor Terry Ryan from Claremont Graduate University, deserves special recognition. Terry was instrumental in more ways than I can think of in the writing of this book. Without his constant encouragement and enthusiasm, I would have never embarked on this journey, and this book would not have been offered to you today. My deepest gratitude goes to him.

Sorin Gudea, PhD
Torrance, California, USA
January 2008

Chapter I

Perspectives on Online Teaching

Introduction

The general focus of the chapter is on the various perspectives of online teaching. Specifically, its objective is to review what has been published in the academic literature about the online teaching environment and its various aspects.

Background

Online education refers to the use of the Internet for teaching and learning. What started many years ago as distance education has evolved to make full use of the technologies available today to enrich the educational experience of the participants (Sherritt & Basom, 1997).

Distance learning programs are constantly being developed by numerous colleges and universities, yet not enough has been done to research the impact of technology on the teachers (Turoff, 1997). As more courses move online, educational institutions and teachers alike are challenged in terms of pedagogy, course content and delivery, and administrative and technology support (Ives & Jarvenpaa, 1996).

An increasing number of colleges and universities offer online programs (Goral, 2001). Distance education is moving into every industry; online training is bigger than online education (Carnevale, 2003). Faculty members are pressured by the changes stemming from education globalization and the potential of information and communication technologies to transform education delivery. This is more of a challenge for teachers who were formed under different circumstances (Clegg, Konrad, & Tan, 2000).

Perspectives on Online Teaching

Distance Education

Information technology (IT) changes the teaching and learning environments dramatically (Massy & Zemsky, 1995). The entire educational environment is affected by advances and changes in IT (Jellinek, 1998; Margolis, 1998). The availability of information and the way it is accessed has changed. Over recent years, there has been an increase in the use of technology to support education. The students who enroll in distance education programs find out that they must learn on their own while the teacher is taking on a facilitator role (Knowlton, 2000; Martine & Freeman, 1999). When teaching online, typically, the teacher posts a syllabus, mini-lectures and course materials, discussion questions, and other assignments for the students. There are deadlines the students must meet in order to receive full credit for their work. However, the students are responsible for their learning, for class interaction, and for the discussions that take place, mostly in written form.

The discussions that occur in the on-ground classroom occur online as well. Yet, one finds that the online discussions follow a more structured format. Starting with an initial question or commentary posted by the teacher or a student, subsequent comments posted by participants appear in order, or in a *thread*. The discussion thread is represented by the message flow, usually in time order: A threaded discussion is simply a hierarchical ordering of messages (Ko & Rosen, 2001). The participants can follow the discussion and reflect on every message that is part of the thread. Unlike spoken conversation, the written form of the discussion allows extended time for reflection and the ability to go back and revisit message fragments, thus supporting an iterative, incremental approach to understanding what is being conveyed in the discussion thread.

The Internet makes it possible to reach across geographical and political boundaries. It offers a great mechanism for disseminating information. Distance education allows the working adult learners to continue their education or stay current in their profession. Students and teachers are separated in space; the classroom reaches across geographical distance (Cyrs, 1997). Online education comes as a natural improvement, where the Internet is the medium used to support distance education. Furthermore, online education affords access to courses that may not be available in a traditional format (Ben-Jacob, Levin, & Ben-Jacob, 2000).

Since the not-so-distant past, the learning environment has steadily evolved from mainly art, to science (Wulf, 1995). Information technology reorganizes and transforms the activities that make up teaching. The role of the teacher is changed by the online environment (Kisner, 2001; Shea, Pelz, Fredericksen, & Pickett, 2001). The teachers must examine how the online environment alters their work, in order to make the most of it.

A Brief History of Distance Education

Teachers have experimented with a variety of technologies since the mid-19th century, with the goal of improving the educational process. The blackboard, textbooks, pictures, correspondence courses, film, radio, and instructional television are only some of the precursors of online education. The advent of the personal computer and the Internet brings a different set of challenges and promises. It is a process still in transition; yet, the versatility of the Internet to bridge information, geography, culture, and language surpasses everything else that has been tried in education before.

It was Isaac Pitman who started the first correspondence course in 1840, when he offered to teach shorthand by mail (Maeroff, 2003). Distance education began, and correspondence courses were offered as early as 1850 at the Illinois Wesleyan University (MacKenzie, Christensen, & Rigby, 1968). In the late 1880s, the University of Chicago established the first major correspondence education program (McIsaac & Gunawardena, 1996). Correspondence education allowed the student and teacher to enjoy a flexible learning schedule. Courses were made available to students who, for one reason or another, could not attend classroom-based instruction. Noble (2001) reported that more than 300 schools offered correspondence education by 1926. Correspondence education, just like today's online education, was seen by many as nothing more than commercial attempts to make education a commodity. It was first targeted at those who were not affluent and could not afford to move to campus, and it was viewed by many educators as an inferior form of education (Pittman, 1991). Of course, correspondence education degrees were challenged; some schools elected not to offer them at all (Noble, 1998). However, even with the drawbacks stemming from the loss of mediated interaction between teacher and student, which arguably diminishes the educational process, correspondence education set to achieve a commendable goal: to bring educational opportunities to the masses. Eventually, the popularity of correspondence education decreased as the quality of the education offered was questioned. More recently, in the 1990s, with the fall of the Iron Curtain, a surge in correspondence education offers started in the former socialist bloc. At the time, to a computer-illiterate and largely uninformed population, this seemed to be a great opportunity to pursue a distance education degree. The Internet eventually offered an alternative.

The next technology to come about was film, which was used in the early 1900s. Paralleling somewhat the growing popularity of the movies, instructional films appeared in the classroom as a symbol of progress. Yet, many educators reacted negatively toward the use of film in the classrooms. Technical issues further contributed to the demise of instructional film (Kisner, 2001). Still in use today, instructional film migrated to new media, such as videotape and DVD.

Radio was not affected by the logistics associated with instructional film. As radio receivers became mainstream, educational radio became popular in the 1920s, and a number of universities (e.g., University of Wisconsin) established their own radio stations (Kisner, 2001). Students in local areas were now able to enroll in school and pursue an education without having to come to campus. Eventually, it was the new technology of television, and the somewhat impersonal nature of the radio broadcast, that led to its demise.

The first instance of instructional television is reported to have taken place in 1953, in Houston, Texas (Cuban, 1986). Used as a supplement to classroom education, instructional television continued to grow slowly, yet it remained an accessory to the instruction in the classroom. The technology continued to advance, and in the 1980s, the Public Broadcast Service (PBS) partnered with several schools offering instructional video courses (Kisner, 2001). In many ways superior to radio, instructional television continues to be used today. However, being a one-way medium limits its potential to becoming more than an accessory tool.

The Internet, which started as a Defense Advanced Research Projects Agency (DARPA) sponsored project, offered universities a convenient medium for sharing computing resources. The National Science Foundation (NSF) funded a research network (NSFNet) that allowed an increasing number of academics to access shared computing resources (Vivian, 1995). The NSFNet eventually grew to become the backbone of the Internet. With its ability to provide users access to distributed information, the Internet became an appealing alternative to classroom education. Unlike its predecessors (film, radio, and television), the Internet supports two-way communication. The global economy and the globalization of education rely on the Internet for dissemination of information and communication. Educational institutions are able, for the first time, to reach geographically remote students in a cost-effective manner. Universities are expanding their boundaries across the electronic frontier, offering online education as an appealing alternative to traditional classroom-based education (Ben-Jacob et al., 2000; P. S. Cahn, 2003; Carnevale & Olsen, 2003).

The Distance Learning Environment

A paradigm shift took place in England in 1969, when the Royal Society established the Open University (OU), an educational institution that democratized access to education by allowing students to enroll regardless of prior academic performance.

The Open University offered credit courses by mail, television, or radio broadcasts serving a population of students who otherwise would not have received an education (Miller, 1998). The OU, established in the UK in 1969, provides higher education to those who wish to pursue a degree by studying part time or who cannot physically attend a traditional university. OU relies on a variety of methods for distance learning, from written and audio materials, CD and DVD, to Internet-delivered courses and television. The majority of the courses have no mandatory face-to-face requirements. The university consistently gets high marks for its programs. In 2005 and 2006 UK government national student satisfaction surveys, OU was rated the top university in England and Wales (BBC News, 2005, 2006; Wikipedia, 2007b).

In the United States, the Lyceum and the Chautauqua movement mark significant moments in distance education. The national American Lyceum was developed in 1831 from lectures given by Josiah Holbrook in Millbury, Massachusetts. It spread through other states as an association for popular instruction of adults and relied on lectures and concerts. The Civil War brought an end to it, but the Chautauqua movement continued its spirit (The Columbia Encyclopedia, 2006; Yahoo, 2007b).

Notably, in 1884, the Chautauqua University was established with guided home reading and correspondence and extension courses. Another offspring, the Chautauqua Literary and Scientific Circle, provided home study by mail and had an enrollment of over 2.5 million students in 1900 (J. S. Maxwell, 2001; Venekamp, 2007). The Chautauqua movement (or the Chautauqua assembly), a popular education movement, offered the general population an opportunity to see and hear speakers, teachers, musicians, artists, and specialists in person. An outdoors summer school, it began in 1874 and lasted through the 1920s. It moved from town to town, throughout rural America, offering intellectual stimulation for the masses. Eventually, improvements in transportations and communications spelled the demise of the Chautauqua movement (Wikipedia, 2007a; Yahoo, 2007a). As radio and movies became readily available, the importance of the Chautauqua movement decreased.

The distance learning environment separates students and teachers temporally and spatially. Time separation is evident when asynchronous environments are considered. Physical separation means the learners and teachers are not in the same room. In fact, they can be at great distance geographically. Educational participants' communication and subsequent interaction takes place mediated by various technologies (e.g., e-mail, fax, video, telephone) (Cyrs, 1997). The physical and time separation characteristics of the distance education environment afford participants certain flexibility in participation, learning/teaching modality, and time schedule.

From a time perspective, distance education can involve synchronous or asynchronous participation. The synchronous form requires participants to interact in real time (e.g., video conferencing, online chat). The asynchronous approach allows students and teachers to *enter* the classroom at their own convenience, with no preset times. The classroom is open 24 hours a day, and the only time constraints (if any) may be those related to student homework assignments and examinations (Cyrs, 1997).

The availability of equipment, technical skills, institutional policies, teaching style, and course goals all concur to affect the distance education environment. At some institutions, the teacher is allowed to decide what technology to use to support distance learning; In-house technology specialists may be available to assist the teacher with technology selection and course development issues. At other institutions, courses are developed by dedicated staff that include subject-matter experts and curriculum and educational specialists (e.g., the University of Phoenix; Farrell, 2003). The teacher takes on a reduced role of simply using the technology and the distance learning environment designed for him or her to engage in teaching students.

Distance learning is growing. As an increasing number of universities consider or already offer distance education as an alternative to traditional, classroom-based education, issues centered on technology use, course content delivery, teaching methods, and teaching styles must be considered (Baldwin, 1998; Cyrs, 1997). Distance education is slowly evolving, driven in part by changes in the technologies used in education. Emerging communication technologies provide cost-effective solutions for disseminating knowledge to an increasing number of learners: the Internet made online education a reality.

In the United States alone, there were 1.9 million students enrolled in online education in 2003. The online enrollment was expected to exceed 2.6 million by the end of 2004 and was estimated to reach 3.2 million in 2005 (Allen & Seaman, 2004; Sloan-C-Resources, 2006). Numerous faculty certification programs exist that prepare teachers to teach online. Yet, faculty members are still exploring their roles as teachers in the online environment and the effect it has on them. As education continues to move online, universities must encourage and support their faculty members to "alter habits and attitudes that have sustained them for their entire careers" (Maeroff, 2003, p. 17).

The Role of the Teacher

As an academic profession, teaching involves various dimensions of academic work: instructing and mentoring the students, performing research, and evaluating and assessing the students' work (Clark, 1987). Teachers take on these roles throughout their courses and are responsible for arousing the students' appreciation for the subject matter and for educating and guiding the students toward mastering the studied subject (S. M. Cahn, 1994). More important, teachers offer students a framework for inquiry in the quest for knowledge.

Technology brings about a potential for enhancing the role of the teacher. Yet, it is not solely the technology, but rather the changes in teaching style that are important. Different environments will call for adjustments to teaching styles. The role of the faculty must change for distance education (Purdy & Wright, 1992). In distance education, the role of the teacher evolves to a constructivist stance—one that requires the teacher to become a facilitator. As multimedia technologies become an integral part of traditional education, the teacher is no longer the knowledge source and instead becomes a knowledge facilitator (Gunawardena & McIsaac, 2004). Rather than filter the access to information, as is the case in the traditional classroom, teachers can recommend additional resources and guide students toward their own discovery. Conceptually, the teacher moves from being in the center of the physical classroom to the periphery of the online classroom. While the environment changes from teacher centered to student centered, knowledge is structured through a cooperative effort involving students and teacher (Knowlton, 2000). The teacher is responsible for framing the course and providing resources and opportunities to supplement the students' interactions. In their revised role, teachers facilitate interaction by engaging the students (Noble, 2001).

It would seem that to a certain extent the online classroom removes the need for the teacher. The student forms a relationship with the text, not the professor. This requires a student-centered approach, appropriate for the nonlinear nature of the course (Knowlton, 2000). Online, the instructional roles and teaching strategies are different (Driscoll, 1994; Knowlton, 2000; J. L. Maxwell, 2001; Purdy & Wright, 1992).

Universities try to determine to what extent business decisions should drive their institutional policies (Wysocki, 2005). Teaching online seems cost effective (Greenblatt, 2001); yet, many faculty members in colleges and universities are embittered: They report feelings of regret, envy, frustration, betrayal, and isolation. This affects their attitudes toward work (Jensen, 1995). One study reports that 32% of teachers would not volunteer to teach online, and 54% of them believed the quality of the courses is lower online. Perhaps another reason for concern is that the number of part-time faculty members is growing faster than that of full-time faculty members (Feenberg, 1999). Nationwide, in 2005, nearly half of all college faculty members were part-timer teachers, up from only 22% in 1970 (Hersh, Merrow, & Wolfe, 2005).

Choices

There is still a lot of controversy around online teaching. Just like any other human beings, the teachers make career choices, and decide what to teach, when to teach, and even whether they wish to continue to teach. Teachers make choices as to whether they choose to teach in certain educational modalities or leave the profession altogether. In one study, most teachers preferred online teaching to the traditional classroom (Cristianson, Tiene, & Luft, 2002). Teachers seek a sense of purpose: inadequate support may diminish their enthusiasm, sense of purpose, and effort. Acute frustration may lead teachers to leave the profession (Baird, 1999).

Some teachers would prefer to teach in regular, on-ground classrooms, while others prefer to teach online; other teachers prefer a hybrid modality. Yet, not all teachers are convinced that online education is effective. There are still questions about whether hybrid teaching can really support quality education (K. P. King, 2002). Consequently, we learn that there are full-time faculty members who are reluctant to teach online (Carnevale, 2004). Teachers resist the effort to be forced into distance education.

In many ways, the use of online education is akin to automating the education process. The use of technology allows for courses to be taught online, either synchronously or asynchronously, reaching a larger number of students and increasing enrollment. Yet, this very technology may be perceived as a threat by teachers, because, often, full-time teachers are replaced with nontenured, part-time teachers (Thompson, 1999). This may lead to a situation where teaching becomes less appealing as long-term employment (Noble, 2001). In fact, many teachers leave the profession after a few years of teaching. They are frustrated by the emotional, physical, and psychological demands of the classroom (Darling-Hammond, 1990). The online environment may have something to do with it.

Administration

Educational institutions and school administrators are equally interested in offering an educational environment that makes efficient use of resources and is conducive to quality learning for their students. In this process, educational administrators have to contend with various personnel issues, such as faculty skills, new personnel needed, and faculty compensation. There is increased faculty resistance to technology because of the perception that it distorts the educational experience (Rayburn & Ramaprasad, 2002). Issues related to faculty members' compensation include money, tenure, release time, and course load. In most institutions, current policies regarding personnel appear to be ad hoc.

A teaching workload has both well- and loosely defined dimensions. While the course load expressed as a number of course credits is clearly defined, other activities, such as student mentoring, course development, and administrative tasks are less well defined. As the education moves from the classroom into different environments (such as online), instructors begin to realize the specific demands associated with course development and delivery (Noble, 2001).

Developing online courses requires a team approach, because it is complicated and takes significant time (Chou & Tsai, 2002). Ershler (2003) advised avoiding a cookie-cutter approach. When offering online courses, the preparation of the online instructional materials requires insight from instructional design, information design, interaction design, and graphic design (Shank & Sitze, 2004). It is a collaborative effort that can be resource intensive, time-consuming, and expensive. According to Farrel (2003), the University of Phoenix uses content experts in addition to a team of 25 curriculum developers; the development of a typical online course requires approximately 12 person-days.

While online education provides students with better access to information and educational resources (Navarro, 2000), it also introduces new concerns and needs for the learners. Lowry, Thornam, and White (2000) advised schools to help their online learners make the most of the educational environment they are in. Online education is great for students who are mature, engaged, and well-organized (Seguin, 2002).

School administrators focus on the fiscal implications of online education. Teachers are concerned with institutional support, interaction, and education quality issues (Bower, 2001). They are concerned with technical knowledge and comfort, and with technological access (Lauzon, Gallant, & Rimkus, 2000). Teachers as well as students need well-developed policies and guidelines for online education (Ershler, 2003).

Learning

Several published studies outline important characteristics needed for successful online learning. Per Pallof and Pratt (2001), most successful course outcomes are being seen in classes that are small and combine face-to-face with online instruction—a "Web-enhanced class" (p. 68). Thus, hybrid learning modalities have the potential to support deep learning (Garrisson & Kanuka, 2004).

Parker's (2003) study showed that online learning may be difficult for some students, and student attrition rate online may exceed 40%. The students who do well online tend to have low anxiety, high tolerance for ambiguity, field independence, and internal locus of control (M. D. Anderson, 2001). Marold, Larsen, and Moreno (2002) found no significant differences in grades between online and on-ground classes. Nevertheless, student performance in examinations varies. Some teachers report their online students consistently receive higher grades compared to those studying in an on-ground classroom; yet, other teachers report the opposite. Weems (2002) found no significant difference for exam averages, but reported a significant decrease of performance of online students across exams.

Successful learning depends on the capabilities of the existing and emergent social networks to form learning communities (Mohrman, Tenkasi, & Mohrman , 2003). These communities encourage problem-solving skills and increasing retention and success for students and faculty alike (Dodge & Kendall, 2004). Yet, effective online communities do not develop easily. It is not enough to lead learners to technology; they must be helped to form communities online—otherwise, they will form them offline (Orey, Koenecke, & Crozier, 2002).

The online environment is a simulated world. Social life develops across on- and off-line networks. Teachers are concerned with technical characteristics of technology, interface features, collaborative tools, and hypertext structures. New modes of communication pose new challenges for understanding collaboration (Hinn, Leander, & Bruce, 2001).

Learning Theories

Historically, in the evolution of mankind, the division of labor and inherent specialization resulted in various trades and a more complex division of labor for the benefit of achieving higher output efficiencies. Specialized occupations required particular skills, as was reflected in Plato's *Republic*: "[The state] will need a farmer, a builder, and a weaver… a shoemaker and one or two others" (Plato, 2003, p. 56). It is this specialization of skills that led to demands for training and education.

Many great minds (Plato, Socrates, Aristotle, Comenius, Rousseau, Pestalozzi, Siegel, Skinner, Piaget, Bloom, to name only a few educational thinkers) have pondered ways to enable people to learn. Among the most important learning theories of the last centuries are *behaviorism, cognitivism,* and *constructivism.*

In general, learning theories attempt to provide explanations for how people learn. Skinner (1950, 1974) associated learning with measurable changes in behavior. The behaviorist view thus held that only the observable behavior was worth studying. Once the predominant school of thought, *behaviorism* was replaced toward the end of the 20th century by cognitivism, which posited that mental states also must be analyzed and taken into account, and that pure conditioning in itself was not enough to ensure learning. The cognitivists focus on the learner by placing more emphasis on factors that are *within* the learner. *Cognitivism* views learning as an active process, characterized by high-level processes; it holds that learning is cumulative and builds on prior knowledge. As of late, cognitivism appears to lose appeal as constructivism becomes increasingly popular.

Constructivism posits that learners build on existing information. As a learning theory, it holds that students can guide their learning through collaboration with others and rely on prior knowledge and experience to construct new concepts and learn by problem solving.

Distance Education Theories

Distance education theories take into account physical separation among students and teacher. Gunawardena and McIsaac's (2004) learned review of the theoretical developments in distance education follows a path from the early mechanistic view of distance education to the need for interaction and dialogue.

An early distance education theory, Peters's industrial production model of distance education combined the imparting of knowledge and skills with the division of labor and the use of technology for reproducing teaching materials and emphasized self-study. Thus, distance education was akin to a structured mechanism. Yet, self-study in itself was not sufficient. Later on, Holmberg (1991), a proponent of guided didactic conversation (i.e., student's interaction with text), emphasized the creation of simulated conversation in educational materials. This is where the issues of interaction and dialogue came up. A more recent development, Moore's (1997) theory of transactional distance pertains to the amount of interaction, the *dialogue,* that occurs among students and teacher. It posits that courses that have more structure and less student-teacher dialogue will have greater transactional distance. As a practical matter, while taking into account the learners' ability to direct their own learning, the teacher has an important role to play in responding to students' application of new knowledge (M. G. Moore & Kearsley, 1996).

Interaction

The distance learning environment forces the teacher to organize and present his or her course materials in an entirely different way (Cyrs, 1997). For the most part, distance education is still mainly text based. Communication style is different due to bandwidth limitations, the asynchronous nature of the medium and reliance on written communication (Smith, Ferguson, & Caris, 2002). The asynchronous dimension of the online environment adds increased complexity, as the teacher must plan now for the proper sequence and the content of the material presented online (Shea et al., 2001). Oliver (2004) noted that the online environment engages the participants in an intense exchange of ideas that are mediated through the computer. At times, teachers need to slow down the interaction (i.e., *chat*) in order to be able to control it (Hameroff, 2003). In the case of a large class, the number of postings can be overwhelming, while in a very small class, the discussions may not go well (Brower, 2003). Collaboration is more than simply exchanging information (Hodgkinson & Holland, 2002). At times, the students' online dialogue is mostly related to personal experiences and does not reflect well-supported reasoning (Angeli, Valanides, & Bonk, 2003).

Teaching effectiveness relies on communication skills and enthusiasm (Johnson & Roellke, 1999). Society and students have changed; from the point of view of students expecting to be entertained most of the time, learning must always be fun. The teachers who use a friendly, honest, humorous style may make students believe they will succeed. Online teaching requires commitment and appropriate interactivity (C. King & McSporran, 2002). Per Paris (2000), the classroom teacher resembles a sage on a stage, where in contrast, the online teacher is more like a guide, on the side of the online classroom. Some teachers say they can form stronger relationships online, while others miss the face-to-face interaction, as there are no classroom theatrics online (Blair, 2002).

Web-based education can simulate face-to-face teaching models successfully, but adjustments are needed in terms of student assessment, faculty training and expectations, and student expectations and motivation (Aggarwal & Bento, 2002). These adjustments affect teachers and students equally and must be adequately supported by schools, because the lack of face-to-face contact may induce online students to feel less pressure to contribute to online class discussions.

The social contexts are different online and in the classroom, and therefore learning designs should be different. Teachers acknowledge uneven online participation and the potential for lurking. Online is more formal, requires more time to think, and there is less teacher control over the social context of learning. Some teachers would like to have alternative procedures for dealing with students' personal problems (e.g., the telephone). Online, new modes of interaction and communication emerge, and monitoring and encouraging participation can be more difficult. Teachers feel that imposing too much structure is detrimental to a value-free environment, as should be the case online.

Teachers often report that online interaction is more difficult to control. At times, a few students can dominate online discussions (Blair, 2002). Students answer messages and post new messages on their own terms online. Yet, the online environment allows for more in-depth discussions: there is more time to formulate answers, and the discussion threads are available for quick reference. The initial anonymity afforded to the online classroom participants evolves into online identities. Perhaps due to the perceived dryness of the medium, reliance on e-mails leads to a much closer relationship. The online forum forces students to communicate frequently with their teachers. As a result, teachers find they must overhaul their teaching strategies: Their ability to write clearly and concisely is important.

Issues

A notable tendency in education is to reformat course materials and learning strategies in order to fit the technology used for delivery. When too much focus is placed on technology rather than education, this approach leads to compromises for both students and the subject being taught online (Minasian-Batmanian, 2002). Teachers themselves are not exempt from making compromises.

The expectations online are exacerbated: Online students expect instantaneous service, while the teachers need significant time to properly respond to students. Teachers have no sick or personal days when teaching online. As long as the technology functions, the course is always on (Laird, 2003). Teachers spend more time teaching online, with no additional compensation (National Educational Association,

2000). This applies to online teaching as well as to course preparation and curriculum development. According to Cristianson et al. (2002), online faculty members spend significantly more time developing Web courses.

Information technology provides a challenge to teachers and course curriculum designers. Despite all the good work, there is still very little experience in developing instruction of course materials for delivery online and for teaching online. Often, teachers have to restructure much of what they have done in the on-ground classroom in order to become effective online (Meyen & Lian, 1997). Without a doubt, the design and delivery of courses that integrate new technologies is challenging. As teachers struggle to use technology, it may end up being used at a superficial level and may not have an impact on the teaching practice (Torrisi & Davis, 2000). As online education relies on technology as the vehicle for delivering education, access to technology becomes an important issue. Technology choices are constrained at times by a school's business goals, the availability of technology support and the very availability of a specific technology (Klobas & Renzi, 2003). For example, the availability of broadband Internet access limits the choices of multimedia material that can be used in an online course.

Educators are concerned with learner expectations, incentives, and content (K. P. King & Dunham, 2005). Online courses require significant effort for development and delivery (Schell, 2004). The production of a virtual course is much more demanding: It requires access to graphical designers, prototypes, adequate choice of technology, and proper budget (Bergstrom, Grahn, Karlstrom, Pulkkis, & Astrom, 2004). Consequently, there is a significant burden to prepare an online course (Chang, 2001). Teaching online is not easy: It requires preparation and hard work. Online course materials require significant time to prepare, and teachers need help in the development and delivery of course materials. Everything must be prepared well before the course starts—not just 1 week in advance (Kubala, 1998).

Teachers realize the importance of integrating technology in classrooms. They enjoy online discussion forums, because the threaded discussions offer more choices, allow more diverse opinions, and lead to deeper analysis (Li, 2003). They learn to focus on interactivity rather than content and to give up some control (Pallof & Pratt, 2001).

Training

Teachers need training to help them move from passive, didactic forms of teaching toward incorporating new teaching methods (Littlejohn, 2002). Faculty members often try to recreate the classroom experience via computer. In traditional education, the teacher handles everything (i.e., course design and development). Online, they need to be the content expert, Web developer, multimedia designer, and system administrator. Those expectations are unrealistic, and teachers should have access to technical support staff (Baker, Schihl, & Aggarwal, 2003). Faculty members feel that they need to receive education on the use of technology and support to develop instructional materials (Rockwell, Schauer, Fritz, & Marx, 2000).

Online teaching requires more technical skills, and the development of online course materials is labor intensive; educational institutions are well advised to have teachers involved in course development. There are significant costs associated with technology aspects of the online environment; online education is not cheap. In many respects, online learning is still mimicking what goes on in a classroom. *Generation Y* students are a natural audience, because they grew up with technology. A possible drawback is that they expect to be entertained (Gehring, 2002).

Teaching

Some teachers are early adopters of distance education, while others are reluctant to integrate technology into their instruction (Grant, 2004). Some teachers fear teaching online because they feel it would erase their presence in the classroom (Banks, 1998). Many teachers who are exposed to both on-ground and online teaching become more conscious of their teaching, both face-to-face and online (McShane, 2004). Some teachers, when teaching online, adjust by being more entertaining and theatrical (Grosse, 2004).

Teachers who decide to teach online must make decisions that will impact their teaching role and strategies. These decisions are shaped by their beliefs and the values they hold about teaching; online education leads teachers to modify their approaches to teaching (Campbell, McGee, & Yates, 1997).

Student assessment online is more difficult, as well. For example, teachers have no way of knowing whether their students study all the course material, or just the material that is needed to complete the assignments (Bergstrom et al., 2004; Parikh, 2003).

Technology

The advantages offered by online education (e.g., access to information, location, convenience) are reduced by drawbacks (e.g., time required for course design, faculty training). Vodanovich and Piotrowski (2001) found that, for many teachers, the use of technology is basic (i.e., e-mail, dissemination of course materials). In contrast to their educators, many of the current and future students are well immersed in technology. Information and communication technologies (ICTs) are a way of life for them (Brown, 2002).

The technology industry is still dictating the needs of education, instead of education dictating the need for technology (Morinaka, 2003). There are concerns about how ICTs are incorporated into the on-ground environment. Teachers must reconsider the relationship of the physical setting to the students' learning experience. Where teaching hands-on aspects of the course is important, computer simulation may be used to replace some labs (Carr, 2000).

Web technology allows teachers to create multidimensional experiences that combine text, audio, and video in a media-rich environment and engage learners (Sensiper, 2000). Students value the flexibility offered by the asynchronous dimension of the class, and the same can be said about the teachers who teach online. The online education participants find that there is more collaboration taking place online as compared to the on-ground classroom (Klipowicz & Laniak, 1999). The online learning environment is more tolerant: It offers the potential to be more female-friendly, its anonymity being a positive aspect. This allows students to interact online without the distracting noise of social conditioning (Sullivan, 2002). Shy students may tend to do better online, because they can craft their communications with very little time pressure and fear of being in the open, in front of the entire class.

Online teaching is not the same as a *canned* lecture: prepackaged, structured, developed, and prepared in advance—a roadmap for the course that has to be followed closely. The online modality allows the teacher to modify content and learning activities throughout the progress of the course, as appropriate. Either on-ground or online, teachers can communicate with their students by private e-mail, voice messages, or phone (T. Anderson, Rourke, Garrison, & Archer, 2001). Some teachers find that when they use technology in the classroom, the use of technology does not necessarily enhance their reaching out to students. What may be working for some students does not necessarily work for the entire class: Students have different communication needs than their teachers—especially the younger students, who prefer speed to face-to-face contact (Arnone, 2002).

The Web allows for two-way communication. Online, the communication style is different due to bandwidth limitations, the asynchronous nature of the medium, and excessive reliance on written communication that is the hallmark of the online classroom. This requires increased clarity of the materials posted online, more time to prepare them, and deeper discussions to explain the course material. The instructor is challenged to rework his or her course materials when developing an online class. The balanced mix of asynchronous (e.g., Listserv) and synchronous (e.g., chat rooms) support in an online course can provide a quality learning experience (Duin, 1998).

It is recognized that the use of technology for distance education affects how learners learn, and how teachers teach (Kisner, 2001). Several studies looked at the work environment of the teacher (Curtis, 2001; Kisner, 2001; Noble, 2001). The attitudes of teachers vary widely with regard to online education. Some teachers fear the changes brought by technology (Turoff, 1997), while others appreciate the added flexibility afforded to them (Curtis, 2001; Cyrs, 1997; Knowlton, 2000). When engaged in online education, the teachers can teach more courses online, for different schools, with less concern for institutional politics, and earn more money (Carnevale, 2004). Online courses are also convenient. They meet academic needs and help students improve technological skills (Leonard & Guha, 2001).

Web technology can help students prepare for the social, academic, and personal challenges of higher education and offer a useful supplement to classroom instruction (Shafer, Davis, Lahner, Petrie, & Calderone, 2002). Online, a deeper level of thinking is noticeable due to written communication; stronger relationships are formed (Smith et al., 2002). However, isolation and lack of contact with faculty members may be a problem to developing effective learning communities (Grubb & Hines, 2000). Loss of personal contact is a concern to teachers and students alike (Weiss, 2000). The online environment makes it difficult for the teacher to help students who are having problems with practical exercises (Bergstrom et al., 2004).

Teachers also report a significant increase in time demand when teaching online. They feel there is at least a two and a half to three times increase in time demand. These figures are similar to those reported by Pallof and Pratt (1999). Online faculty members spend between 1 and 4 hours more per week to teach than they do in the traditional, on-ground classroom. Online, student contact hours increase more than two fold, from 1½ to 4 hours per week. However, other activities, such as lecture, exams, and class and conferencing meetings were the same in terms of time requirements (SchWeber, 2000). Course materials must be kept up to date, yet online courses are more difficult to maintain. Teachers are concerned with the time required to update the course Web site and to interact with students (Hall, 2002). Despite all the difficulties, teachers who are interested in technology will eventually learn how to use it effectively for teaching (Speck, 2000).

Conclusion

The many studies that have been researched and presented in this chapter, in the effort to offer a thorough perspective of online teaching, have left a great deal of unanswered questions.

Understanding of online teaching requires a correct assessment of its positive as well as negative aspects. While many factors may contribute to teachers' attitudes in this environment, evidence abounds that some instructors absolutely love to teach online while others would not want to come near it. This book examines the teachers' perspectives on online teaching in order to provide a grounded understanding of the experience of teaching online. As the author/researcher, I have attempted to identify teachers' attitudes in relation to teaching online and the factors that affect them, as viewed from the perspectives of teachers, using an exploratory design. Given the intent of the study, it seems natural to employ grounded-theory specific methods for theory generation.

As online teaching appears to require more time, effort, and technical skills, schools should increase their support for the online teachers. As the demands on teachers' time are higher, better technology to help teachers assess their students, and to communicate with them effectively, are needed. Online courses require significant effort, and teachers need to be trained in classroom assessment techniques, learning and teaching models, and the use of technology in the classroom.

Using technology for teaching can be a frustrating experience. As technology continues to improve and find its way into the online classroom, teachers may find that their concerns and fears are alleviated. At the very least, the technology used for supporting online teaching should help teachers spend less time reviewing student discussions and grading assignments. For those teachers who miss the energy and sounds of a real classroom, teaching online loses some of its appeal. Perhaps new technology solutions will allow them to regain some of the energy that so many teachers seem to enjoy in the on-ground classroom. As Blair (2002) noted, teaching online is not for every educator; it is a different method of teaching, albeit an exciting one. More work is needed to ensure that teachers are properly prepared to deal with the challenges presented by the online environment, and that educational institutions continue to evaluate new, emerging technologies for use in the online classroom. This means that teachers will have to keep their technology skills current, and adjust their teaching to it. Despite all the difficulties, to side with Speck (2000), it is reasonable to expect that teachers who are interested in technology will eventually learn how to use it effectively for teaching.

References

Aggarwal, A. K., & Bento, R. (2002). Web-based education. In M. Khosrow-Pour (Ed.), *Web-based instructional learning* (pp. 59-77). Hershey, PA: IRM Press.

Allen, I. E., & Seaman, J. (2004). *Entering the mainstream: The quality and extent of online education in the United States, 2003 and 2004*. Sloan Center for Online Education.

Anderson, M. D. (2001). Individual characteristics and Web-based courses. In C. Wolfe (Ed.), *Learning and teaching on the World Wide Web* (pp. 47-73). San Diego, CA: Academic Press.

Anderson, T., Rourke, L., Garrison, D. R., & Archer, W. (2001). Assessing teaching presence in a computer conferencing context. *Journal of Asynchronous Learning Networks, 5*(2), 1-17.

Angeli, C., Valanides, N., & Bonk, C. J. (2003). Communication in a Web-based conferencing system: The quality of computer-mediated interactions. *British Journal of Educational Technology, 34*(1), 31-43.

Arnone, M. (2002). Many students' favorite professors shun distance education. *Chronicle of Higher Education, 48*(35).

Baird, J. R. (1999). A phenomenological exploration of teachers' views of science teaching. *Teachers and Teaching: Theory and Practice, 5*(1), 75-94.

Baker, J. D., Schihl, R. J., & Aggarwal, A. K. (2003). eLearning support systems. In A. K. Aggarwal (Ed.), *Web-based education: Learning from experience* (pp. 223-235). Hershey, PA: Information Science Publishing.

Baldwin, R. G. (1998, Winter). Technology's impact on faculty life and work. In H. K. Gillespie (Ed.), *New directions for teaching and learning: The impact of technology on faculty development, life and work* (Vol. 76, pp. 7-21).

Banks, I. (1998). Reliance on technology threatens the essence of teaching. *The Chronicle of Higher Education, 45*(8), B6.

BBC News. (2005, September 21). *Students rate university courses.* Retrieved October 10, 2006, from http://news.bbc.co.uk/1/hi/education/4265802.stm

BBC News. (2006, August 23). *Student satisfaction survey results.* Retrieved October 10, 2006, from http://news.bbc.co.uk/1/hi/education/5277938.stm

Ben-Jacob, M. G., Levin, D. S., & Ben-Jacob, T. K. (2000, Spring/Summer). The learning environment of the 21st century. *Educational Technology Review,* (13), 8-12.

Bergstrom, L., Grahn, K. J., Karlstrom, K., Pulkkis, G., & Astrom, P. (2004). Teaching network security in a virtual learning environment. *Journal of Information Technology Education, 3,* 189-217.

Blair, J. (2002). The virtual teaching life. *Education Week, 21,* 31-34.

Bower, B. L. (2001). Distance education: Facing the faculty challenge. *Online Journal of Distance Learning Administration, 4*(2).

Brower, H. H. (2003). On emulating classroom discussion in a distance-delivered OBHR course: Creating an on-line learning community. *Academy of Management Learning and Education, 2*(1), 22-36.

Brown, J. S. (2002). Learning in the Digital Age. In M. Devlin, R. Larson, & J. Meyerson (Eds.), *The Internet & the university: Forum 2001* (pp. 65-91): Forum for the Future of Higher Education and EDUCAUSE.

Cahn, P. S. (2003). Number crunching. *The Chronicle of Higher Education, 50*(16).

Cahn, S. M. (1994). *Saints and scamps. Ethics in the academia*. MD: Rowman & Littlefield.

Campbell, N., McGee, C., & Yates, R. (1997). *"It is not out with the old and in with the new": The challenge to adapt to online teaching*. Retrieved April 11, 2005, from http://unisanet.unisa.edu.au/cccc/papers/non-refereed/campbell.htm

Carnevale, D. (2003). Learning online to teach online. *Chronicle of Higher Education, 50*(10).

Carnevale, D. (2004). For online adjuncts, a seller's market. *Chronicle of Higher Education, 50*(34), 31-32.

Carnevale, D., & Olsen, F. (2003). How to succeed in distance education by going after the right audience, online programs build a viable industry. *The Chronicle of Higher Education, 49*(40), 31-33.

Carr, S. (2000). Science instructors ask: Can you teach students at a distance how to use microscopes? *The Chronicle of Higher Education, 46*(32).

Chang, C.-K. (2001). Refining collaborative learning strategies for reducing the technical requirements of Web-based classroom management. *Innovations in Education and Teaching International, 38*(2), 133-143.

Chou, C., & Tsai, C. C. (2002). Developing Web-based curricula: Issues and challenges. *Journal of Curriculum Studies, 34*(6), 623-636.

Clark, B. R. (1987). *The academic life. Small worlds, different worlds*. Princeton, NJ: Princeton University Press, The Carnegie Foundation for the Advancement of Teaching.

Clegg, S., Konrad, J., & Tan, J. (2000). Preparing academic staff to use ICTs in support of student learning. *The International Journal for Academic Development, 5*(2), 138-148.

The Columbia Encyclopedia. (2006). *Lyceum, 19th-century American educational association*. Retrieved March 17, 2008, from http://www.bartleby.com/65/ly/lyceum.html

Cristianson, L., Tiene, D., & Luft, P. (2002). Examining online instruction in undergraduate nursing education. *Distance Education, 23*(2), 213-229.

Cuban, L. (1986). *Teachers and machines. The classroom use of technology since 1920*. New York: Columbia University, Teachers College.

Curtis, M. P. (2001). *Incentives and obstacles for nursing faculty in choosing to teach via distance*. Unpublished dissertation, The Graduate School of Saint Louis University.

Cyrs, T. E. (1997). *Teaching at a distance with the merging technologies: An instructional systems approach*. Las Cruces: New Mexico State University, Center for Educational Development.

Darling-Hammond, L. (1990). *Teacher supply, demand and quality*. Washington, DC: National Board for Professional Teaching Standards.

Dodge, L., & Kendall, M. E. (2004). Learning Communities. *College Teaching, 52*(4), 150-155.

Driscoll, M. P. (1994). *Psychology of learning for instruction*. Boston: Allyn & Bacon.

Duin, A. H. (1998). The culture of distance education: Implementing an online graduate level course in audience analysis. *Technical Communication Quarterly, 7*(4), 365-388.

Ershler, J. (2003). Policy development considerations for administrators and instructors of distance learning programs. *Journal of the United States Distance Learning Association, 17*(2), 1-3.

Farrell, E. F. (2003). Phoenix's unusual way of crafting courses. *The Chronicle of Higher Education, 49*(23).

Feenberg, A. (1999, Winter). Distance learning: Promise or threat. *Crosstalk,* 12-13.

Garrisson, D. R., & Kanuka, H. (2004). Blended learning: Uncovering its transformative potential in higher education. *Internet and Higher Education, 7,* 95-105.

Gehring, J. (2002). Higher ed.'s online odyssey. *Education Week, 21,* 27-29.

Goral, T. (2001). Teaching old dogs new tricks. *Curriculum Administrator, 37*(2), 59-61.

Grant, M. M. (2004). Learning to teach on the Web: Factors influencing teacher education faculty. *Internet and Higher Education, 7,* 329-341.

Greenblatt, E. (2001). The more things change: Teaching in an online classroom. *Christian Science Monitor, 93,* 17.

Grosse, C. U. (2004). How distance learning changes faculty. *International Journal of Instructional Technology and Distance Learning, 1*(6).

Grubb, A., & Hines, M. (2000). Tearing down barriers and building communities: Pedagogical strategies for the Web-based environment. In R. A. Cole (Ed.), *Issues in Web-based pedagogy* (pp. 365-380). Westport, CT: Greenwood Press.

Gunawardena, C. N., & McIsaac, M. S. (2004). Distance education. In D. H. Jonassen (Ed.), *Handbook of research for educational communications and technology* (2nd ed., pp. 355-396). Mahwah, NJ: Erlbaum.

Hall, R. (2002). Aligning learning, teaching, and assessment using the Web: An evaluation of pedagogic approaches. *British Journal of Educational Technology, 33*(2), 149-158.

Hameroff, G. (2003). Keeping the education in online education. *Community College Week, 15*(20), 10-11.

Hersh, R. H., Merrow, J., & Wolfe, T. (2005). *Declining by degrees: Higher education at risk* [DVD]. New York and Washington, DC: Public Broadcasting Service.

Hinn, D. M., Leander, K., & Bruce, B. (2001). Case studies of a virtual school. *Journal of Adolescent & Adult Literacy, 45*(2), 156-165.

Hodgkinson, M., & Holland, J. (2002). Collaborating on the development of technology enabled distance learning: A case study. *Innovations in Education and Teaching International, 39*(2), 89-94.

Holmberg, B. (1991). Testable theory based on discourse and empathy. *Open Learning, 6*(2), 44-46.

Ives, B., & Jarvenpaa, S. L. (1996). Will the Internet revolutionize business education and research? *Sloan Management Review, 37*(3), 33-41.

Jellinek, D. (1998). Distance learning/digital degrees. *The Guardian Weekly*, 21.

Jensen, E. J. (1995). The bitter groves of academe. *Change, 27*(1), 8-11.

Johnson, S. D., & Roellke, C. F. (1999). Secondary teachers' and undergraduate education faculty members' perceptions of teaching-effectiveness criteria: A national survey. *Communication Education, 48*, 127-138.

King, C., & McSporran, M. (2002, July). *Online teaching demands hands-on commitment.* Paper presented at the 15th Annual NACCQ, Hamilton, New Zealand.

King, K. P. (2002). Identifying success in online teacher education and professional development. *Internet and Higher Education, 5*, 231-246.

King, K. P., & Dunham, M. D. (2005, January). Finding our way: Better understanding the needs and motivations of teachers in online learning. *International Journal of Instructional Technology and Distance Learning, 2*(1).

Kisner, C. G. (2001). *The virtual professor: Teaching on the electronic frontier, 1995-1999.* College Park: The Graduate School of the University of Maryland.

Klipowicz, S. W., & Laniak, T. (1999). Hebrew exegesis online: Using information technology to enhance biblical language study. *Teaching Technology and Religion, 2*(2), 109-115.

Klobas, J., & Renzi, S. (2003). Integrating Online Educational Activities in Traditional Courses: University-wide Lessons after Three Years. In A. K. Aggarwal (Ed.), *Web-Based Education: Learning from Experience* (pp. 415-439). Hershey, PA: Information Science Publishing.

Knowlton, D. S. (2000). A theoretical framework for the online classroom: A defense and delineation of a student-centered pedagogy. In E. R. Weiss, D. S. Knwolton,

& B. W. Speck (Eds.), *New directions for teaching and learning. Principles of effective teaching in the online classroom* (Vol. 84, pp. 5-22).

Ko, S., & Rosen, S. (2001). *Teaching online. A practical guide.* Boston: Houghton Mifflin.

Kubala, T. (1998). Addressing student needs: Teaching on the Internet. *T H E Journal, 28*(5), 71-74.

Laird, E. (2003). I'm your teacher, not your Internet-service provider. *Chronicle of Higher Education, 49*(17), B5.

Lauzon, A. C., Gallant, T. B., & Rimkus, S. (2000). A hierarchy of access issues affecting on-line participation by community college students. In R. A. Cole (Ed.), *Issues in Web-based pedagogy* (pp. 317-337). Westport, CT: Greenwood Press.

Leonard, J., & Guha, S. (2001). Education at the crossroads: Online teaching and students' perspectives on distance learning. *Journal of Research on Technology in Education, 34*(1), 51-57.

Li, Q. (2003). Would we teach without technology? A professor's experience of teaching mathematics education incorporating the Internet. *Educational Research, 45*(1), 61-77.

Littlejohn, A. H. (2002). Improving continuing professional development in the use of ICT. *Journal of Computer Assisted Learning, 18,* 166-174.

Lowry, M., Thornam, C., & White, C. T. (2000). Preparing higher education learners for success on the Web. In R. A. Cole (Ed.), *Issues in Web-based pedagogy* (pp. 297-316). Westport, CT: Greenwood Press.

MacKenzie, O., Christensen, E. L., & Rigby, P. H. (1968). *Correspondence instruction in the United States.* New York: McGraw-Hill.

Maeroff, G. A. (2003). *A classroom of one: How online learning is changing our schools and colleges.* New York: Palgrave MacMillan.

Margolis, M. (1998). Brave new universities (The future of academy?). *First Monday, 3*(5).

Marold, K. A., Larsen, G., & Moreno, A. (2002). Web-based learning: Is it working? A comparison of student performance and achievement in Web-based courses and their in-classroom counterparts. In M. Khosrow-Pour (Ed.), *Web-based instructional learning* (pp. 179-189). Hershey, PA: IRM Press.

Martine, C., & Freeman, V. (1999). Combining technologies to deliver distance education. *Educational Technology and Society, 2*(3).

Massy, W. F., & Zemsky, R. (1995). *Using information technology to enhance academic productivity.* Retrieved April 15, 2004, from http://www.educom. edu/program.nlii/docs/massy.html

Maxwell, J. L. (2001). *Faculty perceptions of community in online and traditional courses at catholic colleges.* Unpublished dissertation, University of San Francisco, CA.

Maxwell, J. S. (2001). *The complete Chautauquan.* Retrieved February 12, 2007, from http://members.aol.com/Alphachautauquan/movement.html

McIsaac, M. S., & Gunawardena, C. N. (1996). Distance education. In D. H. Jonassen (Ed.), *Handbook of research for educational communications and technology: A project of the Association for Educational Communications and Technology* (pp. 403-437). New York: Simon & Schuster/MacMillan.

McShane, K. (2004). Integrating face-to-face and online teaching: Academics' role concept and teaching choices. *Teaching in Higher Education, 9*(1), 3-16.

Meyen, E., L., & Lian, C. H. T. (1997). Teaching online courses. *Focus on Autism & Other Developmental Disabilities, 12*(3), 1-17.

Miller, R. E. (1998). *As if learning mattered: Reforming higher education.* Ithaca, NY: Cornell University Press.

Minasian-Batmanian, L. C. (2002). Guidelines for developing an online learning strategy for your subject. *Medical Teacher, 24*(6), 645-657.

Mohrman, S. A., Tenkasi, R. V., & Mohrman, A. M., Jr. (2003). The role of networks in fundamental organizational change. *The Journal of Applied Behavioral Science, 39*(3), 301-323.

Moore, M. (1997). Theory of transactional distance. In D. Keegan (Ed.), *Theoretical Principles of Distance Education* (pp. 22-38). New York: Routledge.

Moore, M. G., & Kearsley, G. (1996). *Distance education: A systems view.* Belmont, CA: Wadsworth.

Morinaka, B. S. (2003). Online education: Where should it be? *Journal of the United States Distance Learning Association, 17*(2), 83-84.

National Educational Association. (2000). *A survey of traditional and distance learning higher education members.* Washington, DC: National Educational Association.

Navarro, P. (2000). The promise—and potential pitfalls—of cyberlearning. In R. A. Cole (Ed.), *Issues in Web-based pedagogy* (pp. 281-296). Westport, CT: Greenwood Press.

Noble, D. F. (1998). Digital diploma mills: The automation of higher education. *First Monday, 3*(1).

Noble, D. F. (2001). *Digital diploma mills. The automation of higher education.* New York: Monthly Review Press.

Oliver, C. (2004). *Teaching at a distance: The online faculty work environment.* Unpublished dissertation, the City University of New York, NY.

Orey, M., Koenecke, L., & Crozier, J. (2002). Learning communities via the Internet à la epic learning: You can lead the horses to water, but you cannot get them to drink. *Innovations in Education and Teaching International, 40*(3), 260-269.

Pallof, R. M., & Pratt, K. (1999). *Building Learning Communities in Cyberspace: Effective Strategies for the Online Classroom.* San Francisco: Jossey-Bass Publishers.

Pallof, R. M., & Pratt, K. (2001). *Lessons from the cyberspace classroom: The realities of online teaching.* San Francisco: Jossey-Bass.

Parikh, M. A. (2003). Beyond the Web: Leveraging multiple Internet technologies. In A. K. Aggarwal (Ed.), *Web-based education: Learning from experience* (pp. 120-130). Hershey, PA: Information Science Publishing.

Paris, D. C. (2000). Is there a professor in this class? In R. A. Cole (Ed.), *Issues in Web-based pedagogy* (pp. 95-110). Westport, CT: Greenwood Press.

Parker, A. (2003). Identifying predictors of academic persistence in distance education. *USDLA Journal, 17*(1).

Pittman, V. (1991). Rivalry for respectability: Collegiate and proprietary correspondence programs. In *Proceedings of the Second American Symposium on Research in Distance Education.* University Park: Pennsylvania State University.

Plato. (2003). *The republic.* New York: Penguin.

Purdy, L. N., & Wright, S. J. (1992). Teaching in distance education: A faculty perspective. *The American Journal of Distance Education, 6*(3), 2-4.

Rayburn, W. E., & Ramaprasad, A. (2002). Three strategies for the use of distance learning technology in higher education. In M. Khosrow-Pour (Ed.), *Web-Based Instructional Learning* (pp. 27-42). Hershey, PA: IRM Press.

Rockwell, K., Schauer, J., Fritz, S. M., & Marx, D. B. (2000). Faculty education, assistance and support needed to deliver education via distance. *Online Journal of Distance Learning Administration, 3*(2).

Schell, G. P. (2004). Universities marginalize online courses. *Communications of the ACM, 47*(11), 107-112.

SchWeber, C. (2000). The "time" factor in on-line teaching: implications for faculty and their universities. In R. A. Cole (Ed.), *Issues in Web-based pedagogy* (pp. 227-236). Westport, CT: Greenwood Press.

Seguin, C. (2002). Games online students play: Building a firewall new instructors (and burned out 'old ones') can use. *TechTrends, 46*(4), 23-57.

Sensiper, S. (2000). Making the case online. Harvard Business School multimedia. *Information, Communication and Society, 3*(4), 616-621.

Shafer, M. J., Davis, J. E., Lahner, J. M., Petrie, T. A., & Calderone, W. K. (2002). The Use and Effectiveness of a Web-based instructional supplement in a college student success program. *Journal of College Student Development, 43*(5), 751-757.

Shank, P., & Sitze, A. (2004). *Making sense of online learning: a guide for beginners and the truly skeptical.* San Francisco, CA: Pfeiffer.

Shea, P. J., Pelz, W., Fredericksen, E. E., & Pickett, A. M. (2001). *Online teaching as a catalyst for classroom-based instructional transformation.* New York: State University of New York, The SUNY Learning Network.

Sherritt, C., & Basom, M. (1997). *Using the Internet for higher education.* (ERIC Document Reproduction Service No. ED 407 546)

Skinner, B. F. (1950). Are theories of learning necessary? *Psychological Review, 57,* 193-216.

Skinner, B. F. (1974). *About behaviorism.* New York: Random House.

Sloan-C-Resources. (2006). *Making the grade: Online education in the United States, 2006.* Retrieved August 10, 2007, from http://www.sloan-c.org/resources/survey.asp

Smith, G. G., Ferguson, D., & Caris, M. (2002). Teaching over the Web versus in the classroom: Differences in the instructor experience. *International Journal of Instructional Media, 29*(1), 61-67.

Speck, B. W. (2000). The academy, online classes, and the breach in ethics. In B. W. Speck (Ed.), *New directions for teaching and learning. Principles of effective teaching in the online classroom* (Vol. 84, pp. 73-82).

Sullivan, P. (2002). "It's easier to be yourself when you are invisible": Female college students discuss their online classroom experiences. *Innovative Higher Education, 27*(2), 129-144.

Thompson, H. (1999). The impact of technology and distance education: A classical learning theory viewpoint. *Educational Technology and Society, 2*(3).

Torrisi, G., & Davis, G. (2000). Online learning as a catalyst for reshaping practice—The experiences of some academics developing online learning materials. *The International Journal for Academic Development, 5*(2), 166-176.

Turoff, M. (1997, April 27-29). *Alternative future for distance learning: The force and the dark side.* Paper presented at the UNESCO/Open University International Colloquium.

Venekamp, L. (2007). *Welcome to Chautauqua.* Retrieved March 10, 2007, from http://www.campusschool.dsu.edu/myweb/history.htm

Vivian, J. (1995). *The media of mass communication.* Boston: Allyn & Bacon.

Vodanovich, S. J., & Piotrowski, C. (2001). Internet-based instruction: A national survey of psychology faculty. *Journal of Instructional Psychology, 28*(4), 253-255.

Weems, G. H. (2002). Comparison of beginning algebra taught onsite versus online. *Journal of Development Education, 26*(1), 10-19.

Weiss, R. E. (2000). Humanizing the online classroom. *New Directions for Teaching and Learning, 84*, 47-51.

Wikipedia. (2007a). *Chautauqua*. Retrieved March 10, 2007, from http://en.wikipedia.org/wik/Chautauqua

Wikipedia. (2007b). *Open university*. Retrieved February 6, 2007, from http://en.wikipedia.org/wiki/Open_University

Wulf, W. A. (1995). Warning: Information technology will transform the university. *Technology, 2*(53), 15-52.

Wysocki, B. (2005, February 23). How Dr. Papadakis Runs a University Like a Company. *The Wall Street Journal, CCXLV,* A1.

Yahoo. (2007a). *Encyclopedia: Chautauqua movement*. Retrieved May 12, 2007, from http://education.yahoo.com/reference/encyclopedia/entry/Chautauq-mv

Yahoo. (2007b). *Lyceum*. Retrieved February 6, 2007, from http://education.yahoo.com/reference/encyclopedia/entry/lyceum;_ylt=Aup2uuRkRtKt3IqYplKDGKRTt8wF

Chapter II

Teacher Profiles

Introduction

This chapter presents a detailed analysis of four in-depth interviews with four selected teachers.

Forty-four interviews were performed for this study, with professors and teachers from all levels of graduate and undergraduate education. It was a difficult task to sort out just four examples that would be most representative for the entire group. Each interview revealed extraordinary personalities, driven in their profession by passion and love toward the act of educating. Nevertheless, to meet the purpose of this chapter, and reflect opinions about both on-ground and online teaching, four teachers were selected. Two of them, Jeremy and Deborah, are practicing only on-ground teaching. The other two, Derek and Sarah, teach mainly online or hybrid courses, but with experience teaching on-ground courses as well. They were profiled in greater depth in order to allow the reader a better understanding of the teachers' teaching experiences and their motivation. The names of the participants profiled, as well as the names of their employers or place of employment, are purposely fictitious or vague, in order to protect their anonymity.

Many of the issues they bring with regard to teaching in general, or teaching online, mirror issues already reported in prior, existing studies. The background section presents a summary of current findings, with regard to this subject, which are reenforced by the findings of this study. Yet, other issues such as the teachers' passion for the profession, the delicate interplay among the various facets of online teaching, and the proposed explanation for teachers' choice of teaching environments are novel to these interviews.

Background

Twenty-one studies researching the theme of teaching online, teachers' experiences and views, and the online learning experience were chosen as most representative. A summary of the conclusions of these studies are as follow:

Teachers are agents of change yet "little is known about how teachers think about the aims of education" (Boyd & Arnold, 2000, p. 23). Nevertheless it is documented that at least some teachers teach less for money and more out of passion (Cahn, 2003). The data derived from the interviews support this view. The contention that teachers take on a constructivist stance when teaching online (Bangert, 2004) is confirmed by the findings.

Teachers report that when teaching online, they experience a significant increase in time demands. Some of them are spending between 1 and 4 hours more per week to teach. Other activities (lecture, exams, class/conferencing meetings) were the same in terms of time (SchWeber, 2000).

Teaching online is not easy. Students expect to be entertained (Gehring, 2002). Online teaching requires teacher commitment and relies on interactivity (C. King & McSporran, 2002). While the classroom teacher may resemble a sage on a stage, the online teacher is more like a guide, on the side of the online classroom (Paris, 2000).

Many teachers are concerned with learner expectations, academic incentives, and course content (K. P. King & Dunham, 2005), and they find that online courses require significant effort for both development and delivery (Schell, 2004). Consequently, they face a significant burden when preparing an online course (Chang, 2001). Online, a different communication style prevails, constrained by bandwidth limitations, the asynchronous nature of the medium, and an excessive reliance on written communication (Smith, Ferguson, & Caris, 2002). Consequently, teaching online requires an increased clarity of the online course materials, more time, and deeper discussions. The initial anonymity evolves into online identities. The instructor has to rework the course materials specifically for the online class. Teaching online requires long hours to respond to messages, e-mail, and evaluate discussions. More time is spent on editing responses (Smith et al., 2002).

Given that the social contexts are different online and in the classroom, it follows that learning designs should be different. The online environment is more formal and requires more time to think; the teacher has less control over the social context of learning. Reusable dialogues can help students learn and reduce teacher workload as the archives of prior discussions are available for review (Nicol, Minty, & Sinclair, 2003). Students value the flexibility that stems from the asynchronous dimension of the online class. In addition, the online learning environment appears to be more female-friendly, its anonymity being a positive characteristic. This allows students to interact online without being distracted by social conditioning (Sullivan, 2002). Teachers note a need to encourage students to contribute actively to the ongoing dialogue; it is this continuous participation that stimulates learning (Bender, 2000).

Faculty members report on factors that affect their use of Internet technologies in class: They do not know how to use it, they have design concerns, and they received inadequate training. They often try to recreate the classroom experience they are familiar with by using the computer. Teachers feel that they need to receive training in how to use the online course technology and require support to develop instructional materials (Rockwell, Schauer, Fritz, & Marx, 2000).

Teacher presence online is reflected in the number and content of teacher postings. These are affected by teaching style, subject taught, class size, and teacher's familiarity with the medium. Online teaching is not the same as a *canned* lecture: The modality allows the teacher to modify course content and learning activities as they find it appropriate throughout the progress of the course. Teachers can communicate with their students by private e-mail, voice messages, or phone (Anderson, Rourke, Garrison, & Archer, 2001).

Technology can be frustrating. Teachers lose the energy and sounds that are present in the on-ground classroom. Although it is an exciting method of teaching, online teaching is also a different method of teaching that is not for every educator (Blair, 2002). Indeed, there are full-time faculty members who are reluctant to teach online (Carnevale, 2004). Those teachers who resist distance education raise concerns pertaining to institutional support, interaction, and education quality (Bower, 2001). For many teachers, inadequate support can diminish their enthusiasm, sense of purpose, and effort. Acute frustration may eventually lead teachers to leave the profession (Baird, 1999).

Teacher Profiles

Among the teachers interviewed for the study, four were selected for in-depth interviews to afford a better understanding of their motivation in the online environment. The issues raised and the views shared by the four teachers profiled are representative of the larger respondent sample. These are two male and two female teachers who speak passionately about their profession. Two of them teach online, while the other two have tried it only to find out it was not working for them. Jeremy is an adjunct faculty member with more than 18 years of teaching experience who chooses not to teach online. Deborah, also an adjunct faculty member, has taught for more than 3 years in the on-ground classroom. Initially, she was excited about teaching online. However, Deborah soon determined that by teaching online she would not have the same exciting teaching experience she enjoys on campus. Derek and Sarah are full-time academics, with 13 and 21 years of teaching experience, respectively. They both teach online courses and are pleased with the outcomes.

When analyzed together, these reports open a rich window into their teaching, with these teachers' unmistakable passion for the profession as the common thread. Their respective profiles follow.

Profile 1: Jeremy

Jeremy is an adjunct faculty member at a large university on the West coast. He has a master's degree in English literature, and he teaches general education, communication, and business courses. He has taught for more than 18 years, all of them in the classroom.

For Jeremy, teaching is a profession. He strives for meaning and personal satisfaction in the classroom: "Teaching to me is a combination of imparting my knowledge to students and hoping that the light comes on, so that rather than just walking away with facts, they're walking away asking themselves and answering the following question, which is 'So what?'"

He is comfortable pursuing this in the regular classroom. Yet, when it comes to teaching online, there are things that he feels would be missing. In particular, the lack of immediate feedback prevents him from enjoying the experience: "Online, I personally do not feel that I can see those lightbulbs turn on, on the computer, communicating that way. In theory, I'd be with them in the beginning and the end, but that would be pretty small. I'm not interested in the money if I can't see the lightbulbs pop on." Personal satisfaction is very important. He is pleased to see that the students actually learned something; to know that he had an impact on making them better people. When he cannot see "the lightbulbs turn on," he experiences disappointment.

Jeremy cares for his students. He is concerned with some students' pursuit of a quick degree, disregarding the time and effort required to learn the material: "I get disappointed every class. There are some students who really don't want to learn. We've still got our share of students who have learned that a college degree will get you through the door. And, as you know that's true, you also know that once you're through that door, you'd better have something besides that piece of paper, or you're not going to get very far through the door. So that's kind of disappointing."

He cares for his teaching and does not consider teaching to be simply a job. While having a paycheck is not something to ignore, it is his passion for helping students that makes him teach: "No, it's definitely not the money. As I have kidded you in the past, Lord knows I will cash the paycheck. But the main thing is the 'Eureka!' When I see the student's face, when I feel they're actually learning something; like I said, when the lightbulb is turning on, flashing, that's my real pay."

His teaching has to be informative and capture the students' minds, making them forget about time: "I like for them to be surprised when it's the first break. I try to have them surprised when it's time to go. In other words, I try to make the time fly. I enjoy when students are actively participating. It's great when students actually do participate."

After graduating from college, his first job led him into teaching. Jeremy remembers how he got started: "In business, one of the places I worked was [xxx], at that time [xxx], two separate jobs, and I was a trainer, teaching marketing and selling classes, customer service, and things of that nature. And it was a kick, it was real kick, and I was good at it, and the students loved it. I was very successful, and they became successful when they went through me vs. some of the other people. I was quite good at something called *telemarketing,* so [xxx] University called me up and said 'We need somebody to teach a master's class in telemarketing. We understand you know telemarketing. Can you teach a 16 week class in telemarketing?' An academic class. Sure, why not? So I put the class together. So that gave me the 'bug' right there."

Teaching online is not even something to be considered. The perceived lack of non-verbal communication cues are a major reason: "Never even considered it [teaching online]. Although they are always asking me to teach online classes, I'm fairly sure I can't see the lightbulbs lighting up online. Exchanging e-mails with friends and relatives and what have you, I rarely see any kind of lightbulb flashing."

Jeremy's aversion to teaching online has nothing to do with the technology. Nor is it related to a lack of computer skills: "I think it has to do with the fact that I don't think I can help students nearly as well as I can face-to-face. Can I help them? Yeah, I can probably help them; I probably can see a flicker, but can I help them anywhere near as much as I could face-to-face; there's no way. I think there are some technological things that can certainly help students on their own, but as far as me being online, communicating with them online vs. going to class—I com-municate with students online, they send me e-mails, I answer back e-mails; it's not like we don't communicate via online, but in terms of it being full-time online, that's what I'm against."

Jeremy does not believe that any technology changes may make him change his mind. He seems pretty determined: "Is there anything that I could possibly think of that would make me want to teach online? The answer is no. The key thing for me is watching people learn and being able to immediately realize it or not. I can see immediately—that's not going to happen online."

Jeremy requires his students to submit homework assignments on paper. This forces students to do a better job at proofreading, if not more: "I tell my students, there's three things you do if you want to do a lousy job of proofreading. One is proofreading right after you've typed it, second is proofreading right off the monitor, and third, proofread it fast. Absolutely."

Teaching has some resemblance to a theatrical performance—it is the "The Show of Teaching." In Jeremy's own words: "At 6 o'clock, it's show time. I could have the worst day in the world. Six o'clock, hey I'm ready to go and I'm there till 10 o'clock. And quite truthfully, when I typically end the class at 10 o'clock, that's when I realize that I'm exhausted. I did not realize that until 10 o'clock, but now I'm offstage, I'm going back to the real world. And it's like 'Oh my God.' Of course I go home, and I get my second wind, but that's another story. One of my greatest rewards is when students come up to me long after the class is over and tell me what I did for them. That's the best reward. Because if they tell you right as the class ends, you don't know if they have an agenda or not. It's nice to hear and yet, why is she saying these things? I haven't issued a grade yet."

He believes in developing rapport with his students. His teaching is effective, and students remember him: "I was at a restaurant about 3 months ago, I was with my wife. Two of my former students, who I didn't recognize in the beginning, as they came closer I recognized both of them but didn't realize they were former students. It turned out I had both of them as undergraduates and had given them complete feedback in writing and so forth. And one is now going for his PhD, and the other is about to graduate with her MBA. And both of them said 'If it hadn't been for you, neither one of us would probably have finished our bachelor's degree. You've really taught us how to work, the purpose of writing.'"

He is really passionate about making an impact on the students. As Jeremy puts it: "If every instructor, you, for example, would give the amount of feedback you could give, because, although you are not a communication or journalism major, you know when students are communicating effectively and when they're not. If every one of us would give the feedback that every one of us is capable of giving, by the time they graduated, not only would they not be afraid of giving a presentation in front of a lot of people, they'd also be able to write effectively. And of course that doesn't always happen, no matter [what university] they graduate from."

Over the years, his teaching style evolved. He has now more patience and a more realistic view of the world: "I realize I can't change the world. I still try, but I realized even though it's still tough to accept, some students, no matter how many times I tell them, aren't going to do something as simplistic as putting five spaces between the header and the page number. No matter how many times I tell them put five spaces—and I never take off for APA, just tell them about it."

When asked to reflect on what makes a good teacher, Jeremy shares these thoughts: "I think a good teacher is somebody who really has the desire to be a teacher and to help people. To help them become better than they are, whatever the subject is. There's too many teachers, so-called, who do this as part-time gigs; so it's like, 'You mean I actually have to be here from 6 to 10? I can't leave at 9:15?' And for what they tell students—for example, when it comes to papers, if they give them any at all,—'I grade on content only.' And that's a cop-out. If I grade on content only, I can skim-read your paper in 30 to 60 seconds, just to see if certain buzz-words are in there. If there is, I give you a good grade; if I give you a good grade, you're happy, and—that's not a teacher. I'm not sure what you call that person."

At times, Jeremy experiences frustration in the classroom: "I'd say the frustration in the classroom would come from the students who don't want to learn and can't just keep it to themselves. Outside of the classroom, it would be the typical stump that one would run into, whether it's in education or business—the administrative overhead that gets in your way."

In Jeremy's opinion, teachers can be trained for success: "Nobody is born to be a leader or a teacher. You make some choices, have some experiences along the way, and from those choices and experiences you meld into either a good, bad, or some-where in the middle instructor. I'm sure you have seen your share of all of those."

Although an adjunct, Jeremy is putting full-time effort into a part-time job. He strives to make his courses fun and informative, and he gives ample feedback on student assignments. Jeremy is very fond of his students. He cares deeply for his students and is happy to see them succeed. It is not so much the money, but the satisfaction derived from teaching—this is what brings Jeremy back to class every day.

Profile 2: Deborah

Deborah is an adjunct faculty member. She has been teaching for 3 years in the classroom and has not taught online yet. She holds a master's degree and teaches science courses at a large university.

For Deborah, teaching is about helping others: "[Teaching] is extending help and assistance and sharing knowledge with others."

She briefly considered online teaching, yet the modality did not seem to live up to her expectations: "I attended the first training session, and then I felt kind of confused, and I really didn't like the attitude that was exhibited in the classroom. I took just the one training session and I never continued."

For Deborah, teaching is a stimulating experience that she truly enjoys. She enjoys being able to help extend the knowledge of her students and share her knowledge with others. Teaching is most rewarding when she can take a step back and leave the students at the heart of the discussion and watch them initiate issues and discuss different perspectives. Facilitation is a natural extension of her teaching approach: "When I step back [and let them talk] I'm on top of the world."

Yet she is comfortable lecturing when she finds it appropriate. She may use lectures to cover learning objectives. In her opinion, pure lecturing or pure facilitation do not exist. Teaching always involves a combination of both. With lectures, she offers information and tackles learning objectives; but this is just about basic information, about laying out the basic foundation on which the students can build. This is where the facilitation part starts, when she poses questions to her students. She then steps back and watches them build and work together, and she only intervenes to help them move on. She provides them guidance, to help them progress within the boundaries that she sets.

Her teaching style changes from class to class, as she constantly monitors the learning taking place and guides her students toward increasingly interesting and involving experiences: she customizes the course to the audience so that her students learn about issues applicable to their situation or context. Deborah is comfortable using technology in the classroom. She uses presentation slides and exchanges e-mail messages with her students. Yet, Deborah is a traditional teacher in some ways: "In my opinion I'm still traditional in my ways. I love to have a book in my hands. I torture my books as much as I cherish them, but I always underline, and this is the way I feel I enjoy the material."

She is nevertheless very passionate about what she is doing. She loves to teach. While some people arrive to teaching by choice, Deborah believes that she was born to teach: "I love teaching, I really do. I think it's the passion of my life, and I'm very, very serious. I think it's something that you either have the capability to do or not. Some people teach, and they give out of their soul, out of their heart and they connect with the students, and you set your students free and they fly with it, they bond with the information. You've established already the contact. I don't know what you call it, really. You set them off, and they're on their own, and you have ignited a torch of interest."

She already has a full-time job, and teaching is a part-time job for her. Yet, it is not the money, but her passion that brings her to the classroom. As she puts it: "And that is because I love teaching, I enjoy it, I enjoy moving forward with the students and getting them somewhere, to a certain dimension, a certain place where I can set them free and they can go on their own."

She loves being in the classroom. She enjoys the interaction taking place, the "meeting of the minds." She finds satisfaction in: "The amount of participation, the number of questions [they ask], the kind of questions, the interest. Are they sleeping or are they wide awake and talking? And then the back and forth communication, you know, like one person is very adamant regarding stem-cell research, with one opinion, you know, the interaction between the students and the length of time. At one point, I was sitting for 1 hour, and it kept on going back and forth and exploring other dimensions."

There are of course frustrations to cope with. First, perhaps her most significant concern is the lack of administrative support for using copyrighted materials (i.e., instructional movies) in the classroom. There are many resources (e.g., videotapes, DVDs, case studies) that she would like to use. Second, she is upset when she encounters students who misbehave, who show a lack of respect for the instructor and their fellow students.

She wanted to teach from a very early age: "I think maybe from high school time or maybe even earlier. I noticed that, I think, from middle school, from middle school on. Because I noticed that I have nieces and nephews, and my most joyful thing is to sit with them and teach them math or teach them science. Science is my big thing. Physiology, in particular, and so on. So it's my joy to sit with them and teach them from their book, and then the payback that I get is when I see their eyes all of a sudden kind of like sparkle and they say 'Oh, yes, okay we got it. This is nice.' And since the very beginning, I always get comments like, 'Oh this was never explained to us this way. You really have the capability to put things in simple terms so we can start to understand.' I got comments today from four or five different faculty members that they have tremendously enjoyed this workshop more than any other workshop. So it's just comments; I never ask for it, but still, it's happening, which tells you that something right, I guess, took place."

Deborah is aware of the need to keep students excited about the material, and focused throughout the learning experience. To her, teaching has no theatrical connotations. Rather than putting on a show, the teacher would be better served to customize the information to the audience: "[Teaching] is not a matter of a show; I think it's a matter of relating the facts in a way that is close to them. I find that when you relate to your fellow human being, in a very honest, down-to-earth way, you don't need to put a show on. You don't need anything else. You are building a bridge on solid ground, a solid foundation. They start trusting you and they start loving what they're hearing, and, then, the other component is freedom, setting them free. The mind is an amazing thing. Imagine how you can just open the door and they will fly through it."

Her teaching style centers on building trust with the students. She does of course follow the lesson plans, the learning objectives. But then she finds it extremely help-ful to give her students examples and let them reach the conclusion themselves. She gives them the information honestly, sticking to the facts. In order to build trust, she brings to class a lot of information. As Deborah views it: "I think also that the key component is when you bring issues from their daily life that you live through, they live through. It just connects, and they say, 'This is not just a professor of science, living somehow in a world of her own; no, this is her daily life.'"

She gives students practical applications for everything they learn in a down-to-earth way: "This would be teaching with both feet on the ground, basically. The students are able to relate everything you say to what's coming across to what would be of interest to them. Applicability and practicality, you know; daily life."

Deborah is aware about the human dimension of teaching and learning: "We're humans, and when it comes to look at it, we're all the same. Not in all ways, but basically we're down to it; we're just human beings whether we come from Africa or from China or the Middle East or from America or whichever."

She started teaching while still in college, several years ago, as a teaching assistant. Her professors always counted on her to assist in the class. And teaching proved to be everything she expected it to be. Her greatest reward is to see her students graduating, marching. She finds particularly rewarding to see some of the students who struggled with personal issues graduate, wearing the cap and the gown.

Deborah would like to see her computer skills improve. While she is computer literate, and versed in the use of basic personal computer applications, she would like to learn more so that she could create more complex course materials, using animation and multimedia. She is aware of the need to keep her skills up to date.

What comes across very strongly are Deborah's uncompromised values and humanity, her sense of direction in her life and her career. She kindly shared the following information with me: "I think the gift of knowledge… is the best thing to give a person. Especially to those of us who do not have much, knowledge—that's power. It's really amazing. Traveling overseas, I went to orphanages where children have nothing, practically nothing, and they're sitting there and they are happy with the pens, the nice pens, gifts. I asked them a question and they all raise their hands and they're jumping up and down and, you know, you get that chance in life to make a difference in their life. I think I'm doing nothing compared to my mother who started the female education in my country so many, many, years ago. The first school for girls that was opened there, was opened by my mother. I can not even tell enough about the stories, things that took place, and how much she fought and how much she worked."

Deborah's recipe for teaching success is quite simple: The joy she derives from teaching is predicated upon her ability to empower her students. To Deborah, teaching is about empowerment.

Profile 3: Derek

Derek has taught for more than 13 years, 7 of them online. He holds a master's degree in business administration, and he currently teaches for three different universities courses in accounting, finance, and economics.

Derek's goal is to help students increase their skills and expand their knowledge in the subject he is teaching. For Derek, the teacher takes on the role of a coach: He cannot really make the students *do* anything; he can only encourage them.

Derek is pleased with his online teaching experience. He describes it as a positive experience. Yet when he first started teaching online, he thought it was a waste of time. He was concerned about how online could replace the classroom and about his ability to adjust to the online modality and answer questions online. In the end, the online environment proved to be more interactive than he expected. His initial expectations were for online education to share more similarity to distance education: "I thought it would be more like, uh, distance education. You know, the old 'you get the book in the mail, you fill out the test, send it in, they grade it, send you back the test' kind of old fashioned work—study-at-home classes."

There are numerous things about online education that Derek likes. First, he saves a lot of time going to and from class. Second, he likes the smaller classes he has online. Third, Derek believes that classroom discussion actually is better online than it is in the classroom, with fewer instances of one student dominating the discussions—it seems harder for online students to take over the class. He lets the students ask all the questions. Online, the teacher takes on a role that is to moderate discussions, to get students to let other people speak. There are shy students online, just as in the classroom. Derek has an endearing term for them: he calls them *wallflowers*—they are the people who sit in the corner and don't say anything; the shyer people. The online environment is safer—the wallflowers find it easier to participate in discussions online. Those who have difficulty communicating in writing can draft their comments online, reflect on and revise them as needed, and submit them at a later time. One notable aspect is that the online environment establishes a sense of anonymity, because there are no pictures (personal photos) online. This perceived anonymity makes the students a little more comfortable sharing in the online classroom.

For Derek, it was more work at first online because he had to draft his lectures and select the assignments: "The first time around, it's a lot of work. However, anytime, the first time you teach a class is a lot of work. You got to use a book, and which assignments to give, and grading, and so on. I think it's more work getting ready for online."

Derek is not pleased that his online classes seem to be getting larger. While in the past he had online classes of between 7 and 10 students, now online classes of 17 or 18 students are common. This changes the dynamics of the interaction from what used to be a *seminar* style, with the graduate students sitting around chit-chatting about topics.

At least one of the universities he teaches for is using what he calls a *canned* lecture, which in a sense, he likes. The canned lecture package provides teachers with an instructor manual and a brief (10 page) outline of what they could teach. The outline becomes the lecture. This is associated with a reduction in the amount of participation the students have to do online and teacher workload. But this may come at the price of having more students in the class, and the teachers' pay stays the same.

The large classes are a concern for Derek, as they make it difficult for the teacher to ensure that every student participates in discussions. The teacher posts the lectures, assignments, and discussion questions. At times he has online students who never ask and never answer a question. When that happens, he counts how many times people do something, and sends them a weekly grade: thus, he just turns into a grading machine, an idea he decries. The students are supposed to participate and answer questions, yet with 17 or 18 students online, the communication can get out of hand. The teacher is forced to choose what questions to address, as he cannot always answer all of them. He has to balance between spending a lot of time answering the questions and grading students, because the university wants the grading done within a certain time (weekly). In general, the larger classes mean lesser attention after a certain point. Yet unfortunately, larger classes seem to be the trend in online education; at least that's what he noticed.

School administration's efforts to alleviate the workload of the teacher typically lead to more group assignments instead of individual assignments. Derek is not entirely comfortable with this approach, yet he appreciates the time savings afforded by taking shortcuts: "If I teach it the old way, I'll be spending 10 hours, 12 hours… I'll be making 10 dollars an hour."

Schools have a reputation to maintain. When teachers do not show up for class, classes get cancelled, and that makes students unhappy. Or teachers may not participate online or answer student questions. He is sympathetic to schools being pressured for profits and for trying to make online education more productive. He agrees with making faculty more productive. Yet, where faculty productivity is addressed by means of the canned lecture, he feels that the approach limits faculty. Rather, better use of technology may be the answer to increasing faculty productivity. Even basic computer simulations would help students learn. They alleviate the need for teachers to answer really basic questions to which the students should already know the answers. Another way technology could help the teacher is by supporting real-time interaction. One of Derek's employers has online chat capabilities for students and for the teacher. The teacher can have office hours and be online, and if somebody comes into the "office," the communication becomes interactive, similar to instant messaging. This allows him to multitask: "I can set it so, I usually wear a set of headsets, so if they enter the classroom, it sets off an alarm; you know, a sound alarm. So I could be doing other work, and then if I hear the alarm, I go into the classroom, answer their questions—it's almost like being in a real faculty office, waiting to see if any students pop by."

His students seem to enjoy a certain amount of real-time online interaction. Derek likes to schedule regular, weekly chats, where the students can show up and ask questions on the assignments and course materials. And even though only 15% of the students in a class may show up, a lot of people who do not show up read the messages saved in a chat archive. This would indicate that vicarious learning is taking place online. Derek has heard from students how valuable the chat archive is.

In particular, it makes up for the fact that this school uses canned lectures. Students regularly access the chat archive for help with the assignments.

The technology used today in online education could be better, Derek says. One school relies on Outlook Express[1] for communication, which Derek thinks it is a horrible product. A second school uses BlackBoard, a product that he likes more. Its features make it easier to organize lectures and assignments, accessible at a click of a button. In addition, there are discussion boards in separate folders, under separate buttons. This segregates the information and makes it much easier for the teacher to monitor the class.

The Outlook Express software makes it more difficult to navigate through and review a large number of messages, and some online classes result in a blizzard of messages. In reaction to a large number of postings, Derek has no option but to limit how many he will answer. He tries to answer the most relevant questions, but often he will let the students resolve some things themselves. Things get worse when his students post PowerPoint presentations to the Outlook Express folders. The teacher may have difficulty opening them: "Outlook Express won't let me look at them because they think there are security risks. So then I have to use the Web browser and go around like the back door and to open the assignment to grade it, which gets to be a real pain in the neck."

In contrast, other schools' systems have a class drop-box feature. Students upload the assignments to the class drop box, where the teacher can see them: "I look at the drop box and I see you know, Sorin's name, Bob's name, Jane's name, and Juan's name. If I wanted to see what you put in there, I just click on it. It shows me all of your assignments. It makes it easier for the teacher. It uses different color to mark those that I looked at, it sort of highlights for you what you've done and haven't done, which I like."

This makes the job of grading much easier because it helps the teacher keep track of what he already viewed. His student assignments involve solving problems. For his accounting classes in particular, Derek does not return graded assignments to students. Rather, he posts suggested solutions at the end of each week. This is easier to do with technology than it is in a classroom, where he would get papers, mark them up, and then hand them back. Online, he can just post the suggested answer, and the students can compare them to the one they got, to see where they went wrong or not.

Derek admits candidly that he likes teaching online, especially given that he lives in a densely populated area, where vehicular traffic can be difficult at times. This can detract from the experience of teaching, as it makes one tired. The online environment offers certain flexibility: One can enjoy a cup of coffee at the local coffeehouse and still teach online over the Internet (using WiFi, for example). Rather than being stuck in traffic, Derek would spend the time on the computer in the online classroom. There is no other real gain for him. Yet, the online education environment allows him to take a vacation, to travel some place, and still teach. As long as he can access the Internet, he is no longer tied to a fixed schedule.

For Derek, teaching online is neither harder nor easier than in the classroom, it is just different. His teaching is pretty much the same. He uses the same materials and student assignments. He might explain things differently online, though, to compensate for the lack of face-to-face communication cues.

One thing he does differently online is to provide more detailed explanations for those things he knows from his classroom experience that need more explanations. He tries to anticipate things, based on his experience in the classroom. Derek likes to teach the same course online and in the classroom at the same time: "I like teaching the class both online and in the classroom at the same time because I can sort of see where people in the classroom are having problems and that helps anticipate problems online."

He believes it is good for a teacher to teach a traditional on-ground class first, before teaching online. This gives the teacher an opportunity to learn beforehand what works and what does not, and what needs more explanations. He can then go online and is aware of what to expect. In Derek's words: "I think that if you just take somebody that never taught in a classroom and put them online, I would think they'd have trouble."

Other than becoming more skilled in using online chat, Derek does not feel he has gained much from the online environment. Certainly, not in terms of his teaching. It is just the flexibility afforded by the online modality that he finds to be a big plus. Building rapport with students is pretty similar, regardless of the modality. Derek enjoys using humor in class. Yet, online messages can be misconstrued easily. Humor helps lighten the load, especially if he is teaching a hard subject: "Online, you do lose some of the social bit of being in a classroom, you know, between the class, maybe at the break, or before the class, you chit-chat with the students and that kind of thing. You don't get that."

Yet Derek keeps plodding away, educating students one by one. He is a teacher, and that is what teachers do: They educate students.

Profile 4: Sarah

Sarah is an academic. She teaches at two universities and has taught for 21 years. She has 5 years of experience teaching hybrid modality (part classroom and part online) and has taught for 2 years online. She teaches instructional technology.

She views teaching as a task of arranging activities to allow others to learn: "Teaching, for me, is arranging a series of experiences so that students are successful at whatever tasks have been deemed important in terms of learning. I see a teacher as kind of an arranger of activities that prompt students to learn."

She describes her online experience as positive. Mainly, she enjoys the interaction with students, and she finds that a greater amount of communication takes place online. There is, of course, the flexibility to teach students across the country and still work a full-time job: "I can teach for an institution that's halfway across the country, because of the flexibilities that the online environment gives me."

Sarah also reports there are negative aspects associated with online teaching. First, she is particularly concerned with the difficulty of building rapport online. She believes that online students find it more difficult to bond. She misses the emotional bond that, in her opinion, builds more quickly in a face-to-face environment. Second, she finds that online teaching is very demanding on the instructor. It takes more time to teach online, and she finds herself spending a lot of time on the computer, due in part to what she perceives as the enhanced online interaction. She spends a lot of time communicating with her students individually as well as in groups. This translates into a lot of work for her, and makes her online teaching very time-consuming.

She finds that she adjusts to the online environment in several ways. She is more organized and provides more information upfront. Not to say that she is less prepared for her on-ground classes; however, she finds a need for more structure online, which she meets by having all her materials ready before the course starts. In an effort to build enthusiasm, excitement, and motivation, she cannot rely on nonverbal cues. Therefore, she has to plan much more for an online class.

She feels that it takes longer for her online students to get to know her. Developing a sense of trust among students and teacher is very important, and that is more difficult to attain online. Trust is very important, and it encourages communication: "I think it's very important as a teacher to start to build that sense of trust so my students, they feel that they can speak up in class and share their ideas."

From her online classes, Sarah learned the importance of getting everyone to participate in the learning experience. In the face-to-face environment, it is so easy to rely on those people who always talk in class; but that does not work in the online environment. In the on-ground classroom, she makes a goal of engaging everyone in some way, at some level. She is much more conscious of getting people engaged in the classroom activity or the learning activity.

That sense of the learning group; it takes so much longer for it to build online. She also misses the nonverbal interaction that adds so much to communication. She misses the body language and the facial expression. She would not abandon online teaching just because of this. Yet, she does miss these nonverbal communication cues.

Sarah compensates for the online environment in a variety of ways. For example, she tries to establish a tone for the class right up front, although she tends to prefer a less formal learning environment.

She discovered when she first started teaching online that it was better to set the expectations right up front rather than wait and see how things were going. The materials she prepares for an online course tend to be very detailed. Her syllabi clearly spell out the expectations and the assignments; she strives to set up the learning experience for her students.

Online, she definitely enjoys the flexibility—being able to interact with each student. As a result, she feels that in the online environment she gets to know her students better, despite never meeting them face-to-face. At the end of the course, as a group, she knows them better. In the face-to-face class, there may be a few students that she gets to know very well. In an online course, the minimum or the baseline for the whole group moves up. While there might be one or two students that she really does not get to know, for the most part, she gets to know the students better overall in an online class. She finds that there is much more communication taking place in the online classes. The asynchronous nature of the discussions allow for better preparation. The students have more time to think about what they want to say. As a result, the interaction is more on target and more thoughtful.

One of her main concerns regards technology. She wishes the technology would improve faster. Sarah seems at ease with using technology; in fact, she frequently used audio conferencing in the past for her courses. She would like to have the option of using real-time communication (e.g., online chat) to enhance immediacy and social presence. Often, the teacher or the students are waiting for replies to their messages. Online, one is never sure when the response may come. The online chat would alleviate this delayed response and help make the interaction more *real*—there would be an increased sense of immediacy that would be a definite plus.

Sarah talks about psychological distance: "We have so much experience seeing people on television that we have no personal relationship with—that we know we'll never have a personal relationship with—there's such a distance there, a real psychological distance."

Technology offers a great way to present information but falls short when it comes to building that bond between teacher and learner. The younger generation of students (the *Nintendo* generation, as she calls them) grew up with the computers and the online gaming and is now entering college; they are bored to death. Many of her students who are just coming into college have a completely separate online persona. They have their gaming role and they might participate in chats. Yet the online environment is not for everybody. But there are some students who should never be in the classroom, just as there are some students who should never be online. That is true about some teachers, too. Some teachers are great in the face-to-face classroom. Some are great online. The online environment can be difficult for everyone—students or teachers alike. It is certainly not a panacea to teaching: "I think it's not for everybody. If you're a bad teacher, going online is not going to make you a good teacher. It's just going to make you bad online."

If she could change anything, Sarah would like to know more about her students before she started teaching the class. Knowing more about students in terms of their background, their learning style, and their strengths would help her tailor things to them better, and it would lead to a more positive educational experience for both teacher and students.

When using online chat, Sarah manages the sessions by calling on students by name. She keeps track of the participation by using a little roster sitting beside the computer. As she calls on people and they contribute, she checks them off. She calls this approach her *speak when spoken to* model, and uses it to control the discussion (chat).

Sarah tries to avoid multitasking when she is in the online classroom; she tries to stay focused, but she notes that her students seem to multitask all the time. In chat rooms, they may have three or four threads going on at the same time. They answer questions, they are doing homework, and follow the course, all at the same time. In the chat [room] there is a certain amount of multitasking going on, just out of habit.

She is very careful about the use of humor online. Because so much of the humor relies on the nonverbal element, she makes sure that people know she is kidding when she says something. Humor is much easier to use in her face-to-face classes, where they do a lot of laughing in class and there is a sort of conversational, informal feeling. Online, humor can be misinterpreted very easily.

Sarah feels that it is harder to teach online and that it requires more work. To her, teaching has a certain resemblance to the sage-on-the-stage cliché: "As teachers, a lot of times we know we have to catch and hold our students' attention. And so a certain amount of what we do is entertaining. We use humor, we grab their attention with, you know, whatever. I think of that as kind of the performance element. If you remove that from the online environment—which you pretty much do—then how are you going to catch, how are you going to get, hold your students' attention?"

It is certainly true that, often, a certain amount of what teachers do in the classroom may qualify as *performance*. The teacher may be perceived as being entertaining yet informative. The online environment poses a challenge in terms of holding students' attention.

When asked to reflect on the effectiveness of the online environment, Sarah is very certain: "The machines aren't what's going to make a difference in whether our students learn or not. We can look at various media, whether it's television or the computer or whatever, and that's not going to make a difference in how students learn. It's the instruction. It's what you do with the online."

In Sarah's opinion, a successful online teacher would have a clear sense of what she wants her students to accomplish. She would constantly think about them. She would be very organized, and a skilled communicator—good at expressing herself with the written word.

Sarah definitely likes to teach. She has taught in the traditional classroom as well as in the online and the hybrid modalities. If she were to choose among these modalities, she feels more comfortable with the hybrid model: "I'd pick hybrid all the time. I think it's just the optimal model. The things that worked best face-to-face, you do in the face-to-face environment. The things that work best online, you do them there. I just think, 'Man! It's the way to go.' I would always pick hybrid."

Conclusion

Jeremy, Deborah, Derek, and Sarah were chosen as representative to profile the teaching experience in general, both in classroom and on-line. The four teacher profiles presented in this section show that faculty members are concerned about their teaching and about the modality that is used to support teaching. The interviews confirm both findings by previous studies and introduce new issues with regard to the teachers' motivation to teach and the online vs. on-ground teaching.

Jeremy has experience teaching in classroom, only. For him, teaching is a profession, not just a job. His personal satisfaction is very important: He is pleased to see that the students actually learned something; to know that he had an impact on making them better people. When he cannot see "the lightbulbs turn on," he experiences disappointment. He feels that the online would deprive him of the experience of directly and personally touching someone's life—of seeing "the lightbulbs turn on"; he is not bothered by the extra time, work, and effort that would have to be put into the process. No technological advancement can make him want to teach on-line. His perception is that on-line environment changes the communication process, preventing him from helping people "become better than they are."

Deborah is a university professor who also has only taught in classroom. For her, teaching is about helping others: "Extending help and assistance and sharing knowledge with others." In her teaching methods, she employs both lecturing, and facilitation. She has considered online teaching only briefly: The modality did not live to her expectations, having left her confused. Deborah has no intention of pursuing online teaching, as much as she is interested in advancing her computer skills and including technology and computer applications in her classroom teaching.

Derek has taught online for approximately half of his 13 years teaching experience. In his work, he is driven by helping students increase their skills and knowledge, coaching and encouraging them. He finds teaching online very advantageous, because it saves him commute time; perceived anonymity improves student communication by allowing shy, *wallflower* students to participate in discussions; access to archive chats helps students with their assignments; student assignment grading is easier online. Some of the drawbacks Derek points out are increased online classroom size, technology difficulties, and canned lectures that may limit faculty approach.

Overall, for him, teaching online is neither easier nor harder than in the classroom; it is just different.

Sarah has taught hybrid or online for 5 of her 21 years of teaching experience. She views teaching as a task of arranging activities to allow others to learn. Her online teaching experience is positive, because she finds that a greater amount of communication takes place online. Some other advantages that Sarah describes are course flexibility and getting to know her students better. Some of the drawbacks that Sarah signals, are missing the emotional bond that builds more quickly in a face-to-face environment; increased time needed to teach online, requiring increased organization and planning; the lack of nonverbal interaction; technology that still requires improvement; the need on the teacher's side to be a very organized and skilled communicator, good at expressing herself with the written word. If she were to choose among teaching modalities, she would pick hybrid.

The interviews reveal changes in education. For many years, education used to be about helping people grow, about grooming students (Dreeben, 1970). Yet, what teachers are telling about their online teaching experiences reflects their focus on knowledge transfer, on helping students acquire skills. The teachers interviewed for the study speak with passion about their work. Online teaching requires more time, effort, and technical skills as well as a change in communication style. It also requires more preparation and hard work. The online classroom feels different in terms of time elasticity. Because the online classroom is always "on," time seems to dilate. As a drawback, the online classroom may feel *empty*, as it is hard to tell who is *in* at any given time. The lack of face-to-face contact may induce online students to feel less pressure to contribute. Teachers acknowledge uneven participation and the potential for lurking. They also feel that imposing too much structure is detrimental to a value-free environment—as should be the case online.

References

Anderson, T., Rourke, L., Garrison, D. R., & Archer, W. (2001). Assessing teaching presence in a computer conferencing context. *Journal of Asynchronous Learning Networks, 5*(2), 1-17.

Baird, J. R. (1999). A phenomenological exploration of teachers' views of science teaching. *Teachers and Teaching: Theory and Practice, 5*(1), 75-94.

Bangert, A. W. (2004). The seven principles of good practice: A framework for evaluating on-line teaching. *Internet and Higher Education, 7*, 217-232.

Bender, T. (2000). Facilitating on-line discussion in an asynchronous format. In R. A. Cole (Ed.), *Issues in Web-based pedagogy* (pp. 381-388). Westport, CT: Greenwood Press.

Blair, J. (2002). The virtual teaching life. *Education Week, 21,* 31-34.

Bower, B. L. (2001). Distance education: Facing the faculty challenge. *Online Journal of Distance Learning Administration, 4*(2).

Boyd, D., & Arnold, M. L. (2000). Teachers' beliefs, antiracism and moral education: Problems of intersection. *Journal of Moral Education, 29*(1), 23-46.

Cahn, P. S. (2003). Number crunching. *The Chronicle of Higher Education, 50*(16).

Carnevale, D. (2004). For online adjuncts, a seller's market. *Chronicle of Higher Education, 50*(34).

Chang, C.-K. (2001). Refining collaborative learning strategies for reducing the technical requirements of Web-based classroom management. *Innovations in Education and Teaching International, 38*(2), 133-143.

Dreeben, R. (1970). *The nature of teaching: Schools and the work of teachers.* Glenview, IL: Scott Foresman.

Gehring, J. (2002). Higher ed.'s online odyssey. *Education Week, 21,* 27-29.

King, C., & McSporran, M. (2002, July). *Online teaching demands hands-on commitment.* Paper presented at the 15th Annual NACCQ, Hamilton, New Zealand.

King, K. P., & Dunham, M. D. (2005, January). Finding our way: Better understanding the needs and motivations of teachers in online learning. *International Journal of Instructional Technology and Distance Learning, 2*(1).

Nicol, D., Minty, I., & Sinclair, C. (2003). The social dimensions of online learning. *Innovations in Education and Teaching International, 40*(3), 270-280.

Paris, D. C. (2000). Is There a professor in this class? In R. A. Cole (Ed.), *Issues in Web-based pedagogy* (pp. 95-110). Westport, CT: Greenwood Press.

Rockwell, K., Schauer, J., Fritz, S. M., & Marx, D. B. (2000). Faculty education, assistance and support needed to deliver education via distance. *Online Journal of Distance Learning Administration, 3*(2).

Schell, G. P. (2004). Universities marginalize online courses. *Communications of the ACM, 47*(11), 107-112.

SchWeber, C. (2000). The "time" factor in on-line teaching: implications for faculty and their universities. In R. A. Cole (Ed.), *Issues in Web-based pedagogy* (pp. 227-236). Westport, CT: Greenwood Press.

Smith, G. G., Ferguson, D., & Caris, M. (2002). Teaching over the Web versus in the classroom: Differences in the instructor experience. *International Journal of Instructional Media, 29*(1), 61-67.

Sullivan, P. (2002). "It's easier to be yourself when you are invisible": Female college students discuss their online classroom experiences. *Innovative Higher Education, 27*(2), 129-144.

Endnote

[1]   Microsoft Outlook is a U.S. registered trademark of Microsoft Corporation. All other product names, company names, or logos mentioned herein may be the [registered] trademark of, and are property of, their respective owners.

Chapter III

What to Expect When Teaching Online

Introduction

This chapter sets out to discover how teachers view online teaching and what they experience when teaching online. It focuses on the stories that the 44 instructors shared with me during the interviews taken for this book. A brief perusal through the literature shows reports of increased time demands, more preparation and hard work, and a need for improved technical skills are just some of the issues that online education was reported to put upon teachers. Yet, as a result of this research, new issues were found, enhancing the knowledge on this subject of online teaching; for example, the extent of the adjustments made by teachers (discussed in greater detail in Chapter VII), the skill gap in technology among teachers and students (covered in Chapter V), and the tradeoffs faced by the teachers when moving to an online educational environment.

Background

A study by Vrasida and McIsaac (2000) shows that teaching online is not easy, because it requires preparation and hard work. It is concluded that teachers should expect to spend more time on course development, student assessment, and other course-related activities when teaching online, as reported by Pallof and Pratt (1999) and by Hall (2002).

Instructors report that online teaching requires more technical skills and that both the use of technology and the course content pose specific challenges. Hence, teachers need help preparing their online course materials, and this could come from professional developers.

The traditional, on-ground classroom is reported to be a much richer media than the online classroom, and to offer excellent support for human communication. In general, human communication is overwhelmingly dominated by body movements over vocal cues and verbal cues (Merrill & Reid, 1981). In terms of learning, written materials rate rather low. Pike (1989) showed that people, in their efforts to learn, generally retain 10% of what they read, 20% of what they hear, 30% of what they read and hear, 30% of what they see, 50% of what they see and hear, 70% of what they say, and 90% of what they teach or do (Pike, 1989, p. 153). This translates into an entirely different approach to communication and teaching when doing it online.

Where the social contexts are different, learning designs should be different. The online environment is more formal in that it relies mainly on writing and hence requires more time to think. It is reported that when online, there is less teacher control over the social context of learning. Nicol, Minty, and Sinclair (2003) suggest that reusable dialogues can help students learn and reduce teacher workload when the archives of prior discussions are available for review.

Text-based communication, prevalent in the online classroom, supports sustained reflection in classroom exchanges. Students develop a sense of accountability from the high visibility of the Web (Sengupta, 2001). In this regard, technology can promote learning in more complex areas of knowledge, such as analysis, synthesis, and creative judgment. Yet, both media richness and social influence affect the media communication choices in Web-based learning (Huerta, Ryan, & Igbaria, 2003).

Students and teachers value the flexibility offered by the asynchronous dimension of the online class. This may result in more collaboration taking place online (Klipowicz & Laniak, 1999). Advantageously, the online learning environment offers the potential to be more female friendly; its anonymity allows students to interact online without the distracting noise of social conditioning (Sullivan, 2002).

With regard to the issue of class size, it is reported that it matters. On one hand, if the class is large, the number of online postings can be quite overwhelming. On the other hand, if the class is very small, the online discussions may not go well (Brower, 2003). As for the quality of the interaction, a study by Angeli, Valanides, and Bonk (2003) found that, at times, the students' online dialogue does very little to support learning as it is mostly related to personal experiences and does not reflect well-supported reasoning. In general, the classes that have the best course outcomes tend to be small and combine face-to-face with online instruction—a "Web-enhanced class" (Pallof & Pratt, 2001, p. 168).

What to Expect When Teaching Online

As indicated in the Preface, the book draws on the results of a study that involved interviews with online teachers. All of the 44 teachers who participated in the study are comfortable with the fact that online education is not a fad; rather, it continues to grow and therefore it cannot simply be ignored. No one expects it to go away: "Online education is definitely here to stay. It is not just a fad; I think it is definitely here to stay. I think there are responsibilities to do it in such a way where the students receive the greatest amount of benefit from that" [09].

Teachers are aware of how quickly online education is growing and are concerned with its impact on the society. One interviewee states that "I'm aware that the online modality is growing dramatically. This whole concept of online teaching is now part of our culture" [12]. Instructors do not see technology as a threat and feel that their profession will continue to play an important role in education for years to come. Quoting one teacher, "I don't think teaching would ever become a commodity. Teaching will always require live instruction, I guess. If that was not so, then people could buy books from the bookstore and learn by themselves. I don't think we'd ever get into a situation where people who like to learn would teach themselves. They want an interactive mode" [36].

It is only natural, then, that teachers continue to reflect on how they can use the online environment and on what can make online teaching desirable and effective. They talk about their online teaching and describe it using terms that touch on the multiple dimensions of the online teaching experience: they talk of theatrics, humor, workload, student quality, media richness, interaction, feedback and assessment, course development issues, time demands, privacy, and the dehumanizing aspects of the online environment.

Course Development

All the teachers interviewed are aware of the economics associated with online education. Online education requires significant setup, and the *administrative* costs can be a burden: "A drawback is the cost of making sure the infrastructure is well developed" [10].

Technology costs are only one concern. A second concern relates to the cost of developing course specifically for the online environment. Most teachers are familiar with courses development techniques. They either develop their own courses or work with professional developers who help them prepare their courses. Course development and design for the online environment can be a particular challenge, at times, as significant difficulties are encountered: "It takes so much work to build a module that you want to build it and let it go. You might want to come back and tweak it and add something here or there, but you never want to rebuild. It took me, when I first started teaching, it took me a year to build the modules and then another year to refine it. It took an extremely long time. That's another disadvantage to the online" [22]. Of particular concern are the situations where multiple people are involved in the design of one course: "We try to do it as a task—created as a committee animal. There is something missing here; a classic problem" [19].

Humor in the Classroom

One teacher, who was very familiar with the theater environment, singles out the powerful energy exchange taking place in the traditional classroom: "I've been in a couple of plays, I've been onstage. I've been in that [theater] environment. I think a lot of teachers get a lot of energy from that kind of setting; when they walk into the classroom, they step up to the podium, or their desk or whatever, there is a whole lot of showmanship, a lot of stage presence" [40]. Some teachers thrive on this classroom energy and strive to recreate it when it is missing from the classroom.

A low-energy classroom may lead to a boring teaching and learning experience. Some teachers notice they encountered students who get bored in the classroom and who seem to be more comfortable studying *online*. This is especially true for the younger students who would seem more inclined to manage their learning time on their own terms. As one teacher puts it, "I know quite a few young people who in a classroom setting would just be so bored right now, whereas online it is their time, they feel comfortable doing it, there was a transition from something fun which was a video game into this. It's fun" [09].

As retaining the attention of the students may be difficult at times, teachers resort to using props to help reach out to the students. This appears to be more important with certain age groups, with younger students in particular. In that case, "The only way to capture students' attention and retain it is by having props" [37]. Props are therefore an important component of the teaching experience, at least for some of the teachers that were interviewed.

In the theater, actors rely on feedback from the spectators to liven up their performance. A similar thing happens in the classroom, where teachers use *humor* in their teaching. Once again, it is all about doing what it takes, within reason, to arouse the interest of the students: "[In the classroom] from the student's expression and from their comments, I can tell that they are understanding what I'm trying to do. It's a show, it's a show, basically. I have to make it interesting, I have to make it attractive, and I have to make it in a way that they want to come back" [32]. When teachers attempt to energize the classroom, some of them resort to certain theatrics in an effort to accomplish this task.

Theatrics

For some teachers, there is a degree of theatrical performance involved in teaching. They compare the classroom experience with acting, with a show. The *theatrical performance* dimension is almost a required accoutrement. As stated earlier, certain students crave an entertaining learning experience or they lose their interest, their focus. Teachers seem keenly aware of the need to keep their students interested: "It becomes somewhat theater. I mean it does. Because you've got to keep them [the students] awake, you have to look for eye contact, or eye avoidance if they've not done the reading, that kind of thing. It is exhausting [for the teacher], but very fulfilling" [23]. Hence, some teachers' inclination to resort to theater-like props and performance in support of their teaching.

The idea of performance is closely related to that of putting on a show—a performance. However, not all teachers agree with the show metaphor: "[Teaching is] not a matter of a show; I think it's a matter of relating the facts in a way that is close to them [the students]. I find that when you relate to your fellow human being in a very honest, down-to-earth way, you don't need to put a show on" [30].

When teachers embrace the *theatrical performance* approach, they do it because they do not want the students to get bored. Once student *boredom* sets in, it may be difficult to regain students' attention. Some teachers make a conscientious effort to present information in an *entertaining* format. The *performance* dimension of teaching is undeniable for some. Yet, the goal is for effective teaching rather than mere entertainment: "Anybody who denies that standing up in front of 30 other folks and trying to keep their interest for 2 hours is not performing doesn't know what they are talking about. But I don't mean it in the sense of having to be theatrical; I mean it in the sense of being effective. It is performance from behind a curtain" [43].

The *entertainment* is especially required for the evening classes, when students come to class after a day of work, and they are presumably tired and eager to get home. In such cases, the theatrical performance seems unavoidable. The effort on behalf of the teacher is significant, yet there are certain rewards for the teacher: "There seems to be this act to pull off, this show. One of my greatest rewards is when students come up to me long after the class is over and tell me what I did for them" [29].

The *theatrical performance* is apparent when teachers strive to keep the students focused for the entire duration of the class. At times, they rely on humor to achieve this objective. One teacher shares his views on the subject: "It is that silly cliché about the sage on the stage, kind of thing. So teachers, a lot of times we know we have to catch and hold our students' attention. And so a certain amount of what we do is entertaining. We use humor, we grab their attention; and I think of that as kind of the performance element" [39].

Some teachers are of the opinion that the theatrical performance is not always necessary in online teaching; rather, it depends on the audience. It is up to teachers to assess their audience and decide accordingly what works best for their class. As in the entertainment world, the audience has a direct impact on the performance: "[The importance of] the 'dog and pony show' depends on the audience, but it can be extremely important" [04]. Whether they are required in the online classroom or not, theatrics may be easier to engage in while teaching on-ground, where emotions can be communicated with greater ease than online.

As discussed previously, some teachers equate their teaching to a show, or on-stage performance. They try to keep their student engaged in the course and in the class activities. Generally speaking, when they teach, teachers are actors playing a specific role: that of a teacher. However, there are other numerous roles a teacher can play. The online teacher takes on a different *role* than in the on-ground classroom. The characteristics of the online medium require an almost one-on-one, tutoring type of relationship among teacher and students. These roles are discussed in greater detail in the subsequent chapters.

When asked to describe how it feels to teach online, the respondents reflect on the *differences between classroom and online* teaching in metaphorical terms. If teaching is a theatrical performance, then the classroom would be the *Broadway show* and the online would be the *movie*. Or, in the words of one answerer, "In the online setting, it is much like a radio drama where you fill in a lot of stuff. In the face-to-face setting, they do see you as an expert, but they also see a lot of the imperfection and so forth" [40].

Time Demands

Teachers note the increased demands on their time when teaching online and describe what they perceive to be a dramatic increase in the amount of time required to teach. One teacher finds that "It is really time consuming to, to read all of these discussions" [08].

As a matter of fact, some interviewees report that online, the increase in time demand can be as high as two and a half times higher, adding to their *teaching demands*: "It is time commitment, to really get it all in, as I said, two to two and a half times more than in a classroom. It is much easier in a classroom" [12].

In addition, instructors note that the *expectations* related to teaching online are not always realistic, particularly from an administrative perspective. The online teacher is subject to a flurry of messages that he or she must respond to. One teacher asks: "How can you expect an instructor to look at 400 messages per week and provide quality responses to even 50% of those? It is not practical" [34].

One possible explanation for the increase in the time required from the teacher is the changed nature of the interaction taking place online. The effect may sometimes be felt at a physical level. As described by one responder, "If you are ever-patient, and you respond to every student every minute, and you are at the computer all the time, and you always think before you write, and you organize everything and present it well, everyone will love you. The school will think you are a great teacher; when they look at your files, everything is organized; and you are just a wreck. You paid the price. That is like being tackled 10 times while you are throwing passes" [05].

Reminiscent of a culture of immediate gratification, online students expect things to happen fast—learning included. The Internet has accustomed them to be able to access information at the click of a button. This quick response time may induce them to have unrealistic *expectations* in terms of communicating with others. Quoting one interviewee: "I've said [to a student], 'Do you realize how many emails I respond to in a day? Do you realize how much time it takes and how much it takes away from other things?' And when I do this, the students are kind of shocked, and then they cut back on what they are trying to do. They are not aware of what demands they are placing on the instructor in the online environment. They are not mean, they are just doing what they feel they ought to be doing, and an instructor, by doing what I did, is taking a risk that they are going to lose the class" [05].

We have already learned from our conversations with teachers that the online time seems to take on a new level of velocity: Time flows differently online. Teaching online is much more *time*-consuming as compared to a traditional classroom. The demands on the teachers' time can be significant. According to one of them, "[Time demand is] just phenomenal. I spend so much more time trying to set expectations in the online course than I ever had to in the offline" [34]. Just as in the on-ground classroom, the teacher must give students the feeling they are not alone in the online classroom; that the teacher is there with them, yet no one can really expect the teacher to be online (and awake) for the duration of the course, 24 hour days: "You have to be there [online] every day. You have to be in a very regular schedule. It is a great cognitive drain. It takes a lot out of you" [05].

In the on-ground classroom, time is indeed of essence: Classes follow a precise schedule. In fact, one of the great advantages of online education is its asynchronous aspect; eliminating time, in a sense, from the equation. The class is "in session" around the clock, with students free to join in any time they please. Therefore, the *perception* of time is different online. There seems to be a certain dilation of time, at least for some respondents. The drawback to this is that it has been observed to affect the students' timely submission of assignments. In the traditional classroom, the passing of time is more evident and the same for everyone. As one teacher says: "It seems like when you are keeping a schedule in the class students mentally keep on track a little better, online it just seems like time is not a factor. It seems like you can do whatever you want forever and it doesn't really make any difference. I would say that time—and I think it is the Internet thing; you can get on the sucker 24 hours a day, so it's a *mañana* factor, 'Oh, I won't do it right now, I can just do it tonight at 12 o'clock, 1 o'clock in the morning.' No, if you are in classroom, you know you have to be there at such and such time" [22].

Despite the perceived time elasticity, which can be very advantageous, online students seem to *expect* immediate feedback and quicker responses from the teacher in general. They seem to see more of a one-on-one communication pathway with their teacher, often forgetting that the instructors also have the rest of the class to communicate with. And, they do expect the teacher to be available around the clock: "There was this one occasion where a student calls me, sends me e-mails, calls me again, stuff like that. I don't count on that nearly to the extent in the offline world, because the students are used to seeing the instructor once a week. So, if it takes you 24 hours to respond to an e-mail, I think they are OK with that. You know, generally speaking. But in the online world, that is not the case" [34]. Online, the teacher is expected to provide immediate responses, regardless of the timing and complexity of the request.

Assessment

Because teachers engage in student assessment as part of their instructional routine, student assessment and evaluation is always present, irrespective of the teaching modality, and is one of the *teaching demands* that is typical of this profession.

In general, it is more difficult for teachers to keep track of students' progress online than it is in the traditional, on-ground classroom. The limitations of the technology employed make it more difficult for teachers to monitor students. As one teacher put it, "When you meet with people every day, you know everybody knows who's there and who's not. I think that when you are in a lab walking around, it's very easy—I can look over a student's shoulder, whereas, online, I don't see things until they are ready for me to see them" [07]. It should come as no surprise, then, that, somehow, student *assessment* seems easier in the traditional classroom. As expressed by another respondent, "In the classroom, it's open book, it's individual effort; I can monitor, and they are told that this is an individual effort. I can see if there is sharing or no sharing going on; I can't see that in the online" [12].

Some teachers resort to on-ground tests for their online students: "Managing exams is still an issue; that is, how do we ensure that students are doing the work by themselves, etc? In [our school], it is required that exams for distance course still be done and managed traditionally" [10]. Proctored on-ground examinations given at the end of the course leave less room for cheating. Another interviewee brings up the issue of cheating as follows: "The assessment process, in general... I'm not talking about just plagiarism, but is it the enrolled student who's taking the online test at a distance? When I give students tests, I assume they are open-book, open-note, and design them that way, and my grading policy that way. I grade on a rubric system, so it's not just the test scores; I look at discussion, lab portfolios, and so on. But I think there's this big question out there with these online students, doing the course from wherever—are they taking the test, or are they hiring someone to take the test for them?" [41].

Students sometimes resort to shortcuts to their schoolwork. At times, they may use someone else's work without much regard for intellectual property. Plagiarism is just as big an issue online as in the traditional classroom, with many teachers being frustrated by this: "That was a real concern in the online environment, where one of the students knew one of her former students and was turning in her assignments. We've had plagiarism software, but because you are not seeing the students on a physical basis, they are not taking tests in front of you, and so it is sometimes a concern whether they are the ones completing their assignments or not. I think that is something we are really going to have to sort out in the online environment, that I sometimes worry about, whether it is actually the student who is the student of record who is completing the assignments or tests" [35].

Students contribute to the learning experience—they are an integral part of it. For our interviewed teachers, student assessment and student quality are related issues. They express concern relative to the quality of the students who enroll in online education, because the quality of the students is paramount for the quality of the teaching and learning experience. This holds true irrespective of the educational modality involved, whether online, on-ground, or hybrid. Online, students seem to have a greater impact on where the course is taking them; therefore, teachers feel increased pressure to adjust the online content to meet the needs of the students, more so than in the traditional campus-based classroom: "Online many times the topics are sprung by the students and every class is very different that way because people's interests are different. And you have to think about it and respond so there is always new work, new thinking and new analysis; it is not packaged sort of the same way as the on-ground class" [36].

Younger students, in particular, seem less prepared and less motivated to think on their own—a requirement in the online environment. One teacher finds that "Younger students, they see themselves as members of the herd, not competitive members of the society" [19]. The younger students grew in a different world than the older ones, and often than their teachers. These students' familiarity with, reliance on, and enthusiasm for *technology* is no match for some of the teachers. Some teachers experience this very acutely: "We didn't have the technology of going online. I've seen it with younger students, with high school students, even elementary school students, where they are doing the chat rooms now, and they are like they are talking to each other on the phone. They are growing up with it, whereas adults, and the adult education environment hasn't grown up with it, and that technology is… they are learning that technology" [26].

The online environment leaves out nonverbal communication cues that are desirable to some teachers. Its reliance on technology yields an environment that could be described as impersonal and bland, a consequence of its low media richness.

One teacher reports that the online environment "It is just less personal. Just by the nature of it. I mean it sort of has to be bland and offend no one. Because it is all out there in print; so you can go back and read things over and over" [27]. These affect both the amount and quality of the feedback available to teachers.

Feedback

Teachers note that the act of teaching may carry significant, intangible rewards, which are instrumental in keeping teachers interested in the profession. They derive satisfaction from "seeing" students learn and understand the course materials. This provides immediate, essential feedback to the teacher, especially in the on-ground classroom: "I enjoy teaching online a lot less. [Online] is very flexible for me, and that is great for this program, but I don't get the positive feedback with the students, I don't get that personal interaction; it is essentially a chain of e-mails" [07]. Teachers like to receive *feedback* in class, and they rely on it to control the learning experience and guide the students. As important as it is for them, feedback is limited in scope in the online environment. One interviewee offered the following reflection: "I personally do not feel that I can see those lightbulbs turn on, on the computer, communicating that way. In theory, I'd be with them in the beginning and the end, but that would be pretty small. I'm not interested in the money if I can't see the lightbulbs pop up" [29].

Some instructors report that online interaction may be more rigid and structured, yet allowing for more flexibility at the same time. The structure is apparent in the need to follow pre-prepared course modules and to not deviate much from the script; this is needed in order to keep discussion focused and class progress on track. As for flexibility, the *interaction* taking place online may take on different directions and/or topics than initially envisioned by the teachers; therefore, more questions may arise, and more topics may be covered. At times, these new topics may diverge from the path spelled out in the course module. One teacher puts it in unequivocal terms: "You have to be more rigid online, but you can be flexible....Well, it is rigid and flexible at the same time. Rigid because there is a certain thing that you cover unless you want to reprogram the whole module, which is a real pain" [22].

Whether on-ground or online, an ongoing concern seems to be the *class size*. Online, however, this appears to be more critical, since it affects the amount of interaction, teacher feedback, and the teacher's ability to establish rapport with their students. This negatively affects the instructors' overall teaching ability. As expressed by one answer, "Excessively large classrooms... online is very demanding: With 15 users, you are a monitor, not instructor. With 15 in the classroom is much easier: If they are doing presentations it takes about 4 hours while online, you must take them one at a time, resulting in tremendous time requirements" [21].

Rapport

Teachers express a need to connect with their students. They try to build *rapport* with the students, a process which is very important to them, and are disappointed when they are not able to. One teacher notes that "I deal with probably the same number of issues in every class. You know students, things come up in their lives, they don't understand, they are not keeping up their end, and they think it is your fault and what-not but, on top of that, I get students who are having a great time, and they are learning, and they come up to me and share things; I see them every day, I get smiles. You don't get that; you don't get that constant feedback, you know, online" [07].

Teachers who are trying to build rapport with their students find the online environment less conducive. Some of them find it difficult to relate in particular to younger students. In the words of one teacher, "I think there is a gap there, generational gap or whatever you want to call it, in translating information for this new generation. Although they are not aware of the content, so they are not content experts, they are bored in trying to learn the content, so they don't pay attention. We don't have their attention. So, I think we should find a different medium to reach them, where we can funnel the content through and see it grab their attention; and maybe computer gaming is a good way. What I've also noticed is that the students are trying to multitask: When they are in class they are trying to use the computer to check e-mail, write messages, write notes, and it seems to me like they are trying to cut the time it takes to do these tasks, to be more efficient. I don't know exactly what that efficiency is going to bring. I don't know what that line if they were to cut all these items' time short, then what? Are they after more leisure time, are they after just chasing themselves, because this is just a mode they are used to. They don't know how to relax. That would be a good question to ask an anthropologist" [37].

More Work

As teachers cope with course development issues, online time elasticity, student feedback and assessment, and attempt to build rapport with their students, they find out that often these challenges result in more work for them.

Teachers prepare for class and teaching online requires more *preparation*. There is a higher degree of improvisation in the traditional classroom than online. Quoting one online teacher as he reflects on why the expectations seem so high, "If you go to the movie, you expect it to be a flawless movie. When you go to a Broadway show, you expect there to be some ad-libbing. In fact, you want it. You like to go to a live show because you like the improvisation—that's the excitement" [13].

Yet, other interviewed instructors report that it seems that the traditional classroom requires more elaborate preparation. In that regard, the online classroom is more forgiving, as it allows the teacher to prepare, and refine her course as it progresses. One teacher finds the on-ground environment is more challenging: "There is a lot more preparation involved in the live classroom... In the online classroom, you can sort of prepare as you go along. You have your lecture ready, you know what questions you are going to be asking students to discuss, but you can be much more flexible as the week shapes up. What you are talking about, the direction the discussion is going to be going. You don't have to have everything in upfront. You can let the classroom shape itself. I like teaching online, because I'm not so nervous" [25].

Teachers recognize that in order to be successful when instructing online, they must make certain adjustments in how they package, and deliver information to the students. They constantly try to look for novel ways to impart knowledge: "But just disseminating information and telling students what they need to know is not the way to go. We know what not to do; we don't know quite what we have to do" [37]. This involves changes to both content and delivery format of their course materials, which translates into more work.

At times, teachers assign additional homework and extracurricular activities to their students in an effort to enhance their learning. In the online teaching, this additional homework that is generated and needs to be graded sums up into more work for the teacher. As expressed in very precise terms by one of our interviewees, "The online students have additional homework, and that means more homework to grade" [16]. To a certain extent, teachers may bring more work upon themselves simply because, online, everything is in written form; there is no verbal communication, such as in the on-ground classroom. Consequently, there is more written material to contend with, including homework, e-mail, and discussion threads.

Expectations

Having said that about the amount of preparation that is needed to teach online, are the expectations any different online than teaching in the on-ground classroom? Online teachers were glad to share their views regarding the perceived expectations associated with teaching online. Some teachers are quite vocal in their beliefs that the *expectations* are higher in the online environment. There is an increased level of professionalism that is required from the teacher who teaches online. Not to say that teachers' professionalism is not already high across the board; after all, it is known that most teachers care deeply about their profession. The online environment just seems to push the expectations up a notch: "Because you go in there [online], you expect because it is professionally edited and it was directed, and maybe you have never seen a movie that's had a problem, have you? I've never seen a movie where someone's had a bad line. It might be a bad movie, but no one starts cracking up" [13].

Most of the interviewed teachers agree that teaching online requires more clarity, more precise content delivery and communication of the course goals and expectations. To this, the teachers make *adjustments*. One respondent shares some of the adjustments he has experienced, as follows: "What I think it comes down to is I'm much more explicit [online]. Whenever I take one of these kinds of courses that was developed offline, and all of a sudden they put it online, I find myself spending significant additional time developing materials to help the student more explicitly understand things in terms of the requirements of the course" [15].

Generally speaking, some of the courses require teachers to demonstrate concepts. However, this is not always possible online, and this leads some teachers to believe that online education is not really working. The truth is that certain subject matters are just more difficult to teach online. In particular, courses that require increased involvement on behalf of the teacher are not good candidates for the online environment. This is a particular concern when students need more coaching, more guidance and hand-holding, as it is often the case with remedial courses: "I could not imagine teaching mathematics online to someone who, you know, could not get through algebra in high school. I couldn't imagine teaching high school algebra [online]. I guess it could be done, but I think it would be difficult. I think that when you are teaching to someone's weakness online, one's weaknesses shine much more. Whereas when you are teaching to someone's strength, I think online is an ideal situation. If it's something I'm interested in and they are interested in, and have some knowledge, they can go through it fairly quickly, but if we were trying to teach programming to philosophy or English majors, I think they would have a great deal of difficulty online" [07]. Not all subjects can be taught online the same way.

Due to either technology constraints or lack of skills in using it on the part of the students and possibly some of the teachers, some things are still easier to demonstrate in the on-ground classroom rather than online. As expressed by one teacher, "The problem they have is they don't, they are not that, uh, familiar with the technology, and that can uh, be very frustrating to them. Because they don't see that in the class, if it was in the class I could quickly show that to them, but they don't see that on the Internet. So, that is the negative thing that comes to mind as well" [08].

Furthermore, given the inherent limitations of the technology available, teachers must carefully consider how these limitations will constrain their teaching online, and the inherent tradeoffs. They must also be aware of the technology that is available to their students, which sets additional constraints. One interviewee reflects on this issue as follows: "Might not be feasible if students don't have adequate infrastructure support—as an instructor issues such as bandwidth and access to PCs could prevent from delivering data-heavy content" [10].

Privacy

The online environment facilitates safer, easier, and friendlier interaction of some of the students in the educational process. This is quite important for the teachers, because it encourages shy students, who otherwise would not contribute to the class, to be more involved and participate more: "You can do things in class in terms of personality, in terms of making people feel at ease; there is a whole bunch of other things you can't do online. On the other hand, some people are more embarrassed in class than they would be online" [17]. This has the potential to foster improved interaction among students and better class participation.

Yet, teachers are concerned with their teaching privacy in the classroom. They do not feel comfortable with others having unlimited access to their online classroom, without their prior knowledge and permission, and under their control. In the words of one frustrated online teacher, "In an on-ground environment, when an instructor goes into the classroom, it is his castle. In the online environment, people can come any time they want and they can do anything they want, and you don't even know that it's going on. That is a big problem" [05].

Other Challenges

The information that has been provided so far throughout this chapter reflects that, without a doubt, teachers have strong feelings about online education in general. Teaching effectiveness, course usability, appropriateness, teaching demands, trad-eoffs, technology constraints, student expectations, control over the teaching process, administrative issues, course design, and class size are just a few of the issues that preoccupy the teachers. For some of them, online education is not quite ready, it does not meet their expectations. Consequently, they doubt its effectiveness and are not interested in teaching online. At least one of the teachers that I talked to, reports a very determined position: "I've been there, I've taken the [online] training, and then I realized that this is as I said, that this is not effective teaching, and I won't be able to do it properly, the way I do it in the classroom; and then find out for me it is not ready. So I won't go up and do it; I wouldn't teach [online]. Because I don't think that I'll be able to be an effective teacher, instructor, you know… my job… is to elaborate and explain and articulate the subject which they are interested and they are required by the curriculum. And if I cannot do it effectively, I wouldn't touch it. That is a moral obligation, and I cannot do it. I stay away from it" [11]. Thus they make choices—to teach online or not.

The experience of teaching online is more abstract in comparison with the traditional on-ground classroom. One teacher believes this is due to the technology compo-nent that is self-evident and permeates the entire online teaching experience: "The technology makes the act of teaching online a more abstract experience" [04]. The channel affects the communication, and teachers notice that online *communication* follows different dynamics as compared to the on-ground classroom. As reported by one answerer, "Everything that you do online takes longer than it would just to speak. Now, speaking is a fairly efficient and quick process, whereas if you are having to write every communication, that takes time. Also, you are not sure if they are reading it the right way" [15].

There are certain dehumanizing aspects brought about by the online education environment. For one, the feedback is different online, and the lack of nonverbal communication cues may have a disconcerting effect on some teachers. Many teachers report deriving satisfaction from having an impact on their students, and that may be more difficult to attain when teaching online. One teacher expresses herself candidly: "I think part of the joy of teaching is being able to relate to people and show them that you care. I think caring and kindness and compassion are what make a great teacher. There's only so much that you can put through in an email message, and teaching with a capital 'T' requires a special kind of person. That special kind of person cannot always express themselves through the distance learning as much as they might want to" [13].

It may be that the over-reliance on what is known about teaching in a traditional classroom is a problem. Teachers are concerned that not all that they are doing—or asked to do—may be appropriate for online education. As expressed by one teacher, "I think what we are doing is putting the cart before the horse there. We are coming up with the modules or the requirements and direction that the online classroom is supposed to be based on what has been historically the classroom environment, and I think that there is not enough thought processes going into it, what is going on online" [26].

As discussed previously, there are some teachers who view teaching as being similar to performing on stage. For these teachers who "perform," teaching online detracts from the teaching experience. There is something missing, they say. Human interaction is diminished online, and some teachers resent the loss. As another one of our interviewed teachers reports that "Taking away the live audience; it diminishes the teaching experience. I get a kick out of... and its part of the perks, part of the motivation of being in the profession in the first place, I get a kick out of being able to crack a spontaneous joke and having a classroom erupt in laughter. It's an immediate sort of reward for teaching" [04].

Yet despite a sense of added flexibility, the online environment can be unforgiving. Perhaps because of its reliance on technology, there is less room for error in the online environment. The teacher better not make mistakes, because in the online environment memories never fade—everything posted online will remain available to scrutiny. Some teachers feel they need to pursue an error-free, machine-like teaching performance online: "Once you remove the person standing there live, the expectation is that this is now some kind of machine. You want to get drawn into a movie, when we don't have live people in front of us, we think about things differently..." [13].

In addition, whether theater-like play, or movie-like setting, the online teaching environment is perceived differently by each individual. Teachers try to adjust their teaching (and behavior) to best accommodate the shortcomings of the environment and to take advantage of its features. While still partial toward the on-ground classroom, a blend between traditional classroom time and online education seems favored by many of our respondents—a *hybrid* environment. One of the teachers notes, "I think a good mix is there, too, because a lot of the quality learning environment is basically interaction, face-to-face interaction, and you lose that somewhat online" [26]. Seemingly, and at least for some online teachers, the hybrid environment offers the optimal approach to online education.

Conclusion

Teachers are aware that as a relatively new and intriguing modality for delivering education, the online environment is different from the traditional classroom. They have an increased awareness of how quickly online education is growing and are concerned with its impact on society. More so, they are aware that as online education continues to grow, it will bring new opportunities and challenges. For some of them, there is a degree of theatrical performance involved in the process of teaching, even though not all teachers agree with the "show" metaphor. They note that some students get bored in the classroom, and feel more comfortable studying online. Sometimes, teachers use props to help reach out to the students. Teachers recognize that in order to be successful in teaching online, they must make adjustments in how they package and deliver information to the students. The expectations are higher when teaching online, because as the online environment relies heavily on technology, it allows less room for error.

As teachers are concerned with the online environment, they continuously evaluate its potential. They ask themselves questions about this environment's characteristics and dimensions, and how it affects their teaching and their effectiveness as teachers. The technology at the core of online education brings about its own challenges.

Teaching online is seemingly time consuming, more so than in the traditional on-ground classroom. The demands on instructors associated with online teaching can be significant. Teachers feel increased pressure to adjust the online content to meet the needs of the students, more so than in the traditional campus-based classroom. More preparation is required from the online teacher. Interaction online is in written form, and some teachers find that to be very beneficial. There is more structure online, yet more flexibility at the same time. The online environment offers a safer, friendlier environment that may help shy students who otherwise would not contribute to the class.

While most teachers still prefer to teach on-ground, some online teachers indicate that a hybrid teaching modality—one that relies on classroom time in combination with online periods—is preferable. In their views, the on-ground portions would allow them to build better rapport with the students and to teach course topics that are more suitable for on-ground and require face-to-face interaction. Further, the online portions would add flexibility and convenience to the course, and would be used to teach things that can be taught well online. As educational institutions move in this direction, experimentation with various subject matters, different ratios of on-ground and online periods, and technologies, are needed to determine the optimal structure of the courses offered in a hybrid format.

Course development for the online environment can be a challenge at times. For certain subject matters in particular, some teachers report that they are not yet convinced that online education is really working. Another ongoing concern seems to be class size. Teachers are concerned with having to teach to large classes, as it negatively affects their teaching ability. It is more difficult for teachers to keep track of students' progress online than it is in the traditional classroom. The teachers participating in the study documented here report that online interaction is more difficult to control, as students answer messages and post new messages on their own terms. However, the online environment allows for more in-depth discussions. Reliance on e-mails leads to a much closer relationship, as the online forum forces students to communicate frequently with their teachers. Consequently, online teachers must overhaul their teaching strategies: Their ability to write clearly and concisely is important. Technology plays an important role in online education.

The teachers who were interviewed for this book provided valuable data that bring attention to an important component of online education, to what teachers experience in teaching online. They agree that they spend more time teaching online, both in preparing for the courses and in assessing and grading student work. They rely more heavily on technical skills, as there is no fallback system; the online classroom is supported by, and depends on, technology. While teachers report a variety of challenges they identify in teaching online, it seems that at times, the answers that teachers seek are not available. The new environment alters teaching to such extent that additional research is welcomed.

As new technologies are deployed to support online education, future studies may help show whether this trend holds. For the time being, it is reasonable to assume that the debate around the effect of the media richness on online education in general, and on online teaching in particular, will continue.

References

Angeli, C., Valanides, N., & Bonk, C. J. (2003). Communication in a Web-based conferencing system: The quality of computer-mediated interactions. *British Journal of Educational Technology, 34*(1), 31-43.

Brower, H. H. (2003). On Emulating classroom discussion in a distance-delivered OBHR course: Creating an on-line learning community. *Academy of Management Learning and Education, 2*(1), 22-36.

Hall, R. (2002). Aligning learning, teaching, and assessment using the Web: An evaluation of pedagogic approaches. *British Journal of Educational Technology, 33*(2), 149-158.

Huerta, E., Ryan, T., & Igbaria, M. (2003). A comprehensive Web-based learning framework: Toward theoretical diversity. In A. K. Aggarwal (Ed.), *Web-based education: Learning from experience* (pp. 24-35). Hershey, PA: Information Science Publishing.

Klipowicz, S. W., & Laniak, T. (1999). Hebrew exegesis online: Using information technology to enhance biblical language study. *Teaching Technology and Religion, 2*(2), 109-115.

Merrill, D. W., & Reid, R. H. (1981). *Personal styles and effective performance.* Radnor, PA: Chilton Book Company.

Nicol, D., Minty, I., & Sinclair, C. (2003). The social dimensions of online learning. *Innovations in Education and Teaching International, 40*(3), 270-280.

Pallof, R. M., & Pratt, K. (1999). *Building learning communities in cyberspace: Effective strategies for the online classroom.* San Francisco: Jossey-Bass.

Pallof, R. M., & Pratt, K. (2001). *Lessons from the cyberspace classroom:The realities of online teaching.* San Francisco: Jossey-Bass.

Pike, R. (1989). *Creative training techniques handbook, tips, tactics and how-to's for delivering effective training.* Minneapolis, MN: Lakewood Books.

Sengupta, S. (2001). Exchanging ideas with peers in network-based classrooms: An aid or a pain? *Language Learning & Technology, 5*(1), 103-134.

Sullivan, P. (2002). "It's easier to be yourself when you are invisible": Female college students discuss their online classroom experiences. *Innovative Higher Education, 27*(2), 129-144.

Vrasida, C., & McIsaac, M. S. (2000). Principles of pedagogy and evaluation for Web-based learning. *Education Media International, 37*(2), 105-111.

Chapter IV

Determinants of Online Teaching Success

Introduction

In this chapter, teachers share their thoughts regarding the determinants for success in online teaching that makes some online teachers successful. A brief review of the relevant published literature is followed by a discussion of the determinants of online teaching success, substantiated by copious citations from the interviews conducted for this book. Several issues identified by our teachers are very important for ensuring that online teaching is successful. Emotional involvement, teacher effectiveness, student quality, and technology reliability are only some of the issues affecting online teaching success. Teachers care deeply about their profession and find that the relatively static design of the online courses leaves little room for experimentation and quick adjustments. Online, they are more effective in helping students improve their writing. In the classroom, they are more effective in helping them reflect on the world.

Background

A brief comparison of the findings of this study to some of the available literature augments the theoretical sensitivity at the core of the study, and helps improve internal validity. For each of the main categories grounded in data, the review of existing published research helps assess the validity of the constructs and their respective properties and dimensions.

Several studies have been researched to identify the elements of success of online teaching and they will be summarized in the body of this chapter. Teaching is a subject of great interest; yet, as teachers are agents of change, "little is known about how teachers think about the aims of education" (Boyd & Arnold, 2000, p. 23). One researched study documents that one of the major forces that drive some teachers to teach is passion, and a lesser force is the monetary rewards (Cahn, 2003). The data derived from this study's interviews support this view. The contention that teachers take on a constructivist stance when teaching online (Bangert, 2004) is also confirmed by my findings. More, the teachers interviewed are caring people, in no way different from what Shulman (2000) found:

The scholarship of teaching reflects a convergence of disciplinary, moral, communal and personal motives. If one is truly devoted to one's discipline, one is committed to transmitting and developing faithful conceptions and understandings of the discipline in students. Thus the integrity of the discipline leads to a sense of what is best for the students. (p. 98)

The teachers interviewed for the study speak with passion about their work. They confirm and delineate the elements described by Rosenberg (2001): "Instruction contains presentation, practice, feedback, and assessment components" (p. 13).

The interviews reveal changes in education. For many years education used to be about helping people grow, about grooming students (Dreeben, 1970). What teachers are telling about their online teaching experiences reflects their focus on knowledge transfer, on helping students acquire skills. Teaching, it seems, has evolved into a facilitation stance, where the teacher directs the class rather than just disseminate information.

Several other determinants of online teaching success exist, from an administrative point of view. Goral (2001) reports an increasing number of colleges and universities offer online programs and that distance education is moving into every industry. Carnevale (2003) found that training online is even more prevalent than online education. In the light of this trend, universities try to determine to what extent business decisions should drive their institutional policies (Wysocki, 2005). Then, tensions exist between research and teaching components of the faculty role (Serow, 2000). Many faculty members in colleges and universities are embittered and report feelings of regret, envy, frustration, betrayal, and isolation, and this affects their attitudes toward work (Jensen, 1995). One study reports that 32% of the teachers would not volunteer to teach online, and 54% of them believed the quality of the courses is lower online. Teachers who used little technology were more likely to hold negative views about online teaching. Faculty members lack appreciation and would like to have better students (Magna Publications, 2004). In addition, per Klobas and Renzi (2003), other issues exist related to inadequate access to appropriate information and communication technology (ICT), excessive focus on business goals, and lack of support.

One area of concern for teachers is that school administrators focus on the fiscal implications of online education. This leads to the number of part-time faculty members growing faster than that of full-time ones (Feenberg, 1999). Nationwide, in 2005, nearly half of all college faculty members are part-time teachers: this is an increase from only 22% in 1970 (Hersh, Merrow, & Wolfe, 2005). Faculty is pressured by changes from education globalization and the potential of ICT to transform education delivery. This is even more of a challenge for those teachers who were formed under different circumstances (Clegg, Konrad, & Tan, 2000).

Another area of concern, very important to ensure online teaching success, is that teachers need well-developed guidelines and policies for online education (Ershler, 2003). They need help in the development and delivery of course materials (Klassen & Vogel, 2003). A teacher is supposed to teach and participate scholarly. Yet, building an online course may require 300 hours and between $35,000 to $55,000 (Carnevale, 2004). Despite all the difficulties, based on the findings of a study done by Speck (2000), those teachers who are interested in technology will eventually learn how to use it effectively for teaching.

From the point of view of institutional administrators, they have to contend with new personnel issues: faculty skills, new personnel needed, faculty compensation, and resistance to technology. Faculty members' compensation includes money, tenure, release time, and course load. Current policies regarding personnel appear to be ad hoc. The increase in faculty resistance to technology is due in part to teachers' perception that it does distort the educational experience (Rayburn & Ramaprasad, 2002).

Determinants of Online Teaching Success

Some teachers are successful in their teaching, and others are not. Or, is it really that simple? From the interviews conducted with teachers who teach online courses, a number of common traits have emerged—traits seemingly characteristics of a successful online teacher. Among them are passion and empathy for the students; knowledge of the subject matter; good communication skills, good writing skills, organizational skills, and time management skills; technology skills; patience and an ability to mentor students; and last but not least, having good students can make a world of difference. A teacher who shares these traits is well positioned to teach successfully in the online educational environment.

There appears to be a general agreement among teachers themselves that not everyone can become a good teacher. Teaching can be a difficult activity, and it is not for everyone: Some teachers believe that subject mastery is not necessarily associated with good *teaching* skills:

The fact that there are relatively few excellent teachers, percentage-wise, is empirical evidence that teaching is hard. A person can master, absolutely master, a subject field, and can keep up with it, too; you know, not just master and solidify, you have to master and then keep up with your field... but still be a lousy teacher... a horrible teacher. I've run into, unfortunately, some of those people... mostly at the university level but also at the secondary level. [04]

If teaching is hard, what are teachers (including those who wish to become teachers) to do? Teachers talk of the emotional involvement in their profession, their effectiveness as teachers, and of their use of technology in their teaching. Each one of these is addressed in the following sections of the chapter.

Emotional Involvement

One common characteristic of the majority, if not of all the teachers interviewed, is that they are caring people. Teachers care deeply about their teaching, their students, and the learning that takes place in the classroom. They want their students to grow as human beings. The failure of any student marks them profoundly, affecting them on an emotional and personal level:

If I went in there and I didn't care, you know... and I didn't care if I just flunked everybody in the classroom... that would be a different story. But for a teacher who cares, it's emotionally and personally difficult to be in that kind of a situation. [04]

Teachers' passion for teaching and potential for empathy is pervasive and colors their teaching.

While the educational modality may affect their teaching, there is more to being a successful teacher: The teaching modality alone will not turn a bad teacher into a good one. As one teacher puts it: "Going online is not going to make you a good teacher" [39]. This statement emphasizes the importance of personal traits over the modality used for teaching.

As mentioned earlier, successful teachers share certain characteristics in that they are open to engage in dialog with the students, have excellent communication skills, are approachable, and knowledgeable. A good teacher converses with her students: "They place a value or importance on their teaching... they engage students in dialogue, which is a two way conversation and not one way" [01].

Continuing to expand on the idea of determining the elements of online teaching success, another interviewee confesses that *what makes a good teacher* are patience, technology skills, time management skills, and willingness to mentor students:

The ability to communicate in a textual environment, the ability to facilitate dialogue rather than lecture, being responsive and giving good feedback. And, of course, all the technological comfort and facility with the technology. And, patience. Willingness to take on multiple roles: sometimes we do a little bit of tech support, sometimes there's a little bit of advising because we are their primary contact. In many regards, we represent the school to the learner. Time management, the ability to coordinate and manage all the deliverables… you have your e-mail, you have your online chats, you have your online discussions and how to manage all those deliverables in a way and do the record keeping, and getting [close to] the students and being responsive and those types of things. I think one of the key things is maintaining the thread of discussion…working with and guiding learners to post responses to each other rather than everyone creating their own threads. These are some of the different types of competencies that an online instructor may need. [44]

According to another respondent, knowledge of the *subject matter* is also very important, as well as communication skills and a caring personality, organization skills, training in teaching, an open mind, a genuine desire to help people, and being a people's person:

Knowledge of the subject matter for one. Ultimately, communication skills—verbal and or written…. Care… care for both the subject matter and for the student and care for the profession of teaching as well. Those things are all required. I also have a lot of training in various classroom techniques and training in acting and training in speech and training in visual arts and written arts as well. So all those things… but that training didn't come easy. [04]

Quoting another teacher, it is equally important for instructors to be open-minded, and to like to learn: "I enjoy learning new things, I've got an open mind… and I think that's very important for us instructors" [06].

Taking the meaning of successful teaching to a different level, one of the interviewees defines teaching as a *vocation*. The idea is that teachers have to be prepared to make personal sacrifices, the reward being a sense of meaningfulness, as their efforts benefit the whole society at large. In the words of one teacher: "That they feel that the work they're performing in the classroom has a value, may be (micro) value for the society and [that] we produce better educated, more knowledgeable, more discerning, more questioning individuals" [01]. Many teachers agree that teaching is an acquired taste. It can be a time-consuming exercise that not everyone will appreciate. For those teachers who are not in it for the money, teaching is definitely a vocation, and vocations require sacrifices, as least in one teacher's opinion: "I had to sacrifice a lot in terms of money and time and attention and effort to mold my raw talent into being a professionally skilled teacher on a high level" [04].

One teacher makes a very powerful statement when concluding that in order to be successful the teachers must focus their *teaching* on the student:

You constantly have to think about them... not being so focused on what you do as a teacher, but what they are doing as a student. I think certainly, a good online teacher is... organized, they're a good communicator, they're good at expressing themselves with the written word... because so much of your communication is written. [39]

Furthermore, it is neither the technology nor the teaching environment that ensures a teacher can teach successfully. It is the teacher's ability to use what he or she has available for his or her *teaching*. The technology alone will not transform a mediocre teacher into a good one: "It's the instruction. It's what you do with the online" [39].

Of course, most people can be trained to become teachers. Yet, the very experience of teaching will affect them in ways they cannot predict. Some folks turn into outstanding teachers, while others remain average, unremarkable teachers: "Nobody is born to be a leader or a teacher. You make some choices, have some experiences along the way and from those choices and experiences you meld into either a good, bad, or somewhere in the middle instructor" [29].

As more answerers ponder on the subject of good teaching, they conclude that it requires good teachers. Those teachers who are genuinely concerned with, and are passionate about their fellow human beings will develop into great teachers: "I think a good teacher is somebody who really has the desire to be a teacher and to help people. To help them become better than they are" [29]. Teachers cannot be good unless they are also humble, show empathy toward their students, and make an honest effort to help them learn—all which are pivotal attributes of the *teaching dimensions*: "I think you have to be empathetic and articulate and clear" [42]. Being a people's person is also very important:

[A good teacher] doesn't have an ego. Well, everyone's got one. But one who can really empathize, understand where the students are at. Who could be a student while being a teacher. Who can really say, "What is the best thing to help these students to learn? How can I take them forward?" Someone who'd rather see the students feel good and strong; in other words, in some classrooms, teachers feel like they have to be in control of the class—who's speaking, how long they're speaking.

But a really good teacher allows the students to take control of the class. He really becomes a person who guides thought rather than disseminates it. [13]

Aside from knowledge, passion, empathy, and an inclination for the profession, teachers must also have excellent interpersonal skills. According to another one of the instructors interviewed for this book, they must be approachable and responsive to students:

Keeping the communication lines open—as open as they can be in an online environment. I think you have to be very responsive. Because now you're having students that are interacting in an online environment 24 by 7. You have to be in a sense more responsive than in the offline environment. I think many of the things that make a good offline teacher or in-class teachers carry over into the online. But I think those are things that the instructor needs, as well as the ability to communicate in writing, those are very, very important. [34]

Being able to build rapport, to connect with students, may be the most important quality a teacher could have: "The ability to connect with a student, the ability to get inside their heads" [27].

To a certain extent, teaching is about influencing students, guiding them through their learning experiences. Yet teachers cannot force students to learn, they can only coach them—and that is only one *role* they may play: "I think teachers are coaches. You know uh, not... not so much... we can't make them do anything, so we sort of encourage them, you know, encouraging and all that stuff is a lot of it, I think" [31]. Once again, interpersonal skills play an important role and can help a good teacher stand out.

Online education relies in large amount on written communication. It is more formal in nature, and a teacher who is more formal in style will fare better online as compared to one that is more informal. As one teacher puts it, "People whose natural teaching style is more formal would probably do better online" [27]. Given the emphasis on written communication, it follows that good writing skills are very desirable and most valuable to a teacher who teaches online:

If the person is a good writer, then it can be an advantage to be online, because the student can type in a rough draft sort of thing, go get a cup of coffee, come back, revise before they post to their discussion; a teacher can do the same thing. The teacher doesn't have to instantly react to something that the student writes... the teacher can read it, step back from it for a minute and go take a shower or something and then come back and respond, after having thought about it a little bit. And if the teacher's a skilled writer, then they can pull that off a little better online. [04]

A second teacher adds his views:

I think mostly, it's to be a good writer. A good writer is a good communicator. A good communicator is someone who thinks for a long time before they say anything. If you're a good writer you think before you write and you communicate well. So people who are really good writers and communicate well are going to be great online instructors as long as they're willing to do it. [05]

Good organization skills, especially teaching online, are essential. About this, one teacher shares a little secret: "To be a successful online instructor you have to be very organized" [08]. In addition, clarity in communication and the way course materials are organized, presented and delivered make a significant difference: "A good teacher has to make himself or herself very clear to them what the expectations are and the material that is taught: teach and explain it in such a way they can relate, put yourself in their place" [32].

For some of our respondents, having good students is very important. They believe that their teaching is vitally affected by *student quality.* As confessed by one teacher: "The students make the instructor. A good instructor doesn't make a good class. A good class makes a good instructor. That's the way it is... that's the way it works" [03].

At least some of the instructors are particularly concerned with the effectiveness of the online environment, with how it affects their teaching and relationship with their students. So far, we have explored some of the determinants of successful teaching and identified some of the traits of a good teacher. Next, let us see how well these traits hold up when teaching online, and how effective they are in this environment.

Teacher Effectiveness

Some teachers reflect on how the effectiveness of the online environment may be taken for granted. Too often one ignores the relatively static design of the online courses. In contrast, in the classroom there is more tolerance for experimentation, adjustments and changes, and for teachers to modify their instruction as they find it appropriate in support of the course goals.

In terms of teaching effectiveness, the *online* environment compares favorably to the traditional on-ground classroom, as much as the opinions are shared. Several teachers note that the online environment is already *effective*, and that it supports their teaching very well:

I personally feel that the online class… the online experience is more effective… in the traditional face-to-face setting, you can walk into a class, you can sit there for 16 weeks and never open your mouth once… You can't do that in online setting and because of the demand of that active participation. I don't have any qualms at all saying that it's more effective because the students are actively engaged. [40]

While the structure is different between the two modalities, some teachers say they attain an acceptable degree of teaching *effectiveness*. Online, they compensate for the differences between the modalities, as seen in detail in Chapter VIII. Some teachers even claim that in fact, they are more *effective* teaching online than in the on-ground classroom: "I think online I'm more effective. I'm getting more and more satisfied students in terms of percentage who learn the most" [36]. Others, however, feel that they are more effective teaching in the traditional on-ground classroom, where there are more communication cues: "[In] on campus classes, I think I'm most [effective]… maybe because I'm just seeing that in their faces, in their expressions… and see that smile on their face. It's such a rewarding thing, and you don't see that online" [08]. For some, teaching online may attain an acceptable degree of *effectiveness*, while still lagging behind the traditional classroom.

Where teachers are used to being spontaneous, and to bring in additional course materials as they find it necessary to enhance the process of instruction, the *traditional classroom* seems to afford them more opportunity to do so: "I do find myself being able to go into additional material I hadn't been able to get to online. Last night… it was the first week of the scripted statistics we actually covered 12 formulas in a span of 2 hours, $2\frac{1}{2}$ hours, and I don't think I could have done that online" [12]. There is more flexibility on-ground for some, compared to online, and there is also seemingly more improvisation, which is important for some teachers. To the extent teachers feel that improvisation and flexibility helps them teach, the online environment calls for different strategies.

As a general statement, a teacher's overall *teaching* effectiveness depends on a variety of factors. Furthermore, there are various dimensions of effectiveness, and teachers describe how these dimensions vary across modalities. Some teachers find that *online*, they are more effective in helping students improve their writing, while in the *classroom* they are more effective in helping them reflect on the world. Once again, *effectiveness* may be expressed in different terms, and by different measures.

Teachers recognize that learning and cognitive traits suggest students would learn better in one modality than the other, and they are aware that having good students would help them teach more effectively. As schools have a fiduciary duty to their customers—the students—to offer them an optimal learning environment, some teachers are of the opinion that students should be evaluated and guided toward the educational modality that best suits their traits, abilities, and skills. In one teacher's opinion:

I think there are students that do better in the online environment, some probably do about the same, and for some it's just not for them. It's definitely not for every student. But there are students who would do better online and would have a harder time in the classroom. It's just a matter of matching the learning style, or opportunities, or social situation of the students with what they would fare better in. [41]

Generalization is difficult, and one must cautiously reflect on teaching effectiveness as related to the educational modality—online or on-ground classroom. Teachers recognize the complexity of the factors at play in each environment, and emphasize the importance of the institutional factors involved:

I think it's possible to be equally effective, but I don't say that as generalization, because I think it depends entirely upon the individuals involved—the teachers and the students, the content material, the level of the course, and again, the extent to which the university or institution has assembled resources that support the teachers and the students. I think it's possible to do well in both, but it does take the right combination of people with the willingness to work in the environment, and put up with the occasional frustrations that you do meet. [43]

As teachers reflect on their online teaching experiences, they share their views and opinions on what they would like to change, or improve, that would help them teach more effectively, and would result in a successful teaching process. Some teachers feel the potential for *change* is minuscule, given there are institutional policies they must abide by: "I may not be able to change anything because there are certain policies that the university expects." [12] Other teachers are just happy with what they have, and find it hard to think about suggestions and recommendation. They are successful at what they are doing, and see no room for improvement: "I don't know if I would change anything that would improve the experience for the teacher. I really think that the way they've got the classes set up really make a lot of sense and make it very easy for the instructors." [28]

Yet, where they offer suggestions, the teachers talk of administrative issues, class size, privacy, teacher compensation, and better technology to support their online teaching.

Many suggestions that teachers offered are administrative in nature and relate to the educational institutions' administrative policies and practices. One thing that teachers would like to control better is program expansion:

I would manage the growth better. I think we try to do too much too fast. For example, they just discontinued [simulations] in my class. I think the reason why they discontinued it is because many students complained about it; it was a 4-hour thing, it took them 17 hours; it was just a grueling thing. They should have perfected it before they implemented it. I think it was a great idea; it's nice to have somebody to talk to on the screen to learn the material when you're at home, instead of just working on the textbook, but perfect the mechanics of it before you introduce it, and I think that would help tremendously. [02]

At some universities, teachers acknowledge they have relative freedom to change the course content and student assignments as they deem appropriate, within the guidelines set by the university. Yet, chief among the things they do not control are class size and student quality. In the opinion of one teacher,

Going back to the smaller classes, and the quality of the homework assignments... We do have the leeway to change the module as we see fit, as long as we achieve the objective. But definitely keeping the classes small, would keep the quality up. When the classes start getting too big, it's overwhelming, you can't keep up, you can't do a quality job... And I think the other drawback is that, in general, most of the online schools have no entrance requirements. Students enroll, yet are not well enough prepared for the environment. [16]

Affected again by class size, online, the amount of communication exchanges increases in direct proportion to the number of students. As one teacher puts it: "[Online, we need] smaller classes. For one class of 19 students... it was four thousand messages by the end of six weeks" [27]. Teachers fear that they may not be able to effectively monitor and address student questions given such large number of messages. Smaller classes of perhaps five to eight students are viewed as ideal for teaching online. Another teacher supports this idea of smaller classes by stating: "The classroom size needs to be small in an online environment as opposed to an on-ground. On-ground you can have larger classrooms because it's mostly done in a lecture-delivery mode" [36].

The classroom has always been the teacher's undisputed domain. The teacher was, and still is to some extent, the authority controlling access to the classroom. Online this changes dramatically, and not every teacher appreciates this change. Rather, there is growing concern relative to privacy, and the perceived amount of *control* they are subjected to. As shared by one of the teachers:

We have to have an understanding with the people who hire us. It's a contractual issue. If somebody says, "I think you're a great teacher, and I want you to come and work for me" you have to be able to say, "Well I want to know who will be looking over my shoulder, and what they're going to do." And I am certainly willing to have somebody look at my performance, or evaluate what I'm doing—in a professional way, in an appropriate way—but I don't want people spying on me online, any more than I want people spying on me in a regular classroom. [05]

While not necessarily the strongest motivator related to teaching effectiveness, teacher compensation does play a role in conducing the teachers to do a good job. A perennial item, teachers' compensation needs to be revised as the demands posed by teaching online call for adequate compensation:

Making sure that a teacher... in addition to be paid an hourly wage for being in the classroom, they also get an office hour... they're paid for at least part of an office hour, depending on their classroom load. That pay should not be stripped just because you're online... just because it's taught online doesn't mean the teacher is spending less time on it than they would be in the classroom... so compensation parity is important. [04]

Since time demands are increased online, more teachers report that they would like fair *compensation* to match. More work should result in more pay:

I want to be paid the 3 hours for my class and another 45 minutes for my office hour as well. Because I still have office-hour duties, whether it be responding to e-mails that students have sent me where they would have just walked into my office and taken care of it there, or grading papers or whatever it happens to be, I want my compensation to be equivalent. [04]

Teachers would like to be recognized and appreciated for what they do:

In an online kind of environment, in order to achieve what I achieve, I have to pay a much more stringent price. I get tremendous responses from the students and they appreciate that, and I get classes to teach, which is kind of a grudging appreciation, but there's very little recognition and there's not the kind of financial return that really makes it worth my while. [05]

Another reported component of success in teaching online is the administrative *support* in terms of curriculum advising. Teachers would like to see more guidelines and more peer collaboration for sharing of best practices, as active participation of all teachers in curriculum design would benefit everyone:

I think that there's not enough curriculum advising; there's not enough direction on curriculum on the college level. While a lot of academic freedom is valuable, and that allows the creative process to take place, I think that it would be nice to have a little more standardization of expectations and, say, learning outcomes and things like that, and I think there's not a lot of that on the college level and graduate level. I think adjuncts don't have as much opportunity to be a part of that process, and adjuncts are picking up an increasing amount of the teaching load. I had many classes taught by teaching assistants. You know they're kind of disenfranchised from the process also, and they're doing the bulk of the teaching. I think it would be helpful to give them more of a voice. [15]

Online teachers are constantly striving to find ways to ensure online teaching is increasing in effectiveness, and technology is a pivotal element. With regards to technology, the opinions are shared when teachers compare the online and on-ground modalities of teaching.

Technology

Several of our interviewees make the point that another needed change that would improve the success of the online teaching process is greater institutional and *administrative* support and increased access to modern technology:

Greater institutional support—investment in right technology and not rely solely on e-mail to conduct online teaching. In addition, giving equal recognition to courses that are thought online vis-à-vis traditional delivery. This is with respect to issues such as teaching credits given. [10]

Technology can be difficult to deal with, especially when student enrollment and growth in general are not well supported by the technology deployed. This can hinder the teaching process and affect it in a negative way. As one teacher sees it, "The online university is growing too fast, it's growing faster than they can handle the server issues" [02].

The very choice of *technology* can be a problem in itself. One teacher shares his frustration:

The technology is a hindrance in itself. Being limited to using Outlook Express and threaded messages, I think there has to be a smoother way of doing it that no one's come up with yet. Using Outlook Express is better than some other things I've tried, other models I've seen in the past, but it's not ideal by any means. So I'd like to see improvement in that area. [25]

More to the subject of the present technology leaving a lot to be desired:

It's not fluid. It would be nice if you could just open up a window on your screen. More like a chat environment, where messages go back and forth fluidly, but the whole thread is captured and kept going all the time. I just find Outlook Express to be very static and not easy to work with. [25]

At the other pole of the issue, some teachers have difficulty in using the technology available to them and find it to be overly complex. Simplicity and *ease of use* are favored over glitzy features. One respondent shares his experience:

We used WebCT… In my thinking it was overly complex. We moved to a less expensive, simpler program… and I'm finding that much easier than WebCT, just logistically, to handle. So I would suggest a simplifying of the technology, a streamlining of it. Rather than trying to have the technology do everything and making it more complicated for the teacher, that's an impediment. [04]

Technology ease of use and simplicity is also favored by this interviewee, who shares the following: "Well, certainly from one perspective the more simple the technology is for the user, the better it is. So anything that would make it transparent, I think would help" [43].

All in all, more teachers find the technology they have to use when teaching online to be impractical and suggest that improvement is needed in order to perfect the process and ensure its success. They would like access to software that supports their teaching better, and to useful online archives. They worry about the *usability* and *appropriateness* of the technology choices made by the schools:

Well, the technology exists… but it's just not practical. But I know it'll come in the near future. I'd like to see more video conferencing. And I'd want to see it in a very smooth, broadband connection, user friendly, easy, integrated into the software systems… I'd like to see more… software systems to improve the teaching… but also software that would allow very easy use of multimedia, and images, and illustrations by a teacher, for live interaction with students… I'd like to see more free repositories of learner object, which just means images, documents, multimedia that teachers or students might use… and it'd just be freely available. [41]

Multimedia

Multimedia, in general, refers to the combined use of various media, such as sound and video in a computer system; the term is also used in relation to applications that combine text, graphics, video, and sound into one package (Dictionary.com, n.d.). Multimedia, as used in this book, refers to the combined use of media, such as videos, audio clips, print, and the Internet, for education.

Another change for more successful online teaching is having access to a certain amount of real-time interaction, which would result in richer *communication.* This is a valuable asset in the online environment, as seen by this teacher:

It would be interesting to have everybody have a Web cam, and get online once a week. It makes a huge difference in talking to somebody if you can see them, see their environment, what's going on, how they look: healthy, not healthy, worried, happy—it makes a difference. There's a lot of body language and visual cues that are really important in connecting with somebody, communicating with them. Teaching is about communicating, that's it. And the online environment without any visual cues is sparse, in terms of communication feedback, ...e-mail and text communication in general is very prone to miscommunication and misinterpretation, because you're missing cues. [25]

Other teachers would like to have some visual tools that would help them monitor student *interaction,* rate (and rank) message content, and gauge student progress in general. One teacher reflects on his situation:

I have the ability to participate in the chat, I can post surveys, you know, come up with multiple choice questions, and I can see a bar graph of that, but something else that would be sort of useful is just maybe a thing on the side that would tell me, you know we're moving too fast or we're moving too slow. [07]

On the same idea of visual tools, this teacher shares that he would like to have support for visual imagery, in order to help him relate to who the students are:

I would have a list of who's in the classroom, and they all have icons, they could very easily, you know, those icons could be different colors and whether they're getting it or not, I could get feedback of who's [there], you know. [07]

Some teachers would like to have access to real-time, synchronous video-conferencing and interactive multimedia content because they feel it would improve their productivity:

The first thing I would like to do… is… interactive media, where for maybe 30 minutes or twice a day for 30 minutes the students could link up with me on video, teleconference, and we can sit there and chat interactively… I would like to be able to talk to my students face-to-face, 30 minutes as a class, for whoever comes on, wants to come on, and do further explanation or answer questions. I think it would be very productive. [12]

They continue to reflect on the subject of *media richness,* found by many to be such a problem in the online teaching. Instructors miss the rich medium of the *classroom* and would like to see richer communication media made available online:

If she was there in front of me, I could tell, okay she can barely stay awake, she's rambling… But in the online environment, I can't tell if she's affected by pain medication, or if she just can't write a sentence that makes sense. [25]

They believe that videoconferencing would help interaction:

Some kind of videoconferencing… with the instructor, with the learning teams, maybe one night a week or something like that would help… I think that would help quite a bit. It would bring a lot more interaction and get the instructors more involved as far as student interaction, also. [26]

They also feel that the students would benefit from seeing their teachers, even by means of a video recording:

Or maybe I could videotape a 30-minute lecture… that I can post in the classroom and I can… show them with visual aids so it's not just me talking but with visual aids, that might be a very powerful learning tool, is having a 30-minute lecture each week that addresses the main concepts. I can get a lot done in 30 minutes. [12]

As much as many of our interviewees report that multimedia technology would allow them to record and offer online lab demonstrations to help students grasp the course material, there are some that are not convinced that support for video would really help them teach online:

I'm not sure that having that little video image in the corner of your monitor would make all that much difference. I think people may become too conscious of that aspect of it, and you'd have to figure out ways to use it efficiently. [43]

Teachers would like to see *technology* that offers them better tools to navigate the online environment in order to be able to easier sort through student messages, have a more intuitive access to information, and to make better use of their time. Whatever makes grading easier is also welcomed by teachers: "Some… programs… that would make it easier for me to grade" [18].

Technology That Supports Better Interaction

Another aspect of the issue of success in the online teaching is the one suggesting that technology should support better *interaction* and student participation in an interactive format: "Truly a multimedia, interactive environment,…the smart classroom, would get people involved a little bit more. It would truly use technology" [22]. The *assessment* of the quality of student interaction is another area where technology was found to be lacking in helping teachers:

You have to have software that evaluates the quality. Because in the classroom, as you're listening, you're able to discern whether so-and-so's comments are quality, or quantity just wanting to say something. But… online, given that students are providing quality feedback, it's certainly much easier and much more easily quantifiable if you just look at the statistics on the server, in terms of evaluating a particular student rather than just relying on your memory of what you recall in terms of what happened in the classroom,… online can be more systematic, more objective. [37]

Teachers feel that increasing the intensity of the *communication* may help them build rapport with their students:

The communication aspect can be more intensified… you get closer, maybe, to people… to know them. There are things that you can't get just through reading somebody's notes. The aspects of the communications that are in voice, that are in body language and you know that they only come out in real time. The good teacher explores those things. You know it says something that somebody gets the glaze in the eyes. You know he's lost. You can't emphasize that and it's a different type of communication. I don't know if you will ever be able to compensate for that, but on the other hand, there are other benefits online that make things enjoyable and they make a lot of sense. [14]

Another teacher has this to say concerning the subject: "We should be using additional technologies to increase interaction online and also just use multimedia for some of our presentations, and online testing" [17].

Perhaps based on what they have experienced in the traditional classroom, teachers talk about how improved technology could help regain some of the lost communication cues, and real-time *interaction*. While the online environment is predicated on space and time separation, teachers feel that even a small amount of real-time interaction would help them teach better:

It would be worthwhile to try to come up with some interactive mechanism online, be it for a 15-minute period schedule or something. I would probably do it with a learning group so we don't have to deal with class members separately; be able to schedule a learning team, maybe for a 15 minute sessions or something like that, if possible, and that way you can interact and you could just ask questions or not, but at least you can use the meeting to do that, and you can provide feedback and get a lot of their questioning answered. [17]

Another respondent supports in his statement the same idea of real-time *interaction*, which he also suggests that it could be scheduled in advance:

I think it is sometimes a good idea to have a special order to the class, so everybody can be online so we can feel like a live class, and we can answer questions and they can chat...like office hours, everybody can be there, so we can kind of visit each other, and this way, for the students that don't log on that much, at least they can be there and feel like they are in a class. Maybe 1 hour, or half an hour. Not 2, not 3 hours. A half an hour is enough; 45 minutes, maximum 1 hour. Every 3 days. [24]

Then, he continues reporting that real-time interaction would also allow the teacher to more effectively answer student questions and to perform student assessment:

We can answer the question right away, I can tell who is in the class, who is active in the class; I can measure their knowledge. They can answer right away if I ask a question. Who answers right away, is there in the class. So I can tell that who is answering the questions, who is answering the quizzes, so it's not like cheating. [24]

Teachers are aware that scheduling real-time sessions are only half the battle, as not all students may show up: "I think I see a lot of people expressing frustrations when they've arranged the session and one or two people don't show up. So the communication leaves a little bit to be desired. But I think it would be useful to have a live conversation once a week" [25].

Either voice- or videoconferencing may prove useful, depending on what the course requirements are: "A teleconference once a week for an hour or 90 minutes, with the whole class where everybody comes together, I think that would help a lot" [14]. Yet, another teacher is concerned with how videoconferencing may be used, and about how well it may work in the end:

Video conferencing...I'm not sure how that would work if everybody's someplace different, but you could hear people's voices, you could have an audio thing. I took a little training session the other day where I could hear any of the other people in the training session and the instructor so at least...they were disembodied voices but that was better than no interaction at all....I think we need to perfect the tools that we use to allow group interaction. [15]

From another perspective, teaching success online is connected by one answerer to something as simple as having an appropriate, ergonomic work environment and access to modern technology. He would like to see the old computers go away, and replaced by modern ones: "It would be nice if the computer I have at work was not 6 years old. And if I had a more ergonomic desk" [42]. Again, technology availability is an issue.

Teachers also suggest that there are limitations related to Internet access. Ideally, students and teachers should have adequate bandwidth *available*. One teacher's wish is to:

Give everybody DSL as part of the tuition,...there's a technology gap: Students will send, for instance, a video clip, and maybe only half the students can actually open it. Online, your technology can be a limiting factor. We're moving ahead on the interpersonal issues, matters, concerns. But, as we get better at that, it's requiring better technology, and not everybody has it. [23]

One instructor suggests that there should be certain *technology*-related prerequisites imposed on students:

Make sure everybody has a Web cam, so I can see them when they go online. I wish I could just see the faces of the students, especially in the chat rooms. I wish I could have a thumbnail view of every one of the students, or that when they're taking a test, I could somehow, see them. We should make it a requirement to videotape them while they're taking their test. I can see their faces, you know. Those are some of the things that I wish would happen. [08]

Another teacher reflects on how unprepared some students are: "Make the student pass technological competency exam before they're allowed to sign up for the course" [04]. Continuing the idea of training in using technology and computers, one instructor suggests that the students themselves would also benefit from a mandatory training:

I would make one computer class on campus that's a prerequisite of taking online classes...or take an introduction to computer course. Uh, so students have actually a thorough knowledge of what you think a computer [does]. Sometimes they drop some classes, not because they don't understand the concepts, but because they do not know how to use their computers. I would definitely change that, make that a requirement. [08]

Technology *reliability* is a general concern for teachers who teach online, because any technological failure can gravely affect the teaching process:

One of the things that can be a real drawback is when the servers go [down]. Because then people are posting and it's not going anywhere and you get online the next day and their stuff isn't there and they panic because it was due the night before. And, usually I'm experiencing the server problems when they do, so I know when the servers are down. But it's been very aggravating to post all of you handouts and then find out that none of them are showing up and then you have to post them all over again! And that's very irritating because that's very time consuming. [16]

Another interviewed subject supports the importance of good *technology*, even if it comes at a cost:

Like I said, if money was spent, people upgraded all their hardware—that's the drain. If people upgraded all their hardware with built-in cameras and fast Pentium 4 three gigs, and everybody's hooked up to broadband, if we could do even a small portion of the smart classroom thing, it would improve like night and day. [22]

Technology, at least in its current form, cannot escape its limitations. In the end it comes down to how it is used, to whether the content taught should even be taught online; this is where the human judgment comes in place and is important:

I think there should be a filtering mechanism where you take and decide what content is appropriate for an online environment. ...There are some ideas that require group interaction. Yet if you want someone to learn the periodic table, or you want them to learn some Information Technology acronyms, that's great. But if you want someone to say "Okay, we're going to take some data and move it into a third normal form"—I'll use a database as an example. To just tell someone step one, step two, give them some examples on the Web, let them try it, see what they come up with, is not nearly as good as being in a room—there are just certain things—that's kind of a medium one, but there are certain things that I think people should sit down and critically say, "Should this really ever be online?" You want to discuss cases online. Are there certain aspects of a lecture that need to be theatrics in order to be effective? [13]

Another teacher shares similar views:

The technology doesn't really enable us to step through what we do on the board when we teach, meaning, when a teacher teaches calculus. The technology doesn't allow us to do that in a way that's acceptable to all students with the technology that you, a faculty member would readily have available. In an interactive way or in a real-time way. [44]

Conclusion

This chapter explores the variables affecting successful online teaching, from the teachers' perspective. They seem to agree that not everyone can become a successful teacher. Teaching can be a difficult activity that is not for everyone; subject mastery is not necessarily associated with good teaching skills. Teachers are caring people, who care deeply about their teaching, their students, and the learning taking place in the classroom. Online education relies in large measure on written communication. For this reason, good writing skills are very desirable and most valuable to a teacher who teaches online. Knowledge of the subject matter is very important; so are communication skills and a caring personality, an open mind, organization skills, training in teaching, a genuine desire to help people, and being a people's person. Teachers have to be prepared to make personal sacrifices, with the reward being a sense of meaningfulness, as their efforts benefit the society at large. To be successful, a teacher must focus on the student.

Second, the chapter explores factors that may help make online teaching more effective. It is not as much the technology, or the environment, as it is the teacher's ability to use what she has available for her teaching. The technology alone will not transform a mediocre teacher into a good one. In terms of teaching effectiveness, the online environment compares favorably to the traditional on-ground classroom. While the structure is different between the online and on-ground modalities, teachers attain an acceptable degree of perceived teaching effectiveness. They compensate for the differences between the modalities.

Some teachers reflect on how the effectiveness of the online environment may be taken for granted. Often, one ignores the relatively static design of the online courses, whereas in the classroom there is more tolerance for experimentation, adjustments, changes, and for teachers to modify their instruction as they find it appropriate in support of the course goals. Online, teachers are more effective in helping students improve their writing. In the classroom, they are more effective in helping them reflect on the world.

Teachers recognize that learning and cognitive traits suggest that students may learn better in one specific modality. As schools have a fiduciary duty to their customers—the students—to offer them an optimal learning environment, perhaps students should be evaluated and guided toward the educational modality that best suits their traits, abilities, and skills.

The classroom has always been the teacher's unchallenged domain. Teachers are used to controlling access to the classroom. Online this changes dramatically, and not every teacher appreciates the change. There is growing concern related to online privacy. Teachers would like to see greater institutional (administrative) support and access to modern technology. Since time demands are increased online, teachers would like fair compensation to match, and they would like to be recognized and appreciated for what they do.

At some universities, teachers acknowledge they have relative freedom to change the course content and student assignments as they deem appropriate, within the guidelines set by the university. Yet chief among the things they do not control are class size and student quality. Technology can be difficult to deal with, especially when student enrollment and growth in general are not well supported by the technology deployed. Some teachers have difficulty in using some of the technology available to them, and find it overly complex. Simplicity is favored over glitzy features.

The factors presented in this chapter and the role they play as determinants of online teaching success paint a rich picture. The teachers who shared their online teaching stories and experiences point to a multitude of things that affect the success of their teaching. As the online environment continues to evolve, these determinants for teaching success need to be reevaluated. Changes in learning and teaching approaches, classroom assessment techniques and methodologies, and in the technology used to deliver online education may affect the factors that are instrumental in online teaching success.

References

Bangert, A. W. (2004). The seven principles of good practice: A framework for evaluating on-line teaching. *Internet and Higher Education, 7*, 217-232.

Boyd, D., & Arnold, M. L. (2000). Teachers' Beliefs, Antiracism and Moral Education: problems of intersection. *Journal of Moral Education, 29*(1), 23-46.

Cahn, P. S. (2003). Number crunching. *The Chronicle of Higher Education, 50*(16).

Carnevale, D. (2003). Learning online to teach online. *Chronicle of Higher Education, 50*(10).

Carnevale, D. (2004). More professors teach by using other colleges' online courses. *Chronicle of Higher Education, 51*(8).

Clegg, S., Konrad, J., & Tan, J. (2000). Preparing academic staff to use ICTs in support of student learning. *The International Journal for Academic Development, 5*(2), 138-148.

Dictionary.com. (n.d.). *Multimedia.* Retrieved August 28, 2007, from http://dictionary.reference.com/browse/multimedia

Dreeben, R. (1970). *The nature of teaching: Schools and the work of teachers.* Glenview, IL: Scott Foresman.

Ershler, J. (2003). Policy development considerations for administrators and instructors of distance learning programs. *Journal of the United States Distance Learning Association, 17*(2), 1-3.

Feenberg, A. (1999, Winter). Distance learning: Promise or threat. *Crosstalk,* 12-13.

Goral, T. (2001). Teaching old dogs new tricks. *Curriculum Administrator, 37*(2), 59-61.

Hersh, R. H., Merrow, J., & Wolfe, T. (2005). *Declining by degrees: Higher education at risk* [DVD]. New York and Washington, DC: Public Broadcasting Service.

Jensen, E. J. (1995). The bitter groves of academe. *Change, 27*(1), 8-11.

Klassen, J., & Vogel, D. (2003). New issues arising from e-education. In A. K. Aggarwal (Ed.), *Web-based education: Learning from experience* (pp. 36-48). Hershey, PA: Information Science Publishing.

Klobas, J., & Renzi, S. (2003). Integrating online educational activities in traditional courses: University-wide lessons after three years. In A. K. Aggarwal (Ed.), *Web-based education: Learning from experience* (pp. 415-439). Hershey, PA: Information Science Publishing.

Magna Publications. (2004). *Gauging faculty attitudes about teaching online.* Retrieved May 11, 2005, from http://www.magnapubs.com/pub/magna-pubs_der/8_5/

Rayburn, W. E., & Ramaprasad, A. (2002). Three strategies for the use of distance learning technology in higher education. In M. Khosrow-Pour (Ed.), *Web-based instructional learning* (pp. 27-42). Hershey, PA: IRM Press.

Rosenberg, M. J. (2001). *E-learning: Strategies for delivering knowledge in the digital age.* New York: McGraw-Hill.

Serow, R. C. (2000). Research and teaching at a research university. *Higher Education, 40*, 449-463.

Shulman, L. S. (2000). Inventing the future. In P. Hutchings (Ed.), *Opening lines: Approaches to the scholarship of teaching and learning.* Menlo Park, CA: The Carnegie Foundation for the Advancement of Teaching.

Speck, B. W. (2000). The academy, online classes, and the breach in ethics. In E. R. Weiss, D. S. Knwolton, & B. W. Speck (Eds.), *New directions for teaching and learning. principles of effective teaching in the online classroom* (Vol. 84, pp. 73-82). San Francisco: Jossey-Bass.

Wysocki, B. (2005, February 23). How Dr. Papadakis runs a university like a company. *The Wall Street Journal, CCXLV,* A1.

Chapter V

The Online Teaching Experience:
Teaching With Technology

Introduction

The chapter explores how teachers use information technology for their online courses, and the possible variations in the meaning they derive from their online teaching experiences. The interviewed teachers share their online experiences and offer several interesting suggestions.

Technology is ubiquitous in everybody's life nowadays, and teachers are no exception to this rule. Whether teaching in the traditional classroom only, or online, the greatest majority of instructors include technology in their teaching process. For example, they prepare course materials on the computer, typing up lectures, student assignments, and presentations. They are definitely not afraid to use technology in support of their teaching, and are not avoiding it. However, the online educational environment is fundamentally different in that it poses specific challenges to teachers. Among the issues that concern them are those related to the instructional processes, media richness, technology reliability, uneven access to technology, and the social isolation of the online teacher. The contents of this chapter should help increase teachers' awareness of what challenges awaits for them in the online classroom.

Background

The available literature researched for this book points to the many facets of the online teaching experience. Blair (2002) indicates that teachers use technology in their teaching whether this takes place in an online or on-ground classroom. Yet resorting solely to using technology in their teaching can be frustrating. Online, teachers lose the energy and sounds of a real classroom: there is no background noise in the online class. Teaching online is not for every educator; it is a different method of teaching, as much as an exciting one.

In another study, Hinn, Leander, and Bruce (2001) reported that the online environment is a simulated world in which social life develops across on- and off-line networks. Teachers are concerned then with the technical characteristics of technology, interfaces, collaborative tools, and hypertext structures. The new modes of communication pose new challenges for understanding collaboration.

With regard to student participation, the lack of face-to-face contact may lead online students to feel less pressure to contribute. Teachers acknowledge uneven participation and the potential for lurking; however, they feel that imposing too much structure is detrimental to a value-free environment, as should be the case online. Some teachers would like to have alternative procedures for dealing with students' personal problems (e.g., the telephone). Online, new modes of interaction and communication emerge, and monitoring and encouraging participation can be more difficult. Despite this, there is better feedback online in that more time for reflection is available (Nicol, Minty, & Sinclair, 2003).

Vachris (1999) shows that the online technology promotes a more cooperative learning environment. Yet the interaction is more costly in terms of instructor time, in addition to online teachers spending two to three times more time delivering a course online than on-ground.

Information technology (IT) artifacts are widely used in education. Computers are ubiquitous, and many people rely on the Internet for communication, information, or to improve the quality of their lives. However, this increased reliance on technology leads to unexpected consequences: There is a price to pay for living "on the grid." While the computer age has given us many reasons to rejoice, "and is often compelling, powerful and productive—it is unprecedentedly fast, even frantic; it is relentless. The price of digitization's information and fun is frustration; it always needs to be rebooted or relearned" (Henninger, 2005, p. A1). Whatever the case, there is no doubt that the Internet is deeply embedded in the social fabric (Hoffman & Novak, 2004). People are comfortable using the Internet as a source of information and as a communication and socializing tool (Stafford & Gonier, 2004).

The Role of Technology in Supporting Online Teaching

To some teachers, it appears that the technology industry is still the driving force who prescribes the needs of education instead of education dictating its own technological needs (Morinaka, 2003). Naturally, this is a cause for concern. Additional concerns arise from how information and communication technologies (ICT) are incorporated into the on-ground educational environment. Teachers must reconsider the relationship of the physical setting to the students' learning experience. Students and staff need to be allowed to shape their places of teaching and learning, just as they shape the curriculum (Jamieson, Fisher, Gilding, Taylor, & Trevitt, 2000).

New technologies are constantly developed and become mainstream. Universities are augmenting distance education with telecommunications media (Stadtlander, 1998). The Web allows for two-way communication: sending and receiving messages moved to real-time with the advent of instant messaging software and audio and video messaging. Today's students are always multiprocessing (Brown, 2000). They grow accustomed to sharing their lives with the computer, which becomes a natural extension of their persona. Web technology allows teachers to create complex, multidimensional experiences that combine text, audio, and video in a media-rich environment, and engage the learners (Sensiper, 2000). Teachers can take advantage of this. However, the advantages offered by the online environment (e.g., access to information, location, convenience) are reduced by drawbacks (e.g., time required for course design, faculty training). Vodanovich and Piotrowski (2001) reported that for many teachers, the use of technology is very basic and limited to e-mail and dissemination of course materials. In contrast, many students are well immersed in technology. For them, ICT has become a way of life (Brown, 2002). Furthermore, a study by the Kaiser Family Foundation found one third of children use blogs and social networking Web sites regularly, unlike their parents (LeClaire, 2006).

Teachers are trying to reach out to their students, yet the use of technology does not necessarily make it easier. The ability to connect emotionally with students makes for a "special" professor. Students have different communication needs than their teachers, especially the younger students, who prefer speed to face-to-face contact (Arnone, 2002).

Teaching With Technology

Information technology is at the basis of the process of teaching online and is bound to impact the overall online teaching experience. Teachers use technology all the time, not only for their online courses but for the on-ground courses as well; they have used technology to teach courses inside and outside the classroom. As one teacher puts it, "The online education is already a part of the classroom. Everybody is wired. Everybody has their own Web site. You can even go to your classroom and you have wiring there and you can get on your Internet" [05]. *Technology* is pervasive and almost ubiquitous. All our interviewed teachers were quick to note that technology has found its way into both the on-ground and online classroom.

Teachers and Technology

Teachers do not fear technology. They are not afraid to rely on it for their teaching, and are certainly not avoiding technology; yet they recognize that teaching online involves more than just technology. As one instructor pointed out,

I think there are some technological things that can certainly help students on their own. But as far as me being online, and communicating with them online vs. going to class [on campus]—I communicate with students online, they send me e-mails; I answer back e-mails, it's not like we don't communicate online. But in terms of it being full-time online, that's what I am against. [29]

Another interviewed instructor notes that in the end, it is not as much what *technology* they have access to, as it is how they use the technology they have available, and what they do with it:

[Online] gave me an opportunity to expand my own abilities, it's a little bit different form of teaching and I have no regrets, you just got to slow down a little bit. I support online. It's as good as the faculty makes it, the same in the classroom though. [12]

As they reflect on how they use technology to teach online, teachers note that technology can help them reuse course materials; yet, it affects how courses are designed, and it places constraints on student assessment processes. They talk of instructional processes, media richness, synchronicity, reliability, uneven access to technology, and the social isolation of the online teacher.

Using Technology Effectively: A Hit-and-Miss Exercise

Teachers reflect on whether the online classroom can be used effectively for teaching and learning, and point to *administrative* concerns that they feel are important and need to be addressed to ensure online education continues to improve. Mainly, these pertain to technology and curriculum choices such as those that are typically made by educational institutions' administrators. One teacher shares his hopes: "If the technology is right, and the curriculum is developed appropriately, there's no reason why an online education couldn't be comparable or even better than an on-ground experience" [05].

When asked to think about their teaching, and reflect on their *effectiveness* teaching in the online classroom, three distinctive views have been expressed. One group of teachers report they do not feel that the different environment affects their ability to teach; the technology-intensive online classroom does not diminish their ability to teach. Others note that their effectiveness varies with the environment: "I feel that I am more effective, as a teacher, in the classroom" [14]. And a third group of teachers does not believe the online environment is appropriate for teaching. These teachers, who do not believe it is working, are concerned with their teaching effectiveness, as expressed in this confession: "[Online], my primary objective of transferring knowledge fails: They don't get it, and they get a grade that does not reflect it" [19]. As we can see, the views of the teachers diverge, and some teachers feel the online educational environment imposes quite dramatic constraints on their teaching.

An example of course design and administration issues that highlights the many ways in which technology can hinder the teaching process is the situation of the course development being fraught, despite all the efforts, with miscommunications among teachers, software developers, curriculum developers, and Web designers. One teacher vents her frustration stemming from attempting to develop a course as a group:

The new e-learning team... they supposedly knew how to develop courses and could help the teacher.... Well, what they wanted was a PDF file; what I wanted was to have 100% interaction. I thought I could send them a Word document and they'll do the rest... not so! I ended up subcontracting for the e-learning team. They wanted a different product than mine, and when they put all the pieces together—it's their product...in the end—it's not my product anymore. As far as I am concerned, this was a wrong strategy, and wrong implementation from the very beginning. [19]

As this example illustrates, the initial setup of an online course is critical. Aside from setting up the technology component of the online classroom, teachers must find ways to ensure that the course development process flows as smoothly as possible, and that all the parties involved agree on what has to be done, and by what means. This is similar to what a project manager faces, when managing a project that involves multiple stakeholders who have to achieve consensus on the scope and substance of the project.

In the teaching process, teachers often reuse course materials such as lectures bits, case studies, exercises and problems, and homework assignments. The online environment is particularly well suited to allow *reusability* of course materials, as these are stored in electronic format. Once the course materials are online, they can much easier be reused for other courses, whether online or on-ground. One teacher notes the omnipresence of the computers:

And since people often are teaching both online and on-ground you can attach materials that come from the online environment in between classes that you're teaching on-ground. The so-called on-ground classes really have a strong computer and Internet component to them. [05]

This statement emphasizes the technological component at the core of the online educational environment.

Technology skills, as well as technology itself, carry over between educational modalities and environments and have a positive effect in the overall teaching experience. Teachers feel they are gaining from being exposed to different teaching modalities. There are things they learn to transfer between the on-ground and the online classroom and vice versa. As one teacher puts it,

In the online classes, I taught we used Blackboard, and now, in my situation I am using WebCT as an adjunct tool with the face-to-face class that I do teach... and I have found ways to use it very effectively to save time and, I think, to help students get better prepared, and allow me to assess student progress in an ongoing process. So I think the carryover was thinking about ways I could use technology in my traditional classes. [43]

Teachers stand to benefit from teaching in different modalities, as they can find out for themselves what works better in a specific environment and can "borrow" teaching materials and techniques to use in other environments.

Constraint Creep

In general, teachers appear to condone a certain degree of entertainment, of fun, in education. They observe that such things do not translate well in the online teaching environment, because the showmanship is different online. When the "entertainment" factor fails to communicate, something is amiss. In the words of one participant in the study,

I have to think, "Ok, if you remove that [the entertainment] from the online envi-ronment... which you pretty much do, then how are you going to catch...how are you going to get...hold your students' attention?" Because now you can't rely on, "Hey, I heard this great joke. ..." I mean, you've just really got to think about how you are going to grab them. [39]

The technology component of teaching online does, to a certain extent, have a nega-tive impact on spontaneity. For this reason, online is more difficult for the teacher to keep students focused and/or entertained. For one teacher,

A certain amount of that we have done in the past with sort of this performance...be-ing entertaining. Well, can't really do that online, so...well, how are you going to hold your students' attention? It's a challenge. How are you going...how are you going to get them to stay focused on the content, and stay on task? [39]

Some teachers adjust well to the lack of spontaneity that, at times, may be perceived as a nuisance. The extended time that is available for teaching (and learning)—a 24-hours-per-day class schedule—calls for different approaches to keeping students focused: It is no longer feasible to entertain them for such an extended period of time.

When teaching online, teachers become quickly aware of the constraints introduced by technology itself, and the list continues to grow as they achieve more experience online. Perhaps the most significant constraints stem from bandwidth—in terms of requirements and availability. Teachers report a need to modify the design of their courses as they try to compensate for the shortcomings of the online media and to take advantage of what they perceive to be potential benefits. One teacher shares his approach:

I have taken a specific stance in how I design the course. I design it for the lowest common denominator...for students that don't have anything but a dial-up, I want to make sure they can access the materials so I try and avoid using a lot of video. I can use some video but it is going to take a while for them to access it. I use a lot of graphics. I use images and text and then I embed in the text hyperlinks that will give them additional information or additional viewpoints. [40]

As briefly mentioned early on, among the most important determinants of online education success, the initial setup is perceived to be a critical one. However, teach-ers note that even if everything is done right, *technology* is not an answer to all the questions. Its role is to support the quest for knowledge. There is no silver bullet, so to speak:

I think you use technology. I think you use PowerPoint. I think you use computer systems to find out information and to give you direction and the data, but I don't think that it becomes the end all so that there isn't any kind of verbal and penetrating and subjective consideration of what's going on. [01]

It is perceived by some teachers that the use of technology takes away from, and limits the instruction process. The teachers have more options in the classroom: "Your imagination, your creativity, your probing, your ability to be incisive, all of these are factors which I think perhaps are not possible in a computer-based, purely technology system" [01]. In that regard, some teachers agree that a certain amount of multimedia technology can help the online teaching process. When they say they need more audio-visual support, clearly, teachers are referring to a certain *media richness* that they feel is needed in the online classroom:

I am thinking of having a short video clip on the server and the students can click on it and download the streaming video… that might be a way that I could do my demonstrations, for instance, so that they are watching the poppet beads and the telephone chords fold up into the proteins as I am talking. So that would let me to do some of what I can do in the face-to-face class and bring it to the online environment. [42]

Relying on Technology

Developing courses around a specific technology may be of increased risk, because technology may fail you when is most needed. More, just because a certain technology is available does not mean that all students will have equal access to it. Online education relies on students and teachers having access to the Internet, and it is directly affected by Internet service outages. Furthermore, the participants—students and teacher—may be using various types and versions of software on their computers. This may be a problem, especially when functionality is affected:

The technology can fail, and that can be a problem. My online courses are deliberately low on the bells and whistles because our students have very slow dial-up connections or very old computers, so they have a textbook and I refer to figures in the book as opposed to putting a lot of images online in the course. So I suppose that's a constraint, but I've been able to work around it pretty well. There's always some student who really appreciates that they never see each other and there are always some students who really would like to meet face-to-face at least once, so balancing all those needs is hard. [42]

The current technology some teachers have access to is, in many ways, too basic and could be improved. In addition to that, the simplistic ways in which technology is often used are obvious:

Our technology is pretty basic... We don't use the chat room feature or even the discussion boards. We really post lectures that are released for a certain amount of time, usually about 4 days. We have seven assignments that we give, and those are pre-released... We also have assigned readings, and those are available through an electronic reserve... All the communication between the professor and student is through e-mail... All assignments are turned in via e-mail. [35]

As a consequence of relying solely on communication technologies, a fairly common occurrence when teaching online is that, to a certain degree, online teachers feel socially isolated from their peers. They wish they had more opportunities to interact with fellow teachers. One teacher notes there is some support from the school's administration:

Our administration has set up [online] a faculty lounge. It's where all the online faculty go and we have our own discussion boards. And that's helped tremendously with the social isolation. So we can meet on the Internet and share the good, the bad, the ugly—frustrations, problems, solutions. Occasionally even I'll say, "Let's meet up this Friday over at this place for a margarita or something...." To actually meet up with the other online faculty, I just really appreciate that. [41]

The human interaction is diminished in, and by, the online environment.

The Asynchronous Medium: Controlling the Interaction

While the typical online environment is asynchronous, some teachers report a quest for added synchronicity. Online chats, either organized or ad hoc, become part of the classroom. People "talk" online: "We do online chats. We do e-mail, we do asynchronous discussion, but we also do synchronous real-time chat; but even with that, the students... they still wanted the audio... that idea of immediacy" [39].

Technology can help regain the *synchronous* aspects some teachers miss in the online environment. Yes, some teachers really like synchronous communication:

What I would probably explore is using instant messaging, or I would explore using net meeting... so that you do spend time with the students and you do have an interactive session with the students… at least have a time when you're all online interactively with a group of students, because that will clear up, make things much more efficient. That, I think it would be very, very helpful. Even if you have an hour a week to meet with them… I think overall it would be much more effective. [17]

Some teachers are used to videoconferencing with their students. This is another example of how technology can be used to increase the synchronicity of the interaction. One teacher shared his experience using multimedia communication equipment: "I used to use audio conferencing a lot... and I really miss it. And the students do too. They really liked having that element of hearing voices. You know, they heard my voice, they heard their classmates' voices. You know, we'd been on sort of an audio bridge" [39].

Some teachers use technology to help enrich interaction and establish rapport with their students by supporting a sense of presence, by reducing the social distance. As one of the interviewees related,

The more real you can make that person, whether it's the teacher, the classmate, whatever… The student starts to build this relationship more quickly. There's this obvious presence, and I think that's one reason why they like the real-time chat… There's this real sense of immediacy that there's actually a real person responding to them right now, and so I think that's a real plus in the online environment, to have this good strong sense of immediacy. [39]

In contrast, other teachers do not miss real-time interaction and do not believe that synchronous communication would help their teaching online. They are more partial to the flexibility afforded by the online modality and to being able to choose the time and timing of the interaction with their online students. One teacher is of the opinion that

Most students don't want to be locked down to a specific time or place, and I certainly don't think it would be appropriate to do that for a 3-hour stint… But if a… the instructor needs to do a demonstration, that could be done in a way that would be interactive. I think any type of synchronous learning needs to be limited, just because, I think… people become online learners for the convenience. [44]

As the control over the timing of the interaction shifts from teacher to students, the dynamics of the interaction change.

A chief grievance reported by many teachers when assessing the two teaching modalities (on-ground and online) is related to teacher-student interaction. For those in the online classroom, in particular, the interaction is very different. This is noted by many teachers to be the greatest difference among the teaching modalities. In the words of one teacher,

There is a big difference between teaching online and teaching in class. ...The biggest difference is the interaction, as of today. As of today, the interaction is lacking [online]. There are some tools that are supposed to have interaction, such as the bulletin boards and chat. But for person-to-person interaction, there just have not been any tools as yet in order to bring that up to the same level as what you would have in a class. [22]

It would seem that teachers would welcome technologies that would enhance interaction and improve the communication with their students.

Teachers note the different types of communication taking place online. Traditional classroom teaching relies on communication broadcasts, yet online one-to-one communication is often present. This reflects a uni-cast type of communication, and Socratic teaching is not far off: "We're headed into the one-on-one situation, where numbers don't put a constraint anymore" [33].

Teaching with technology makes it hard at times to see whether learning takes place. Those teachers who teach on ground often resort to nonverbal communication cues—such as looking at students' faces—to assess learning progress. As these nonverbal communication cues are missing from the online environment, some teachers note that learning does take place online: "Students taking the online or the hybrid course perform as well, or better, than students that take a pure lecture course" [38]. However, a second teacher finds that "[Classroom students] learn more than your online students. Of course, definitely. Also, as a teacher, teaching online classes,...when I taught on-ground classes, I learned much more than online. 100%" [24].

For another instructor, the quality of the outcome is less of a concern: "Students do learn just as well [classroom or online]" [39]. Still, other teachers continue to be unconvinced:

Even though probably 15% of students in a class show up, a lot of people that don't show up read...[messages] saved in a chat archive. So say, like, you were late so you couldn't come to tonight's chat, but after it's over, you go online, you go in, and you could read the chat archive...I hear from a lot of students that they read those to help them with the assignment. [31]

As this citation shows, learning takes on many forms. Yet, immersion and vicarious learning take place more often in a traditional classroom, taught on-ground rather than online. It is beneficial for students to be on campus, in the on-ground educational environment:

[In classroom] you learn things in the hallways, in the corridors. You learn things from other students. You learn things by going to lectures and events that pop up that the online student doesn't have access to. I think, most specifically, just interacting with other students—friendships don't develop. You don't have online that collegiality that we have [on-ground]. [25]

Viewing Students Through the Technology Lens

In terms of student assessment, there are some teachers who feel that using technology helps them assess students' progress. They report that the use of technology helps them grade student assignments. One answerer reports that "[Technology] it makes the job of grading much easier, because it sort of keeps track of what you've viewed and what you haven't viewed" [31]. Yet other teachers indicate that the technology they use forces them to make adjustments in how they monitor their online students. The environment is different enough from the on-ground classroom, to warrant—to require, in fact—some changes:

In a classroom I can see whether a person is going through some distress or having some personal issues and not learning or doing things that he/she should be doing. In an online environment, because we don't have that physical presence, I have to read the postings that these people will make and make those connections, and that has been a learning experience also. [36]

Those teachers who taught online courses are not surprised to see their classes shrink significantly, as students drop out. The technology used in online education often results in an impersonal environment, one that is not necessarily student friendly. While student retention is an issue that transcends educational modalities, and students may drop courses for any number of reasons, the dropout rate appears to increase for online courses. This is a cause of concern for some teachers, while for others it is simply an example of evolutionary adjustment, likely attributable to student quality. In the words of one teacher,

The dropout rate in online or hybrid instruction is probably greater than in lecture-type classes. This is because students have the option to realize either they're not up to the material, or that they're less interested than they thought they were at the start. It's harder to do that in a lecture class, it's harder to drop it. [38]

Some of the teachers interviewed find it more difficult to teach online, while others do not. One teacher feels the change is minor: "[Online] it is a little bit more difficult than in an oral environment" [35]. However, another teacher feels the change is significant: "And [online] you really have to become a 24 by 7 instructor almost. But at least the, you know, 16 by 7" [34]. Teaching with technology may lead to a somewhat mechanistic view of teaching. Where talking of the show-like aspects of teaching, one teacher notes how much he enjoyed performing in the on-ground classroom: "When I taught face-to-face, it was like going on stage, and I would perform. I would perform very well, and I would enjoy that" [40].

Online, things are a bit different. For one, the expectations increase dramatically; everything is more impersonal, mechanistic in a sense. Teachers react accordingly:

When we don't have live people in front of us, we think about things differently. A live person standing up there, before you boo at them or before you get upset, most people will stop to think about "This is a human being up there." You're a professor in front of a classroom, your students are there they see you as a human being, if you act like one, if you're a good faculty... and you're kind, they develop a relationship with you. They don't develop a relationship with faculty online like that. If you send a mass e-mail or you don't answer their e-mails, they take that as neglect. But when you write e-mails, when I look at the grammar, the spelling, is there anything in this e-mail that might be misconstrued, I spent a half hour on an e-mail that's two paragraphs long, especially if it's the first step that's going out to the whole class, to make sure that e-mail is perfect. I have a little checklist for myself to make sure I've done over e-mail. I never think that hard about a classroom. [13]

By carefully crafting communications, teachers find ways to use technology to their benefit and enhance the chances of building the kind of rapport they seemingly need to ensure the quality of their teaching.

It can be said that, to some extent, a technology-based educational environment allows students to "hide": Teachers have less opportunities to actually learn about their students and to assess correctly their learning progress. Thus, the issues associated with student assessment are amplified.

Chief among the assessment issues brought up by our teachers is the issue of plagiarism. While present at times in the campus-based classroom, plagiarism takes on a new life in the online environment: It is difficult for teachers to verify whether the student is the one actually doing the homework or taking the test online. One online teacher shares his concerns:

When I post the applications quiz for the week I do not know for sure if there's lateral communication offline with students who are helping them. I did find in one case a

couple months ago where two students had the same paper turned in with specif-
ics, and it was so obvious one did it and the other just rode the coattails, because
they had the same typos. ...I haven't figured out how to ensure that plagiarism isn't
rampant in statistics in the online as it is in the classroom. That's a challenge for
any faculty to try to deal with. Fighting plagiarism is sometimes difficult to prove,
and it's a concern because the Internet is such an accessible tool for them. [12]

It Feels Different Being Online

Teachers note that in many respects, they find the online environment to be quite different from the on-ground classroom. As one teacher says, quite candidly,

It's sort of a difference between listening to a radio drama and watching a television
show. In a radio drama, you know, you fill in all the blanks. You fill in the imagery of
the character, you fill in the setting and so forth; where in a television show, it's all
provided for you. In the face-to-face instruction, it's all provided. There's no filling
in, there's no guess work. But the online environment, because, from a visual point
of view, the only thing they ever see of me personally is the picture I have posted...on
the online syllabus for the course. There's a lot of anonymity. ...We don't know what
each other looks like. [40]

The differences between online and on-ground teaching are more evident when teachers consider the different subject matters they teach: Technology usability and appropriateness come into question when considering that some courses can be taught well online, while others are more difficult to teach online. One teacher shared her thoughts:

Personally, I feel online classes could be very useful for certain topics, but I think
the key is blended learning. I think taking the students and having them not see each
other at all, may not work as well as if you have a situation in which you bring them
together maybe two or three times over the course of the semester to get face-to-
face interaction time with the faculty to answer some of their questions in person,
maybe get to see some of the other classmates that otherwise they may have not
had the chance to see, and so they can put a face with the e-mail, they know who
they're talking to. [37]

Teachers are concerned with the appropriateness of the online environment, of how well it supports their teaching. They seem to agree that online education is not for everyone—whether teacher or student. Rather, student quality reflected in personality and cognitive traits factor in to explain why some students fare better online while others do not:

I'm convinced that the online student is not made of the same gene as the classroom student. I'm almost convinced that everybody's not made for online learning. It's not just that the teacher has to be ready to teach online and the student has to be ready to be taught online, because the students are much more self-motivated, self-starter, and not afraid to open the book themselves and read and ask questions, whereas the traditional students in a classroom are kind of passively waiting with the book in front of them, maybe hoping that the teacher will point out the important section, pages so they can read them. So, it's the passive versus active students. [36]

Teachers continue to teach and strive to prepare their courses and to improve their teaching for the online environment.

Where Technology Should Help

Teachers spend certain amounts of time preparing their courses, and most of them agree that teaching online can be very time-consuming. They have to prepare their materials with greater care, and this adds to their teaching demands. It is just more work to do: "It's much more of a challenge from an instructor's standpoint, because now you're putting things in writing, everything's in writing" [34]. For another teacher, teaching online, "It just takes a lot of time to get it done, so it's time-consuming" [12].

Using technology to teach requires teachers to spend more time *planning* the course materials; there is definitely more planning involved. As one teacher states,

[Online] I do the same things with a regular classroom course, except that I think more about the questions that I'm asking online. ... When you're in front of the class, the interaction is very quick; you don't have to think as much because the time comes up as it goes, and when you're doing things online, because it is not interactive, you have to plan things out a little more, and you have to ask questions that are going to make them think and that requires more in-depth analysis on their part. [17]

In addition, teachers report that the online environment is very demanding in terms of writing skills. As written communication is the norm, students and teachers alike benefit as they hone their writing skills. Teachers reflect on how online teaching has benefited them:

We all wish that students were better writers, had better writing skills. One of the things that the online experience does is to very much encourage improvement in writing skills. And, writing the dialogue over a period of time, several semesters... what's that expression? "What doesn't kill you makes you stronger." [23]

While focusing on educating their students, teachers continue to grow also, and improve their teaching as they acquire more experience teaching online.

At the end of the day, teachers feel they have a duty to offer their students an adequate environment for learning, one that is optimal and compensates for student differences. One teacher is very frank about his values:

As an academic, I would never counsel someone who is capable of attending an actual campus, not to do it. I would never counsel someone to choose an online education if they can afford, in any way, to go to a traditional campus. There's just no substitute for it. [25]

Whether enrolled in on-ground or online education, students can be a challenging audience, given their prowess with technology, short attention span, desire for immediate answers, and multitasking practices, all which impact the teaching demands:

It's getting almost impossible to teach a group of students if they have computers in front of them. The reason being, they're the computer generation, they're used to their own computer and that their own interpersonal interaction going on with that medium, and to try to instruct a group is impossible to do because they just want the personal one-on-one. [15]

This is particularly relevant in the online educational environment, where teachers' prowess with technology is not only expected, it is paramount to allowing the teacher to function as efficiently and be as effective as intended.

The Emotional Angle

The teaching demands associated with the online environment can be significant. The intensity of the effort required to teach online is described by one teacher in very graphical terms:

I guess it's kind of like, you were the quarterback, and you threw four touchdowns, and your team won, but you also got sacked 13 times. And every bone in your body ached. You're glad you won the game, but you sure wish that your offensive linemen had blocked a little bit better. [05]

As human beings, teachers have emotional needs to meet. Yet, teaching can be frustrating in many ways. Some teachers approach teaching with pragmatism: "You're not here to change the world; it's either this, or [work in the] the industry" [19]. Teachers enjoy their memories of events that took place in the classroom. They note that their memories from on-ground courses last longer. As one of the interviewed teachers candidly shared, "I've forgotten my online class students a lot quicker than I have my on-ground class students. And I know a certain thing, or certain experience that happened on-ground, I remember a lot longer than when they happened online" [26].

In response to their teaching experiences, teachers make choices about how to do their teaching and react to the modality in behavioral and attitudinal terms. As one teacher puts it,

[The teachers] may not be wanting to teach any more online because of some administrative stuff that goes on. But the people who have taught online and have quit, I think in 100% of the cases that I know about, it's because of administrative stuff, not because of students, per se. [29]

Teachers may not always be able to make an informed decision regarding the on-line environment and are concerned about their ability to teach using technology: "Faculty may not realize what they're getting themselves into when it comes to [the] technological aspects of teaching online" [35].

Teachers' inner motivation is instrumental in how they view teaching and perhaps in how much effort they are willing to put out in order to teach online. At times, and for some teachers, it feels just like any other job: "For some of the people who are here on a part-time basis, this is a part-time gig. They're not concerned, it just happens to be teaching" [29]. Some teachers are adamantly refusing to teach online. They feel that the online environment may detract from their teaching experience, and they choose to avoid teaching online: "It's a little bit like community building; it's a little bit about the faculty having a chance to see these students face-to-face, so they seem real, as opposed to an e-mail address" [37]. One teacher was very blunt: "I like the smell of chalk" [38]. No one could really argue with that. Another teacher feels she does better in the on-ground classroom: "In the on-ground, I can get students really, really excited about what we're doing" [05]. And, in addition, teachers are concerned that "Online, I don't develop the personal relationship with the bulk of your students. And they're a name and an assignment, whereas, you know, when you're sitting in front of, for so many weeks, you associate names and faces, and I think you develop a better personal relationship" [07]. The choices made by teachers are discussed in more detail in Chapter VIII.

Frustration by Technology

Teachers reflect upon, and are concerned with how online education may have a negative impact on society. Yet, there is not enough evidence that this is happening:

It would seem that what we're doing is in a sense segregating an element of the population. You're in this socioeconomic group, therefore you can't be with us live; you can do it online. Yet, my experience in three different universities working online is [that] we don't, it's not done that way. Mostly, online has to do with distance. [23]

For many online teachers, teaching with technology can be a frustrating experience, and one instructor vents her frustration as follows: "Technology is not there yet. So, if technology is not there yet, we are not ready for it, and if we are not ready, then we shouldn't practice" [11]. As much as technological advances found their way in the classroom progressively over the years, some teachers feel that technology cannot capture the essence of the physical presence in the classroom. Quoting one of the participants in the study,

We used videotape 10 to 15 years ago [for distance education]....It failed the same way with different people....Why? There's something in learning about you being in classroom with other people that have the same goal as you—we don't know how to capture and capsule it. [19]

Other teachers do not believe that the current technology can adequately support online education and voice their concerns regarding the usability and appropriateness of the various technologies used in online education. Another teacher shares her frustration: "I think online teaching right now is very lacking" [26].

Some teachers observe the risk of allowing technology to play too large a role in education. In their view, the technology has the potential of becoming a great mediator in the online teaching experience, had it not been for inherent technological problems: computer crashes and unavailable systems can detract from the experience. One of the participants in the study makes this point as follows:

The moment you go online, you have technology mediating the entire experience. A big detriment to the online experience, it's folks not having access to a computer, or the computer is down, or the network is screwed up, or something like that; folks have planned on spending X number of hours a certain day of the week, and if there's a problem technology-wise where they can't do that, that is a downfall of this, and I don't know how. ...That's the other thing, too; you don't know how much of it is really an excuse vs. something that's real. [26]

More Challenges

As mentioned earlier, the technology used for teaching online brings with it a fair number of challenges. For example, when teachers state they would like to have access to better technology, they also agree that more bandwidth is needed for everyone in their online classes; this is something they would like to change. This is viewed by one instructor as follows:

Uh...the challenges that we have in working with the students that we engage with is...really comes down to something as simple as bandwidth. If we had an unlimited bandwidth, not only from our source, you know from the university or with regards to the university, but the students have unlimited bandwidth to work with, then the communication tools, the...the, uh, the potential for interactivity would obviously increase accordingly. And, uh, I think that would solve a lot of the challenges that we've had to deal with or have to deal with on an ongoing basis. [40]

The temporal flexibility associated with asynchronous communication is appreciated by teachers, as they feel they have more freedom to choose their work schedule. However, they also feel that, online, they have to carefully control the evolution of the course. Flexibility in itself is not enough: The teacher is responsible for providing an adequate structure for the course. As one teacher notes,

There's flexibility: It is much more there online when it comes to time, but structure has to be there for the teacher. The students probably just get the benefit of the flexibility, but they have less access to the instructor. And they have less opportunity to ask questions, less opportunity to be given help, when they are online. [07]

Yet, other teachers believe that technology makes online teaching too inflexible and inefficient. In their own words,

I also don't find the online class to be as efficient as everybody thinks it to be. One of the motivations for online learning is that you can get efficiencies, and you allow technology to do a lot of the work. But when you start communicating with students

by e-mail rather than face-to-face, having to repeat things by e-mail rather than face-to-face, when your online materials have to be programmed in rather than something you can quickly change in your notes or quickly change in your Power-Point presentation... not to mention all the back shop that has to be put into place to support a Web site... I question this idea of efficiency. [20]

As a mediator to the online education process, technology provides support for teaching online and for the students to access the online classroom and course materials. Availability of and access to technology varies and leads to different results for the participants. Students' excuses for missing homework assignments have evolved to keep up with the times. As exemplified by a teacher,

I know some of my students have broadband, and they seem to be able to get more things done than those who only have dial-up, and their computers keep crashing. It used to be the dog who ate the homework; now it's the printer who ate the homework. [35]

Technology as a Friend

According to one teacher and his reflections on the issue, adding a technology component to teaching is beneficial: "[The online portion] came in as a natural addition, a natural enhancement to the classroom... and that's very positive. It's so positive that it's not talked about; it's just taken for granted. We just assume it" [05]. The traditional on-ground *classroom* continues to evolve, and teachers report an increased reliance on technology. An interviewed teacher feels that "As technology improves and as the capability of communication gets spread more and more, it's not so much an issue of online or on-ground but effectively integrating technology-based education services into instruction...improving effectiveness. That's the real issue" [05].

Being cognizant that some schools may mandate online teaching, the instructors just breaking into online teaching should give themselves time to adjust. With regard to this issue, administrative pressure to teach online is not appropriate. While there is a trend for educational institutions to offer online education as an alternative, student and teacher participation should not be mandatory. Online teaching is an acquired taste. Nevertheless, reality shows that some schools do mandate teaching online:

Online was going to be part of the way they do things. And so all of the schools announced that this was, everyone, participation was mandatory. And when I saw that, I freaked. I said, "I am not good at this," "I don't want to participate," "how boring

could that be…" all these kinds of things. If it hadn't been mandatory, I probably never would've volunteered for it. And I've grown with the technology; I've grown with my own experience, and experience of the students in the classes. [23]

Conclusion

The experience of online teaching has many facets, and the teachers' perceptions are equally varied. Teaching online is not for every teacher, and neither is the online classroom appropriate for every student. Some instructors adamantly distrust this form of teaching; others see it as a good alternative and adjunct to on-ground teaching, while others appreciate the flexibility of online teaching. The issues brought up by the teachers interviewed and that are discussed in this chapter relate to the technology aspect and its effect on teaching.

Teachers use technology all the time. Whether they teach on-ground or online, teachers use computers and the Internet to prepare for class and to communicate with their students. Given this reliance on technology, some instructors agree that it is not as much what they have access to in terms of technology as it is how they use the technology they have. Yet other teachers note that access to multimedia technology can help their online teaching, and they find the limitations of the current technology to be quite significant. The teachers interviewed also report that in the online educational environment, they have more difficulty to keep their students focused and/or entertained. In order to alleviate this, as well as to enhance their teaching, some teachers participate in videoconferences with their students. In that regard, they find that technology can help regain the synchronicity that some of them miss in the online environment. In contrast to this, there are other teachers who do not miss the real-time interaction characteristic of the on-ground classroom and do not believe that having access to synchronous communication would help their teaching online. Summing up, numerous teachers agree that the current technology they have access to is, in many ways, too basic.

The general conclusion that could safely be drawn might be that online teaching is wonderful for some teachers and students, yet it is not for everyone. As technology continues to become ingrained in education, it is more and more often used to enhance the on-ground classroom. As for the online educational environment, technology *becomes* the classroom: As the technology at its core changes, so does the online classroom and online education as a whole. For now, the issues brought up by our teachers continue to concern them.

Teachers continue to make choices as a result of their exposure to, and experiences in, the online environment and with the use of technology in their process of teaching. Today's online teachers may feel they are socially isolated from their peers. Nevertheless, online education continues to evolve and is growing fast. As technology, course content, learning and teaching philosophies and approaches, and class assessment techniques continue to develop, teachers will revise their positions vis-à-vis online education in general and online teaching in particular.

References

Arnone, M. (2002). Many students' favorite professors shun distance education. *Chronicle of Higher Education, 48*(35).

Blair, J. (2002). The virtual teaching life. *Education Week, 21,* 31-34.

Brown, J. S. (2000, March/April). Growing up digital. How the Web changes work, education, and the ways people learn. *Change,* 11-20.

Brown, J. S. (2002). Learning in the digital age. In M. Devlin, R. Larson, & J. Meyerson (Eds.), *The Internet & the university: Forum 2001* (pp. 65-91). Forum for the Future of Higher Education and EDUCAUSE.

Henninger, D. (2005, February 18). 21st century art makes its escape from the toilet. *The Wall Street Journal, CCXLV,* A1.

Hinn, D. M., Leander, K., & Bruce, B. (2001). Case studies of a virtual school. *Journal of Adolescent & Adult Literacy, 45*(2), 156-165.

Hoffman, D. L., & Novak, T., P. (2004). Has the Internet become indispensable? *Communications of the ACM, 47*(7), 37-42.

Jamieson, P., Fisher, K., Gilding, T., Taylor, P. G., & Trevitt, A. C. F. (2000). Place and space in the design of new learning environments. *Higher Education Research and Development, 19*(2), 221-236.

LeClaire, J. (2006). *Kids and tech: How much is too much?* Retrieved August 25, 2007, from http://www.technewsworld.com/story/52677.html

Morinaka, B. S. (2003). Online education: Where should it be? *Journal of the United States Distance Learning Association, 17*(2), 83-84.

Nicol, D., Minty, I., & Sinclair, C. (2003). The social dimensions of online learning. *Innovations in Education and Teaching International, 40*(3), 270-280.

Sensiper, S. (2000). Making the case online. Harvard Business School multimedia. *Information, Communication and Society, 3*(4), 616-621.

Stadtlander, L. M. (1998). Virtual instruction: Teaching an online graduate seminar. *Teaching of Psychology, 25*(2), 146-148.

Stafford, T. F., & Gonier, D. (2004). What Americans like about being online. *Communications of the ACM, 47*(11), 107-112.

Vachris, C. (1999). Teaching principles of economics without "chalk and talk": The experience of CNU online. *Journal of Economic Education, 30*(3), 292-307.

Vodanovich, S. J., & Piotrowski, C. (2001). Internet-based instruction: A national survey of psychology faculty. *Journal of Instructional Psychology, 28*(4), 253-255.

Chapter VI

Online Teaching Demands

Introduction

Teachers are aware of and reflect on a variety of issues related to teaching online. In responding to the demands they notice, they highlight certain things they would like to change—things they feel would improve their online teaching. Without a doubt, their use of technology in the classroom affects their teaching. As technology continues to improve, its usability, availability, and actual use are ongoing concerns. The same can be said for curriculum development, course design, and faculty training. As the teaching profession is changing, different challenges are posed to teachers and universities.

Background

As they teach, educators are subjected to various teaching demands. This chapter presents some of the factors that teachers perceive as relevant in setting the stage for and affecting their teaching. From interviews we learned that instructors report somewhat similar sets of demands: Online teaching requires more time, effort and technical skills as well as a number of changes in their communication style. The academic literature pertaining to teaching demands in the online environment that was reviewed for this book, and the findings derived from interview data are generally in agreement.

Teachers acknowledge that teaching online is not easy, because it requires increased preparation and hard work and results in overall increased time demands. Those instructors interviewed by this author feel they need two to three times more time online, as compared to teaching in a traditional classroom. Pallof and Pratt (1999) reported similar figures, finding that online faculty members spend more time teaching online, from anywhere between 1 and 4 hours extra per week. Online, student contact hours increase more than two-fold: from $1\frac{1}{2}$ hours to 4 hours per week. Other activities (e.g., lecture, exams, class or conferencing meetings) posed similar time requirements (SchWeber, 2000). In addition to spending more time teaching, instructors note they spend more time updating their course Web sites and interacting with students (Hall, 2002).

Online teaching also requires more technical skills on both the student's and instructor's side; there is a perception that there is not enough teacher participation in course development. Furthermore, online education is expensive, and despite all the monies spent, online learning still tries to imitate what goes on in a classroom. The younger students—"Generation Y"—grew up with technology and therefore form a natural audience. However, there is ample evidence that they expect to be entertained (Gehring, 2002).

Online, the communication style is constrained by bandwidth limitations, the asynchronous nature of the medium, and excessive reliance on written communication. This requires an increase in the clarity of the materials, more time, and deeper discussions to support the online teaching process. Other issues related to this are that the initial anonymity of the participants evolves into online identities; that the instructor is challenged to rework his or her course materials when developing an online class; that teaching online requires long hours to respond to messages, e-mail, and evaluate discussions; and that more time is spent on editing responses (Smith, Ferguson, & Caris, 2002).

More issues pertaining to demands when teaching online address the educators, who are concerned with such issues as learner expectations, incentives, and content (King & Dunham, 2005). Moreover, the development and delivery of online courses requires significant effort (Schell, 2004). The production of a virtual course requires access to graphical designers, prototypes, appropriate technologies, and budget (Bergstrom, Grahn, Karlstrom, Pulkkis, & Astrom, 2004). There is a significant burden to prepare an online course, because they are much more demanding (Chang, 2001). Last, students should be evaluated using multiple methods to compensate for lack of face-to-face interaction (Vrasida & McIsaac, 2000).

Online Teaching Demands

Together with the instructors that were interviewed, I sought to find possible answers to several questions: How do teachers, in an online setting, view teaching? How do they view it otherwise? What do they think the expectations are? What are the demands? From the interviews conducted with fellow online teachers, a complex picture emerges. Teachers reflect on the demands associated with teaching online and point to a number of different things. Among them are class size concerns, multitasking, and student expectations; expectations set by school administrators; student motivation, assessment, and grade inflation; and course design. They identify areas for improvement and highlight that they would like to receive more faculty development and training, have better access to their peers, learn more about their students, and be able to give and receive better feedback.

Definitions of Teaching

Teaching generally refers to imparting knowledge or skills—to giving instruction: It is the act, practice, occupation, or profession of a teacher (Dictionary.com, n.d.; *Merriam-Webster's Collegiate Dictionary,* 1993; *Webster's II New College Dictionary,* 2005). Online teaching then refers to teaching by using a computer, either connected to a network or through a commercial electronic information service, or the Internet.

Educators reflect on what teaching means to them and provide a *teaching definition* that has multiple attributes. As their stories unfold, it becomes evident that teaching is a demanding profession. There are multiple ways to look at teaching, from providing information to interactive participation and facilitation:

Teaching has multiple meanings all wrapped up into one. One basic idea of teaching is the conveyance of information and or skill, from one person to another. However, it's not just straight line conveyance like a person reading a book or getting a lecture off a TV screen. It's more of an interaction and, to use a buzzword, facilitation of a learner acquiring new information or skills. That's what the role of the teacher is… to help that process along. There's also the inspirational and/or motivational aspect of teaching, which is part of the facilitation… the teacher helping the learner make relevant meaning for that learner's own individual circumstances. [04]

In the opinion of another participant in the study, teaching is "Providing students an education based on your own experiences and what you have learned through formal instruction" [26]. Or, it could be as simple as "Imparting knowledge" [32].

Perhaps the words of one faculty member offer the best conceptualization: "Teaching is a process of learning for both the teacher, as well as the students whether there is extensive dialog and discussion" [01].

Teachers play an important role in assisting students in their quest for knowledge. Hence, teaching is about *knowledge transfer*: "Transferring knowledge, as helping others obtain their goals, you know, in terms of profession, in terms of bettering themselves" [02]. It is also about reaching out to students: "Extending help and assistance and sharing knowledge with others" [30].

Irrespective of how they word their answers, our respondents define teaching in unequivocal terms: as being centered on the transfer, or sharing, or conveyance of knowledge. It is always knowledge that they refer to, and not simply information: "The transfer of both information and knowledge from the provider to the recipient. As a goal, teaching, in my view, refers to improving [students'] understanding of a particular subject domain" [10]. For others, it is clearly about sharing knowledge: "The conveying of knowledge and experience, judgment, and intuition to another party" [34]. Teaching requires educators to engage in various behaviors: They help people learn; they provide, and facilitate access to knowledge; they motivate and encourage learners.

Teachers like what they are doing: They like to help people reach their goals, be it professional or educational, or simply in terms of helping them improve themselves. They seek to provide applied knowledge, one that would help enhance the students' ability to think and learn, and also be able to solve problems and to apply their knowledge to something or some situation they are in. In unequivocal terms, teaching is about helping other people grow. Teachers function as guides, leading students throughout their education journey. They guide students, and help them: "Helping to guide them to a learning objective… helping students achieve self-discovery" [25]. More so, "Teaching is helping people figure out how to learn things" [27]. Some teachers describe teaching as a very concrete experience: "I think that—a simple way to say this is that I consider it 'the show time'" [11]. Teaching, in this particular example, involves theatrical performance and showmanship.

Teaching and Learning

Some participants describe teaching as being a learner-centered approach. In that case, teaching implies the teacher as being a facilitator. The facilitator is responsible for capturing the students' strengths, and helping them build on those strengths within the framework provided by the course; allowing them (and supporting them) to access new knowledge. As such, *teaching* can be construed as being about providing guidance to the learner: "It's guidance… it's a more effective way to get somebody in the right direction" [14].

Educators strive to make students interested in the subject studied:

Using your knowledge and experience in a subject or in some kind of profession to get a student, a person who's interested in this, to explore things, to start thinking about things, maybe in a different way or in a new way or in a way that you are suggesting based on your experience. [15]

Once again, they help their students acquire more skills: "Help students increase their skills in whatever the subject is… try and expand people's knowledge" [31]. In that sense, at times *teaching* may involve optimism and hope:

Teaching to me is a combination of imparting my knowledge to students and hoping that the light comes on, so that rather than just walking away with facts, they're walking away asking themselves and answering the following question, which is "So what?" [29]

Since the early days of education, teaching in person, face-to-face, in some sort of on-ground classroom, has been by far the most common approach to teaching. Thus, the various aspects of on-ground teaching have already been explored, and are understood quite well. For example, the participants are always clearly visible, and reachable, in the on-ground classroom. Teaching *online*, however, is quite different. For example, the amount of knowledge to transfer may be the same, yet the audience, and the class dynamics may be different: "Make sure a minimum amount of knowledge transfer to all students; have a minimum level of knowledge" [19]. Or, as perceived by another teacher: "[Online] you don't know what you have in the room… after you've been teaching 5 or 6 years, you walk in a room and you can tell right away what you've got. But online, it takes a lot longer to figure out" [27].

The Role of the Teacher

When teaching, the instructor may play many *roles;* the teacher may be perceived as a coach, facilitator, conductor, director, mentor, provider, tutor, or disseminator of knowledge:

The instructor is kind of a coach. He's not the imparter of knowledge. The materials that are given to the student are assumed to be mastered by the student, and then the student will come back and present things—and then it's the job of the instructor to kind of create some kind of a spark, some kind of an acquisition of new information or new ideas from the student through the interaction. [05]

The teacher can also become a facilitator: "Being a facilitator, a guide, a provider of knowledge so that I can help enlighten students and help them learn about a particular topic" [20].

When they take the lead, guiding their students along the road to knowledge, teachers resemble a conductor: "With the classical definition of disseminating information, teaching has evolved into more facilitating nowadays. Which is basically being a conductor, someone who directs the class" [22]. For those who relate teaching to a set of predefined experiences, the teacher is the director: "Arranging a series of experiences so that students are successful at whatever tasks have been deemed important in terms of learning. I see a teacher as kind of an arranger of activities that prompt students to learn" [39]. Students are individuals who stand to benefit from the attention and guidance provided by the teacher. The teacher takes on the role of a mentor: "Teaching for me is to mentor individuals so that they can learn something, update, or upgrade, or create something in their memories, in their experience" [33].

Education implies access to educational resources, and teachers play a very important role as educational providers: "Providing the opportunity for learners to learn. Providing the resources, the materials, the information necessary for learners to learn the specific content or the curriculum that they're there for" [44]. More teachers refer to teaching in terms that emphasize imparting knowledge: "Some of it has to do with knowledge, and some of it has to do with skills. So, I suppose the first thing that leaped into my head was imparting knowledge, but in my online course it's much more about constructivist model than imparting sense" [42]. At times, in depth attention, guidance, and perhaps counseling must be bestowed upon students, and the teacher plays the role of a tutor:

You're almost a tutor and maybe that's kind of an idiosyncrasy of the type of course we teach and our ways of communication but it's almost like your instructor is your tutor. It's kind of that one-on-one approach, rather than you are the teacher and you have thirty other students that are looking at you from the class. [35]

Whatever roles they may end up taking on, teachers always strive to help their students: "I give them the basic skills and the information they need to get through" [06]. Or, as another teacher puts it: "Transmitting the subject matter to those that don't have it and make sure they understand it" [21]. Yet, another teacher sees it slightly differently. His role is to "Interpret the course curriculum in a satisfactory manner that provides a maximum value to all students" [23]. For another teacher, "I'm giving the students the skills they need to move ahead in the world or to survive in the world" [35]. Teaching is also understood as the "Ability to help learn. Not so much the content, but learning how to learn" [37].

All educators have different traits, and unavoidably, some teachers are better than others. Great teachers are those that do not have an ego and can empathize with the students, as described by one of our study participants:

A Teacher with a capital **T***, one who doesn't have an ego. Well, everyone's got one. But one who can really empathize, understand where the students are at. Who could be a student while being a teacher. Who can really say, "What is the best thing to help these students to learn? How can I take them forward?" Someone who'd rather see the students feel good and strong, in other words, in some classrooms, teachers feel like they have to be in control of the class—who's speaking, how long they're speaking. But a really good teacher allows the students to take control of the class. Not one or two that dominate, but really becomes a person who guides thought rather than disseminates it. You can have students read articles, read books, but when you bring them together, if you really want them to learn, they have to be learning on their terms. In other words, they have to be extending their own cognitive mapping through information you give them and through facilitation you give them. But an instructor should not be trying to design the cognitive map of the students to look like them. It's like a good parent. A good parent will have a good attitude like, say you're a spiritual person, you'd say "We're helping God raise our child." That would be a really insightful parent who believes the good forces, whatever they want to call it. And they're there as sort of a guide to keep the child from stepping [out] into the street, but really the child is doing it. The parents to me that are not mature, they'll say "Oh, I'll have to do it." The word* **I** *comes out.* **I** *have to prepare their food;* **I** *have to make sure they do their homework;* **I** *have to make sure they know right from wrong. They live like an expert who's going to make that little person just like them. Some people have to be like that. Some people that are really good parents or really good teachers are ones who let them learn, who coach them, support them, who give them positive feedback. That's a capital* **T***. [13]*

Teaching Demands

The subsequent section discusses various demands that our study subjects have identified in the interviews, with regard to their online teaching activities. The teachers that were interviewed report having to contend with students' and university's expectations, student quality, course design, curriculum, and other issues—all multiple sources for the demands they face in teaching online.

Related to teaching, educators have developed and continue to develop their own sets of expectations. Initially, they expect the workload to be the same as in their on-ground classes, which teachers soon find is not true. Chief among teachers' concerns is the fact that a lot more *preparation* is required when teaching online. As acknowledged by one of the respondents:

It takes more thought, you have to, it's not like hours, if you're saying, okay I don't have to, I got my presentations to them I know where I want to go I've taught this class five times, I'll start off and we'll give them these things to do and I'll still have to do that, so what happens is you just go. But online you have to prepare better because you don't have enough shots at it. [17]

Time

Then instructors expect to spend time preparing course materials, grading assignments, and providing feedback and support to their students. However, the demands on teacher's *time* when doing the above tasks shift dramatically when teaching online: "I find myself spending same or even more time online. I do save on driving. That's one thing. But I think that I spend that time rereading my e-mails" [14]. Another demand of time comes from the elastic nature of the online classroom. To explain, the on-ground class schedule is well defined: Students and teacher meet for a couple of hours every week, for the duration of the course (be it a trimester or a semester) accompanied by several hours of individual work outside the classroom. In contrast, the online class is open for extended periods of *time*:

When you teach in the class once a week—you prepare—you can do a really good job on students. Online is 7 days a week—you don't get a breather, you got to be there every day... after the first week is over, you got a tremendous workload. On-ground, you don't have that. [21]

Continuing on what makes the online environment more demanding, is that it requires the teacher to spend too much of her *time* on class administration, and this is time that would be better spent on teaching. As relayed by one teacher,

I'd like to see more of my time, more of an instructor's time, able to be dedicated towards the class. What has happened is that classes are seen as once they're set up to go, its kind of on auto-pilot, so therefore you should be able to teach a number of those classes as well as other classes, because they're all done and all ready to go. But at least, in a class like mine, I think it's a sort of subject that constantly has to be revisited and updated with current examples and information. And I sometimes feel like the material starts getting stale... examples are outdated, things could be improved... so I sometimes wish there was more time to spend on online classes. I think it just takes more time dedicated to an online class than people think it does. Technology-wise I know there's new bells and whistles and ways of interacting with the students and ways of managing the content on your website and things... there's probably some things that could definitely add some efficiencies that way, but I just can't tell you exactly which ones. [20]

As this teacher spends all her time trying to teach, she finds it too easy to miss the big picture; that there is not much time left for experimentation, for finding out new ways to do things online.

Teachers expect the online class to flow as planned. In a sense, they feel they have more *control* when teaching an online course. In the words of one teacher:

Online is going to go pretty much the way you prepared... the chat may go a little bit different than I planned, but pretty much you know, I make these announcements in class so it's much less flexible, it's what I plan on... I feel much more comfortable giving them a little bit of information in a classroom and seeing how far that takes them. And then giving them a little bit more and a little bit more and little bit more. Whereas online it's much faster. I have much less contact with them.....The end product in an online classroom is much closer to what I planned. There just isn't the flexibility there. [07]

Course Design

Often time, courses taught on-ground seem to be ported to the online environment without much change or consideration as to what works or not in this different educational modality. Hence, some teachers raise *course design* issues:

I don't think that enough attention has been paid to curriculum development for the online environment... the courses that have been developed are just taking what you would teach in the classroom and say, "Okay, now you're going to teach this online." And even the way that the course materials are set up for us, the course materials are exactly the same, whatever environment you're using. Some of it just doesn't translate. So I don't think very highly of the curriculum developers at the university where I teach, but I think that overall more attention should be paid to how the curriculum should be developed for the online students. Definitely more attention needs to be paid to that. [25]

Furthermore, teachers are of the opinion that "Different subject matter should be taught differently because of technology support." [05] Not all courses should be taught using the same approach, and not all subjects should be taught the same way:

Taking a cookie cutter approach and just saying that this buffet of materials is something that must be mastered and must be taught by instructors, and must be learned by students in the same way, makes no sense for statistics. It may work fine for a lot of other programs that they have, I'm not competent to comment on that, but it doesn't work for my kind of stuff. [05]

Another instructor expands on the issue that not all *subject matters* should be taught online the same way:

Most of the kinds of classes I teach, which are project-based classes; you have to sit them [the students] down and say, "Ok, this is how you look things up, this is how you put a project together and how you do a creative project." And the only real exception to that I teach is the math classes, that you sort of more um, therapy for the math frightened....I found it hard enough; I decided I wasn't going to do it...I teach a creativity class...I really had a hard time with [online] and that's my favorite class to teach on-ground...I tried it three or four different ways online, it always falls flat. [27]

As mentioned earlier, educators do not always agree with *course design*, with how the curriculum is developed, and with the course content. They feel they should have more say in how universities approach these issues: "I would change the curriculum...here and there. I guess I can modify the syllabus there for a few classes... I don't agree with what they say there and what they ask their students to do... that's what I would change" [03].

When teaching *online*, form and structure are important elements:

In the online environment much of the instruction is hard coded, if you will. So the students are able to navigate, and if the course is well-designed, move through the instructive components at their own rate, and in the sequence that they find most effective for their learning style. Whereas, in the traditional classroom, instruction tends to be imparted by the faculty member, or the instructor. Until we move toward using more robust media in the traditional classroom, we're seeing that the faculty is still the person who is responsible for somehow putting the instruction out there. [44]

Teachers would like to have access to technical assistance and *course design* specialists to help them customize their online courses. Courses could be augmented by adding streaming audio and video feeds, yet not all teachers know how to use these technologies to improve the design of the online courses they teach:

In a perfect world... you could use streaming audio and streaming video, and I would be able to do that. I don't know how to create those files, and the technical support we have at my institution is really not that good. They have people who know the technology but not the instructional piece. I would really like an instructional designer who's an educator first and a technologist second, who could help me design tools that would work. That, I don't have. [42]

The *online* classroom should blend a variety of rich information, in various formats. Aside from typical text-based content, multimedia formats including video, audio, and rich online simulations would be beneficial for the online experience:

Maybe not only text and pictures but... online could utilize... short videos, tutorials, walkthroughs, and things of that nature... simulations... would help a lot, as a replacement for being able to go to a lab. But I think you would have to narrow in on the specific subject... I do really think that there's a big difference when you are trying to teach somebody business or you are trying to teach them how to be a good designer or engineer. [14]

Expectations

In addition to having their own expectations and demands, the *expectations* set by the administration are another very important issue that the educators encounter in their daily work. These administration expectations are desired to be less restrictive and to allow teachers to modify the assignments and student requirements in the online courses as considered appropriate by the instructor. One situation that can be exemplified is that often times there is not enough flexibility in assessing students' prowess:

I would disband the 120 word subject response to discussion questions for the whole course, and just get into an interactive discussion where the length of the answer is not preset... I think the word limit requirement is better suited for courses that are not technical... Someone else would have to decide that, but maybe there's an opportunity to shift the way we communicate and get off these what sometimes seems mundane questions that may have value but I would rather they learn something from the material that they're being tested on… I could be more effective if I could waive that requirement and get into a discussion of formulas, concepts, back and forth and see if that works. [12]

Education continues to resort to graded assignments as a method of assessment of student progress. At times, the grades do not quite reflect the realities of the classroom, or course. Grade inflation is one of the *issues* that transcend educational modalities. One teacher shares his concerns:

There's an overall atmosphere…in education right now that students want to come in and get an A but not do anything, or do little, or the least amount. So there isn't that level of excellence maybe that I feel is going on. I think that is exacerbated in online [education], because they think being online…they think it's going to be easier; but no, it's harder. And they need to understand that. Because it takes a lot of self-discipline…Anybody who has a lot of self-discipline would do very well online. If there was some way you could measure self-discipline among students, I bet you can make an exact correlation to those people who had high self-discipline to doing very well online. And if you could somehow measure students who had a low self-discipline level or were lazy, I bet there would be a direct correlation to doing bad online. [22]

The quality of the online students is of great concern to this teacher.

Teachers reflect on community building as an important aspect of their teaching. They are further concerned with ethical *issues*, and with student plagiarism:

They would have to introduce themselves to the class so we really thought of ourselves more as a class…so that there was more personal interaction between the students…One of the big problems that we're kind of concerned about here is plagiarism and I know that my colleague had instances of that during the spring semester. [35]

In order to better address plagiarism, some teachers suggest giving students online quizzes that are timed; again, they would like more flexibility within the *assessment* process: "I would give students tighter deadlines; smaller chunks of information; questions that are quick timed" [19].

With regards to the issue of what teachers would like to see their students improve upon, and how their students impact the online teaching experience, they feel that students should have access to a minimal computer configuration. One teacher would prefer to resort to

The least common denominator rule. So if you said that everybody had to be technically up to a standard, and equipment had to be technically up to a standard, it would give you a lot more flexibility in what you were doing in an online environment. [05]

Clearly, teachers would like to make sure that students have access to adequate technology infrastructure, because online education can be very difficult for some students. Not all students learn the same way: those students who have a tendency to procrastinate need special attention. Furthermore, the quality of the student population has a direct effect on the online teaching and learning, as experienced by this online participant: "Sometimes it takes a lot longer than planned, and you can't really... fault them on that...So, it's very difficult. One thing that would be helpful would be some mandatory contact every week" [07].

Certain demands come from the students, and teachers report that the students' *expectations* are higher in the online environment: "The students do expect it to be more perfect online" [34]. Then, in the on-ground classroom, questions posed by students typically receive immediate answers. On a similar vein, online students expect short response time from their teachers, ignoring the fact that the teacher cannot possibly be available every moment of the day—this raises the demands placed on the teacher: "In the online environment students want instantaneous response" [34]. It would almost appear as that online, the students drive the interaction. This is different from the on-ground classroom, where the teacher is pretty much in charge and controls the interaction. It is for these reasons that teaching online seems to require teachers to work harder to motivate their students. As one teacher puts it:

In the classroom, because everyone's there together, you have to say what's right and wrong. There's this pervasive equity issue because a group is present. Everybody can't be right. But when you're doing one-on-one in an asynchronous, online classroom, everybody can be right. It's just degrees of rightness. I've found that because the social capital takes longer to build in an online environment, you have to keep positive reinforcement running; you have to keep motivating people. Otherwise they get a minimalist approach to the class and they don't really get much out of it. [13]

As we saw earlier, teachers play multiple roles when teaching. Despite the variety of these roles, and of their desire to motivate students, teachers cannot force students to learn, and this is where student quality comes again into play, as one of the demands of online teaching:

Teaching is really facilitating the students' assimilating the information. You have to help guide the students through activities, and testing, to actually incorporate that information into their knowledge set rather than just presenting information. There's a "taking a horse to water" analogy. You can't force them to learn, you can only facilitate that...that's what I see my role as instructor. To help, facilitate them on their uptake of the information. [07]

This example illustrates how facilitation becomes the norm in online teaching.

Other demands stem from how technology is used. The online environment shies away from the teacher being in the center, as it is the case in the on-ground classroom. Teaching online centers on facilitation, and some teachers find that to be a challenge:

Right now they just have this Macromedia flash thing....But I think that they need to do something, some more guided practice, things that would allow them to experiment a little bit more. I, all I get is these big assignments...there's no way to test for understanding along the way...right now, like I said, I'm just a facilitator...I'm coming in and trying to fix what they left out, but I can only fix what they, people have identified as problems...lecture made sense, but, I don't know how to apply that to this problem. [07]

Large classes are more demanding; teachers reflect on the class size, and note that the smaller classes are somewhat easier to teach. Class size does seem to matter: "The bigger classes kind of just mean lesser attention, after a certain point. When you have 20 students... you can't look at every assignment the same way you could if you had 10" [31]. Teachers find their teaching is affected by the size of their audience, with *class size* having an impact on their effectiveness, irrespective of the modality. For one teacher:

I think I'm effective online....Yet I'm probably a little stronger in the classroom than online. And the reasons for that probably is just the way the modality is, in terms of needing to be online so much to ensure that there's a good communication for understanding. Classes are fairly good size, fortunately I don't have the same class size online as I do in the classroom. In one of my classes I have 24 students right now...that's the second time I've had 24. That's too many. If I have 12 or 14 in the classroom, that would be ideal for me. Online, I like 7 or 8, sometimes 12 or 13. [12]

A different type of demand pertains to classroom energy, which is important to some teachers and they look for ways to keep that energy going. They thrive on the energy they find in the classroom:

Energizing, reenergizing, deenergizing, and in my mind, I'm thinking I'm in a classroom and that's fine; I can see them, I think I can handle that part, but online "My God," that's a class they meet for 7 days 24 hours a day. [23]

By some accounts, there is hardly any energy online, where classes are open around the clock. On the same subject, there are teachers who try to bring more energy to class by being entertaining in their teaching. In the on-ground classroom in particular, there is a certain degree of showmanship; teachers find that it helps to provide information in an *entertaining* way: "There would be a little bit more of what I call 'edutainment' or entertainment involved. So [in the classroom] you get a little bit more showmanship and presentation as opposed to the… to the online environment" [44]. This teacher finds it more difficult to engage in edutainment in the online classroom.

Some teachers feel the online teaching demands reduce their *effectiveness*, and that they are more effective in the classroom:

I am more effective in my on-campus classes,…because I'm seeing that in their faces, in their expressions, that they really got it, and see that smile on their face. It's such a rewarding thing, and you don't see that online even though you can't see that on their assignments, you're never sure. [08]

Another teacher feels she performs better in the traditional classroom: "I think I'm better on-ground. I think people learn more. Probably because they're more focused. You know, you have their full attention" [27]. However, another teacher is not overly concerned with his effectiveness: "A little less effective online, but still, um, pretty effective" [18]. Because their effectiveness is reduced, teachers need to find ways to compensate for, and mitigate the demands. The adjustments they make are discussed in greater detail in Chapter VIII.

Other teachers do not feel the online teaching demands are significant. They are comfortable with their *effectiveness* in both modalities (on-ground and online), with a slight preference for the traditional classroom. As one teacher puts it: "I think I'm very effective in both places [classroom and online], but I think I'm probably more effective…I'm more effective online. Definitely" [43].

Typically, in the online environment, all of the information posted online remains available for the entire duration of the course and can be viewed by students and instructor alike. Despite all this increased scrutiny the online environment fosters, some teachers find the online environment to be more forgiving; they perceive that to be a benefit and they grew to appreciate it:

You can get away online a little bit with sort of coming in and doing this, and if somebody is rear-ended in a chair for four hours, it's in their interest to be entertained. And if you can get them the first week, and get them engaged and get them entertained you know, then they'll... just because they're nailed to the floor for four hours, in self-defense they might just learn something. I think it's easier to blow the class off online. [27]

Course Outcomes

For some teachers, the online and on-ground classrooms are equally effective modalities for teaching. As one teacher sees it,

I'd say there's no significant difference. In some ways, online may be more effective if you're doing something that requires the use of multimedia or learning over time, it actually may be more effective. But I would say overall, I think they're comparable. [44]

Other teachers feel that they have an increased ability to assess their effectiveness in the classroom: "I can see my effectiveness in the classroom more visibly" [12].

Or, they may be more *effective* online: "I think online I'm more effective. I'm getting more and more satisfied students in terms of percentage [of] who learn the most" [36].

All that being said, there are *differences among* the *modalities* in terms of outcomes. As one study participant notes:

[Online] I'm more effective in getting students to improve their ability to write and think. In the classroom, I'm more effective in getting students to really challenge their preconceived notions of the world of technology and the world of business. I can help a few on a particular project or assignment—help them write better, or help them improve their analysis a little bit. But I think in the classroom I can really help them think about the world in a more expansive way. [13]

Teaching effectiveness is enhanced by the existence of rapport between teacher and student, and some teachers report that having the ability to establish this *rapport* with their students is very important. Students tend do better when relationships exist:

For example, if they have to do teamwork because that is part of the structure of the school where they go, then if they feel that "belonging" they will participate with their team, and they will provide their teammates with the material that they need. If there isn't that sense of belonging, where they really don't care, they let somebody else do all the work. [09]

For teachers to feel effective, they must be able to rally students: "If you make them feel that they are part of the team... then one helps the other learn" [09].

Online, building rapport is more difficult.

Instructors rely on feedback when teaching online and otherwise. Feedback is important to teachers, both in giving and receiving it; they are supposed to provide feedback to students, yet stand to gain a great deal from receiving feedback themselves: "Having some kind of feedback...just to increase that level of feedback" [07]. They would like to have immediate feedback, in order to be able to assess how students are doing when they are presented with the information—whether they understand it correctly. Teachers feel that online they need to know more about their students beforehand, so they can better address their strengths and weaknesses. There seems to be a certain lack of information available to the online teacher: student background and learning style are not immediately obvious and teachers crave having this type of information available beforehand as it would help them improve the online educational experience:

It would help me to know more about my students before I started teaching the class. In higher education, that's pretty hard. I think that knowing more about my students in terms of their background, their learning style, their strengths, would help me to then tailor things to them better. I just think it would be a more positive experience for both me and my students. [39]

Challenges

Keenly aware of the challenges facing them in the online environment, teachers try to address them as best they can. It is true that sometimes, the students enrolled in a traditional on-campus program may end up taking online courses, yet they are not always prepared to deal with the different modality. However, the same can be said about their teachers. Not all teachers are prepared to transfer between modalities. One teacher reflects on his overall performance:

I think I'm still less effective [online]. And I say that because I think what it really comes down to is the self selective thing in the sense that students that are taking these courses have opted for an offline program, an in class program, and they're all of a sudden put into an environment that now is online, and that was not their preference. They may not be the right students to really be most effective in that learning environment, from a learning standpoint. There's a lot of learning that I still have to work on as to what works well in an online course. What may be very effective in class but not as effective using the identical structure online, where it has to be somehow tweaked, modified, to work well in the online. [34]

Given the demands, some instructors note that teaching *online* may not be for everyone. In one teacher's opinion,

It feels strange to teach online. Every teacher has a certain temperament. There are teachers that love teaching online because they don't want to have interaction with students. Basically I like dealing with students. I like dealing person to person, so it's more difficult for me to be online. [22]

Some teachers are better prepared to teach online, while others should remain in the traditional classroom. As they approach the online teaching modality, teachers should be offered adequate training so that they can be just as effective in the new teaching modality they engage in, as in the more traditional, on-ground classroom. Institutions that offer online courses stress the new role played by teachers, who online become facilitators rather than knowledge gatekeepers:

It's a university, and there are a third of the courses that are online, because that's their nature, that's part of the pedagogy if you want to say, it can be learned that way... I would change what gets selected to go online. And... really spend a lot of time coaching faculty that if you go online with the mentality that it's instructor-centered, I'm the knowledge expert, I'm here to disseminate, don't bother, because those things are just awful. You really have to be learner-centered. If you're not learner-centered, if you're not a "Teacher-with-a-capital-T," don't even try online. You might be able to blow a lot of smoke in the classroom and impress people with your authority and reputation, but that doesn't translate on the online classroom at all. [13]

More on the subject, some teachers perform better in an on-ground classroom, while others excel in the online environment; different teaching environments call for different types of teachers:

I would change the teacher, a different brain, a different kind of teacher. One who is schooled in instructional design. Two, a teacher who knows how learning takes

place. Three, a teacher who knows that their role is just how to mentor. To mentor people so that they can go find things, go learn on their own…Learning is very, very personal. You can't force anybody to learn anything, but you can create a climate where they are excited to learn…maybe we need to groom or grow a different kind of teacher. Some of us will go to the elements, and others will know how to do it properly. [33]

Furthermore, educators recognize that some of their peers are better fit to conduct research, rather than be in the classroom, educating students. One of our respondents comments on this:

In statistics there are people who are mathematically oriented statisticians, and then there are research scientists who use statistics. They have radically different approaches to instruction that are of great value to students. Students of either instructor could benefit greatly from that, but they could know that in advance. Are you interested in a research approach? Then go to Professor A, B, and C. If you're more interested in a mathematical, problem-solving approach, then go to that kind of thing; and it would just be a natural part of the program—which is how it is at regular universities. [05]

For those teachers who continue to teach online, training can help them deal effectively with most of the demands of the online educational environment. The majority of the teachers interviewed welcome training in several areas, including technology, student assessment, and teaching techniques.

Faculty Development

It is acknowledged that teachers need ongoing *faculty development* and training. Training should cover technology use in the online classroom, and should be taught in a manner that is appropriate for those being trained:

Better training for the teachers in technology. I've…they gave me little…technology training workshops in the world of teaching are notoriously awful, mainly because they bring in these techno-heads who don't know how to teach, and they start going off on all these tangents about all these technical things and it doesn't really address the needs of the people in the workshop. [04]

Further on the issue of faculty development, the technology that instructors have available—that they must use for the online courses—can test their skills and patience. Teachers are honest about their technology skills: they feel proper training is essential to help them take advantage of its potential and they are eager to learn how to use technology. Yet, they feel they do not always have adequate training and access to *faculty development* opportunities:

My skills online are not where I want them to be. So I feel I'm definitely more effective in the classroom. However, I would like to be as effective online and I hope to be that way down the road when I develop the skills and learn more about taking a lot of the logistics out of it and just make it applicable to the learning experience. [26]

Teachers' effectiveness could be improved through better training.

Moreover, training instructors in teaching and assessment techniques is important, as one of the interviewees shared:

There's a lot of learning that I still have to work on as to what works well in an online course that may be completely new concepts or may be alterations to techniques used in a classroom environment. What may be very effective in class but not as effective using the identical structure online, where it has to be somehow tweaked, modified, to work well in the online. [34]

One thing that would be of particular help in decreasing the demands the online teaching imposes, would be to provide teachers with improved access to other fellow online teachers. This would allow them to learn from the online teaching experiences of their peers. In seeking a higher level of peer support, teachers hope to be able to learn from what other teachers are doing online, to share tidbits of teaching related information, and to find ways to improve their online teaching:

We don't have any peer review here. I don't think many schools have peer review and so if I'm teaching something, I've never seen anybody else teach that. I have no idea how they teach it. If I...could see how things are covered by other people...I'd be able to improve. [17]

Then, a certain degree of specialization is necessary to better help instructors cope with the demands associated with teaching multiple subjects. Teachers would prefer to focus on a limited set of online courses taught; they would like to see specialization: "I'd have instructors that would just teach a few classes; and they'd teach them over and over and over again, and it'd be their classes. And it wouldn't be the same if another teacher taught the class" [05]. Once again, they would like to see better technology training: "Training on how to teach online effectively which includes the use of right media and how to deliver content effectively" [10]. In addition, teachers would like to have some form of ongoing teacher evaluation. Course evaluations—in terms of teacher performance—offer valuable information that teachers can use to improve their online teaching:

I would definitely change…the kind of preparation that instructors get or don't get. At my institution the courses have to go through a curriculum process for online, but the instructors don't. Some instructors are doing a good job and some are doing a terrible job. [42]

For those teachers that have been exposed to different teaching environments, their preferences seem to converge toward an educational modality that mixes the on-ground, face-to-face classroom with an online component; this is the *hybrid* modality:

If I could, I would probably make all my classes into hybrids. I can manage a class better if it's a hybrid…I would just have all my students submit their assignments to the online module and I could administer it better. It would cut out the paper a lot of times. If everything is electronic I can just pull it up on screen,…while in class many times I get paperwork. Except for the Web class where they just publish it. They publish or ftp it and I can just check it by clicking on a link. The grading is a lot better also, because the grading is all built in. That's a nice advantage. The administrative tools are very, very nice for teachers. They're also nice for students because since it's built in they know the ongoing progress they're making. [22]

Changes in education affect the modalities involved, course materials, teaching philosophies, technologies, and learning styles. Teachers reflect on how the *teaching* profession is changing:

Let's look at the movie industry. Let's use this Broadway/Movie thing—I think it's the perfect way to talk about it. In the movie industry, you have a lot of specialized people. Who are the actors? The actors are the brand…the university is a brand.…So, you want to look at the future, you bring in somebody who's an expert in five different areas of security. An expert in five different areas of—and you ask them each to prepare a module for you. And you hire someone else to come in as a producer, and edit it down to whatever it needs to be, and then you have your special effects people who bring in a multimedia thing.…Maybe postgraduates will do this. And their job is, you tell them what you want, and they produce the multimedia. The Blackboard people take care of the Web site. They actually build the Web site for you. What you give them is ideas and they turn it out. I can see that happening. I can see teaching becoming like movie production. [13]

Conclusion

Whether on-ground or online, teachers view themselves as participants in the act of learning. They take on various roles, as providers of knowledge. The role they play in the online classroom becomes more assistive in nature; as facilitators, they face teaching demands that are either unique to the online environment or amplified by it. These include demands associated with or stemming from class size concerns, multitasking, and student expectations; expectations set by school administrators; student motivation, assessment, and grade inflation; course design; and curriculum development issues. Teachers view some of the demands as beneficial, while others are more difficult to fathom. Some of the more important demands reported are presented in Figure 1.

Then, some teachers view teaching as being similar to imparting knowledge. They find there is more structure online, and they adjust their teaching accordingly. Not all subject matters can be taught online with the same effectiveness, and technology support varies across courses. There is a certain degree of showmanship in the classroom, which is more difficult to replicate online. Teachers find the online environment to be less conducive to communication, and to hamper their efforts to

Figure 1. Balancing among teaching demands

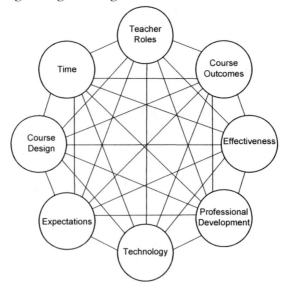

build rapport with their students. Faculty development is an ongoing requirement for those who wish to teach online, with emphasis on classroom assessment techniques, course design, curriculum development, technology, and communication.

Teaching provides learning opportunities for teacher and students alike. In a way, teaching is about transferring knowledge and reaching out to students. Teachers like what they are doing: they like to teach others. When teaching, the instructor plays many roles: He or she can be a coach, facilitator, conductor, director, mentor, tutor, or provider. Whatever their roles may be, teachers strive to help students. Some teachers feel that their effectiveness online is reduced, that they are more effective in the classroom. Teachers are honest about their technology skills. They feel that proper training is essential to help them take advantage of its potential, and they are eager to learn how to use technology. However, they do not always have adequate training. Online students expect short response time from their teachers, ignoring that the teacher cannot possibly be available every moment of the day. Some teachers find the online environment to be more forgiving. When teaching online, in response to the demands they face, teachers make certain adjustments to how they teach. For example, they may spend more time preparing the questions provided to students, to compensate for the slower speed of the interaction; in addition, they may find themselves adjusting how they monitor their online students. Teaching online requires teachers to work harder to motivate students.

Teachers are aware of, and reflect on a variety of issues related to teaching online. Where they would like to change things, at times administrative pressures hamper their efforts. Technology continues to improve, yet its usability, availability, and actual use are ongoing concerns. The same can be said for curriculum development, course design, and faculty training. As the teaching profession is changing, different challenges are posed to teachers and universities. These challenges need to be constantly reevaluated and addressed in order to allow for improved teaching and effectiveness of the online educational environment.

References

Bergstrom, L., Grahn, K. J., Karlstrom, K., Pulkkis, G., & Astrom, P. (2004). Teaching network security in a virtual learning environment. *Journal of Information Technology Education, 3*, 189-217.

Chang, C.-K. (2001). Refining collaborative learning strategies for reducing the technical requirements of Web-based classroom management. *Innovations in Education and Teaching International, 38*(2), 133-143.

Dictionary.com. (n. d.). *Teaching*. Retrieved August 28, 2007, retrieved from http://dictionary.reference.com/browse/teaching

Gehring, J. (2002). Higher ed.'s online odyssey. *Education Week, 21,* 27-29.

Hall, R. (2002). Aligning learning, teaching, and assessment using the Web: An evaluation of pedagogic approaches. *British Journal of Educational Technology, 33*(2), 149-158.

King, K. P., & Dunham, M. D. (2005, January). Finding our way: Better understanding the needs and motivations of teachers in online learning. *International Journal of Instructional Technology and Distance Learning, 2*(1).

Merriam-Webster's collegiate dictionary, 10th ed. (1993). Springfield, MA: Merriam Webster.

Pallof, R. M., & Pratt, K. (1999). *Building learning communities in cyberspace: Effective strategies for the online classroom.* San Francisco: Jossey-Bass.

Schell, G. P. (2004). Universities marginalize online courses. *Communications of the ACM, 47*(11), 107-112.

SchWeber, C. (2000). The "time" factor in on-line teaching: implications for faculty and their universities. In R. A. Cole (Ed.), *Issues in Web-based pedagogy* (pp. 227-236). Westport, CT: Greenwood Press.

Smith, G. G., Ferguson, D., & Caris, M. (2002). Teaching over the Web versus in the classroom: Differences in the instructor experience. *International Journal of Instructional Media, 29*(1), 61-67.

Vrasida, C., & McIsaac, M. S. (2000). Principles of pedagogy and evaluation for Web-based learning. *Education Media International, 37*(2), 105-111.

Webster's II new college dictionary, third edition. (2005). Boston: HoughtonMifflin.

Chapter VII

Gains and Losses

Introduction

This chapter reviews the gains and losses experienced by teachers who teach online courses, and the choices they make relative to teaching online.

Background

Teachers note gains and losses related to the process of teaching in the online environment. As they teach online, they learn from the experience and increase their awareness of what works well online. They adjust to the online environment, in an attempt to maximize the gains and mitigate the losses. Some of the adjustments they make are for the better, while others are for the worse. Based on these adjustments, these teachers make choices whether they continue to teach one modality vs. another, or leave the profession altogether.

Gaining

Several advantages attract educators to teach online. The research literature points towards some aspects of online teaching instructors find advantageous, and these aspects are presented in this section.

One of the mentioned advantages is that teachers can teach more courses online, and for different schools; they can earn more money and have less concern for institutional politics (Carnevale, 2004). Then, online courses are convenient: They meet academic needs and help students improve their technological skills (Leonard & Guha, 2001). Web technology can help students prepare for the social, academic, and personal challenges of higher education and offer a useful supplement to classroom instruction (Shafer, Davis, Lahner, Petrie, & Calderone, 2002).

Instructors that choose to teach in more than one modality find that they can supplement their on-ground instruction with technology from their online classes (Woods, Baker, & Hopper, 2004). Some teachers report that a deeper level of thinking is noticeable online, due to written communication. Stronger relationships are formed (Smith, Ferguson, & Caris, 2002).

Giving Up

By the same token, several disadvantages make teachers reluctant to stay into online teaching, or even to try it at all.

According to Carr (2000), teaching online is not for everyone because of a steep learning curve; then, online instruction requires regular contact between teacher and students. Something that worries professors is that online, students can fall behind because they are "invisible." More, preparing online course materials require significant time, and everything must be prepared well before the course starts, not just one week in advance (Kubala, 1998).

The loss of personal contact concerns teachers and students alike (Weiss, 2000). The online environment makes it difficult for the teacher to help students who were having problems with practical exercises (Bergstrom, Grahn, Karlstrom, Pulkkis, & Astrom, 2004). As Bonk (2004) reported, online discussions are difficult to establish and coordinate.

Choice

As introduced earlier, the teachers mostly choose between four options: to teach on-ground, to teach online, to teach hybrid, or to leave the profession altogether.

Many teachers leave the profession after a few years of teaching. They are frustrated by the emotional, physical, and psychological demands of the classroom (Darling-Hammond, 1990). Full-time faculty members are reluctant to go online (Carnevale, 2004). Teachers resist the effort to be forced into distance education; they are concerned with the level of institutional support, interaction, and education quality issues (Bower, 2001). Inadequate support can diminish teachers' enthusiasm, sense of purpose, and effort. When it sets in, acute frustration may lead teachers to leave the profession (Baird, 1999).

In one study, most teachers preferred online teaching to the traditional classroom (Cristianson, Tiene, & Luft, 2002); some teachers preferred hybrid. Yet, there are still questions whether a hybrid modality can really support quality education (King, 2002).

This book finds that the majority of the teachers interviewed feel very strongly about their preference for a hybrid model. They consider it to be the optimal teaching modality. However, the on-ground classroom still ranks highest in their preferences.

Gains and Losses

The teachers who were exposed to different educational modalities appear to gain a richer perspective of the demands within each modality. They try to teach effectively—and adjust their teaching to fit the environment—the educational modality. However, as they adjust, they notice there are things that they have to give up; in a similar manner, they notice gains made possible by the online environment. In the following section, online teachers discuss some of the gains and losses they perceive with regards to online teaching as well as the choices they sometimes make.

Without a doubt, there are teachers who truly enjoy teaching online: "I find most enjoyable the fact that you can do it [teach online] all from your home. You can do it anytime that you want" [05]. However, other teachers find that the online environment limits their options: from teaching to support materials, things may be difficult to deal with online. One of the study participants expresses her disappointment as follows:

I feel locked: a soldier fighting the wrong war with a wrong general, and every way you move they shoot at you. ...We have gone back to not having textbooks...to such a basic level, it's depressing. There is nothing online—even though the modules are there, but they're not ready by then. ... I don't even have more time. It increased the email questions to a level that is sad: the substance isn't there. [19]

Some teachers find their motivation dwindles as they continue to teach online. The reason is that while they feel they do an outstanding job online, the *incentives, rewards and appreciation* seem to be lagging:

[Online] nobody really cares whether you write and do a terrific job at this kind of thing, or you just make token responses, or you have some clichés that are built

out that you can put in there. Nobody will notice the difference. You may have one instructor who's extremely conscientious and actually contributes greatly to the educational experience of the students—and somebody else who just has prepackaged responses to everything that's going on. The instructor that has available all the prepackaged responses uses very little cognitive effort—since they're all prepackaged he just cuts and pastes and puts them in as he goes—and gets the same amount of money. There's very little reward for being an outstanding online teacher. [05]

Yet the experience of teaching online has the potential to enrich the teacher, as we can see in the following section.

Gains

The gains derived from teaching in the online educational environment can be substantial. Teachers benefit from exposure to a different environment, and *gain* additional skills and insight:

[Online] it induced me to think a little bit outside of the box by the nature of that modality. I think you have to be a little bit differently focused on what you're doing than you are in the classroom. You're going to teach the same material but because of the modality you have to be conscious of the whole idea of online, and what it requires that is different than in the classrooms, specifically the communication, the asynchronous aspect, and the support that they need. You have to do it a little bit differently online. I'm starting to do, I'm starting to collect my long responses to common questions so I can have some pre-planned generic response, I'm trying to get more efficient. In the classroom someone will ask a question, I'll give it to them, and in the online I do the same thing but it doesn't get conversational as much as in the classroom so it's more challenging. It's induced me to be thinking differently on how to facilitate and enhance the learning environment. [12]

Clarity

One teacher reflects on what he has gained from teaching online:

In terms of the things I've gained I think it's how I view the importance of being very, very clear in your communication and that in using terminology it's very important to define that terminology, that to assume that a person has the same interpretation of a word or set of words may not be the same interpretation that you have. So it's really helped me in terms of framing my communication. Some of the other things

I've changed in terms of my style is that I think for an online course to truly be effective, it is now literally a 7-day-a-week job. It's important in an online environment that you are in some way visible to the students, almost daily. If there is a discussion board that you are participating in at some level and guiding them in the discussion board fairly regularly.... It's literally very ongoing, very intimate. ... You need to make it very intimate to make it work. ...Certain methodologies that may have been effective in a classroom setting need to be altered or adjusted to be effective, and in some cases completely dropped; you just can't make them work in the online environment. [34]

Among the *benefits* they report is an increased clarity in the materials they prepare for class. As acknowledged by one of the interviewees: "I feel that the quality of the material, as far as them being able to clearly see it, I think is many times clearer in my online lecture" [06]. Then, one must know the course materials better: "Online—we're taking this to a deeper level of preparation, if I may" [40].

The educator becomes more sensitive to the level of formality present in certain environments. One teacher reflects on the increased degree of formality: "Writing, even typing in a chat room seems to be, has a little bit higher level of formality" [07]. All the written communication forces the teacher to edit everything very carefully:

And when you put something on the paper, it has to be perfect. The mistakes, you know can't be there, you have to check your grammar. You worry about how you are expressing yourself. ...When you write something down and post it as a note...I find that personally to be rewarding for me. To write something down because you know you find new ways to formulate something. [14]

In addition, teachers are aware that teaching online requires them to provide numerous course details upfront:

The materials I prepare for an online course tend to be very detailed.... I try to really be as clear as I can about what my expectations are...the content is the same but I think I'm just more clear about what I expect from the student. You have to set up the experiences that you've said you want your students to have to learn. I think I've really internalized that for online teaching, even more than I have for face-to-face. [39]

The online environment functions as a central archive, where all course materials are stored and categorized, readily available to teachers:

I have templates, because after the first semester [online] I downloaded all the discussions as one long file and I saved it, so if I remember that I have a similar situation I can go back and see how I worded it, and that's very helpful. [42]

Teachers are pleased with, and *enjoy* the fact that they can reuse materials created for online courses, and bring them into the on-ground classroom:

You actually can create things in the online environment that are very helpful in the on-ground classes. And you have all sorts of projects and papers and other things that students make available to you, that are things that you can use for future classes. Since everything is being written back and forth, you're able to save things that are good.....Almost all the materials that I use in the on-ground environment I created in the online. [05]

Personal Growth

Instructors note that there is additional training offered to those who teach online, and they appreciate the opportunities for *faculty development*: "There're a lot of opportunities for faculty development through being an online instructor that *can* happen on-ground, but not to the extent that they happens in online" [05]. Training opportunities are valuable, as they allow the educators to learn or improve new skills.

Our respondents report being aware that the online environment poses particular challenges, yet they also acknowledge certain *benefits*. One teacher admits that

Certainly, teaching online requires you to learn some new skills and think about how to use the technology. So that environment does require you to think about how you could use the technology, about the extent to which whatever strategies you've used before are credible in that situation, about how you might have to adapt. So I certainly think that that kind of exposure provides gains for anybody who does it. [43]

It is exactly this type of exposure that leads them to embrace new strategies and ways of thinking.

From their exposure to the online environment, teachers learn to be more aware of their cognitive changes and of what they are *gaining*. For one teacher,

The online environment is also teaching me to be much more cognizant of what I say and to really think through what I say or what I write. So it has its downside; it's more challenging from that stand point, if you want to call it a negative, but I also see it as more of a challenge. I actually think it helps improve my overall teaching abilities. [34]

Time Elasticity

Time expands in the online classroom. Teachers gain temporal *flexibility* when teaching online: "I think that there's temporal flexibility" [07]. This view is shared by others: "I am gaining flexibility in teaching" [10]. For our respondents, the flexibility found online is a big plus: "It provides you more options to do things... I can reach back to a discussion board at 2:00 in the morning" [34]. This newly found temporal flexibility allows participants to spend more *time* in formulating their messages. One teacher notes that,

Online, you have time,...in a discussion setting, you have time to reflect on your response to the question. You have time to incorporate the kinds of things that have been discussed or that are being discussed or that have been presented. You've got time to incorporate them into your actual day to day practice that you often don't have in a typical face-to-face setting. [40]

Furthermore, there is more *time* for teaching online, while in the on-ground classroom, the teacher is usually limited for time. Online, they can stretch out 4 hours of instruction over the course of an entire week. Because there is more time to do everything, they feel there is less pressure *online*, in comparison to the on-ground classroom. One teacher finds that,

First of all, that pressure is not there—that you have to answer immediately, otherwise forget it. And secondly, there is a trace of everything so you can go back and sort of make it like an open book—you can go back to any page and read something and respond. [36]

Anxiety

Another significant gain is that the online environment allows the teacher to project a professional image even in situations she may have difficulty doing that:

What I posted online was never anything that reflected off my real mood, which would have been a lot harder to hide that in a classroom, because your body language and your expressions are just going to give you away. [16]

Thus, it can be said that the online environment is more forgiving for teachers. Among other *benefits*, there is more error-tolerance online: "Teaching online protects me from feeling the slight touch of discomfort when I have not had the time to fully prepare to deliver a 3-hour face-to-face session" [10].

Some teachers report that the online environment reduces anxiety for all participants—a definite *benefit* for all those involved: "Teaching online, for the better but shy students, enables me to engage in a continuous discussion with my students, which otherwise I would not have been able to [do] in a face-to-face session" [10]. One teacher continues on this issue:

I don't think there's as much of a worry online of, "Gee, I'm going to say something wrong." Whereas on ground, people might be afraid to speak up because… "What if I say something stupid?" kind of thing… it's a safe environment; nobody's going to make fun of them. [16]

Then, physical safety is higher online; the online environment is safer for all the participants:

The other advantage I think is the lack of stress, or lack of fear for the students to respond. In a physical environment there are always people who are aggressive and capturing much of the class time; whereas there are other students who are a little timid or shy and not able to, or maybe communication-wise they're a little lacking, and in an online environment those stresses aren't there. And you can respond freely. Nobody's hogging anybody else's time. [36]

Discipline

At times, teachers have to deal with students who misbehave. As we are told, *disciplining* online students is easier online, in the sense that private communication is easier to attain when necessary. In the words of one teacher:

I find it much easier to be able to write the note because then I can control the tone that it comes across in. And uh, you know, the student who got offended, …I sent him a quick message saying, "Just want you to know that I'm handling the situation. I saw it. Please don't be offended or be aware that I know you've been offended.

Hope you're not going to drop the class. Um... but I've taken care of it... so hang in there." But it would be a lot harder face-to-face because it would be very easy to get angry,... especially if the other student got rude. [16]

Expanding on the subject, the online environment allows instructors to discipline students in a less stressful manner. One teacher recalls,

Some students...I had one that posted on the very first day: "I don't know why I have to take this class. I know everything there is to know about this topic and this is just a colossal waste of time so I know I'm not going to learn a thing." And everyday this person was posting [similar things] and I just... ugh! I couldn't WAIT for the last day of the course where he finally got to... maybe Monday or Tuesday of week five, "Gee, I think I've learned something after all." But boy, when I posted those final grades, I thought "Whew... see ya!" (laughs) "Good riddance!" (laughs) But I mean, I could do that behind the scenes because I was never face-to-face with the student. [16]

Diversity

Another gain stems from having a more diverse student population online. Online classes are more diverse and teachers feel they are *gaining* from this diversity:

[Online] I have students who are right now serving in the Gulf or in Europe and from many different countries. So, I get insight, a lot of these people online are working in the industry, so I get a lot of feedback from people who are as seasoned as I am or more so. [07]

At least, for this reason, some teachers perceive the *interaction* taking place online as superior. They consider that online discussions are better:

[Discussions are better online]... it's really tough to do, in a sense, unlimited discussion in the classroom. I almost have to cut short some of the questions in discussion, because you have to get through so much material in the 50 minute or whatever lecture period it is. [On-ground] There's a limited amount of Q&A you can do if you really want to get through the lecture material. You really can't have any student to student discussion in the classroom to any great degree; that takes away from the lecture time. [41]

Reinforcing this idea, some teachers find that the *interaction* is better online, both in terms of quantity and quality. As expressed by one teacher: "I am gaining the ability to generate more discussions online" [10]. Another teacher agrees: "[Online] we can discuss…in a lot more depth" [16].

Quality

In addition to having better interaction online, some teachers report their online students submit better homework:

[Online] I get absolutely marvelous work from students who… perhaps there wouldn't be that same type of discussion as there would be in person because they're shy or they just don't like to think in front of a group of people. [Online] they can speak in front of other people in writing. It is so interesting really to see what kind of background, what people come in, depending on what geographic area they're from as well. That is really very, very interesting. I really enjoy that. [09]

Notably, a different type of gain is reported by those teachers who enjoy having demanding students. Where the online students are more demanding, and expect more from their teachers—there are *teaching demands* to contend with:

It's more demanding cognitively… it's more rewarding in the online environment because you tend to get students saying smarter things and doing better things. But of course that challenges you to do smarter things and better things—and you end up getting exhausted doing it. [05]

Teachers report having an increased awareness of the teaching and *learning* taking place online: "I'm more aware of the learning process… how my students are learning and what's working for them and what's not working for them" [42]. When having better students leads to better teaching, the teacher learns and grows with the experience.

Time Management

As the online environment separates teaching from physical location, online teachers can spend less time commuting to campus. It is only natural then to learn that online teachers report better overall quality of life. One teacher is quite glad to teach online: "I don't have to travel or to drive" [36]. On the other hand, they have to prepare better for their online classes, and be more thoughtful in their teaching: "I had to think through things…put scenarios together so that I could present things and then have people analyze [them] to try to get at specific situations which I didn't have to do in class" [17]. Then, since everything is now in writing:

Online I have a whole barrage of sort… template information that I will give the class, because it's information that I know they have to have…it would be something I could say in ten minutes on-ground. [Online] I have to write it all out…it would have to be all systematic. Then I'd post those throughout the class. I wouldn't do that on-ground. I would just have a discussion on-ground. [18]

The almost exclusive reliance on written materials leads to an increase in time demands, which most teachers perceive as a loss. However, as they spend more time and effort developing the materials for the online courses they teach, teachers are *gaining* overall from the experience:

Working to develop the materials, the content, for the online class, and having to write things out… it forced me to have to think through exactly what I was saying about a particular topic. It might be something in lecture I was just talking about, but when I had to write it down, in a number of cases I found that what I was saying in lecture might be somewhat vague, and the online classes forced me to be clear and more exact about whatever topic it was. So I think it strengthened and made me clear about what I do in the lecture [on-ground] class. So sometimes what'll happen is I write it down, something I said in lecture, and then I look and think, 'What the heck does that mean?' And so I have to think it through a little more, dig a little more, get a little more information to strengthen it. The online helped me to be stronger in what I did in lecture. [20]

Indeed, those teachers who teach both modalities (online and on-ground) feel it *benefited* their career: "You must know both modalities… Increase knowledge… Flexibility in being a professor… Any school you go to now asks if you teach online" [21]. Teachers gain from the new, online experience, through self-analysis of their teaching style, which leads to increased creativity:

I guess it's just so easy to go in [classroom] and use the chalk board and use whatever models or demonstrations that I've got collected over the years and just talk with them. When I do lectures it's very interactive and I'll break it up with a lot of pairs or triplet activities… I'm thinking more creatively about it, about how to teach. [42]

Another instructor sees the gain as follows:

I certainly did some things differently, and I think I gained some insights into the means of my students that I wouldn't have been able to do otherwise… with respect to my own teaching in a sort of general way, it put me into a new environment so I had to do some reflection on my own teaching, which is always helpful. [43]

Satisfaction

In addition, educators build on what they learned it works with their students; they expand their teaching techniques and adapt them to the current teaching environment: "There are some online techniques that we discovered in online courses that we found to be, uh, extremely beneficial for classroom use" [23]. For example, when they teach on ground, they try to enhance the learning experience by bringing online activities to their students:

I did find that the online activities enhanced the classroom experience… a lovingly yes. Having these discussion groups online, they [the students] can access them on a day when they feel rested and attentive, and they can read what everyone else has said and maybe what they've already said, and get more of a context or a synthesis of the information. [23]

They bring this enhanced experience to their on-ground classes, for the benefit of the students. One teacher reflects on what he had learned:

Teaching online has made me a better classroom facilitator as well. It's certainly given me the technology tools to do some neat types of things… using some of the things that are available on the web, using different types of multimedia, and allowing students to navigate and find their own types of things that are relevant tot them and tie it into whatever it is the learning outcomes are. [44]

All these gains can lead to a very satisfying online teaching experience: "I get a lot more satisfaction from teaching online" [40]. However, despite all the potential gains, some teachers do not feel they actually gain much from teaching online. One teacher sees it as:

I don't think that you can gain much because you're having a classroom teaching, all the tools that are available online are still available to you. What you get is convenience, and efficiency. For example, using the Internet for online teaching, is exploring the medium to the larger degree than you would just when you do the classroom teaching. But classroom teaching doesn't prevent you from using every-thing that's on the Internet. And vice versa, obviously is not true. Doing the online in the classroom is not relevant. I think that there are certain aspects and benefits to classroom teaching that are unique. [14]

Losses

Despite all the benefits previously discussed, teaching online also means that the educators are constrained by the limitations of the online environment: They give up certain things they enjoy in the classroom. Some losses are emotional in nature, while others center on interaction, communication, time management, and teaching.

The Soft Touch

Teachers have emotional needs; they like to bond with their students, and they find that to be more difficult to do online:

I miss that sort of emotional bond that you build more quickly in a face-to-face en-vironment....That sense of the group that you build when you're with your students face-to-face, I think it just takes a lot longer to build that online. [39]

In particular, teachers find the *rapport* with students as very important for their teaching, and they deplore the difficulty of building rapport online. As one teacher puts it,

Opportunity, day to day, the face-to-face meetings, the interactions you have with your students, and you know them, they talk about their lives, you miss all of those...even though the first discussion topic is "introduce yourself" and most of them will write actually three, four paragraphs about themselves. The day to day interaction between the teacher and student is missing. But I see these students that I might have for two semesters [online] in my classes and I don't know them, I don't—you don't bond to your students really the same way that you do with your on campus classes. [08]

They also deplore the lessened ability to inspire their online students. One teacher shares: "[Online] I loose the warmth of face-to-face discussions... the ability to be more articulate, as in a face-to-face setting, and my ability to inspire students by virtue of being a physical role model to students" [10].

Energizing Students

There are instructors who resort to humor in their teaching. Those teachers who like to use *humor* in the classroom find it more difficult to do so in the online classroom. One teacher reflects on it:

[I loose] my ability to be more gregarious, more humorous...online. You have to be really careful,...especially since people are from different cultures, you don't know if they understand the sayings, you don't know if they are going to take it wrong or they're going to understand the humor. So I've definitely pulled back on [it]. [18]

Teachers may use humor to motivate students or, they may be attempting to increase the level of energy of the class.

There is an *energizing* effect in the traditional on-ground classroom, and some teachers miss this energy. For one teacher:

There is some energy that comes from bringing a group of people together in a physical space. I'd say it's, I think you can recreate a similar experience, for to achieve outcomes you know from a learning efficacy, I think you can create an equivalent learning environment. But in the sense of if you're a person that gets energized by group dynamic in a physical space, which I do, I do enjoy that, so that is a tradeoff. You don't get that rush of, "Wow, that was a really good discussion." And the energy that builds in that physical space. You don't really get that. So I miss that. [44]

The lack of classroom energy may explain why some teachers find online teaching less satisfying: "Most faculty members who are uncomfortable not having that face-to-face interaction are those faculty members who really get their energy...they derive their satisfaction from the social interaction that goes on in the classroom" [40].

Another significant loss pertains to the amount of control that teachers can exert in the online environment:

In the classroom you can immediately take control, whereas online it'll take some time. You can take control, but it'll take some time. By the time everyone reads...or

the posting you just placed to stop something, it could take a few days before some-
one decides to read it. [09]

Control is therefore harder to attain, and it takes longer to go into effect online.

Course Flexibility

Teachers also find that they have to give up on some teaching aspects, when teaching online:

Online, it is a little more frustrating because [it's] "How can I show this person?"
That's where the visual part comes in, if I could show this person differently...
whereas in the classroom you can definitely show that person, whether it's through
a book, or some picture, some graph, some matrix, some something...but online by
the time, again, you get that message you don't know where they're at, and there
can't be that concentrated moment of clarification, if you will. So you don't know by
the time you got back to them where their mind went. I mean it could have gone way
out there and by the time you bring them way back again—that sometimes could be
frustrating. Not being able to grab them immediately to clear something up. [09]

There are certain things that teachers can do in a regular on-ground classroom,
but they cannot do them online; for example, they try to enhance and clarify the
information being taught:

Sometimes it's nice to be able to do a demonstration. I can sort of talk them through
a thought experiment by posting something. But I can use telephone cords and pop-
pet beads to explain how proteins fold up and they watch all these toys, or I have
other toys that I can use for molecules diffusing or I'll get the students to come up
front and go through a couple of the steps and all of a sudden you just see the light
go across their faces and they've got this concept. I can't do that online. [42]

The characteristics of the online educational environment are such that conveying
ideas or demonstrating things is difficult.

Often times, the online course does not always pan out as planned by the teacher.
One interviewed subject recalls: "I do my lesson plans, I look at, you know, here's
where they should be, here's where they need to be, I try and get here, they are
almost never where they need to be at the beginning" [07]. Continuing the idea,
the *planning* that teachers engage in appears to work much better in the on-ground

classroom; the online environment loses at this issue and is described to resemble an assembly line. As one teacher sees it:

A good teacher does a lot of planning, but the class that you ended up doing versus the plan that you had are radically different. And I think sometimes, the further they are from your original plan, those are better classes, I think I did a better job [on-ground] because I adapted them more to the needs of the student. It's not just an assembly line. Where online tends to be much more assembly line. [07]

Given the amount of preparation required, some teachers find that the online courses are too inflexible. As everything must be specified upfront, it cannot be easily changed afterwards, and many instructors do not seem too happy about it. As one teacher puts it,

Because of the students coming in and their need to know what everything is, basically at the beginning of class… they're willing to work on the assignments, but you can't change what the assignments are, you can't change, adapt to the particular group of students you have. [07]

Communication

There are also losses associated with the type of communication supported by the online environment, stemming from the characteristics of the technologies used to support online education. A common concern is that the lack of nonverbal communication cues will subject online communications to easy misinterpretation—a consequence of employing communication media that have low *media richness*: "The emotions you give up, the emotional value of discussions, voice inflection: When someone says something online, or states something online, it can be perceived several different ways possibly" [26]. Furthermore: "You really need to watch your tone [online]… it's easy to offend people" [16].

Online, teachers must also give up the nonverbal communication cues they so much enjoy in the traditional classroom. The lack of face-to-face communication cues is painfully obvious. The educational modality affects their *rapport* with the students:

Because there is no face-to-face interaction, the rapport must be set up entirely on the screen, on the computer. The absence of body language and…voice tones are all missing. And that goes both in the receiving and sending end of the communication.

At times, it makes it harder to get a point across online. Sometimes, it's harder to get at what the students are asking and what their reactions are. [03]

The amount of *feedback* for the teacher is also much reduced online:

Teaching online you're without all the feedback from the student, except for the students who are vocal enough to say you know, "Hey I don't understand that." Online you can spend all your time dealing with one very vocal student where everybody else needed help in a completely different area. [07]

Teachers gain a great deal of *feedback* from observing students. Online, this is not possible:

If you have been trained to observe and to listen and to watch a person when they are speaking, you can get a great deal from that observation that you can't do online. And indeed there are many, many different clues that will tell you about how someone is reacting, and these are well documented in the literature. And they are definitely helpful, and that you cannot do online. [38]

The lack of *face-to-face* communication cues is found challenging and a loss for the student-teacher interaction. For one teacher, "A big challenge is not seeing the students... how, what is the best way of measuring students?" [11]. The online teaching modality affects negatively the instructors' ability to *assess* and measure the progress of their students. One study participant shares her views:

In a classroom I can see whether a person is going through some distress or having some personal issues and not learning or doing things that he or she should be doing. In an online environment, because we don't have that physical presence, I have to read the postings that these people will make, and make those connections, and that has been a learning experience also. I was not very good in that myself, or used to that kind of feedback before. [36]

Collaboration

Some teachers feel that there is less collaboration online; this is reported by one respondent:

I'd like for there to be more learner to learner collaboration. Although technically we say we can do that, and people post to bulletin boards sometimes, and they respond to it, I've been involved in online classes where, if someone posts something, like there's a question, and everybody's post something, and some more thoughtful people will read the existing post and when they post they reference that, but it stops. It reminds me of http—you get your Web page, and it comes back, and the connection is gone. So it's not like the relationship extends beyond one transaction. I post something, maybe somebody reads it. Very rarely do people respond to people's posts, and do you develop the kind of collaboration you get in the classroom. It's technically possible, but I haven't seen it happening. So I guess what I really don't like about online learning is that you miss that learner-to-learner interface. [13]

To some extent, the online environment is found to be dehumanizing due to the loss of direct human interaction: "You're giving up a lot of human reaction, a lot of human relationships, or relationships [among] students and instructor. And it's that [face-to-face] interaction I enjoy. You don't get that online" [26]. The perceived dehumanizing effect detracts from the social interactions instructors *enjoy* so much: "[The online environment reduces] social interaction, and the immediate feedback I give to the students" [32]. For example, spontaneity is easy to notice in the traditional *classroom,* but not so online: "Spontaneity... when you're in the classroom, you can tell a shy person who has the light bulb on, and it's very subtle... you know they've got something to share" [23]. Not only for this reason, there are teachers who miss having *synchronous,* real-time communication with their students: "You lose the real time, synchronous collaboration between students. I know you can electronically attempt to do that, but it's not the same" [13]. The same loss of real-time interaction leads some teachers to find it harder to maintain *discipline* in the online classroom: "It's a lot harder to maintain discipline, at least I found it's a lot harder in a purely online environment" [27]. In this case, the type of interaction characteristic of the online environment hampers teachers' efforts to maintain class discipline.

In our subjects' opinion, the dynamics of the traditional classroom and that of the online one are dramatically different—there are significant *differences*:

The dynamics are just different in the classroom vs. online. It's simply more dynamic in the classroom...online, someone can write—either I as the faculty member, or the students—something one night and they won't get a response until the next day many times, and vice versa. [09]

The long wait for message replies is unnerving.

Time Dimensions

Online educators expend a greater amount of *effort* in their teaching: "The effort required in the online course is significantly higher from an instructor's standpoint than in the offline" [34]. Despite all their efforts, some instructors have difficulty controlling, and guiding the students:

What I didn't enjoy was that, the discussion or comments would go into one [direction], and homework in another. At that point there was no way to completely avoid it going to different places. So I did spend an awful lot of unnecessary time trying to sift through. As much as you can scan through something, you still have to scan through it. And instead of spending, as I said, an hour I would spend 4 hours, and that was far too much time, because it wasn't necessary. It really wasn't necessary to do so. [09]

Everything requires patience and more time, online.

The *time* demands are of significant concern to the online instructors: "I'm spending much more time [teaching online], probably three to four more hours a week than with the on-ground class" [36]. Clearly, there is more work to do: "I am giving up all my free time. I think [teaching online] it's three times the amount of work" [13]. Teaching online is much more time consuming:

Teaching online just takes more time. I spend a lot of time sitting at a computer... partly, that's because the interaction is so enhanced that I spend a lot of time communicating to my students individually as well as in groups or whatever. So it's a lot of work. It's very time consuming. [39]

Given all the demands, teaching online affects the quality of life of the teacher: "I've given up free time with my family. I could be doing other things. I've given up pretty much all of my personal time for things that I love to do [teach]" [02]. Teachers try to manage their time better, yet *time* management is difficult online, where the class is open around the clock: "How you manage your time....That's another challenge. Because time is "money." Because after all, you have to be balanced" [11].

Choices

The changes that teachers go through when teaching online, determine some of them to choose whether they wish to continue teaching online or not. Cognizant of the differences between classroom and online, teachers concur that the ideal environment would be synchronous and asynchronous at the same time. Yet, that is nothing short of an oxymoron. As one of our subjects puts it,

The other thing that you cannot do in a lecture room is provide the flexibility of interaction so that you don't have to be in the same time or space for the student to be able to work. And it's often convenient for students to work on their own, but then to have to wish if at all possible to be able to communicate with their instructor synchronously or asynchronously. And to provide a seamless way of linking—of providing those opportunities, both synchronous and asynchronous—they turn out to be something that is impossible to do in a classroom. [38]

When asked whether they would make a *choice*, if they had to, the interviewed teachers gyrated toward any of the three possible choices: online, on-ground, or hybrid. Some instructors preferred the *hybrid* environment, because it offers the best of all worlds: "I'd pick hybrid all the time. I think it's just the optimal model. The things that worked best face-to-face, you do in the face-to-face environment. The things that work best online, you do them there" [39]. A second teacher reflects on her preference towards the hybrid environment:

Because it [hybrid] offers the best of both worlds. There are times when face-to-face is useful.…But…the lecture is a lousy way to transmit information, and a hybrid course allows you to use lectures or labs in a very limited way with active discussion and participation, but not to rely on them as an [exclusive] means for delivering content. [38]

Other respondents elected to remain in the *classroom*:

I would say classroom only. I would say. I love the people, I love the day to day interaction with my students. That is why I started teaching.…If I have to choose, I would go one hundred percent on campus. [08]

A second instructor agrees: "The great majority of my experience has been in the classroom. Now, [my] experience online has taught me the value of that modality to whit it adds value to the classroom. However, my preference is still the classroom" [23]. Another instructor would choose to teach on ground in order to avoid repetitive stress syndrome risk factors:

A factor…would the carpal tunnel syndrome, in addition to having time for revising the course. I don't [want to] ruin my wrist. And if I had to teach four courses

a semester I think it would be too much. It would be being online constantly and I don't think I could stand that. So I think if I had to give up one or the other, I'd probably give up the online, but that's hard to imagine now. [42]

The vivid on ground classroom holds appeal:

I like the classroom teaching, because I like to go among people. I go there, I kind of enjoy having, you know, 20 people, having a conversation—it feels very different. You can forget sometimes that you are doing a job. It can be a really enjoyable experience. [14]

At the other end of the debate are the teachers who feel very comfortable teaching *online*. They would choose to teach purely online: "I think truthfully my answer would be that I'd almost prefer to teach online" [34]. Some instructors note how their views of the online environment have improved:

Online. Two years ago you would have asked me and I would've said "No way." But now I see the satisfied students. I see that what I'm doing is worthwhile, making a change in somebody. I still see people coming in with a fear of quantitative things, and they leave happy and they learn something. They have not learned everything but they've learned something and it's not all that scary. It's quite useful in their lives. So I can see that happening without being able to see any of them physically. [36]

Another teacher shares the following: "I would definitely stay online. Absolutely. I think I've found that balance by doing it in a mixed environment, in the sense that my specialization is online, but I'm part of a larger university setting" [44].

Some of our interviewed subjects would prefer not to have to choose one modality over the others:

I don't think I'd want to do only one kind. I think I'd prefer to go back and forth, try some hybrid, and do something new. If you stick to only one kind of situation, I think, maybe, you can get tired of it. [43]

Others are more candid about how they would make a *choice*:

There would be one determinant, and that would be "time." I would prefer a classroom, because I just like being with people. However, online sometimes, because of time, scheduling, and again, putting in the commuting and all of that, sometimes it's

Table 1. Gains and losses: A few examples

Gains	Losses
Temporal flexibility	Course flexibility
Quality of life	Quality of life
Interaction	Interaction
Awareness of the modality	Communication
Discipline	Discipline
Safety	Privacy
Formality	Improvisation
Diversity	Humor
Teaching time	Time management
Clarity	Face-to-face communication cues
Less pressure	Efficiency
Error tolerance	Synchronous, real-time communication
Quality	Quality

possible and other times it's not. And if you can't, a lot of times, teach classroom, instead of the alternative being not teach at all, I would teach online. [09]

Conclusion

This chapter explores the gains and losses reported by teachers who teach online. It also presents the choices that teachers would make if asked to choose one modality of teaching. Some of the more important gains and losses reported are presented in Table 1.

In sum, teachers who teach online gain flexibility, satisfaction, quality of life, additional skills and insight, structure, clarity, and an increased awareness of the higher degree of formality that characterizes the online environment. Teacher's perceptions of the teaching demands they face online vary. Where they feel less pressure online, the online environment appears as more forgiving and seemingly more error-tolerant than on ground, where erroneous statement cannot be retracted easily, as it is the case with an online message. The one-on-one communication that is achieved online makes it somewhat easier to discipline students, as private communications are very easy to attain.

Some teachers do not feel they gain much from teaching online. They miss having synchronous, real-time communication with their students, and believe that the online courses are too inflexible. Everything must be specified upfront, and they do not seem too happy about it. Yet others report a greater level of satisfaction associated with online teaching. The online environment functions as a central archive, where all course materials are stored and categorized, and are readily available to teachers.

Not everyone agrees that there is more quality in online discussions. Any online communication must be carefully formulated, as it is subject to misinterpretation. Online teachers give up the emotional bond with their students, control, flexibility, and humor. Online, the face-to-face communication cues are lost and some teachers report that feedback is reduced, and that they are less capable to inspire their students. While teachers end up spending more time to develop their online courses, they also spend significant time teaching: The online educational environment is time consuming. Time expands in the online classroom, yet time management is difficult online, where the class is open around the clock. The online environment is quite different, and may lead a teacher to feel that she has limited options available. From teaching to support materials, things may be difficult to deal with. As teaching demands add up, they have an unavoidable effect on teachers' quality of life.

When asked whether they would make a choice if they had to, teachers gyrate toward any of the three possible choices: online, on-ground, and hybrid. Some teachers prefer the hybrid environment, as it offers the best of all worlds. Other teachers elect to remain in the classroom. Yet other teachers feel very comfortable teaching online; they choose to teach purely online. In this vein, some teachers who don't feel that the online teaching meets their personal needs for interacting with students, seeing the lightbulb turn on, and so on, turn to teaching multiple modalities: They choose to teach some classes online, some on-ground or hybrid (part of adjusting to the new trend in teaching, or coping mechanism, or choice). The last choice for the instructors that cannot adjust is to leave the teaching profession altogether, as noted by Baird (1999). However, none of the subjects interviewed by this author expressed this choice.

The online educational environment will continue to evolve, driven in part by technology advances or by new approaches to teaching and learning. Teachers will continue to face day-to-day decisions on how to adjust to this ever-changing environment. It is therefore to be expected that both the nature of these adjustments and their relative magnitude will change as well. Teachers' views of online teaching continue to evolve: New challenges may be identified, while existing ones may be no longer a concern. As online education changes, further research is warranted to help provide an understanding of how the adjustments made by teachers evolve as well, in response to the ever evolving environment. The gains and losses that teachers will continue to identify, and the subsequent adjustments they will undertake in their teaching need to be researched further in order to allow the online teaching environment to reach its full potential.

References

Baird, J. R. (1999). A phenomenological exploration of teachers' views of science teaching. *Teachers and Teaching: Theory and Practice, 5*(1), 75-94.

Bergstrom, L., Grahn, K. J., Karlstrom, K., Pulkkis, G., & Astrom, P. (2004). Teaching network security in a virtual learning environment. *Journal of Information Technology Education, 3*, 189-217.

Bonk, C. (2004). I should have known this was coming: Computer-mediated discussion in teacher education. *Journal of Research on Technology in Education, 36*(2), 95-102.

Bower, B. L. (2001). Distance education: Facing the faculty challenge. *Online Journal of Distance Learning Administration, 4*(2).

Carnevale, D. (2004). For online adjuncts, a seller's market. *Chronicle of Higher Education, 50*(34).

Carr, S. (2000). *After half a course, a professor concedes distance education is not for him.* Retrieved May 10, 2005, from http://chronicle.com/free/2000/03/2000032801u.htm

Cristianson, L., Tiene, D., & Luft, P. (2002). Examining online instruction in undergraduate nursing education. *Distance Education, 23*(2), 213-229.

Darling-Hammond, L. (1990). *Teacher supply, demand and quality.* Washington, DC: National Board for Professional Teaching Standards.

King, K. P. (2002). Identifying success in online teacher education and professional development. *Internet and Higher Education, 5*, 231-246.

Kubala, T. (1998). Addressing student needs: Teaching on the Internet. *T H E Journal, 28*(5), 71-74.

Leonard, J., & Guha, S. (2001). Education at the crossroads: Online teaching and students' perspectives on distance learning. *Journal of Research on Technology in Education, 34*(1), 51-57.

Shafer, M. J., Davis, J. E., Lahner, J. M., Petrie, T. A., & Calderone, W. K. (2002). The use and effectiveness of a Web-based instructional supplement in a college student success program. *Journal of College Student Development, 43*(5), 751-757.

Smith, G. G., Ferguson, D., & Caris, M. (2002). Teaching over the Web versus in the classroom: Differences in the instructor experience. *International Journal of Instructional Media, 29*(1), 61-67.

Weiss, R. E. (2000). Humanizing the online classroom. *New Directions for Teaching and Learning, 84*, 47-51.

Woods, R., Baker, J. D., & Hopper, D. (2004). Hybrid structures: Faculty use and perception of Web-based courseware as supplement to face-to-face instruction. *Internet and Higher Education, 7*, 281-297.

Chapter VIII

Teaching Tradeoffs

Introduction

This chapter explores possible tradeoffs teachers identify in relation to online teaching. Instructors, in the process of teaching, have to constantly interact with their students, with their peers, with academic departments, with school administrators, course developers, and many others. The environment in which they function—the form of teaching—poses specific challenges they need to recognize and manage in order to maintain their effectiveness as teachers. The subjects who were interviewed for this book share their perceptions and experiences regarding the potential and actual tradeoffs to online teaching. They try to compensate, for example, for the lack of visual communication cues factual in the online environment, by modifying the design of the presentation slides they use in class and by changing the format of the course to adapt the materials to the different modality. They also note behavioral changes and gains in communication, with some teachers reporting changing to a completely different online persona. The tradeoffs lead to adjustments that may affect the instructors' communication style, teaching style, and even their entire teaching philosophy. Ultimately, these affect their career choices.

Background

Review of some of the published research literature referring to online teaching reveals that teachers who teach online are quick to identify differences among the online, hybrid, and on-ground forms of teaching. As this author found, teachers make adjustments to their style, delivery, teaching, course materials, and philosophy when switching teaching modalities.

One of the observed and reported differences are cognitive changes when teaching online. In this environment, teachers appear to shift to a deeper level of cognitive complexity (Walters Coppola, Hiltz, & Rotter, 2002). Furthermore, the instructional roles and teaching strategies are different, with a dramatic increase in demands on both teacher and students being noted. Online conversations are much more time-consuming; inducing collaboration online requires a different design structure for activities, discussions, and assignments. Thus, how to create a supportive and stimulating cognitive environment online remains a significant challenge for teachers. While different, teaching online does not require a whole new approach to teaching. Yet for the online teacher, taking on a social moderator role is critical (Wiesenberg, 1999). Online faculty members change their role to focus on facilitation and collaboration (Klassen & Vogel, 2003).

For some, the classroom dynamics are the same (Greenblatt, 2001). Other teachers feel that online, everything takes place at great speed; that it is a young person's medium; at times, teachers have to slow down the interaction (chat) in order to be able to reclaim control (Hameroff, 2003). A study done by Ohler and Theall (2004) shows that teachers do not seem to have operationalized the differences between online and face-to-face instruction to adjust their teaching and assessment strategies. In contrast, this author finds that teachers do make certain adjustments in how they teach in order to compensate for the differences among modalities, as is obvious from the pages of this chapter.

In a way, the online classroom removes the need for the teacher: The student forms a relationship with the text, not the professor. This requires a student-centered approach, appropriate for the nonlinear nature of the course (Knowlton, 2000). This leads to teaching online seemingly being more cost effective, which becomes an important factor for the school administrators (Greenblatt, 2001).

Faculty members are influenced by intrinsic factors (e.g., convenience, comfort, common interests, future purposes) and extrinsic factors (e.g., external pressures) when deciding whether to consider online teaching, or not. Not surprisingly then, some teachers are early adopters of distance education, while others are reluctant to integrate technology into their instruction (Grant, 2004).

Campbell, McGee, and Yates (1997) also found out that in response to the online teaching environment, teachers make adjustments. They concluded that online education leads teachers to modify their approaches to teaching.

Teachers who decide to teach online must make decisions that will impact their teaching role and strategies. These decisions are shaped by their beliefs, and personal values regarding teaching. They often adjust by being more entertaining and theatrical, according to Grosse (2004). However, this author found that in fact, teachers become less theatrical and rely less on humor when teaching online. Instructors become more conscious of their teaching, when combining face-to-face and online teaching (McShane, 2004).

Integrating technology in the classroom is important for the teachers. They enjoy the use of online discussion forums, as the threaded discussions can lead to more choices, more diverse opinions, and deeper analysis (Li, 2003). Online, they learn to focus on the interaction rather than content, and to give up some control (Pallof & Pratt, 2001).

Teaching online is not for everyone (Carr, 2000). Instruction in the online environment involves a steep learning curve. Furthermore, teacher and students need to be in contact on a regular basis, for the courses that are taught online. By the nature of the online educational environment, students appear to be "invisible" and can very easily fall behind in their studies. In addition, there are indications that the online course materials require a significant amount of time to prepare as everything has to be prepared well before the course starts, and not just a short period of time (i.e., 1 week) in advance (Kubala, 1998).

Weiss (2000) shows that teachers and students alike express concerns regarding the loss of personal contact that is associated with online education. Isolation and lack of contact with other faculty members may be a problem to developing effective learning communities (Grubb & Hines, 2000).

Teaching Tradeoffs

In the process of switching the teaching modality, or just contemplating the change from instruction in the traditional on-ground classroom to the online one, teachers are aware of and report various tradeoffs they have to make in the process. These tradeoffs are a response to the online environment and they reflect the differences between the two teaching modalities. The interviewed subjects believe that the tradeoffs they have to make affect their teaching. What follows is an account of these tradeoffs and the subsequent beliefs expressed by this study's subjects.

The instructors who have taught in more than one modality were in a good position to make comparisons and draw their own conclusions. Still, it was observed that even those teachers who have never taught in more than one environment had developed an awareness of the issues they face with regard to this subject. This following quoted instructor reports that different ingredients make up the two teaching modalities:

Here's where the two things really separate, in the case of the online interaction, the quality of writing and the quality of thought and the patience that an instructor has are all ingredients in success. In the on-ground kind of experience, it's spontaneity of the interaction between the people that's the success of the thing. ...There are really different ingredients in the online and the on-ground success. You're a completely different teacher in the two, ...In the on-ground type of experience, there's a buildup to the time that you're in the classroom, there's kind of a letdown after the classroom, and then there's a buildup again. So there's kind of a scalloping that goes on in a direct classroom experience. It doesn't really happen online. [05]

Teachers this author talked to have strong feelings about online education, and report that the compromises affect many aspects of online teaching. To some of them, the potential tradeoffs are uneven, from the very beginning, and are not worth making. Some teachers do not believe the online environment allows them to meet their teaching objectives. They reflect on how their role as providers of knowledge is mismanaged in the online environment. One teacher is quite vocal in expressing his frustration: "Killing 3 out of 4 [face-to-face] lectures makes it an impossibility to teach effectively" [19].

This following interviewee reports being keenly aware that she cannot avoid making *tradeoffs*, as she attempts to adjust to the online teaching modality:

I think that there is always a tradeoff...to make. To make the course online and to get through what you wanted to get through. We have modified it within the past year but that is something that we haven't gotten to. There is something that you sacrifice for convenience. There isn't the constant reminder there and it's easier to procrastinate in the online course. Sometimes you do feel very isolated because you're not in contact with other students...there isn't the communication or support network there that you are used to having. [35]

In the online environment, in particular, instructors have to balance between the separation of work from physical location and the increased time demands they face.

Time

One significant *tradeoff* reported by teachers relates to the time demands they experience online. The real-time communication that takes place in the on-ground classroom has definite appeal as it usually takes place within well defined time intervals—the scheduled class time. As one teacher puts it, "Because of the asynchronous nature of it, I can find myself spending a lot more time than I would for the same class on the ground. Because on the ground, there is a definite, set class time" [04]. In this situation, the tradeoff is in the ability to work online at any time chosen by the teacher. Technology use can be addictive, at least for some online teachers. They feel drawn to checking their messages often. Yet, perhaps not as much for the sake of using a specific technology, as for the sake of staying current on what develops in the online classroom....In the words of one teacher, "I'm back online checking to see what the latest postings are and stuff like that. So it can be seductive in that regard and suck up a lot of time" [04]. Here, the tradeoff is between trying to stay current on what goes on in the online classroom, and the time required to accomplish this task.

More teachers note increased demands on their time, imposed by the online environment, due to the requirement of an extended presence. They must make themselves available for an extended amount of time as their students expect them to be there, with them. One teacher reflects on her staying teetered to the online classroom: "I'm constantly logging into the computer, probably three or four times a day, 6 days a week" [42]. Another teacher sees the apparent elasticity of the time online, as an advantage and a positive tradeoff of teaching online:

Because the class is not synchronous, I can put my online time in any time of the day. I can supposedly answer and respond to students at one o'clock in the morning...anytime...on a Sunday. It doesn't make any difference. [03]

Having more time to dedicate to class activities can be quite beneficial. A second teacher shares his views:

There are things that you can do online that you cannot do on-ground and...vice versa. For example there are activities that we can do online that can run through the week or even longer in an incremental manner—that in the classroom we have to do something while we are there, and finish it; we can't really carry it on through the week because nobody is around....Topics-wise, we cover the same topics but the activities we do are somewhat different. [36]

Teaching course topics that require an extended amount of time is taxing yet satisfying for teachers, as it allows them to spend as much time online as they need to cover the topic and not be constrained by class hours.

Even more on the subject of the perceived time elasticity that appears to characterize the online environment, it is reported that it may have a positive impact on the type and volume of feedback available to the teacher. Thus, the related increase in demand on teachers' time may pay off through improved teacher feedback. Since teachers rely on class feedback to assess not only how students are learning, but also to constantly evaluate their teaching and improve upon it, this is an important tradeoff. Reflecting on the differences in class *feedback* between teaching modalities: "Online you get immediate feedback—continuous over 1 week. Classroom [on-ground] is only once a week" [19]. Other teachers as well are in consensus that they get better feedback online from their students; that being the case, they exhibit a certain preference for the *online* environment. As stated by one teacher:

I think that I have a better feel for the progress of the students online because you are in touch with them virtually everyday...or at least every 2 days and [on-] ground class is once a week and you don't know where they stand... 'til they show up and turn in their work and it's too late. They've screwed it up and you have to correct it. So, online is better for that reason. From a student's point of view, they get better interaction from the instructor. [03]

For this teacher, there is a distinction between the online feedback, which he calls "continuous," and the classroom feedback, which is "discrete."

Learning

Whether they teach in the on-ground classroom or in the online environment, teachers are concerned with the learning that takes place. Teachers reflect on student involvement in the *learning* process. One teacher shares his views of how online students learn (or not):

I think the students typically, come to the class, they are there physically and then for the rest of the week they are pretty much gone—and they are busy in their work, they are busy in their personal lives. The amount of study they've done, the amount of work they've done is minimal. Whereas in the online environment they're present all the time and you can almost see how they're progressing, how they're participating and learning. So you have sort of this 24/7 availability feature both ways I guess. In an on-ground environment you don't have the control, so I like that part of the online [classroom where] you have more control on people's learning. From a remote location you can control that, which I like. I can almost see who is putting in the work and learning and who is not and try to change that and encourage them. On ground environment I've lost them for weeks. [36]

Almost all the respondents agree that more feedback is preferable, and as this teacher states, there can be good feedback online. However, overall, many of them thought that the type of feedback they received online was leaving a lot to be desired. Nevertheless, as we can see here, there may be some value from offering teachers a means of assessing the progress of their students more often, as compared to what is provided by the weekly on-ground class sessions.

Other *tradeoffs* refer to, and are associated with, the timing of the interaction. The asynchronous nature of the online environment makes it possible for students and the teacher alike to log on and engage in learning at the times that are most convenient for them. After all, the online environment affords temporal and spatial flexibility. Work (i.e., teaching and learning) and location are separate entities in the online environment. And, despite the increase in the amount of time required to teach online, there is a certain flexibility granted by the extended class period. As the online classroom is open around the clock, it is the coursework deadlines that are really important. However, this sense of continuous class time may be frustrating for those that have to wait, and wait, and wait for a response to a question they posted online. As reported by one interviewee:

Because of the timing, first of all. The different times they answer, they ask questions, I answer the questions. Different times, they don't get right away the answers to questions. They have to wait 3 hours, 4 hours, 5 hours, and some of the instructors after 12 hours they answer the question. So the students will get lost for 12 hours, and it's not easy for them. [24]

The tradeoff here is between the benefits of the asynchronous communication and the delay between online messages, which can be a nuisance.

Interaction

Teachers appreciate having the improved communication and student interaction; yet, online this comes at the expense of having to spend more time and do more work. The sheer volume of the messages that may end up posted online can be quite large. This author heard some teachers complain of receiving more than 4,000 messages in a single online course. The discussion threads, posted as online messages, can provide a great deal of material that the instructor feels compelled to assess and critique. Yet, some teachers find themselves spending too much *time* analyzing discussion threads unnecessarily. One teacher reflects on his approach to evaluating the discussion threads in her online courses:

With the online class, I sometimes find myself going back to the discussion forums unnecessarily [and] excessively. I'm only getting paid so much for this class, but

I'm spending way too many hours on this thing just because I want to check in at nine in the morning, and at eleven in the morning, and at one in the afternoon, and just before dinner, and before I go to bed. [04]

Where the interaction gets better online is that the parties involved have more opportunities to refine and edit both the format and the content of their communications. When teaching online, teachers have ample time to prepare and edit their messages. This is a plus, and teachers *enjoy* having more time doing it. However, all over again, there is an unavoidable increase in the amount of *time* teachers have to spend online:

You have more time to compose your thoughts but at the same time it takes longer for you to put together your message and it takes longer for the students to respond to you and vice versa. That's one of the tradeoffs you get for convenience is that the students may not see the message, they may not check their email for another twelve hours and so they may not see the message and not respond to it by then. It's just [that] there's a time gap, I think that's one of the big tradeoffs for the convenience factor. [35]

To be fair, even in an on-ground classroom the volume of information exchanged among teacher and students can be significant. We all can probably recall instances of class discussions where everyone got excited about the subject and the entire class participated in the discussion for an extended length of time. This can very well happen online, too. In fact, some teachers are of the opinion that the volume, and perhaps the intensity of the *interaction,* is greatly increased online. As shared by one respondent, "[Online] the communication network is multiplied 5-6 times. The students have a better chance to ask and receive response....Often, there are 8, 9, or even 10 answers per question—that does not happen in the classroom" [19]. Much of the learning taking place in the classroom revolves around the interaction among teacher and students. Often times the teacher is the one who tries to start the discussions and to keep them going in order to achieve the learning objectives they have agreed to. The interviewees note the lack of *interaction* spontaneity in the online environment:

The delay in between the discussions... there are delays, it's not spontaneous. There's a lot to be had by spontaneity in a [on-ground] class versus online. In a classroom environment folks are going to at that time tell you what they feel and there's more... they can also make some changes to what their comments are based on feedback from other students and the instructor too, at the same time. [26]

For this teacher, the classroom interaction seems more fluid, and perhaps of higher quality. In this sense, the lack of spontaneity noticeable online is countered by the increase in the volume of interaction. At times, class discussions take on a slowly start: Significant effort may be required to stir up the interaction, to get the students to participate in the debate. This may happen to anyone. The teacher must find ways to keep the discussion going—he is the one responsible for guiding her students. To this extent, interacting *online* is more difficult for all the parties involved.

Persona

Faced with teaching in an environment that is dramatically different from the real world, online teachers acknowledge an image compromise. Some teachers report they have different online teaching style and *persona*. As one teacher admits,

I'm different online. I mean, when I'm on-ground, I'm an entertainer. Sometimes I even sing to my students in class, I try to get them emotionally up, when I teach the class. And I'm very, very dialectic. I like to dialogue with my students, and they learn very quickly that everybody is going to be called upon and everybody has to be prepared, and they get prepared for that kind of thing. And in the online environment I mimic that, but the key to the whole thing is to occasionally write long responses, or to ask questions, to present other materials for students to look at, and to provide the kind of an atmosphere for learning. But the direct interactions, and… creating excitement is not done the same way [online]. And I don't think students online come and for 15 minutes or for half an hour get emotionally wrapped up in what's going on, but they do in the on-ground [classroom]. In the on-ground I can get students really, really excited about what we're doing. [05]

Some teachers enjoy the presence of humor in the classroom. They feel that the use of humor helps them connect with their students. Yet, it is difficult to convey humor online. One teacher admits: "I am a very energetic speaker, and so, on-ground, I… there's more humor involved… it's hard to get humor online" [18]. This teacher would have a different online persona —a tradeoff involving a loss of energy and humor while teaching online.

More tradeoffs are evident when considering how teachers teach different subjects online. Some courses call for a certain type of teaching, where the teacher has to be able to easily grasp where the class is going; to demonstrate things and work out problems in small, incremental steps, and rely on class feedback at every step. Clearly, this seems difficult to achieve online, at least for some teachers: "I don't know how successful I would have been with those classes where you have to show them step by step what to do" [08]. Another teacher shares his views with regards to this subject, in great detail:

Some people who would argue that you can't teach statistics at all online. One of the problems in an online kind of environment, with statistics, is that you have to write formulas and symbols which aren't regularly available on the computer, and if you're putting them into these interactive chat or communications you can't write them in by hand or do anything like that. ...Whereas if you needed to do a formula and you're in a face-to-face class, you just go write it on the board. ...The argument that a lot of people would make, is that if you're teaching statistics, you need to have the immediate feedback rather than long term feedback in order for people to understand exercises and understand problems. You need them to be presented step by step in time. Giving somebody a solution that isn't done step by step isn't going to do them much good. [05]

Then, teachers conclude that perhaps some *subject matters* should not be taught online at all: "[When teaching] finance, you're looking at being analytical. ...You're trying to put together all the pieces. And that's a really difficult thing to get across" [02]. A second teacher confirms this:

Certain courses are really conducive to teach online. An accounting course would be a very good online [course] to have contact suitable more for online. I'm trying to teach a strategy course online. It is very difficult to teach strategy online. [43]

Teachers feel compelled to take some of the best features from each of the environments they have taught in and to combine them. This approach would create a "super" environment, which would take advantage of the benefits noted by teachers while allowing them to minimize losses. This appears to be the case with today's *hybrid* environment, which blends online and on-ground instruction. The *hybrid* environment seems to offer the most appealing environment for teaching, with the fewest tradeoffs reported by teachers. In the words of one teacher:

Obviously the ideal solution is some combination of the two [on-ground and online] environments. There need to be times when you get together and meet face-to-face and have interactions, and then take that into a learning environment where you're interacting with computers. That kind of model is obviously the ultimate model that you're going to achieve. [05]

Safety

When in the on-ground classroom, students tend to avoid subjects that may be offensive or objectionable. Perhaps the relative anonymity afforded by the online environment, coupled with the physical separation among students may lead them to engage deeper in the interaction. Not necessarily to say they are more daring; yet, the online environment seems less threatening to shy students, who typically would not participate in discussion in the on-ground classroom. *Interaction* online has less bias and is safer. As one teacher puts it:

I think it's less bias, you can't see the person that you're talking to. You don't know if they're big or small or what race they are, what nationality they are,...sometimes you have to figure it out but for the most part it's "blind," and I really think that [is] a good thing. [02]

The tradeoff is that they give up on communication cues, in return for gains in discussion quality—because there's less bias.

Some teachers are of the opinion that overall, the online environment is more conducive of *communication*. As substantiated by one of our interviewees, "It's easier to communicate online, all you do is take a message and click and respond. You can respond where everyone can see it, or you can respond offline, where nobody knows that you're doing it" [05]. Yet, other teachers disagree. They are of the opinion that the online communication is an inferior form of communication, because

It takes longer to communicate ideas. When you're in a classroom, when you're communicating orally, oral communication is pretty fast comparatively, where this you're going through e-mail, we're not in a chat room environment and so communication takes longer and the communication is asynchronous too, I mean it's not live, and so there's always that time gap that I was always a little bit worried about. [35]

Another one of the teachers agrees that online, the communication is less effective:

It's just as you are having a conversation with somebody in person, when they ask you a question, you provide a response, you can physically see sometimes, how well they're assimilating your response, based on their body language and their non verbal communication. You don't have that in the online environment. [34]

The tradeoff for teaching online is evident, as concluded by another respondent: "The biggest tradeoff is lack of face-to-face interaction" [04].

Continuing on the idea of how missing nonverbal cues affect communication online as well as the element of rapport between the teacher and student, it appears that different teachers view the issue differently. One of our subjects feels that the tradeoff is not worth it, because it can skew the meaning of the message: "A person can use the same words, but say them in completely different ways in terms of their tone, their pace and so forth, and have very different connotations" [04]. For many online teachers, this is a significant issue. More, they feel that the lack of support from nonverbal communication cues significantly impairs their ability to build *rapport* with the online students, as so honestly shared by a teacher: "[Online] it's a great way to present information and that sort of thing but in terms of building that... bond... between teacher and learner, I don't think that [the online] will do it" [39].

Yet, some teachers seem to appreciate the lack of *face-to-face* communication cues. They feel it encourages student participation. This is because

That same lack of face-to-face interaction might be a strength in some regards, if it can remove...the shyness factor. If someone is shy and doesn't like to participate and open their mouth in class, for whatever reason... Being online... may actually encourage that person to participate more... because they don't feel threatened by having to physically encounter somebody and have someone looking at them while they speak. So that's one of the advantages of online for the shy people of the world... give them an opportunity to stay hidden but nevertheless participate word-wise. [04]

As it was mentioned in the previous paragraph that the online environment appears to be less threatening, and to reduce the stress level of those students who are too shy to participate in a face-to-face discussion, it seems that there is better interaction online: In the words of one teacher:

Because it's more focused. Course requirements and requirements for every week, folks are sitting down and going online and writing about things. They are more focused on meeting those requirements vs. just trying to shoot in the dark, possibly, in the classroom, just trying to act like they really know what they're talking about, and in many cases they really don't. They can BS their way through it, which is a lot harder to do online. Because people will see it and it's also documented. People can go back and look at it several times, and it's, "What is this person thinking or trying to convey?" [26]

In addition, as the discussions evolve, their respective message threads continue to expand, while all the messages that are part of the discussion thread are also available for all to review as they wish: "In the online environment... you're reading what everyone has to say. You have an opportunity to look at everything in a written form that people are just talking about in the on-ground for a fleeting second" [05]. In response to the flurry of the online interaction, students feel compelled to participate: It may be the awareness that their lack of participation would be easily noticed by the others, and that may cause them to get a lower grade than they would have received otherwise. They could also feel that they can have a one-on-one conversation with their teacher. As one teacher puts it,

[Online] there's a lot more individual attention than you get from the students. There's a very individual level of communication whereas the communication in a classroom is more of a group communication, in my opinion. I think that's something that is really positive. [35]

The individual level of communication does lead to an increase in communication, which results in more work for the teacher, who now has to answer every message.

Some teachers find that teaching in the online environment is friendlier, less threatening than the on-ground classroom. The online students perform better, their homework is of better quality, and the learning experience improves for all participants. Yet, the teacher must exercise caution and remember that feedback cues can be misguiding at times. As we are warned by one teacher:

The positive side in online is that there's no peer pressure. You can't have people ganging up on you like they will in an on-ground class, and de facto dictating a lower standard. Students have to meet a standard or disappear, in the online kind of environment. So in general the standard that students have to meet online is higher than the standard that they have to meet on-ground. Since you're trying to meet a higher intellectual standard in the online type of environment, it can be very rewarding. And the quality of the content can become very, very high. And under those circumstances it's very, very good. You can also get into the situation where even the best students are having difficulty with what you're doing, and then frustration can build up and it's very hard for you to get people back on track in that kind of environment. Whereas in a face-to-face [environment], you see the frustration quicker and you're able to head it off before it becomes more of a problem. [05]

In this example, the tradeoff is between an improved learning experience and the possibility of missing out on cues related to student frustration and students who may be falling behind.

Empathy

Teachers care about their students, about their profession. They are empathetic to their students and keep the students' best interests at heart; because of this, they find the amount of *emotional involvement* to be lower online. As one teacher shares his views, he highlights what the joy of teaching consists of:

I don't think students online...get emotionally wrapped up in what's going on, but they do in the on-ground. In the on-ground, I can get students really, really excited about what we're doing. ...So in the online environment it may take you three or four weeks to set up the educational experience where the student all the sudden will have an "Ah hah!" [05]

It is about the moment of truth, the moment when it becomes obvious that the transfer of knowledge to the student was successful: The students' grasp of the course material has materialized, as evidenced by the enlightenment reflected on their faces. This, for some teachers, is a priceless experience.

A certain level of intimacy develops in the on-ground classroom, intimacy which seems not to be replicated in the online environment. We are told that there is less intimacy *online*:

There's sort of an intimacy that involves the group that comes about and, at least in the type of course that I teach online, that really isn't something that happens. Because it's only a one unit course that we teach so we don't really have any group discussions and so the students don't usually have a lot of contact with each other. I think that's one of the things that's missing from our course vs. the traditional setting that would make it less intimate. The student interaction is very much a part of the classroom that, at least for the online course that I taught, was not really there. [35]

And this decrease in intimacy may be one of the factors that reduces teachers' ability to establish *rapport* with their online students. On the other hand, one teacher reports enjoying teaching to online students because they are just simply better than their on-ground colleagues and he finds it easier to build rapport with them. In his own words: "Online students seem friendlier,...because they're more conscientious,…they're more dedicated. I think it's easier to get in and establish a rapport with them than with a face-to-face class, [on-] ground class" [03]. A second teacher shares his views on how important is to structure the online course properly, and the role played by the initial setup of the online course. As he puts it,

When you teach online, you first try to develop a positive attitude by making welcoming comments, or telling jokes, or something like that. You post biographical information, you share biographical information; you do all kinds of things to establish rapport. And it's all through writing…and through interactive exchanging of e-mail, essentially. And in that kind of environment—if you establish rapport at a fairly early stage—then your communication from then on really depends on how much you communicate, and how much thought you put into the exchange of messages, and the on-ground kind of experience you need to establish rapport. There's a certain minimum contact you need to establish with students,…but the on-ground environment is a lot more forgiving than the online. [Online] Either it goes or it doesn't go, and it's very, very difficult to change it because it takes so long between messages to communicate things back and forth. If you set up things right then it goes well—but if you set things up wrong it's very hard to recover. [05]

Student Quality

In the paragraphs presented above, teachers discuss various tradeoffs that involve among others a lack of nonverbal communication cues and a loss of intimacy, balanced against gains offered by an educational environment that can be perceived as safer, friendlier, with less bias, and less threatening than the on-ground classroom. Its unique design may afford the online environment the capability to function as an academic filter, in a sense. *Student quality* is an ongoing concern for teachers, and they are happy to find that the students taking courses online appear to prepare better for the classes: only the more disciplined, and determined students survive online. As one teacher puts it,

There can be a self-selective sort of process that occurs in online education. If a student is going to take an online class, at least they know how to use a computer, you'd hope so. They're at least somewhat technically sophisticated in that way. [04]

Most teachers are more comfortable when their students open up to communication, and some teachers believe that they get to know their online students better, because of this improved level of communication:

I feel that I know my online students better than the classroom ones.... I think at the end of the course, as a group, I know them better. In the face-to-face class, there will be a few students that I get to know very well. In an online course, I think the minimum or the baseline for the whole group moves up. Um, there might be one or two students that I really don't get to know but for the most part, I get to know the students better overall, in an online class. And I think that's just because you know, I feel like there's just so much more communication... you know, individually... in the... you know, with the online classes. [39]

It seems easier to teach to good students: "If you're lucky enough to get the good class, it's going to be phenomenal" [34].

That does not happen all the time, though. Often, the teacher finds herself in an unenviable position; she approaches the end of the semester only to realize some of her [online] students have fallen so far behind in their coursework that it would take a miracle to bring them back on track. The apparent disconnect between the expectations of the students and the reality of the course is reason for frustration:

They run into trouble, because you know, they're, they want to get A's and B's and they don't really see you... they don't attend the lectures, they don't read over the lectures, they don't look at the class material. And so yeah they do the assignment but it's not really 'A' material... it meets the basic definition of the assignment so it's a passing grade, but it's nothing more. So I think that... [if] you just don't have that one-to-one contact, it's very easy for the students to get a lot less out of the class than they should be. [07]

Neither the students who are failing, nor the teacher who grades them are happy to find themselves in this type of a situation. Whatever other tradeoffs they make, teachers will not accept those that reduce the quality of the education received by their students.

As teachers reflect on the quality of their students, they ask themselves whether everyone could be taught, and should study online. The response is quick to materialize: Teachers admit that the online environment is not for everybody. One teacher finds that the online environment "Is good for some students, the same for some students, and worse for some students" [41]. The argument can be taken further, by questioning whether online teaching is for every teacher as well; the answer is negative, as evidenced in the following interview excerpts:

I think it's not for everybody. I think you know, you have all those caveats... you know, if you're a bad teacher, going online is not going to make you a good teacher.

It's just going to make you bad online. So I think, you know, people are going to learn from good instruction period. [39]

Moving from the real world, present in the on-ground classroom, to the virtual realities of the online realm can be a difficult, complex journey. Not everyone, teacher or students, will succeed in making the transition. There are numerous impediments stemming from the very different nature of the environments and of the media involved. Quoting one teacher,

My background is as a linguist, and so the importance of tone of voice and body language when it comes to linguistic communication is extremely important. It's far more important in a lot of cases than the words that are actually spoken. That means there's a new sort of environment that's going on. For some that's a positive because they are very good at communicating effectively when it comes to the written format... sometimes it's much easier to communicate in the written format and know how you want to formulate things as compared to the oral environment. For some people that really does make for such a sterile environment especially in today's world. Until recently, the oral nature of our society, when it comes to politicians and other things, it's very much a part of our culture. Email has maybe started to change things where writing wasn't as stressed and now it seems to be very much stressed, where it's more that you're able to communicate effectively in a written environment. I think that some people really regard that as sterile. Some are so used to having the face-to-face conversation with another human being, whether it's your instructor or fellow classmates, and I think that could make it very difficult for some people. [35]

Universities continue to invest in online education for a number of good reasons. For one, they strive to attract students. There are costs involved in the teaching process, and online education holds certain appeal because is scalable: once an online course is developed, it could be taught to any number of students. In general, this results in better online economics, yet, some teachers fear that universities may expand online teaching for the wrong reasons:

One of the things I'm concerned about is that as administrators see that their profit margins are greater for online classes, I don't know for sure if this is the case right now, but I could see it maybe becoming the case... that the drive to encourage online education may fall victim to the wrong motives... that the cost efficiency will take a more prevalent role in the decisions about what kind of classes to offer. That the administrators will see that if they offer an online class, then they don't have to put air conditioning in this building, so they can save money on the overhead.

And if I do an online class I won't have to pay the janitor, so I don't need janitors. And if I do online classes... maybe... you know, those types of issues. The reason for having the online classes will be because the administration feels they are more cost efficient, rather than offering online classes because they are more flexible or because they are more superior for a particular subject area or a particular class. Choosing to offer online classes for the wrong reasons, mainly money... I see that as a danger. [05]

This respondent favors a cautionary approach that would not allow cost to be the main factor in deciding to offer online education, forsaking tradeoffs to quality education.

Teaching online relies on technology; it is dependent on the computers used, on the Internet, and on the communication that is conducted online. However, in the end, the quality of the instruction is more important than the educational modality. One of the teachers interviewed stated in no uncertain terms that

The machines aren't what's going to make a difference in whether our students learn or not. We can look at various media, whether it's television or the computer or whatever and that's not going to make a difference in how students learn. It's the instruction. It's what you do with the online. [39]

Conclusion

This chapter explores the tradeoffs and adjustments teachers make, as well as their beliefs regarding the effect of the tradeoffs on their teaching. A summary of these tradeoffs is presented in Table 1.

Overall, teachers benefit from exposure to a different environment and gain additional skills and insight. They note behavioral changes: Their communication style changes, they structure their courses differently, and they are more sensitive to the level of formality present in certain environments. In reaction to the online environment, teachers make adjustments. For example, they modify the design of the graphical materials they use in class. In addition, they may change the format of the course to adapt the materials to the different modality. Some teachers do not believe that the online environment allows them to meet their teaching objectives. They note that significant tradeoffs are related to the time demands they experience online.

Teachers quantify their effectiveness in the hybrid and in the online modalities as somewhat inferior to what they experience in the on-ground classroom. Teaching online requires an extended presence. Tradeoffs refer to, and are associated with,

Table 1. Teaching Tradeoffs

Online	Description	On-ground
More	Level of formality	Less
More	Temporal flexibility	Less
Less	Communication cues	More
More	Course preparation	Less
More	Level of structure	Less
Less	A sense of classroom "energy"	More
Less	Humor	More
More	Personal safety	Less
More	Privacy	Less
Less	Personal time available	More
More	Amount of work required	Less
Less	Degree of control over the course direction	More
Less	Ease of controlling the interaction	More
Less	Ease of establishing rapport	More
Less	Feedback amount, quality, and timeliness	More

the timing of the interaction and the availability of feedback. On one hand, teachers enjoy having more time to prepare their online messages. On the other, this only increases the amount of time they spend online. Often, teachers find themselves spending too much time analyzing discussion threads unnecessarily. Some teachers report they have a different online persona, and a different online teaching style.

Teachers' accounts reveal rich experiences in teaching in the on-ground classroom, online, or using hybrid modalities. Aside from the tradeoffs they identify, there are numerous factors that contribute to the teaching experience, and views vary among the teachers interviewed for this book. However, several recurring items are noticeable (e.g., satisfaction, frustration, availability and use of technology, class size, teaching modality, media richness). The categories derived from the interview data are examined in detail in the next two chapters.

Teachers find themselves facing tradeoffs as they try to adjust their teaching to fit the modality—online or on the ground. As they strive to find the better fit between course activities and the modality they teach in, they choose to teach parts of a course on ground, and parts of it online. In order to be able to move between the two modalities, without jeopardizing the quality of their teaching or their quality of life, teachers focus on the process of instruction itself, around which they handle technology and administrative issues. It is to be expected that future technology improvements, changes in curriculum, and improvements in learning and teaching models will affect online teachers' views of the online teaching environment, and of the tradeoffs they will associate with their teaching online. Further research is needed to keep pace with these changes and to inform on the potential gains and losses, and on the tradeoffs reported by online teachers.

As teachers report that the tradeoffs they are forced to make affect their teaching, it is important that educational institutions find ways to support their online teachers reduce the magnitude of the tradeoffs; to help them gain more, and loose less when teaching online. Teachers continue to play an important role in online education, and helping them improve their online teaching experiences would go a long way towards helping online education approach its full potential.

References

Campbell, N., McGee, C., & Yates, R. (1997). *"It is not out with the old and in with the new": The challenge to adapt to online teaching.* Retrieved April 11, 2005, from http://unisanet.unisa.edu.au/cccc/papers/non-refereed/campbell.htm

Carr, S. (2000). *After half a course, a professor concedes distance education is not for him.* Retrieved May 10, 2005, retrieved from http://chronicle.com/free/2000/03/2000032801u.htm

Grant, M. M. (2004). Learning to teach on the Web: Factors influencing teacher education faculty. *Internet and Higher Education, 7,* 329-341.

Greenblatt, E. (2001). The more things change: Teaching in an online classroom. *Christian Science Monitor, 93,* 17.

Grosse, C. U. (2004). How distance learning changes faculty. *International Journal of Instructional Technology and Distance Learning, 1*(6).

Grubb, A., & Hines, M. (2000). Tearing down barriers and building communities: Pedagogical strategies for the Web-based environment. In R. A. Cole (Ed.), *Issues in Web-based pedagogy* (pp. 365-380). Westport, CT: Greenwood Press.

Hameroff, G. (2003). Keeping the education in online education. *Community College Week, 15*(20), 10-11.

Klassen, J., & Vogel, D. (2003). New issues arising from e-education. In A. K. Aggarwal (Ed.), *Web-based education: Learning from experience* (pp. 36-48). Hershey, PA: Information Science Publishing.

Knowlton, D. S. (2000). A theoretical framework for the online classroom: A defense and delineation of a student-centered pedagogy. In B. W. Speck (Ed.), *New directions for teaching and learning. Principles of effective teaching in the online classroom* (Vol. 84, pp. 5-22).

Kubala, T. (1998). Addressing student needs: Teaching on the Internet. *T H E Journal, 28*(5), 71-74.

Li, Q. (2003). Would we teach without technology? A professor's experience of teaching mathematics education incorporating the Internet. *Educational Research, 45*(1), 61-77.

McShane, K. (2004). Integrating face-to-face and online teaching: Academics' role concept and teaching choices. *Teaching in Higher Education, 9*(1), 3-16.

Ohler, S., & Theall, M. (2004, April 12-13). *An exploratory study of teacher opinions about teaching and learning on-line and face-to-face: the instructional choices of a sample of faculty in computer science.* Paper presented at the Instructional Evaluation and Faculty Development Conference, San Diego, CA.

Pallof, R. M., & Pratt, K. (2001). *Lessons from the cyberspace classroom: The realities of online teaching.* San Francisco: Jossey-Bass.

Walters Coppola, N., Hiltz, S. R., & Rotter, N. G. (2002). Becoming a virtual professor: Pedagogical roles and asynchronous learning networks. *Journal of Management Information Systems, 18*(4), 69-89.

Weiss, R. E. (2000). Humanizing the online classroom. *New Directions for Teaching and Learning, 84*, 47-51.

Wiesenberg, F. (1999). Teaching on-line: One instructor's evolving 'theory-of-practice.' *Adult Basic Education, 9*(3), 1-10.

Chapter IX

Central Ideas:
Teaching

Introduction

In the previous chapters, teachers shared their online teaching stories. They talked about how the online environment affects them and their teaching, about the trade-offs they find, the issues associated with technology and teaching online, and about the adjustments they feel they make. They also shared the benefits and the losses they notice as a result of their teaching online. While all these data are fascinating, it is now time to put things in perspective and find out how, if at all, these stories intersect and help us coin a better understanding of the teachers' experiences in the online environment. This chapter focuses on the central ideas that are related to teaching and will discuss the first four core categories identified: Teaching, Teaching Demands, Teacher Needs, and Teaching Dimensions.

Background

Forty-four teachers were interviewed for this book and shared their stories. As their stories unfolded, themes were identified that evolved into categories. By constantly moving between the interview data and the emergent categories, through a process of constant comparison, these categories were continuously refined in light of the new data gathered from interviews. New categories were identified, together with relationships among the existing categories. Eventually, when no new categories emerged from the interview data, 10 high-level categories were identified and used to generate a theory of the online teaching experience presented in Chapter XI.

Table 1. Initial categories

Adjustments	Learning	Availability
Administrative	Media Richness	Job
Assessment	Multitasking	Knowledge transfer
Choice	Other Profession?	Office Hours
Class Size	Peer Support	Benefits
Differences Between Online And Classroom	Incentives/Appreciation/Rewards	What Makes A Good Teacher
Discipline	Vocation	Role
Ease Of Use	Satisfaction	Reusability
Teaching With Technology	Show/Theatrical Performance	What Would You Change
Efficiency	Student quality	Why Do You Teach?
Effort	Subject Matter	One Word: *Teaching*
Emotional Involvement	Support	Online
Energizing	Synchronous	Persona
Enjoy	Teacher Needs	Classroom
Entertainment	Teaching	Interaction
Expectations	Teaching Definition	Why
Face-to-face	Teaching demands	Rapport
Faculty development	Teaching dimensions	Communication
Feedback	Effectiveness	Control
Flexibility	Technical support	Course design
Frustrating	Technology	Planning
Gaining	Time	Reliability
Giving Up	Touchy-Feely Stuff	Deep Learning
Humor	Tradeoffs	Preparation
Hybrid	Usability/Appropriateness	Issues
Improvisation	Boredom	

Central Ideas: Teaching

Transcript Analysis

The interviews were recorded for authenticity and were immediately transcribed. The transcripts were compared to the audio recordings, edited for accuracy, and coding started right away.

Once the transcripts of the interviews were confirmed accurate, they were loaded into ATLAS.ti, qualitative analysis software, and coded for themes and emerging categories. This first step generated a number of categories that were grouped under each research question to facilitate further exploration. As the line-by-line analysis of the transcripts progressed, I recorded my thoughts in memos that helped me make comparisons among concepts. The ATLAS.ti software helped present categories systematically and compare them across questions. Subsequent readings confirmed category significance. Seventy-seven initial categories evolved from the analysis of the transcripts and are listed in Table 1.

Further analysis helped aggregate the categories presented in Table 1 into more general categories and delineated relationships among categories. Concepts that appeared to be similar were grouped under a higher order, more abstract concept or category, based on its ability to explain the phenomenon of interest.

The main outcome of the analysis was the emergence of 10 core categories: Teaching, Teaching Demands, Teacher Needs, Teaching Dimensions, Teaching With Technology, Technology, Differences Among Modalities, Issues, Adjustments, and Choice (see Table 2).

As central themes emerged from data, the focus of the researcher shifted to saturating the categories. Once no new properties, dimension, or relationships were found in the data collection, theoretical saturation was achieved.

Table 2. Main categories

Teaching	Technology
Teaching Demands	Differences Among Modalities
Teacher Needs	Issues
Teaching Dimensions	Adjustments
Teaching With Technology	Choice

Figure 1. Main categories and relationships

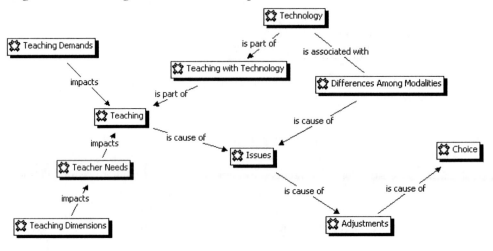

Core Categories

The 10 main categories and their respective relationships are presented in Figure 1.

These core categories were further developed in terms of properties, dimensions, and relationships, resulting in a theory. The theory presented in Chapter XI integrates this set of categories to explain the online teaching experience.

Teaching

Without a doubt, for many teachers teaching is a labor of love. Schmier (2005) was able to describe the essence of teaching in a moving way:

I love being on my campus. I love walking it. I love the students… I love what I do and am doing what I love. What is teaching? To me, it's more than merely transmitting information. It's more than merely preparing students to take some exam. It's more than helping them get some professional credentials… There's more, much more, to teaching than all that… The notion that there is a moral obligation to be kind, helping, respectful, just, and compassionate at all times and in everything we do, including that which we do on our campuses and in our classrooms, is embedded in all of the great religions and secular philosophies… to make the world a more peaceful, loving, creative, respectful, intelligent, and caring place. That's being a teacher! That's the teacher's mission, purpose, and meaning: giving time and en-

ergy consciously to leave this world of ours a better place than when we found it. Being a good teacher involves doing good for students and helping them learn to do good and to do well. As teachers, our challenge, then, is to make every day in that classroom, as well as on our campus, a good deed day. Teachers should help people learn as they have not learned; they should help people to do with what they know as they have never done; they should help people to feel as they have not felt, to believe as they have not believed, to think as they have not thought, to hope as they have not hoped, to behave as they have not behaved, to be mindful as they have not been mindful.

Teachers define teaching in various ways, with all definitions being facets of this very complex activity: for some, teaching means helping people learn. Other teachers define teaching in terms related to knowledge transfer or rather as mentoring; others feel that teaching is about facilitating students' learning.

When teaching is about transferring knowledge, it is with the understanding that the teacher will be helping others obtain their goals in terms of profession and to better themselves. Teaching may also mean to "Mentor individuals so that they can learn something, update, or upgrade, or create something in their memories, in their experience" [33]. For some teachers, teaching is coaching somebody so that they can learn something and make use of it. On the same note, teaching could be referred to as facilitating others to capture and to learn the subject matter in a way that will make it useful and practical for them. This is true regardless of what the subject matter may be. Yet, teaching certain courses (e.g., economics) may have immediate practical applications, rather than being just academic.

As the analysis of the categories continued, this main (core) category—Teaching—was saturated and resulted in four properties: Knowledge Transfer, Show/Theatrical Performance, Role, and Improvisation. The property *Knowledge Transfer* revealed

Figure 2. Category: Teaching

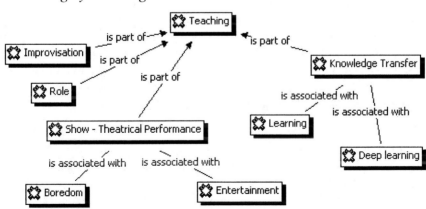

two associated sub-properties: *Learning* and *Deep Learning*; and the property *Show/Theatrical Performance* revealed two sub-properties: *Entertainment* and *Boredom*. All these are presented in Figure 2, including their respective relationships.

Knowledge Transfer revealed two sub-properties: *Learning* and *Deep Learning*. Teachers seem to agree that Learning is available to students and teachers alike, regardless of the modality. By attending on-ground courses, students and teacher alike learn things in the hallways, in the classrooms, and on campus in general. Students learn from other students, from going to lectures, and other events. These may be activities that the online students cannot attend. There is more learning on-ground than online, then. The dimensions of Learning are from *little* to *more* learning.

Of course, there are different levels of learning. Teachers refer to *deep learning* and admit it does not seem to happen often online; *surface* learning does. Seemingly, it is easier for teachers to develop a relationship in an on-ground class, where communication is a lot deeper and the level of trust among participants may be a little bit higher than online: "Because trust kind of works with communication; if they trust you then they're more likely to open up themselves to you" [22]. Hence, there is not much deep learning online.

Teachers talk about teaching online in terms of a *Show/Theatrical Performance*. They find the classroom lecture to be theatrical, which is not the case in online environments. In the classroom, it appears they often "put on a show"—but not to entertain the students; rather, it is a directed experience, something a director does, making sure everything flows well in the right direction: "The way I approach my in-class is information entertainment. I'm really there to get them enthused about the subject… to try to entertain them" [06].

Following the same idea of Show/Theatrical Performance, some teachers are quite adamant: "Anybody who denies that standing up in front of 30 other folks and trying to keep their interest for 2 hours is not performing doesn't know what they're talking about" [43]. Yet, while the Show/Theatrical Performance appears to be fairly common occurrence on ground, it does not occur online.

This could be because the on-ground classroom is more tolerant to improvisation. Just as it would be the case in a theatrical performance—should the actor use slightly different words from show to show, it would not matter much. The audience is more forgiving should an actor make a mistake, forget his or her line, improvise, stutter; not so online: It seems the expectations for excellence are higher, as it would be with a movie. Watching a movie, one expects to see no mistakes of any kind; everything is supposed to go by the book (script), and provide something in the end: Education, that is.

Adjunct faculty members seem to show concern for the "show," for entertaining, for the "dog-and-pony" show. Academic faculty members though, do recognize the fine nuances brought in by the degree of improvisation necessary: "It's a show, it's a show, basically. I have to make it interesting, I have to make it attractive, and I have to make it in a way that they want to come back" [32]. If and when the show occurs online, things are not quite the same: "Online is performance from behind a curtain" [43].

Show/Theatrical Performance reveals two sub-properties: *Entertainment* and *Boredom*. Some teachers make a conscientious effort to present information in an *entertaining* format:

The way I approach my in-class is information entertainment. I'm really there to get them enthused about the subject…to try to entertain them. I've gotten to the point now where I'm really making an all out effort to do most of my classes in PowerPoint too…just to give that extra effort for them. [06]

When teachers embrace the theatrical-performance approach, they do it because they do not want their students to get bored. They do not want boredom to set in. Once the students become bored, it is difficult to regain their attention:

Unless our brains are used to multitasking, part of that is disabled, their ability to focus on a single task and be in tuned enough to actually absorb the information. When the boredom sets in, and it's a waste of effort, basically; they're just not into it. [37]

Teachers notice that some students get bored in the classroom and feel more comfortable studying online. It is perhaps because in the traditional on-ground classroom, quite a few young people would just be bored easily, as they must spend time in the classroom. Online, it's really their time: The students feel more comfortable engaged in learning and transiting from one activity to another. Who knows; there may be a few video games in there too, just for fun.

When teaching, the instructor may take on multiple *roles*. He or she could be a coach; a facilitator, guide, or provider of knowledge; or a conductor, someone who directs the class. In the same vein, the teacher becomes a director, arranging a series of experiences so that students are successful: He or she is an arranger of activities that prompt students to learn. The teacher can be a mentor: He or she mentors individuals so that they can learn something. The teachers feel they have the responsibility to provide the opportunity for learners to learn. They must provide the resources, the materials, and the information necessary for learners to learn. Then, at times, the teacher is almost a tutor. The property *Role* is dimensioned along discrete values: *coach, facilitator, conductor, director, mentor, provider,* and *tutor.*

There is certain amount of *improvisation* present in the traditional classroom. Online, it may be quite a different story, as described in subsequent sections of this study.

As teachers prepare for class, there is a higher degree of improvisation in the traditional classroom than there is online. Online teaching requires more preparedness. One teacher puts it quite convincingly:

If we go back to the idea of preparedness, it's like when you buy a movie ticket, like the analogy of the movie and the Broadway show—you go to the movie, you expect it to be a flawless movie. When you go to a Broadway show, you expect there to be some ad-libbing. In fact, you want it. You like to go to a live show because you like the improvisation—that's the excitement. You go to the Comedy Store. When you pay the same money for a course online as a classroom, people think this is cheap; you put it on a Web server and you download it—the cost to the university is nothing. They don't think about all the design time, they don't think about the faculty they pay. When they go to a classroom, they say here's a multimillion dollar building, all the people that maintain it. I want to know why that makes sense. I can see the artist on stage, you are getting quick feedback. ...They don't know exactly what's happened, if the spectators liked it. If they make a mistake, they're human, we know that. ...I think about the movies, the movies are developed for a much, much larger audience than the Broadway. You don't customize the movie as much as you could customize a play. ...Think about how much money goes into it, how many people are involved. If you think about a movie, you've got sound, stage hands, you have to go out and get permission to sell everywhere. [Is it] $10 million? I don't know what they charge to make a movie. A Broadway show, you've got this one room, and you build some stuff there, and people are involved, and the lead time might be the same, but the number of resources in a movie have got to be financially higher, I would think in most cases. [13]

Teaching online may feel strange in a way, because in the online environment the time seems not to be a factor. Online students must be constantly reminded of deadlines, and of the assignments that are due. The teacher has to keep on the students, and constantly pursue them, and remind them; this, for some teachers, feels it is like babysitting. In the words of one teacher,

It is the Internet thing again; it is "on" 24 hours a day, so it is a mañana factor: "Oh, I don't have to do it right now; I can just do it at 12 o'clock, 1 o'clock in the morning." While in the classroom, you know you have to be there at such and such time. [22]

The teacher can cover a lot more in an online class if the students want to. The modality is a lot more flexible, as much as requires more preparedness and allows for less improvisation. It can be said that, in the classroom, one only has the details of a book, while in an online classroom, the book is the entire Internet. Time-wise, online it is a 24-hour class, so, theoretically, students may be afforded more time for assignments. To some teachers, the experience of teaching online resembles writing a book:

You can talk about something, and know the material, but when you put something on paper, it has to be perfect. There can be no mistakes; you worry about how you express yourself...while in the classroom, you always have a second chance. Not so online. You do not just go there and just present hard concepts and throw them out there. You sometimes pause; you break down your delivery and look for certain opportunities to present materials at certain times. Online, this is more difficult to accomplish. [14]

There are also benefits that transcend the educational modality: Face-to-face instruction can help the teacher become more sensitive to online learning, while online instruction can help the teacher to become more sensitive to mentoring students in a face-to-face situation.

With respect to dimension, the property *Improvisation* ranges from "more improvisation on ground" to "less improvisation online."

Figure 3. Category: Teaching demands

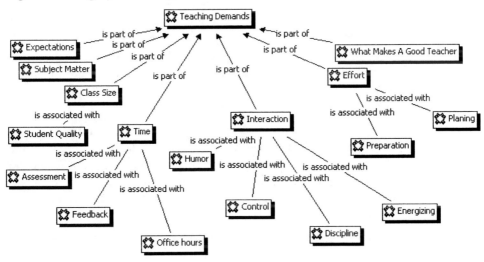

Teaching Demands

This second core category reveals seven associated properties: *Expectations, Subject Matter, Class Size, Time, Interaction, Effort,* and *What Makes Good Teacher* (see Figure 3).

Class Size developed a sub-property *Student Quality. Time* developed three sub-properties: *Assessment, Feedback,* and *Office Hours.* The property *Interaction* developed four subcategories: *Humor, Control, Discipline,* and *Energizing.* The property *Effort* developed two sub-properties: *Preparation* and *Planning.*

Well, all these are good, but *What Makes A Good Teacher?* Online education relies in large measure on written communication. For this reason, good writing skills are very desirable and most valuable to a teacher who teaches online. Knowledge of the subject matter is very important, but so are communication skills and a caring personality, organization skills, training in teaching, an open mind, a genuine desire to help people, and being a people's person. Teachers have to be prepared to make personal sacrifices, with the reward being a sense of meaningfulness, as their efforts benefit their students and the society. To be successful, a teacher must focus on the student. The associated dimensions are *writing skills, knowledge of the subject matter, communication skills, a caring personality, organization skills, training in teaching, an open mind, a genuine desire to help people,* and *focus on the student.*

Pertaining to the *Expectations* issue, some teachers are of the opinion that students do not seem to take the online environment very seriously. According to them, the online expectations are such that the Internet is supposed to make everything easier; a search engine type of mentality. Or, there is this mindset that online learning is supposed somehow to be similar to online shopping: Students just come in and click a couple of buttons and pass a class. E-commerce Web sites try to make the online shopping experience as easy as possible, but as far as teaching and learning online, it is a lot more difficult. The assignments still have a due date, yet students can turn them in any time, and that gives them a little bit more flexibility.

A major misconception in expectations is that online education is simply the "electronic classroom." That is false. People think that just because something is online, all of a sudden learning is going to be easier. Yet, there are things that one cannot get from watching the computer. Somebody has to be there and show you. Consensus among some teachers is that conveying information is simpler in the on-ground classroom; teachers can disseminate or get ideas or give examples of creativity in the classroom, but they cannot do that online as well.

It is up to the students who take online courses to learn, more or less. Student quality is not an issue as long as self-selection is allowed. The dropout rate is higher online, and this is likely because students have the option to realize they are not up to the material; sometime they lose interest in the course. While it is harder to drop an on ground class, that is not true for the online environment. The students that have difficulty in an online course seem to simply disappear when they drop out of the course, or drop out altogether from the online environment.

Teachers find that the students' expectations concerning response time are often unrealistic in the online classroom. Online, students are given the freedom to do a class in a 24/7 environment; therefore, they seem to expect the instructor to be available the same way. For example, students may post something online on Monday at 1a.m., but they are not really expecting to get a response on Wednesday at noon: NO! They want to see some response quickly, within hours. One teacher shares the story of a student who sent her an e-mail one afternoon at 2 p.m. At 3 p.m., as she did not get a response, the student called the teacher on the phone. Within the course of 3 hours, she left 4 voicemail messages, the last one being, "I have e-mailed you, I have left several messages, why haven't I heard back from you?" [34]. This situation, where the students want an instantaneous response, appears to be quite prevalent in the online environment, which can be very aggravating for teachers.

To some extent, online students seem to think that just because something is online, it is a kind of computer simulation, or something similar—that all of a sudden learning is going to be easier. Consequently, they do not exert the same amount of cognitive effort, to memorize something or to get a particular framework in the brain. They think it is easier to study online, and as a result they do not learn much. Teachers indicate there are "low learning expectations online."

On the other hand, some subject matters can be taught online extremely well (e.g., literature, languages, critical thinking), whereas other subjects (e.g., biology, chemistry, sports) are a lot more difficult. The same may apply to programming, statistics or math courses. In some respects it all depends on the teacher, as anything that requires drawing on the board or working a problem on the board is difficult to accomplish online. While the entire solution or diagram can be provided to students up front, it does not seem to be the same as in the on-ground classroom.

Teachers agree that training for skills is *doable* online, as much as education may be a bit different. Even subjects that develop motor skills can be taught online with certain success. For example, violin can be taught online using multimedia (Scherer, 2004). The teachers interviewed indicate that the online environment is great for material that anyone can grasp on their own. It follows that some subjects are appropriate for teaching online while others are inappropriate for teaching online.

One factor affecting teaching is the class size. Online classes tend to be large in the beginning, with 50 to 60 students on average. Yet, the online retention rate can be dismal, with one teacher reporting less than 10 students still remaining by the end of the course. If the class size becomes too large, then managing students' requirements online can become difficult. Teachers seem to agree that the ideal number for an online course is between 10 and 15 students. This would appear to be the optimum point for effective management of an online class. Teachers find their level of commitment to online teaching falls significantly when they get too many questions (sometimes similar ones) from many students who also happen to expect the teacher to respond immediately. The teachers I talked to indicated they experienced online class sizes from a low of 6 to a high of 70 students.

The *Class Size* associated property developed a sub-property, *Student Quality*. The teaching experience is affected by the quality of the students in the class: The students "make" the instructor. When the students are highly motivated, and highly independent, usually they are very successful. The property *Student Quality* is dimensioned as "high" for the online classes.

Time is another property of *Teaching Demands*. Teachers indicate that they are spending more time and effort developing the materials for the online courses. Time expands in the online classroom. There is more time for teaching, yet time management is difficult online, where the class is open around the clock. Online teachers expend a greater amount of effort in their teaching: The online environment is time consuming and affects the quality of life of the teachers who teach online. Overall, some teachers require more time, while others require less time to teach online.

As the online class continues for an entire week, the teacher manages to stretch out 4 hours of instruction over 7 days. That means folks have more time to think about what is going on. The teacher has to become a 24/7 instructor, almost; it is no surprise, then, that teachers find the online teaching very time consuming.

The property *Time* developed three sub-properties: *Assessment, Feedback,* and *Office Hours*. Different modalities call for different assessment and testing strategies. Some of the teachers report having different kinds of tests in each educational modality. For example, good students are easily identified on-ground: One can recognize them in a classroom environment, just by their interaction and by how other students treat them. This type of assessment is more difficult to do online. *Assessment* is harder online. It is tougher for the teacher to assess the student's involvement within their learning teams online than it is in the classroom. The associated dimension is "harder online."

Feedback is important for teachers: Online it may be more difficult to know whether what they are saying is getting across, because online they do not have good feedback. In the on-ground classroom, teachers can tell by the students' facial expressions, behavioral cues, and the like. The teachers benefit from the immediate feedback existing in the on-ground classroom. Online, this advantage does not exist because of lack of face-to-face interaction. Online, if there is something that is not clear for the students, it takes a lot longer and more focused time from the part of the teacher, to clarify it. The associated dimension is "reduced/limited online" feedback.

Online, just like in the on-ground environment, teachers find that they need to set aside time for *Office Hours*. Some of the more successful faculty members schedule chat time for students to communicate synchronously. Just like in the on-ground environment, if nobody shows up (i.e., signs up for the chat session), the teacher can use the time to check his or her mail or to read a book or do something else. Yet, they are available to students, should they wish to chat. Office hours are therefore "useful."

As far as *Interaction* is concerned, teachers find that in the online environment, students are less likely to communicate with the teacher. Because there is no face-to-face interaction, the rapport must be set up entirely on the screen, via the computer. Meeting in person greatly enhances the opportunities for the student to know the instructor, and vice versa. This is true even when only 5% of the communication may be in person and 95% online. Even a limited amount of interactive communication between the instructor and students is beneficial. On the other hand, there are some teachers who think "That same lack of face-to-face interaction is a strength of online teaching if it removes—or helps remove—the shyness factor" [04].

Continuing the *Interaction* property, online communication is not as intense as in the classroom: There are things that one cannot get just from reading somebody's notes. A good teacher tends to explore the communication cues present in voice and body language, and these only come out in real time. The "glaze"—the clue that tells when someone is lost—is not available online. In order to mentor students well, and to make sure that they understand the subject, it is helpful for the teacher to be able to see the nonverbal cues apparent in the face-to-face conversation.

There is a "collective brain" online. One can create groups, but the technology has not advanced to a place where one can have more than four or five people in a group and still be effective. As individuals take advantage of the group, they co-create knowledge. Yet somehow, people are more effective making this happen live.

The dimensions reported for *Interaction* range from "little interaction" to "lots of interaction." The property *Interaction* developed four sub-properties: *Energizing*, *Humor*, *Control*, and *Discipline*.

Some teachers note the classroom to be *Energizing*, which has a positive impact on participants. Classroom energy might cause time to slow down, or as one teacher puts it,

In a high-energy environment... frequently, we'll go half an hour after the class was supposed to end. It's night time, and this is the last class... yet no one will notice that we've gone a half an hour over. [23]

The property is dimensioned as "more energy in the on-ground classroom."

Teachers use *Humor* in class. Yet, less humor is used online. One teacher tries to use humor "a little bit" in order to personalize the experience, to let people know that there is a real human being at the other end of the keyboard. However, humor has to be used with great caution: One must be really careful, as words can easily be misinterpreted: "You have to be real careful too... on what you put down and what you say and how it's said" [26]. Nevertheless, humor can be very useful as a way to lighten the load, especially if it is a hard subject. Other teachers do not believe that humor is all that important in the classroom. The associated dimension is "less humor online."

Some teachers expect the online class to flow as planned. They indeed feel they have more *Control* online, where everything goes pretty much the way is prepared. Yet, other teachers note a perceived lack of control in the online environment: They can immediately take control in the on-ground classroom, whereas online it requires them increased time and effort.

The classroom has always been the teacher's unchallenged fiefdom. The teacher was, and still is to some extent the authority, controlling access to the classroom. Online, this changes dramatically and not every teacher appreciates the change. There are privacy concerns. In the words of one teacher,

I'm certainly willing to have somebody look at my performance or evaluate what I'm doing in a professional way, in an appropriate way, but I don't want people spying on me online any more than I want people spying on me in a regular classroom. [05]

The associated dimension is "less control online."

Along the same idea, teachers find it harder to maintain *Discipline* in the online classroom. The associated dimension is "difficult to maintain online."

Continuing to branch off the second core category, *Teaching Demands,* online teachers expend a greater amount of effort in their teaching. The effort required in the online course is significantly higher from an instructor's standpoint than in the offline, on-ground classroom. The property *Effort* developed two sub-properties: *Planning* and *Preparation*.

Planning for the on-ground classroom is a lot easier and leaves more room for improvisation. Based on this study's interviewed subjects, a good teacher always does a lot of planning. However, the class that he or she ends up teaching often turns out to be radically different than originally planned. What the teachers point out is that, many times, the further the class is from the original plan, the better the class becomes; that teachers do a better job when they adapt the course to the needs of the students. Yet, in the opinions of some teachers, the online classroom tends to be much more akin to an "assembly line," not allowing for much improvisation. The course follows the prescribed, planned path, with little deviation from what was defined well in advance. The associated dimension is "more planning online."

More *Preparation* is required when teaching online. Teaching online requires more thought and teachers have to prepare better because they must get things right from the first attempt: They do not get multiple opportunities to make things right, as

Figure 4. Category: Teacher needs

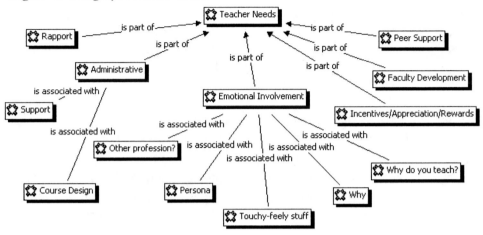

they do in the on-ground classroom. The associated dimension is "more preparation online."

Teacher Needs

This third core category revealed six properties: *Rapport, Administrative, Emotional Involvement, Incentives/Appreciation/Rewards, Faculty Development,* and *Peer Support,* as depicted in Figure 4.

The property *Administrative* has two sub-properties: *Support* and *Course Design.* The property *Emotional Involvement* has five sub-properties: *Other Profession, Persona, Touchy-Feely Stuff, Why,* and *Why Do You Teach?*

Teachers find it hard to build *Rapport* with their online students. Online, they do not manage to develop a personal relationship with the bulk of their students; the students are just a name and an assignment. Opposite, in the on-ground classroom, after sharing the classroom for many weeks with their students, teachers associate names and faces and develop better personal relationships with their students. Teachers seem to care about developing rapport with their students. As one teacher puts it,

Without [rapport], I just don't see how you could be successful in a classroom, especially. To me it's completely important. And I think it's vital to the success of the students actually… being able to finish the class and do the work up to the par that you expect. [16]

The associated dimension is "hard to build."

Teachers are concerned with *Administrative* issues. For one, they are concerned with the fact that school administrators see that their profit margins are greater for online classes, and that drives to encourage online education for the wrong motives. The teachers worry that the cost efficiency will take a more prevalent role in the decisions about what kind of classes are offered online. Another issue is that teachers often feel that they do not get enough appreciation for what they do online. Faculty compensation is a perennial issue, yet some faculty members do not believe that the money they get is worth the effort they expend teaching online. The property *Administrative* has two sub-properties: *Support* and *Course Design*.

Having adequate administrative *Support* is important: Some teachers take advantage of having access to instructional specialists online, who can help find solutions to dealing with the students or course related issues. The associated dimension for the property *Support* is "adequate."

A second dimension of *Support* pertains to course development. Teachers would like greater support for *Course Design*. At times, communication breaks down among teacher, course developers, technology experts, and administrators. When this happens, things can go bad quickly and a frustrated teacher is the least that can happen. Teachers seem to agree that not enough attention has been paid to curriculum development for the online environment. The associated dimension is "inadequate."

Teacher training is important and the online teachers would benefit from receiving more training and better access to *Faculty Development* opportunities. Some schools offer teacher training, while others do not. One adjunct professor complains about the fact that she got absolutely no training before she was given an online teaching assignment. More technology training allows teachers to take advantage of the technologies supporting the online environment. Some schools do offer comprehensive faculty development programs for their online teachers. The dimensions associated with the property *Faculty Development* range from "not available" to "excellent."

There is *Emotional Involvement* among teacher and students. Teachers are sensitive, caring people. They care about educating the students. For some, teaching is everything. The educational modality makes a difference: Some teachers report that in the on-ground classroom they can get students really, really excited about what they are doing; yet there are teachers who choose to teach online because they are not as nervous as they would normally be in the on-ground classroom. The property *Emotional Involvement* has five sub-properties: *Why Do You Teach?*, *Why*, *Touchy-Feely Stuff*, *Other Profession*, and *Persona*.

Teachers choose to teach for a variety of reasons: Some are hoping to be a catalyst of positive change; others are quite frank about their motivation:

I teach online because of the monies—I'm getting paid for it. And I teach online because I like the administrative tools. I did not like online teaching when I first taught it—I hated it. But once I built my module, I loved it, because it was easy for me. [22]

Some teachers savor those moments of enlightening, evidence of the students' understanding of a complex concept: "My main motivation is going back to seeing that light come on. That really is very gratifying to me, to realize that I helped somebody be able to understand something that they didn't understand before" [25]. Or, it could simply be the joy that teaching brings about:

I enjoy it. Going back, I've always wanted to be some kind of instructor through the years, either training or something like that, and I always wanted to be an actual classroom-type instructor for folks that want to learn and want to go further in their education vs. just regular training. So I enjoy the environment, and I enjoy the experience I get out of it. I learn a lot from the interaction of the students. [26]

Some teachers are very passionate about what they do:

I love teaching, I really do. I think it's the passion of my life, and I'm very, very serious. I think it's something that you either have the capability to do or not. Some people teach and they give out of their soul, out of their heart, and they connect with the students and you set your students free and they fly with it, they bond with the information. You've established already the contact. I don't know what you call it, really. You set them off and they're on their own, and you have ignited a torch of interest. [30]

Teacher motivation is a complex function that includes more than just the monetary rewards. I came across many teachers who did not appear to care much about financial gains. One teacher had this to say:

I wouldn't do it just for the paycheck, because I'm not going to get paid more as a teacher than I am as an IT manager. Over the years, giving presentations and training session and teaching has been something that I found very rewarding—more so than managing people, or writing books. [25]

A second teacher added,

It's definitely not the money. As I have kidded you in the past, Lord knows I will cash the paycheck, so it's not thoroughly for no money. But the main thing is the "Eureka!" When I see the student's face, when I feel they're actually learning something; like I said when the light bulb is turning on, flashing—that's my real pay. [29]

Yet, another teacher made even stronger statements:

I think it's an addiction. Teachers don't make much money, but some of them could make a lot of money. But they teach. So I think it's an addiction of some kind, neurotics of wanting to improve other people's lives. It's a social orientation. [33]

There are also psychological elements mentioned by the teachers: the *Touchy-Feely Stuff* is absolutely essential, at least for some teachers:

I think it's absolutely essential. I wouldn't get into psychology and all that kind of stuff, the monkey that would rather be held than eat, you know. I'm trying to think of a Mother Theresa quote that I just came across. She said that the people in the third world would rather be acknowledged and hugged than given food. ...I find it relevant to the classroom that we need that touchy-feely stuff. [31]

For the majority of the teachers interviewed, teaching is a passion they would not trade for *another profession*: In the words of one teacher, "I can't imagine it, I really can't. I cannot. I, I don't know" [08].

One other teacher reported that had he not been teaching, he may have chosen to be a professional trainer, working independently and contracting out to train employees at other companies. Obviously, this person would continue to work with people and help them learn new things.

Teachers reflect on the image they project in the online classroom, on their online *Persona*. Some feel they project the same image, irrespective of the educational modality they are involved in. Yet, they recognize they may end up being more detailed online. Others feel their real self comes across only in the on-ground classroom; their online students do not know their teacher that well. While they may project the same persona online and on-ground, students may get to know more about their teacher, much more quickly in the face-to-face environment. The associated dimensions are "same," and "different."

When teachers feel they do an outstanding job online, the incentives, rewards, and appreciation that teachers would like to receive seem to be lagging. One teacher is quite frustrated with the facts:

Online nobody really cares whether you write and do a terrific job at this kind of thing or you just make token responses; or you have some clichés that are built out that you can put in there. Nobody will notice the difference. You may have one instructor who's extremely conscientious and actually contributes greatly to the educational experience of the students and somebody else who just has prepackaged responses to everything that's going on. The instructor that has all the prepackaged responses to things uses very little cognitive effort, since they're all prepackaged he just cuts and pastes and puts them in as he goes and gets the same amount of money. There's very little reward for being an outstanding online teacher. [05]

Since time demands are significantly increased online, teachers would like fair compensation to match these demands:

I want to be paid the 3 hours for my class and another 45 minutes for my office hour as well. Because I still have office hour duties, whether it be responding to e-mails that students have sent me where they would have just walked into my office and taken care of it there, or grading papers or whatever it happens to be, I want my compensation to be equivalent. [04]

Furthermore, they would like to be recognized and appreciated for what they do:

In an online kind of environment, in order to achieve what I achieve, I have to pay a much more stringent price. I get tremendous responses from the students and they appreciate that, and I get classes to teach, which is kind of a grudging appreciation, but there's very little recognition and there's not the kind of financial return that really makes it worth my while. [05]

Since online teaching is more labor intensive, teachers feel that is only natural to expect that more work should result in more pay: People should get paid more for teaching online because there's more work. The associated dimension is "inadequate" incentives, rewards, and appreciation for the online teachers.

Online teachers feel socially isolated from their peers; they crave peer support. When they are offered a means to socialize with their peers, teachers are quite happy to take advantage of the opportunity:

Figure 5. Category: Teaching dimensions

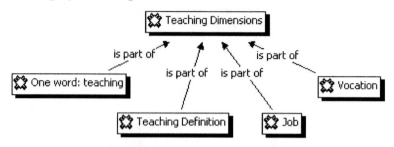

I was actually thinking how great... our administration has set up [online] a faculty lounge. It's where all the online faculty go and we have our own discussion boards. And that's helped tremendously with the social isolation. So we can meet on the Internet and share the good, the bad, the ugly—frustrations, problems, solutions. Occasionally even I'll say, let's meet up this Friday over at this place for a margarita or something....To actually meet up with the other online faculty, I just really appreciate that. I remember thinking today, at the end of the semester, how great that resource is. [41]

The associated dimension is that peer support is "desirable."

Teaching Dimensions

The majority of the respondents express the passion they have for teaching. They feel it is mainly a vocation; yet, teaching can also be a job. Or, it could become a job under certain circumstances. Perhaps this explains why some teachers leave the profession. Dreeben (1970) talked about teachers as being passionate people, and this passion is evident in the majority of the interviews conducted for this book.

This category saturated with four properties: *One Word: Teaching, Teaching Definition, Job,* and *Vocation* (see Figure 5).

Teachers are very specific about how they view teaching in general. Some view it as an extensive dialog and discussion of new exciting concepts, of new things that are taking place within a society, and they do not think that this can be done online. They may be annoyed by the perceived neediness of the online students, and feel like they have to chaperon their students excessively. Others resort to convenience as a qualifier: "I would say efficient... convenient. *Convenient* would be the real word for all involved, students and faculty" [16]. Others prefer to view teaching as theatrical performance: "I think that a simple way to say this is that I consider it 'the show time'" [11]. Yet, others find online teaching to be better defined by such terms as *challenging* or *time-consuming*. One teacher refers to the frustration experienced while teaching online: "In the very beginning it was very frustrating; now it's less frustrating" [22]. For other teacher, teaching online is very satisfying: "For me, it's a joy, and for my students, it's empowerment" [30]. Or, it is about how much work it takes to teach online: "It's a lot more work. Really, it's a lot more work" [35]. Others tend to refer to interaction as one of the key aspects of online teaching:

It's the interactivity. If designed properly, [it] is a very rewarding learning opportunity. And I think that it should be student-centered, activity-driven, and there should be human feedback. And the human feedback is the element that makes or breaks a really successful online [teaching] experience. [38]

For some, teaching online is simply magical: "*Shazzam*" [41]. Others feel it is a dull experience, by design: They find the online environment is intentionally bland in order to not offend anyone. For those who find online teaching gratifying, it can be an exhilarating, satisfying experience. The property is dimensioned along discrete values: "efficient," "convenient," "challenging," "time-consuming," "frustrating," "joy," "more work," "rewarding," "*shazzam*," "bland," "exhilarating," and "satisfying."

When asked to think of teaching in general, irrespective of the modality involved (on-ground or online), the teachers interviewed offered definitions that are indicative of their genuine interest in the profession. For one teacher, teaching is "The transfer of both information and knowledge from the provider to the recipient (the desiring recipient). As a goal, teaching, in my view, refers to improving students' understanding of a particular subject domain" [10]. Other teachers offered their view of teaching as a means for helping people grow or providing students an education based on the teacher's own experiences and on what the teacher has learned through formal instruction. They view teaching as a way of imparting knowledge that is relevant and can be applied to a real-life situation; teaching is about practical application of the knowledge transferred in the classroom. Other teachers make reference to their mentoring roles: "Teaching for me is to mentor individuals so that they can learn something, update, or upgrade, or create something in their memories, in their experience. For me, teaching is coaching somebody so that they can learn something" [33]. The associated dimensions are "transferring information," "providing education," "imparting knowledge," and "mentoring."

Teaching can be a job, or a vocation: it depends on the teacher. For the ones for whom teaching is simply a job: "I don't have a teaching philosophy, for me it's a job" [19]. Yet, the majority of the teachers interviewed feel really strongly about teaching as a vocation:

I love teaching, I really do. I think it's the passion of my life, and I'm very, very serious. I think it's something that you either have the capability to do or not. Some people teach and they give out of their soul, out of their heart, and they connect with the students, and you set your students free, and they fly with it, they bond with the information. You've established already the contact. [30]

Triangulation: Literature Comparison

The four categories discussed (*Teaching, Teaching Demands, Teacher Needs,* and *Teaching Dimensions*) offer a colorful picture and an understanding of how teachers view teaching, off- and online. Teachers speak of their passion for teaching, of the issues that both frame, and constrain their teaching. Of particular interest are their thoughts related to teaching online.

Teaching

It is documented that at least some teachers teach less for money and more out of passion (Cahn, 2003). The data derived from the interviews support this view. The contention that teachers take on a constructivist stance when teaching online (Bangert, 2004) is also confirmed by the findings. The teachers interviewed are caring people who care deeply about their students and their teaching; they speak with passion about their work.

The interviews reveal changes in education. For many years, education used to be about helping people grow, about grooming students (Dreeben, 1970). The teachers I interviewed certainly attest to this: They enjoy helping students learn new things and grow as human beings. Yet, what teachers are telling about their online teaching experiences reflects their focus on knowledge transfer, on helping students acquire skills. This is somewhat different from the classical definition of disseminating information. The change from a knowledge provider to an enabler is evident. Teaching, it seems, has evolved into a facilitation stance, where the teacher resembles a conductor, someone who directs the class. The teachers that were interviewed acknowledge these changes, and the majority of them seem to accept them. However, certain feeling of nostalgia is evident, particularly among those teachers who spent a significant amount of their teaching career in the on-ground classroom.

Teaching Demands

The published literature shows that online courses require significant effort and resources; in particular, for course development and delivery (Schell, 2004). Given the technology-intensive nature of online education, the production of a virtual course is much more demanding. Course development for the online environment becomes a resource-intensive endeavor that requires access to a plethora of resources, such as graphical designers, prototypes, and budgets, together with adequate technology (Bergstrom, Grahn, Karlstrom, Pulkkis, & Astrom, 2004). Our teachers reflect similar thoughts in that oftentimes they find themselves facing limited budgets and technology that does little to help them teach online. One of the comments they constantly make is that they would like to have access to course developers that are well versed in technology. Many times the teachers are put in a situation where they develop their online courses on their own, without being trained to use modern communications technology and multimedia. Their reports agree with Chang's (2001) findings that the burden associated with preparing online courses is significant. Hall (2002) shows that teachers are concerned with the time required to update course Web sites and to interact with students. These activities, as our teachers indicate, lead them to spend between 1 and 4 hours more per week to teach online as they do on-ground.

Teachers are used to answering student question in the classroom. They strive to answer all of the questions raised by their students, and they find it easier to do so in the on-ground classroom. They also note an increased ability to redirect discussions, an opportunity to divert and to follow a specific discussion thread while teaching in the on-ground environment. In contrasts, such behavior is more difficult to achieve online, where the teacher appears to have less control over the discussions and the direction they are taking. Some of the teachers interviewed indicate that, online, the teacher can only ask a few questions and get a few responses, and that is it. For those teachers who prefer to lead the discussions, and to exert tight control over their development, the online environment appears to pose additional constraints, ones they are ill-equipped to contend with.

Teaching demands increase in direct relation to the volume of the discussions taking place in the classroom. Time and time again, the teachers interviewed describe what they perceived as an overwhelming amount of communications they have to deal with online. In this regard, the findings from the study agree with Brower (2003). When the class is large, the number of postings can be overwhelming. However, if the class is very small, discussions may not go well. All of the teachers interviewed agree that class discussions played an important part in their teaching.

Teachers expressed interest in learning from peers about what works, and what does not work in teaching online. They are interested in discussing a wide range of topics with their peers and complain of a lack of adequate support from their peers and of not having access to peer support groups. As they see it, school administrators could do a better job at fostering this type of support groups by enabling access to other teachers. These sentiments echo those findings reported in a study by Babinski, Jones, and DeWert (2001), that access to a support group is welcomed by teachers, as it would allow them to foster a sense of community where they can share experiences, knowledge and reflections. This finding is quite sensible, and it could prove to be a cost-effective approach to educating teachers on the *do*s and *don't*s of teaching online.

Time flows differently in the online classroom, as noted by the teachers interviewed for this study. They note a sense of time elasticity present online. Because the online classroom is always "on," time seems to dilate. Some teachers view this as a positive aspect of teaching online, as they have more time to teach. However, others deplore the feeling of emptiness brought about by a class that is open around the clock. They have a hard time telling who is "in" at any time.

Teacher Needs

Society, teachers, and students change over time, as does everything else in the surrounding environment. The teachers I interviewed note that they find their students expect to be entertained most of the time. In that sense, learning must have a "fun" component, and teachers must adapt their teaching or risk losing their students' attention. This must be observed when teaching online: Teachers must adapt to the online environment, yet continue to use a friendly, honest, humorous style that make students feel encouraged, energized, and believe in their success. In line with the findings reported by King and McSporran (2002), our teachers agree that teaching, whether online or on-ground, requires commitment and appropriate interactivity. Yet the approach they use is different, and specific to the educational modality. Their role is somewhat diminished online, where they resort to facilitation, while they still take the center stage in the on ground classroom. This appears to affect their ability to build relationships with their students. Some of our teachers say they can form stronger relationships online, yet the majority states the contrary.

Those teachers who rely on classroom theatrics are at disadvantage when teaching online, as the online environment is not conducive of face-to-face communication cues. The data collected in the study provides support for Blair's (2002) findings that there are no classroom theatrics online. Many of the teachers that were interviewed for this book speak of their enthusiasm for teaching and expressed concern that their teaching effectiveness may be negatively affected by the online environment and by the communication constraints imposed by it. As Johnson and Roellke (1999) showed, teaching effectiveness is predicated upon communication skills and enthusiasm. While our teachers' enthusiasm is pervasive, their concerns for the quality of the communication they are able to achieve online are worthy of further consideration. As the role played by the teacher changes with the educational environment, teachers need training to help them incorporate new teaching methods and move away from more passive, didactic forms of teaching (Littlejohn, 2002).

Technology training is needed as well. One of the chief complaints raised by teachers is that they do not know how to use Internet technologies in class, in addition to having course design concerns. It should come as no surprise that, those teachers who indicate they do not received adequate training question the usefulness of the Internet in the classroom. The rapid shift to online, resource-based learning is hampered by poor course design. By offering teachers training to help them keep pace with modern technology, teaching methods, and course design in the online environment, universities can help their teachers become more effective and more comfortable with teaching online.

Teaching Dimensions

The online environment has been reported to affect the communication style due to bandwidth limitations, the asynchronous nature of the medium, and reliance on written communication (Smith, Ferguson, & Caris, 2002). Yet, some of the teachers interviewed value the flexibility offered by the asynchronous dimension of the online classroom. Klipowicz and Laniak (1999) found that there is more collaboration taking place online. In contrast, the research conducted for this book found that teachers differ on whether there is more collaboration in the online classroom as well as on the quality of the collaboration taking place online.

The teachers participating in the study report that online interaction is more difficult to control, given an asynchronous environment. Students answer messages and post new messages on their own terms. To the extent the online environment confers certain anonymity to the participants, it encourages participation. Some teachers reported they found the online environment to be beneficial to shy students, who found the online environment less threatening. Thus, the online environment offers the potential to be more student-friendly, its anonymity being a positive aspect—one that allows students to interact online without the distracting noise of social conditioning (Sullivan, 2002).

Conclusion

The overall conclusion indicated by the respondents is that the on-ground environment is better than the online one. The interview data supports the findings reported by other researchers in that online teaching requires more time, effort, and technical skills as well as change in communication style.

Teachers' enthusiasm continues to play a significant role and to be instrumental in their effectiveness as teachers. As teachers become aware of the limitations of the online teaching environment, they adjust their communication style to accommodate bandwidth limitations and the asynchronous nature of the medium. Online, their teaching involves written communication almost exclusively. This requires increased clarity of the course materials. In fact, the instructor often has to rework course materials when developing an online class. This, of course, leads to more work.

Online teaching poses increased time demands on teachers, due to the asynchronous nature of the communication. Many of the responses provided by teachers are on a one-on-one basis, as they specifically address student questions. Thus, teaching online requires long hours to respond to messages, e-mail, and to evaluate class discussions.

Oftentimes faculty members attempt to recreate the classroom experience via computer. In traditional education, the teacher handles everything (i.e., course design and development) and takes on a multitude of roles—ones that most teachers are comfortable with. Yet, online, some teachers find the same demands overwhelming. They must take on new roles—such as content expert, Web developer, multimedia designer, and system administrator—all in the same time. It is for this reason that teachers should be offered adequate training to help them cope with the increased demands stemming from the online environment and to help them be as efficient in their online teaching as they are in the on-ground classroom.

References

Babinski, L. M., Jones, B. D., & DeWert, M. H. (2001). The roles of facilitators and peers in an online support community for first-year teachers. *Journal of Educational and Psychological Consultation, 12*(2), 151-169.

Bangert, A. W. (2004). The seven principles of good practice: A framework for evaluating on-line teaching. *Internet and Higher Education, 7*, 217-232.

Bergstrom, L., Grahn, K. J., Karlstrom, K., Pulkkis, G., & Astrom, P. (2004). Teaching network security in a virtual learning environment. *Journal of Information Technology Education, 3*, 189-217.

Blair, J. (2002). The virtual teaching life. *Education Week, 21*, 31-34.

Brower, H. H. (2003). On emulating classroom discussion in a distance-delivered OBHR course: Creating an on-line learning community. *Academy of Management Learning and Education, 2*(1), 22-36.

Cahn, P. S. (2003). Number crunching. *The Chronicle of Higher Education, 50*(16).

Chang, C.-K. (2001). Refining collaborative learning strategies for reducing the technical requirements of Web-based classroom management. *Innovations in Education and Teaching International, 38*(2), 133-143.

Dreeben, R. (1970). *The nature of teaching: Schools and the work of teachers.* Glenview, IL: Scott Foresman and Company.

Hall, R. (2002). Aligning learning, teaching, and assessment using the Web: An evaluation of pedagogic approaches. *British Journal of Educational Technology, 33*(2), 149-158.

Johnson, S. D., & Roellke, C. F. (1999). Secondary teachers' and undergraduate education faculty members' perceptions of teaching-effectiveness criteria: A national survey. *Communication Education, 48*, 127-138.

King, C., & McSporran, M. (2002, July). *Online teaching demands hands-on commitment.* Paper presented at the 15th Annual NACCQ, Hamilton, New Zealand.

Klipowicz, S. W., & Laniak, T. (1999). Hebrew exegesis online: Using information technology to enhance biblical language study. *Teaching Technology and Religion, 2*(2), 109-115.

Littlejohn, A. H. (2002). Improving continuing professional development in the use of ICT. *Journal of Computer Assisted Learning, 18*, 166-174.

Schell, G. P. (2004). Universities marginalize online courses. *Communications of the ACM, 47*(11), 107-112.

Scherer, B. L. (2004, December 30). Bowing to technology: Fiddling in cyberspace. *The Wall Street Journal, CCXLIV,* D8.

Smith, G. G., Ferguson, D., & Caris, M. (2002). Teaching over the Web versus in the classroom: Differences in the instructor experience. *International Journal of Instructional Media, 29*(1), 61-67.

Sullivan, P. (2002). "It's easier to be yourself when you are invisible": Female college students discuss their online classroom experiences. *Innovative Higher Education, 27*(2), 129-144.

Chapter X

Central Ideas:
Technology

Introduction

In the previous chapters, teachers shared their experiences and feelings about online teaching; we have seen some of the perspectives related to online teaching and to teaching in general. Teachers talked about how the online environment affects them and their teaching style; about the tradeoffs they find; the issues associated with technology and teaching online; about the adjustments they feel they have to make; and about the benefits and the losses they notice as a result of their teaching online. Thus this chapter tries to put things in perspective and find out how, if at all, these stories intersect. The chapter also focuses on the central ideas that are related to technology and its use in the online classroom, ideas that have been derived from the interview data.

Background

Forty-four teachers were interviewed in the study that is the basis of this book, and they shared their stories. As the stories unfolded, themes that evolved into categories were identified. By constantly moving between the interview data and the emergent categories, by a process of constant comparison, these categories were continuously refined in light of the new data gathered from interviews. New categories were identified, together with relationships among the existing categories. Eventually, when no new categories emerged from the interview data, the categories evolved into 10 high-level categories, which were used to generate a theory of the online teaching experience.

Central Ideas: Technology

Chapter IX shows that the analysis of the interview transcripts generated 10 main categories: *Teaching, Teaching Demands, Teacher Needs, Teaching Dimensions, Teaching With Technology, Technology, Differences Among Modalities, Issues, Adjustments,* and *Choice.* Of these, *Teaching, Teaching Demands, Teacher Needs,* and *Teaching Dimensions* were discussed in Chapter IX. The remaining categories are discussed below.

Core Categories

This chapter continues the discussion of the core categories identified in Chapter IX. It presents in detail the remaining categories: *Teaching With Technology, Technology, Differences Among Modalities, Issues, Adjustments,* and *Choice.*

These core categories are further developed in terms of properties, dimensions, and relationships, resulting in a theory that is presented in Chapter XI. The theory integrates this set of categories to explain the online teaching experience.

Teaching With Technology

Technology is used in education on a daily basis. It is not exclusive to the online environment. Teachers constantly think about how they can use technology in their teaching in order to enhance the transfer of information. For example, many teachers

Figure 1. Category: Teaching with technology

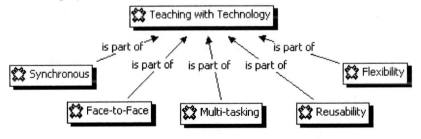

use software to prepare class presentations and discussion slides. They use computer systems to search for information they will take to the classroom and share with their students; yet, they do not look at technology to become the end-all solution. Even if the traditional on-ground classes have a strong technology (e.g., computers, Internet) component to them, teaching involves more than the use of technology; it requires a large degree of verbal communication and subjective consideration of what is being discussed or presented in the classroom.

Teaching With Technology reveals five properties: *Synchronous, Face-to-Face, Multitasking, Reusability,* and *Flexibility* (see Figure 1).

Synchronous vs. asynchronous time in the online environment is a disputed issue among the teachers; some teachers find it useful to integrate synchronous time in the online teaching, while others disagree. The on-ground environment is definitely more *synchronous* than the online environment: In the on-ground classroom, teaching flows pretty much the same for all students—all participants share the experience in real time. A book is linear; the drawback is that it is difficult to accommodate different types of learners if they are following the same book. The online environment is asynchronous, and that is an advantage in many respects. Online, there are many more degrees of freedom, which can help accommodate different types of learners; nevertheless, this makes for added complexity and increased difficulty. Hence, it does not work the same for everyone, students and teachers alike. Some of the interviewed teachers believe there is a need for some level of synchronous communication (interaction) online. They talk about telephone conferences, instant messaging, having office hours (online), and Web cams. However, by design, the online environment accommodates participants without concern for geographical location and time zone. Thus, synchronicity in the online environment is not something that is encouraged by everyone. Some teachers find it to be a good thing, as an asynchronous environment slows down the feedback cycle with the students. Others are bothered by the asynchronous nature of online teaching.

The benefits derived from synchronous communication cannot be ignored: One teacher reflects on the matter and finds that synchronous interaction is key to experiential learning: "You have to make it synchronous, because in an asynchronous environment, the input you need from person X may come 4 hours later; that is 4 hours too late" [37]. On the other hand, other teachers abhor synchronicity online:

The synchronous [online], it's not good. Sometimes they are in different time zones and they have difficulty to get in touch; for example, after hours, or she has to wait for responses of other students. So it takes time. But group activity in the class, same time, so they are together, they do something together, and they help each other, they can show each other how to solve it. For online it takes time; 3 hours time, sometimes 5 hours. [24]

Another teacher agrees:

Everyone needs to be on at the same time, but no, unsynchronized works better than synchronized because of the pressure to be available and ready to participate exactly at the same time. An asynchronous environment works better than synchronized. Some universities I know use a synchronous approach, and simply require that for several hours, from 7 to 8 o'clock, everybody be there. [36]

Some teachers find that having real-time communication online helps them teach. Yet, again, as some teachers believe the very concept of online education is founded on the idea of avoiding (or simply not needing) synchronous interaction, they agree that any attempt to seek synchronous interaction in that kind of setting (i.e., online) becomes extremely challenging. The associated dimensions are "desirable," "undesirable," "useful," and "useless."

One of the reported benefits of the on-ground teaching involves *Face-to-Face* interaction among participants. When teaching by example, the teacher may have to repeat the same thing a couple of times, and the most efficient way is just to be there and see; the teacher does not move forward with the instruction until he or she sees that the students mastered or understood the steps. Online, most of these communication cues are missing. The richness of the media is lacking: Teachers must compensate for that lack of face-to-face communication cues to avoid making the online classroom very impersonal. To be truly effective in the process of instruction, the teacher has to find a real substitute for being able to draw something on the blackboard and talk about it, and also for not having people to look at it in real time and get their reactions, get their questions, and provide answers and explanations. In the words of one teacher,

If the student was there in front of me, I could tell that she can barely stay awake, that she is rambling, and that she should be home in bed because she has been in this accident. But in the online environment, I cannot tell if she is affected by pain medication or if she just cannot write a sentence that makes sense. [25]

In addition, teachers also appreciate the value of the nonverbal communication cues they observe in the on-ground classroom:

Oh, it's valuable because it's part of communication. Somebody can, you know... if, if an instructor says "You understand?" and everybody nods their heads and you take a look at the body language of somebody that, that seems to convey that they don't, you can ask them... you can ask follow-up questions. [28]

It should come as no surprise that teachers believe it is the visual communication that allows them to establish the roles they have in the classroom. In the on-ground classroom, it is very clear from the onset who is the teacher, and who are the students, and who is the figure of authority (hopefully, the teacher). That kind of rapport is not quite so easy to establish in the online environment. Teaching online is associated with "low" face-to-face communication and interaction.

The subject of multitasking is viewed by many of the interviewed subjects as one of the advantages of the online teaching. On-ground, there may be some multitasking involved mainly on the part of some of the students, but this is easily controlled or corrected by the class instructor. Online, there is multitasking for both teachers and students alike. Multitasking while teaching online can be quite beneficial:

[Online] I can multitask. This office hour thing; I'm there waiting, but I do other stuff while I'm waiting. I mean, if no one shows up, then I get to do something else. If someone shows up, then I get to take care of whatever their thing is. [31]

While some teachers make a conscious effort not to engage in multitasking when teaching online, they nevertheless are keenly aware that their students multitask quite often.

One of the advantages of teaching with technology is that it alters in a positive way the *Reusability* of course materials, which ranks high with the teachers. Once they have their course materials online, it is much easier for teachers to reuse them in the on-ground classroom. This is particularly convenient for those teachers who are teaching both online and on-ground courses. They can take course materials that were prepared for the online environment and use them—with modifications, as needed—in the on-ground classroom. As all of the online course materials are stored in electronic form, they can be modified easily and customized as appropriate. The on-ground classes are not technology impaired; they can have quite a sizable technology component in them, as evidenced by the use of the Internet for research and communication between class meetings. Unfortunately, the reverse may be more difficult to achieve, as course materials must be modified for online teaching. Therefore, the *Reusability* of the online course materials is "high."

The *Flexibility* afforded by the online environment also ranks high with teachers who chose to teach online. Teachers find that they gain flexibility when teaching online, as they can manage their time with fewer restrictions. The online environment also provides them with more options: They can reach back to a discussion board at 2:00 in the morning, or log on at different hours every day. They can even reprioritize the tasks on hand and spend variable amounts of time teaching online, as the course progresses and as they determine it to be necessary. Yet, other teachers report they are also giving up a great deal in terms of teaching style and flexibility. This is the case with the online courses that are "canned," for which the teacher has limited ability to change content and structure, or establish the expectations. The associated dimensions are "less flexibility online," and "more flexibility online."

Technology

Teachers use technology all the time in the process of instruction, both in the on-line, and in the on-ground teaching environment. Several views exist with regards to technology. One is that it is not as much what they have access to in terms of technology, as it is how they use the technology they have. Another view is that the current technology that the teachers have access to is, in many ways, too basic; the limitations to using technology are quite significant.

The category is saturated with multiple properties: *Technical Support, Reliability, Media Richness, Synchronous, Usability/Appropriateness, Ease of Use,* and *Synchronous* (see Figure 2).

Uneven access to technology and variations in the *Availability* of technology across institutions is an element of disadvantage that mainly affects the online teaching process. Many times, the choices available to teachers are limited, if at all available. For some teachers, the available technology is adequate. Yet, others express frustration:

If you have seen the possibility of true interactive online communications with high bandwidth, and virtual classrooms, and all sorts of live feeds that are coming in that have existed for 30 years, for goodness sake, and you're exchanging e-mails and calling it online learning, we are pretty primitive. [05]

Another concern related to technology, and variable that has to be controlled in order to ensure an optimal process of instruction, is that technology can only be used effectively if all participants know how to use it. One teacher reports,

Figure 2. Category: Technology

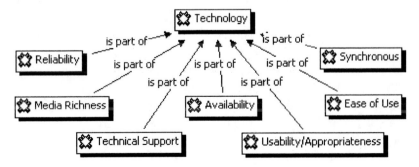

[The technology] it's adequate. ... Our students are also a little bit behind the curve when it comes to the technology or hardware or software they're using as well. Several of them may be using dial-up and our particular platform, Blackboard, does not interact well sometimes when it comes to dial-up. [35]

At times, the issue is that there are no sufficient resources available in the institution responsible for the process of instruction: "And they just said, we're not going to buy new computers" [27]. Another reported concern is that the academic policies are not quite optimal: "I may not be able to change anything because there are certain policies that the university expects" [12]. The property is dimensioned as "unacceptable" and "acceptable."

The level of *Technical Support* available to online teachers varies. Some teachers are quite satisfied with the level of technical support they receive. Yet others report they often encounter problems with their online system, which can be frustrating for the students and sometimes for the instructor alike. Those schools that are growing their online education department too fast are more likely to run into capacity problems with their online servers, which cannot keep up with the increase in load. The associated dimensions are "none," "satisfactory," and "excellent."

The *Reliability* of the technology used for online education varies from "low" to "high." Teachers report there are technical glitches affecting the servers and long, unacceptable server response times that result in connection timeout for the client computers. As one teacher put it,

One of the things that can be a real drawback is when the servers go down. Because then people are posting and it's not going anywhere and you get online the next day and their stuff isn't there and they panic because it was due the night before. And, uh, usually I'm experiencing the server problems when they do, so I know when the servers down. But it's been very aggravating to post all of your handouts and then find out that none of them are showing up and then you have to post them all over again! And that's very irritating because that's very time-consuming. [16]

At times, the problems are blamed on administration: "They moved the course Web site to another server; we had an exam on Tuesday, the Web site was down Saturday through Monday" [19]. When students do not have the ability to get to their online material, frustration sets in. When the servers are unavailable, or freeze up, as they often do, that may lead students to contact the teacher and ask for help: In particular, when they are in the middle of taking an online test, "That means the student has to contact me to unfreeze the test and then they have to start all over again" [35]. Based on what was reported by online teachers, *Reliability* can be construed as either "low" or "high."

Once again, on the issue of synchronicity, the opinions are split between desirable and not desirable, or something in between. Some teachers do not care much for *Synchronous* communication: "I think any type of synchronous learning needs to be limited, just because I think you're going to—people become online learners for the convenience" [44]. However, other teachers prefer synchronous communication because "Online you lose the real time, synchronous collaboration between students. I know you can electronically attempt to do that, but it's not the same" [13]. Other teachers indicate that the ideal environment for teaching would support varying degrees of synchronicity. Such an environment would be very convenient for students and teacher, as they would be able to communicate with their instructor and each other synchronously or asynchronously as deemed necessary.

As was discussed in Chapter IX, teachers indicate that the *Media Richness* is relatively low in the online environment. They say that they are missing the visual component of the instructional process. Some teachers report that a truly multimedia environment would help get people involved a little bit more. The asynchronous communication tools in use today are somewhat of a constraint. For good measure, the chat rooms and e-mail systems and all the other types of asynchronous communication that we use today are nothing more than a crutch. We are probably only using only a very small percentage of what we should really be using. Bridging the gap between the on-ground and the online classroom experience can help improve interaction significantly. The visual cues are important. Online, teachers have to compensate for that lack of face-to-face communication cues. It is the low media richness associated with today's online environment that can make the online classroom seem quite impersonal. If history is a lesson, there is something that is missing: Videotape was used in education 10 or 15 years ago, and some would agree that the experiment was not quite an unchallenged success. By other accounts, the use of video was a failure. Why? There is something special about being in classroom with other people that share the same common goals: As of this moment it is not known how to capture and capsule that "something."

Online, many teachers are quite fond of using audio-visual materials and audio or video technology to support their teaching. Yet, the process is imperfect, especially in certain course specialties, and could stand improvement:

Having a short video clip on the server and the students can click on it and download the streaming video, so that might be a way that I could do my demonstrations; for instance, so that they're watching the poppet beads and the telephone chords fold up into the proteins as I'm talking. So that would let me do some of what I can do in the face-to-face class and bring it to the online environment. You could potentially do a lab demonstration, a short demonstration, so they could see some data. [42]

The lack of, or inadequacy of feedback online frustrates the teacher:

It's that the visual and speech aspects are missing, obviously. I feel that I need to stop and recapture them [the students]; that I need to explain maybe one more time; that I need to find out why did they get lost in the sequence in the explanation. It's important to me that I have this constant, that we are connected. In classroom, you want to be connected to all students, all the time. [14]

And the difficulty of learning more about the students, about their abilities, skills, talents, of who they really are, bothers teachers:

You can still get a person's personality through e-mail. That will come through, but there's this whole aspect of human interaction that is absent. The way you look and the way you feel, your facial expressions and body language, and for the most part I think that that's lacking. I think that's unfortunate, but there may be those few instances where that's actually a bonus because it doesn't get in the way of just purely looking at the person's work. If someone has something they do that kind of is annoying to you that's probably not going to be there in the online environment. I don't know if that's good or bad. [15]

Using technology can be difficult and not always user friendly; teachers are concerned with the technology's *Ease of Use.* They report being overwhelmed by systems that seem unnecessarily complex, and they try to avoid them. When they find they cannot use it successfully, they move to a less expensive, simpler system—one that they find easier to use than what was initially offered by the school and was too much for them to handle. They prefer to have access to systems that integrate smoothly, take advantage of the broadband connectivity available to students—are user friendly, easy to use, and connected to other software systems. At times, limitations introduced by the technology choices made by the school are unwarranted. There are universities that choose to stick to a one vendor solution, especially in this day and age, when all of the tools they use are platform independent. Teachers can be quite critical of the technology strategy behind the choice made. In many instances, the things that make life difficult for the teachers tend to be resolved when frustrated faculty members complain loudly enough. Teachers seem to agree that the *Ease of Use* of the technologies implemented to support online teaching is "low."

Teachers reflect on how the technology they have available does or does not appropriately support teaching. Overall, they seem to believe that current technologies are not quite ready to support online education. In the words of one teacher, "Online teaching now is very lacking: While the tools we have could do a half-way decent job at providing content and information, they do not do a good job as far as anything else" [22]. The appropriateness and usability of the technology comes into question as there are two sides to it: Teachers, on one hand, are finding it most frustrating to have to work with primitive technology provided by the school. Yet, on the other hand, they oftentimes have students who have not even mastered simple technology.

Another aspect of technology usability and appropriateness is the desirability of a good fit between subject matter and the technology used to support online teaching. One teacher explains how different subjects need to be taught differently online:

One of the problems in an online kind of environment with statistics, is you have to write formulas and symbols which aren't regularly available on the computer, and if you're putting them into these interactive chat/communications, you can't write them in by hand or do anything like that....If the technology is right, and the curriculum is developed appropriately, there's no reason why an online education couldn't be comparable or even better than an on-ground one. [05]

Differences Among Modalities

A hybrid education modality seems ideal by the account of many of the interviewed participants. Teachers like having a tool that allows them to move seamlessly back and forth between synchronous and asynchronous modes of interaction. Interactivity, if designed properly, leads to a very rewarding learning opportunity; the human feedback is the element that makes or breaks a really successful online experience. From talking with the interviewed teachers, it becomes obvious that there are things they can do online but not on-ground, and vice versa. For example, there are activities that online can run through an entire week or even longer in an incremental manner. In contrast, in the on-ground classroom they have to do something while everyone is present, and finish what they start. Activities cannot really carry on after class is dismissed. While teachers may cover the same topic online and in an on-ground classroom, the activities they do are somewhat different. Of course, the role of the teacher changes with the modality, from a "knowledge giver" on-ground to a "knowledge discusser" online. Both on-ground and online classes are dynamic, in the sense that things happen online as well as in the classroom. Yet, while in the on-ground classroom teachers can immediately take control of a particular situation, online it will take them some time to achieve the same result. They can still take control, but it will require a longer amount of time.

This category evolved from the initial *Differences Between Online and Classroom*, which was later renamed *Differences Among Modalities* to better reflect the properties associated with it. Three properties were saturated here: *Classroom, Hybrid,* and *Online* (see Figure 3).

Figure 3. Category: Differences among modalities

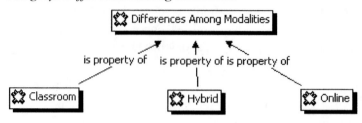

Current trends seem to point towards *Hybrid* modality as becoming the preferred approach to education, in general. Even in the on-ground classes, students are often turning in their papers as attachments to e-mails, and they are communicating with their teacher and fellow students outside the allotted class time using e-mail. The traditional on-ground class takes on features that are the hallmark of the online classroom yet it does not become an online class.

Some of the subjects of this study also support this trend, favoring the *Hybrid* teaching environment which blends online and on-ground instruction and viewing it as the best modality for education and teaching. Quoting one teacher, the hybrid modality

Is nice because on the first day, you can see them and you know what you've got. Also, they have a chance to socialize… and they can't be too obnoxious because they know they're going to have to face you again in the end, unlike in a purely online environment. [27]

Teachers reflect on the *Online* teaching environment: Because of the lack of the face-to-face communication cues, they must rely mainly on written text. In the case of the online interaction, the quality of writing and the quality of thought and the patience that an instructor has are all ingredients of success. The apparent online "distance" between teacher and students requires that students are able to take responsibility for their learning. It makes it difficult for the teacher to motivate and to assess students' learning progress. Because of all the communication aspects associated with the online educational environment, the teacher does not develop personal relationship with the bulk of the students.

For teachers who teach online, it is a lot more work involved. The teaching process requires a lot more time, and expediency. Teachers report they have to almost become 24 by 7 instructors. In addition, because the online teaching modality is not interactive, teachers have to plan things out a little more and they have to ask questions that are going to make the students think; that requires more in-depth analysis on the part of the teacher. One teacher reports that she is

Spending all my time facilitating discussions and grading. I have rubrics, the students have access to all the rubrics so after each discussion closes out I'll grade that set and then I send each student e-mails telling them more qualitative feedback than just a number. And so I end up having a lot of discussions with the whole class and the e-mail correspondence with them, there's a lot more contact. [42]

Overall, teachers find online teaching to be quite different from what they experience in the on-ground classroom: Personal interface is lacking, and often times the study groups' accountability is not at the highest level. Yet, by teaching online, a teacher's anxiety of having to face a class that is shy in contributing to class discussions is significantly reduced.

With regard to teaching in the on-ground *Classroom*, one teacher finds it more advantageous because

The on-ground environment [is] a lot more forgiving than the online. Either it goes or it doesn't go, and it's very, very difficult to change it because [online] it takes so long between messages to communicate things back and forth. If you set up things right then it goes well, but if you set things up wrong it's very hard to recover. [05]

A drawback of the on-ground classroom teaching is that the teacher has to abide by time and schedule constraints. When, for example, there are only 4 hours of class time and there is much material to cover, the teacher cannot take the time to deviate from the lesson plan. Classroom discussion must be carefully timed, and any off topic conversations must be relegated to break time. Online, there are chat rooms available, which offer a discussion forum for any off topic conversations.

Some teachers find that the need for a lot of improvisation in the on-ground classroom may be a disadvantage. When they are in front of the class, the interaction is very rapid; there is not much time to think things through in the on-ground classroom. Online, on the other hand, ample time is available. Yet, some teachers believe that the success of the on on-ground teaching modality is owed to the spontaneity of the interaction. In the on-ground classroom, the communication is not one-on-one; rather, to borrow a telecommunications term, it involves *broadcasting*. Online, on the other hand, teaching may feel like a one-on-one exercise, akin to uni-casting.

Issues

This category revealed seven properties: *Effectiveness, Satisfaction, Frustration, Communication, Efficiency, Change,* and *Tradeoffs.* The property *Change* stems from the initial category *What Would You Change?* which was renamed for clarity (see Figure 4).

Figure 4. Category: Issues

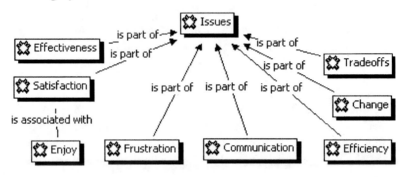

The property *Satisfaction* developed one sub-property, *Enjoy*.

When it comes to assessing their online teaching *Effectiveness*, teachers' opinions vary. One teacher finds that "Online teaching is in its infancy. People are trying to find more effective ways to make online work" [05]. Yet, online, another teacher finds that she is more effective in getting students to improve their ability to write and think. In the on-ground classroom, she is more effective in getting students to really challenge their preconceived notions of the world of technology and the world of business. That being said, she agrees that she seems to be more effective on campus, in the on-ground classroom. The property is dimensioned as "effective" and "ineffective."

Teachers derive *Satisfaction* from their teaching: They enjoy seeing students take what they learn in the classroom and use it. After all, that is what teaching is about: transferring the knowledge and being able to apply it. Teachers report being excited. In the words of one teacher, teaching online is

Exciting. I really feel like I'm on the cutting edge of transformational educational modality here, and it's attractive enough to me, with all my gripings about the lack of face-to-face interaction, you know, I've been doing the face-to-face interaction for 15 years or more as far as being a professional teacher, in addition to all those years I spent in the classroom as a student. [04]

The inner satisfaction of being a teacher can be very gratifying; in particular at the end of the day when the teacher feels that she had accomplished something. In her own words, "I see those goals straight away and the students come back and tell me so many stories about their life as to how I had helped them, and that just makes my day" [32]. The property *Satisfaction* developed one sub-property, *Enjoy*.

Teachers *enjoy* teaching. As one teacher puts it,

Your greatest gratification comes when you finish your class or your weekend session and you have a wonderful glowing tiredness because you have put in so much of yourself to what has transpired, at least I do, and you see the faces, the response, you see the reaction of the students and that you've learned something and they've learned something and it's been a very strong meeting of the minds, and that doesn't always happen, but when it does, it's really an exciting and gratifying moment. [01]

In spite of the feelings of joy that it can elicit, teaching can be frustrating at times. One reason of *frustration* may be the poor quality of the online dialogue that sometimes contains little more than token responses and answer clichés. Another reported reason of frustration is the potential of an issue of safety, related to the online teaching modality: "When I first started, I had some students who would borderline harass me, who wouldn't have done that if we were in a classroom" [06]. Online teachers can also become frustrated by the perceived loss of human interaction, or by students that keep asking the same question in their e-mails. In the on-ground classroom, an announcement could be made once and for all, answering the question for all students. Limited access to adequate technology infrastructure by the students, preventing them from making full use of the course content, is another reason of frustration reported by the interviewed teachers. When this happens, course materials almost must be prepared to the lowest common denominator, which can turn into an extremely frustrating exercise for the teacher. Another frustrating issue reported is that the time demands loom large:

Online, you can spend a half hour answering a student's question. Typing up a meaningful e-mail, going through their work, and that's only good for that student. If you've got to do that 20 more times, your Saturday is gone. And that can happen every week. If you want to do anything challenging, give them interesting assignments, you really have to provide the support. Whereas in a classroom, you can say okay, today I'm going to spend the first half hour of class going through this, and you solve it in a half hour. [13]

When the online classes are allowed to be too large, it soon becomes impossible for the teacher to keep up with the messages posted by the students. The teachers become, in a sense, removed from their students, which only increases teacher frustration.

Teachers identify some of the *tradeoffs* associated with teaching online. By far, the biggest tradeoffs relate to the increased demands on teacher time. In the words of one teacher,

I miss that sort of emotional bond that you build more quickly in a face-to-face environment—that sense of the group that you build when you're with your students face-to-face. ... I think also teaching online just takes more time. I spend a lot of time sitting at a computer partly because the interaction is so enhanced that I spend a lot of time communicating to my students individually as well as in groups. So it's a lot of work. It's very time-consuming. [39]

A second teacher finds the tradeoff to be worthwhile, while discussing the time issue:

It's a tradeoff, you know. I'm constantly logging into the computer, probably three or four times a day, 6 days a week. But I trade that off for not having to be in class at a particular time for lecture. So I don't think that's worse; it's just different. [42]

The associated dimensions are "interaction,", "time," and "emotional bond."

Teachers reflect on what aspects of online education could be improved, and on the *changes* they would like to make. The information gathered reflects that they would definitely like to manage the growth of the online education in a better way. They would like to make curriculum changes and have their students pass a technological competency exam before they are allowed to sign up for the online courses. They would like to see more feedback online, in their course. They would also like to see more institutional support and investments in the right technology and not rely solely on e-mail to conduct online teaching. In addition, the teachers would like to receive the same recognition for teaching online as for on-ground courses and to receive equal credit for both. With regard to use of technology, the teachers would like to be offered training on how to teach online effectively, including how to use the right media and how to deliver content effectively. Support for using interactive media is a must, at least for certain course activities. The technology can be a hindrance in itself. Both teacher and students should have access to adequate technology infrastructure. In the words of one teacher,

In a perfect world every one would have high speed Internet connections so you could use streaming audio and streaming video and I would be able to do that. I don't know how to create those files, and the technical support we have at my institution is really not that good. They have people who know the technology but not the instructional piece. I would really like an instructional designer who's an educator first and a techy second, who could help me design tools that would work. That I don't have. [42]

In addition, better tools for managing students online are needed, which involves smaller online classes in order to allow teachers to focus on the students and the progress they are making. Access to technology that makes it easier for the teachers to assess students, and to grade assignments and class participation, would also be a needed change. The property *Change* is dimensioned as follows: "growth," "institutional support," "curriculum," "feedback," "prerequisites," and "technology."

When asked to assess *efficiency*, some teachers believe that online classes are inefficient:

I also don't find the online class to be as efficient as everybody thinks it to be. One of the motivations for online learning is that you can get efficiencies and you allow technology to do a lot of the work. But when you start communicating with students by e-mail rather than face-to-face, having to repeat things by e-mail rather than face-to-face, when your online materials have to be programmed in rather than something you can quickly change in your notes or quickly change in your Power-Point presentation… not to mention all the backshop that has to be put into place to support a Web site…. I question this idea of efficiency. [20]

For others, they find them efficient: "It's pretty efficient" [16]. The associated dimensions are "inefficient" and "pretty efficient."

With regard to the issue of communication, teachers feel that increasing the quality of the *communication* may help them build better rapport with their students:

The communication aspect can be more intensified. That you get closer, maybe, to people, to know them. There are things that you can't get just through reading somebody's notes. The aspects of the communications that are in voice, that are in body language and you know that they only come out in real-time. The good teacher explores those things. You know it says something that somebody gets the glaze in the eyes. You know he's lost. You can't emphasize that and it's, uh, different type of communication. I don't know if you will ever be able to compensate for that, but, on the other hand, there are other benefits on online that make things enjoyable and they make a lot of sense. [14]

The online environment in its present form is not conducive of communication. In the words of one teacher,

One of the things is that it takes longer to communicate ideas. When you're in a classroom, when you're communicating orally, oral communication is pretty fast comparatively, where this you're going through e-mail, we're not in a chat room

environment and so communication takes longer and the communication is asyn-chronous too; I mean, it's not live, and so there's always that time gap that I was always a little bit worried about. So that is one of the things you give up. It's a lot harder to communicate. [35]

The property is dimensioned as "reduced online" and "increased online."

Adjustments

The differences between the online environment and the on-ground classroom, and the demands associated with teaching online, pressure teachers to make adjustments to continue to be effective in their teaching. Some of the adjustments pertain to how they design course materials, delivery, and communication.

For example, they modify the design of the PowerPoint presentations they use in class. In addition, they may change the format of the course to adapt the materials to the different modality. They structure their courses differently and are more sensitive to the level of formality present in certain environments, and they prepare their course materials with more clarity. Teachers spend more time and effort developing materials for the online courses. They strive to improve their time-management skills to better cope with the fact that they are spending more time engaged in teaching activities online, where the class is open around the clock.

Overall, teachers benefit from exposure to a different environment and gain additional skills and insight. They note behavioral changes and changes in their communication style. Online, teachers must give up the nonverbal communication cues they so much enjoy in the on-ground classroom. The lack of face-to-face communication cues is painfully obvious and forces them to adjust. Yet, the online environment is quite different than the on-ground classroom, and may lead a teacher to feel he has limited options available. From teaching to support materials, things may be difficult to deal with. Teachers strive to maintain control online, where discussions easily can go off track. In their attempts to bond with their students, some teachers try to put a human touch on their online presence and interaction. For example, they may post photos or a digital image of a cookie for their students.

Figure 5. Category: Adjustments

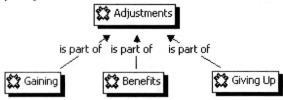

The category is saturated with three properties: *Gaining, Benefits,* and *Giving Up* (see Figure 5).

Some of the things that the interviewed teachers report as having *gained* from their online teaching are organization and time-management skills; increased awareness of what works online and what does not; new ideas to try in the classroom; technology skills; flexibility; and time. Teachers find that they can actually create things in the online environment that they can also use in future online or on-ground classes. They end up with all sorts of projects and reports and other things that students make available to them in a digital format, and they can use these things for future classes. They also feel that the quality of the course material is much improved in the online lectures they make available to their students. There is a lot to gain from the temporal flexibility afforded by the online environment. Teaching online protects the teacher from feeling the slight touch of discomfort associated with not having had the time to fully prepare to deliver a 3-hour face-to-face session or from feeling the time constraints of the on-ground classes. Somehow, the online environment appears to be stress-free from the point of view of the students' access to communicate with the teacher. At least there is a certain lack of fear for the students to respond. In the on-ground classroom, there are always people who are aggressive and may capture much of the class time, whereas there are other students who may be too shy or simply unable to communicate. This does not occur in an online environment; this type of stress does not exist online. Students can ask questions and respond freely. Nobody is hogging anybody else's time. Teachers who teach online seem to be more aware of the learning process, of how their students are learning and what is working for them and what is not working for them. They are a bit more creative in their methods, in how they teach. The associated dimensions are "organization," "time-management skills," "awareness of what works," "new ideas," "technology skills," "flexibility," and "time."

As part of the adjustment process, the teachers also have to *give up* things in order to adjust to online teaching, such as flexibility, time, control, quality of interaction, feedback quality and quantity, and satisfaction. For one teacher, teaching online takes a heavy toll from the time point of view:

I've given up free time with my family. I could be doing other things. I've given up pretty much all of my personal time for things that I love to do.... I probably shouldn't give up so much, but I just really enjoy it. [02]

Again, with regard to time, for another teacher, teaching online means giving up "Free time: all my free time. I think it's three times the amount of work" [13]. Giving up on face-to-face interaction means that communication suffers online: At times, it makes it harder to get a point across online. Sometimes it's harder to understand what the students are asking and what their reactions are. There is a certain warmth stemming from face-to-face discussions and an ability to be more articulate in a face-to-face setting. Some teachers who try to inspire students and be a role model may turn from a physical to a virtual role model online. Also, online, the spontaneity of the interaction is changed. One must give up a lot of human reaction, a lot of human relationships, or relationships between students and instructors, or among teachers themselves. Teachers may have to give up, and miss, the sort of emotional bond that one builds more quickly in a face-to-face environment; that sense of the group that teachers build when they are with their students face-to-face. While this sense of belonging, of rapport, can be built online, it takes longer. The associated properties are "flexibility," "time," "control," "interaction quality," "feedback," "satisfaction," and "emotional involvement."

Teaching online is not without _benefits._ The clarity of the presentations is higher online. The amount of structure varies, from less structure to mainly more structure. The timing of the information preparation is different, as all requirements must be specified up front. One teacher reports that she benefited significantly from being an online instructor as online teaching forced her to become more organized. For some teachers, the asynchronous nature of the online environment is appealing:

The asynchronous nature on online teaching is also attractive in that regard. If I'm not feeling well at noon on Wednesday, I don't have to do my online facilitation at noon. I can either do it tomorrow on Thursday, or do it later in the evening, after I've rested up, or whatever it happens to be. So I'm not locked into a particular time or a particular place to have to function as the teacher. [04]

Teachers who teach online find out that they have to exercise a certain amount of patience when teaching online and that sort of carries over to the on-ground classes they may also teach. Another reported benefit is that some online classes have better students—at least from some teachers' point of view. Sometimes, naturally, one may have to teach to classes who are not of the highest quality. Yet, on the average, online classes have better students than the on-ground ones. This is because students that have difficulty in an online environment will drop out. Then, when the students are working adults, there is a great wealth of knowledge to be shared among students and instructor alike. Teachers appreciate the convenience of teaching online because they could work from home. Online teaching offers a certain degree of flexibility to the teacher. Given the asynchronous environment, she can go online when she finds it convenient, whether that is early in the morning or late at night. The teacher can take the day off and avoid long commutes in heavy traffic or inclement weather. The associated dimensions are "higher clarity," "structure," "flexibility," and "timing."

Choice

When asked to make a choice, teachers turn toward any of the three possible choices: online, on-ground, and hybrid. Some teachers would prefer the hybrid environment, as it offers the best of all worlds. Other teachers would elect to remain in the classroom. Yet other teachers feel very comfortable teaching online and would choose to teach purely online courses.

Teachers may choose to teach in multiple modalities (i.e., online, hybrid, or on-ground), teach only one modality, or leave the profession altogether. Some teachers report they do not have a *choice* at all, while others would clearly prefer to teach in the on-ground classroom, with online as their second best option:

There would be one determinant, and that would be time. I would prefer a class-room, because I just like being with people. However, online, sometimes—because of time scheduling issues and putting in the commuting and all of that—sometimes it's possible and other times it's not. And if you can't, a lot of times, teach classroom, instead of the alternative being not teach at all, I would teach online. [09]

Other teachers would choose the hybrid modality, while others would prefer to teach online. The associated dimensions are "classroom," "hybrid," "online," and "no choice."

Of the 44 teachers interviewed, 4 teachers stated they would choose to teach in a hybrid modality, 4 would teach online, and 13 would prefer to stay in the classroom. The remaining 23 teachers did not answer the question.

Triangulation: Literature Comparison

Technology can be frustrating. Teachers lose the sounds and energy of a real class-room. Teaching online is not for every educator; it is a different method of teaching, albeit an exciting one (Blair, 2002). The online environment is a simulated world; teachers are concerned with technical characteristics of technology, interface features, collaborative tools, and hypertext structures. The online technology promotes a more cooperative learning environment. The interaction is more costly in terms of instructor time. Online teachers spend two to three times the amount of time delivering an on-line course (Vachris, 1999).

The lack of face-to-face contact may induce online students to feel less pressure to contribute. Teachers acknowledge uneven participation and the potential for lurking. Teachers feel that imposing too much structure is detrimental to a value-free environment, as should be the case online. Some teachers would like to have alternative procedures for dealing with students' personal problems (e.g., telephone). Online, new modes of interaction and communication emerge, and monitoring and encouraging participation can be more difficult. There is better feedback online in that more time for reflection is available (Nicol, Minty, & Sinclair, 2003).

There are concerns about how information and communication technologies (ICT) are incorporated into the on-ground environment. Teachers must reconsider the relationship of the physical setting to the students' learning experience.

Universities are augmenting distance education with telecommunications media (Stadtlander, 1998). The Web allows for two-way communication. Today's students are always multiprocessing (Brown, 2000). Web technology allows teachers to create multidimensional experiences that combine text, audio, and video in a media-rich environment and engage the learners (Sensiper, 2000). The advantages offered by online (access to information, location, convenience) are reduced by drawbacks (time required for course design, faculty training). For many teachers, the use of technology is basic (i.e., e-mail, dissemination of course materials) as reported by Vodanovich and Piotrowski (2001). In contrast, many of the current and future students are well immersed in technology. ICT is a way of life for them (Brown, 2002).

Teachers report cognitive changes when teaching online. Instructional roles and teaching strategies are different. Dramatic increase in demands on both teacher and students are noted. Online conversations are much more time-consuming. Inducing collaboration online requires a different design structure for activities, discussions, and assignments. A significant challenge for teachers is how to create a supportive, stimulating cognitive environment online.

Many faculty members in colleges and universities are embittered: They report feelings of regret, envy, frustration, betrayal, and isolation. This affects their attitudes toward work (Jensen, 1995). Teachers who used little technology were more likely to hold negative views about online teaching.

Institutional administrators have to contend with personnel issues: faculty skills, new personnel needed, faculty compensation, and resistance to technology. Faculty members' compensation includes money, tenure, release time, and course load. Current policies regarding personnel appear to be ad hoc. The increase in faculty resistance to technology is due in part to teachers' perception that it distorts the educational experience (Rayburn & Ramaprasad, 2002).

The design and delivery of courses that integrate new technologies is challenging. Technology may end being used at a superficial level and it may not have an impact on teaching practice (Torrisi & Davis, 2000). Information technology provides a challenge to teachers and course curriculum designers.

Developing online courses requires a team approach; it is complicated and takes significant time (Chou & Tsai, 2002). Course designers are well advised to avoid technology limitations and design courses for maximum effect. Teaching, learning, and evaluation must reflect the differences between modalities (Ohler & Theall, 2004).

The expectations online are exacerbated: Online students expect instantaneous service, and teachers need significant time to properly respond to students. Teachers spend more time teaching online, with no additional compensation (National Educational Association, 2000). Online faculty members spend significantly more time to develop Web courses (Cristianson, Tiene, & Luft, 2002).

Assessment is difficult. Teachers have no way of knowing whether their students study all the course material. Instructors would like to know more about their online students (Meyen & Lian, 1997). Online is great for students who are mature, engaged, and well-organized (Seguin, 2002).

Teachers who decide to teach online must make decisions that will impact their teaching role and strategies. These decisions are shaped by their beliefs and the values they hold about teaching. They adjust by being more entertaining and theatrical (Grosse, 2004). However, I found quite the opposite: Teachers adjust by becoming less entertaining and theatrical online. Teachers become more conscious of their teaching when combining face-to-face and online teaching (McShane, 2004).

Teachers realize the importance of integrating technology in classrooms. They enjoy online discussion forums, as the threaded discussions offer more choices, allow more diverse opinions, and lead to deeper analysis (Li, 2003). Teachers supplement their on-ground instruction with technology from their online classes (Woods, Baker, & Hopper, 2004). They can teach more courses online, for different schools, with less concern for institutional politics, and earn more money (Carnevale, 2004). Online courses are convenient, meet academic needs, and help students improve technological skills (Leonard & Guha, 2001). Web technology can help students prepare for the social, academic, and personal challenges of higher education and offer a useful supplement to classroom instruction (Shafer, Davis, Lahner, Petrie, & Calderone, 2002). Some of the teachers interviewed for this book report opposing views: They feel that online courses do not meet academic needs.

Teaching online is not for everyone (Carr, 2000). There is a steep learning curve, and online instruction requires regular contact between teacher and students. Online students can fall behind because they are "invisible." Course materials require significant time to prepare, and everything must be prepared well before the course starts (Kubala, 1998).

Loss of personal contact is a concern to teachers and students alike (Weiss, 2000). The online environment makes it difficult for the teacher to help students who are having problems with practical exercises (Bergstrom, Grahn, Karlstrom, Pulkkis, & Astrom, 2004). Online discussions are difficult to establish and coordinate (Bonk, 2004). The teachers interviewed by this author stated opinions that confirm these findings.

Many teachers leave the profession after a few years of teaching. They are frustrated by the emotional, physical, and psychological demands of the classroom (Darling-Hammond, 1990). Teachers resist the effort to be forced into distance education. They are concerned with institutional support, interaction, and education quality issues (Bower, 2001). Inadequate support can diminish enthusiasm, sense of purpose and effort.

In one study, most teachers preferred online teaching to the traditional classroom (Cristianson et al., 2002). Some teachers preferred hybrid. Yet, there are still questions whether hybrid can really support quality education (King, 2002). This being said, this book finds a certain preference for the on-ground classroom, despite the fact that some teachers view hybrid education as a superior modality.

Hybrid learning modalities have the potential to support deep learning (Garrisson & Kanuka, 2004). Most successful course outcomes are being seen in classes that are small and combine face-to-face with online instruction—a "Web-enhanced class" (Pallof & Pratt, 2001, p.68).

Conclusion

There is very little experience in developing instruction for delivery online, and for teaching online. Teachers have to restructure much of their course materials. There is a tendency to reformat materials and learning strategies to fit the technology. The use of technology does not necessarily enhance the reaching out to students. As teachers are concerned with the technology availability and bandwidth, they design their course materials in a conservative manner to ensure equal access for their students. The ability to connect emotionally with students makes for a "special" professor. The online classroom removes the need for the teacher. The student forms a relationship with the text, not the professor.

Ohler and Theall (2004) showed that teachers do not seem to have operationalized the differences between online and face-to-face instruction to adjust their teaching and assessment strategies. However, I found that teachers make certain adjustments to how they teach in order to compensate for the differences among modalities.

A majority of the teachers interviewed are very vocal about their preference for a hybrid model. They consider it to be the optimal teaching modality. However, the on-ground classroom still ranks high in their preferences.

References

Bergstrom, L., Grahn, K. J., Karlstrom, K., Pulkkis, G., & Astrom, P. (2004). Teaching network security in a virtual learning environment. *Journal of Information Technology Education, 3,* 189-217.

Blair, J. (2002). The virtual teaching life. *Education Week, 21,* 31-34.

Bonk, C. (2004). I should have known this was coming: Computer-mediated discussion in teacher education. *Journal of Research on Technology in Education, 36*(2), 95-102.

Bower, B. L. (2001). Distance education: Facing the faculty challenge. *Online Journal of Distance Learning Administration, 4*(2).

Brown, J. S. (2000, March/April). Growing up digital. How the Web changes work, education, and the ways people learn. *Change,* 11-20.

Brown, J. S. (2002). Learning in the digital age. In M. Devlin, R. Larson, & J. Meyerson (Eds.), *The Internet & the university: Forum 2001* (pp. 65-91). Forum for the Future of Higher Education and EDUCAUSE, 2002.

Carnevale, D. (2004). For online adjuncts, a seller's market. *Chronicle of Higher Education, 50*(34).

Carr, S. (2000). *After half a course, a professor concedes distance education is not for him.* Retrieved May 10, 2005, from http://chronicle.com/free/2000/03/2000032801u.htm

Chou, C., & Tsai, C. C. (2002). Developing Web-based curricula: Issues and challenges. *Journal of Curriculum Studies, 34*(6), 623-636.

Cristianson, L., Tiene, D., & Luft, P. (2002). Examining online instruction in undergraduate nursing education. *Distance Education, 23*(2), 213-229.

Darling-Hammond, L. (1990). *Teacher supply, demand and quality.* Washington, DC: National Board for Professional Teaching Standards.

Garrisson, D. R., & Kanuka, H. (2004). Blended learning: Uncovering its transformative potential in higher education. *Internet and Higher Education, 7,* 95-105.

Grosse, C. U. (2004). How distance learning changes faculty. *International Journal of Instructional Technology and Distance Learning, 1*(6).

Jensen, E. J. (1995). The bitter groves of academe. *Change, 27*(1), 8-11.

King, K. P. (2002). Identifying success in online teacher education and professional development. *Internet and Higher Education, 5,* 231-246.

Kubala, T. (1998). Addressing student needs: Teaching on the Internet. *T H E Journal, 28*(5), 71-74.

Leonard, J., & Guha, S. (2001). Education at the crossroads: Online teaching and students' perspectives on distance learning. *Journal of Research on Technology in Education, 34*(1), 51-57.

Li, Q. (2003). Would we teach without technology? A professor's experience of teaching mathematics education incorporating the Internet. *Educational Research, 45*(1), 61-77.

McShane, K. (2004). Integrating face-to-face and online teaching: academics' role concept and teaching choices. *Teaching in Higher Education, 9*(1), 3-16.

Meyen, E., L., & Lian, C. H. T. (1997). Teaching online courses. *Focus on Autism & Other Developmental Disabilities, 12*(3), 1-17.

National Educational Association. (2000). *A survey of traditional and distance learning higher education members.* Washington, DC: National Educational Association.

Nicol, D., Minty, I., & Sinclair, C. (2003). The Social dimensions of online learning. *Innovations in Education and Teaching International, 40*(3), 270-280.

Ohler, S., & Theall, M. (2004, April 12-13). *An exploratory study of teacher opinions about teaching and learning on-line and face-to-face: the instructional choices of a sample of faculty in computer science.* Paper presented at the Instructional Evaluation and Faculty Development Conference, San Diego, CA.

Pallof, R. M., & Pratt, K. (2001). *Lessons from the cyberspace classroom: The realities of online teaching.* San Francisco: Jossey-Bass.

Rayburn, W. E., & Ramaprasad, A. (2002). Three strategies for the use of distance learning technology in higher education. In M. Khosrow-Pour (Ed.), *Web-based instructional learning* (pp. 27-42). Hershey, PA: IRM Press.

Seguin, C. (2002). Games online students play: Building a firewall new instructors (and burned out 'old ones') can use. *TechTrends, 46*(4), 23-57.

Sensiper, S. (2000). Making the case online. Harvard Business School multimedia. *Information, Communication and Society, 3*(4), 616-621.

Shafer, M. J., Davis, J. E., Lahner, J. M., Petrie, T. A., & Calderone, W. K. (2002). The use and effectiveness of a Web-based instructional supplement in a college student success program. *Journal of College Student Development, 43*(5), 751-757.

Stadtlander, L. M. (1998). Virtual instruction: Teaching an online graduate seminar. *Teaching of Psychology, 25*(2), 146-148.

Torrisi, G., & Davis, G. (2000). Online learning as a catalyst for reshaping practice—The experiences of some academics developing online learning materials. *The International Journal for Academic Development, 5*(2), 166-176.

Vachris, C. (1999). Teaching principles of economics without "chalk and talk": The experience of CNU online. *Journal of Economic Education, 30*(3), 292-307.

Vodanovich, S. J., & Piotrowski, C. (2001). Internet-based instruction: A national survey of psychology faculty. *Journal of Instructional Psychology, 28*(4), 253-255.

Weiss, R. E. (2000). Humanizing the online classroom. *New Directions for Teaching and Learning, 84*, 47-51.

Woods, R., Baker, J. D., & Hopper, D. (2004). Hybrid structures: Faculty use and perception of Web-based courseware as supplement to face-to-face instruction. *Internet and Higher Education, 7*, 281-297.

Chapter XI

A Theory of the Online Teaching Experience

Introduction

This chapter sets out to present a theory of the online teaching experience, as viewed by the teachers of online courses. It draws on the core categories presented in the previous two chapters ("Central Ideas: Teaching" and "Central Ideas: Technology"). The chapter proceeds by validating the core categories by means of triangulation with other published research, by identifying relationships and interplay among the 10 core categories, and by formulating the theory in narrative form.

Background

A brief comparison of the findings presented in this book to the literature augments the theoretical sensitivity at the core of the study, and helps improve internal validity. For each of the main categories grounded in data, the review of existing published research helps assess the validity of the constructs and their respective properties and dimensions.

The in-depth analysis of transcripts generated 10 main categories: *Teaching, Teaching Demands, Teacher Needs, Teaching Dimensions, Teaching With Technology, Technology, Differences Among Modalities, Issues, Adjustments,* and *Choice*. These categories are presented in greater detail in Chapters IX and X.

Teaching

The first category, *Teaching,* is a subject of great interest and has been researched and discussed in many published specialty studies. Despite this, as reported by Boyd and Arnold (2000), "little is known about how teachers think about the aims of education" (p. 23). Cahn (2003) documented that at least some teachers teach more out of passion and less because they are driven by monetary gains; the data derived from the interviews conducted for this book support this view. The contention that teachers take on a constructivist stance when teaching online (Bangert, 2004) is also confirmed by the findings. The teachers interviewed proved to be caring people, in no way different from what Shulman (2000) found:

The scholarship of teaching reflects a convergence of disciplinary, moral, communal and personal motives. If one is truly devoted to one's discipline, one is committed to transmitting and developing faithful conceptions and understandings of the discipline in students. Thus the integrity of the discipline leads to a sense of what is best for the students. (p. 98)

The teachers interviewed for this book speak with passion about their work; they confirm and delineate the elements described by Rosenberg (2001) that teaching contains elements pertaining to presentation and practice and to feedback and students' assessment.

What is significant about the interviews is that they reveal changes and new trends in education. Dreeben (1970) asserted that education was all about helping people grow, about grooming students. Yet, what teachers are telling about their teaching experiences reflects their focus on knowledge transfer and on helping students acquire skills. This is somewhat different from the classical definition of teaching as disseminating information. Teaching, it seems, has evolved into a facilitation stance—where the teacher resembles a conductor, someone who directs the class.

In the on-ground classroom, one has to respond to whatever questions are presented. Yet, there is some opportunity to divert and follow a thread. Online, this is more difficult to achieve. The teacher has to follow a more structured format, allowing for the exchange of fewer questions and answers. The online classroom also feels different in terms of time elasticity. Because the online classroom is always "on," the time seems to dilate, with potential creation of a feeling of emptiness, as it is hard to tell who is "in" at any time.

Teaching Demands

The second category, *Teaching Demands,* groups factors that teachers perceive as relevant in setting the stage. The data offered by the teachers show similarities with previous studies in that online teaching requires more time, effort, and technical skills as well as a change in communication style.

Demands

Time is one of the most critical factors that the teachers report, with an increase in time demand by two and one half to three times when teaching online. These figures are similar to those reported by Pallof and Pratt (1999). This translates into online teachers spending between 1 and 4 hours more per week to teach. One of the reasons of why this happens is that, online, student contact hours increase from 1 $\frac{1}{2}$ to 4 hours weekly, or a twofold increase. Other activities such as lecture, exams, conferences, and class meetings were found to require the same in terms of time (SchWeber, 2000). Teachers also express concern with the time required to update the course Web site and to interact with students (Hall, 2002).

Another demand when teaching online is the need to change the communication style, with almost sole reliance on written communication. This requires increased clarity of the materials, with the instructor being challenged to have excellent writing skills and to rework his or her course materials when developing an online class. Teaching online also requires long hours to respond to messages, e-mail, and to evaluate discussions. More time is spent on editing responses (Smith, Ferguson, & Caris, 2002). Because it is based on technology, the process of online teaching is also limited by bandwidth characteristics and by the asynchronous nature of the medium.

Course Development

Educators are concerned with learner expectations, incentives, and content (K. P. King & Dunham, 2005). Online courses require significant development and delivery efforts (Schell, 2004). The production of a virtual course poses significant demands: It requires access to graphical designers, prototypes, adequate choice of technology, and proper budget (Bergstrom, Grahn, Karlstrom, Pulkkis, & Astrom, 2004). Consequently, there is a significant burden to prepare an online course (Chang, 2001).

Teacher Needs

The third category, *Teacher Needs,* encompasses several factors that are important to teachers. Among them are interaction, learning aspects, face-to-face communication cues, and faculty development and training.

Interaction

In general, human communication consists of 7% verbal cues, 38% vocal cues, and 55% body movements (Merrill & Reid, 1981). In terms of learning, written materials rate rather low. Pike (1989, p. 153) showed that people, in their efforts to learn, generally retain 10% of what they read, 20% of what they hear, 30% of what they read and hear, 30% of what they see, 50% of what they see and hear, 70% of what they say, and 90% of what they teach or do.

The on-ground classroom is much richer than the online classroom and offers excellent support for human communication, because all essential elements of learning are present: verbal, written, vocal cues, and body movements. The teachers participating in the study report that online interaction occurs with more difficulty because of the main reliance on written communication. Yet, the communication and learning in the online environment is facilitated through elements that are not commonly encountered in the on-ground process. Specifically, text-based communication has been shown to support sustained reflection in classroom exchanges (i.e., messages). Online is more formal, requires more time to think, and there is less teacher control over the social context of learning. Reusable dialogues can help students learn as the archives of prior discussions are available for review (Nicol, Minty, & Sinclair, 2003).

The online forum forces students to communicate frequently with their teachers, while reliance on e-mails leads to a much closer relationship among participants. Klipowicz and Laniak (1999) also found out that there is more collaboration taking place online. Students develop a sense of accountability from the high visibility of the Web (Sengupta, 2001). The online learning environment has the potential to be more female friendly, anonymity being a positive aspect. This allows students to interact online without the distracting noise of social conditioning (Sullivan, 2002). Technology can also promote learning in more complex areas of knowledge such as analysis, synthesis, and creative judgment. Some of the online teachers note the high quality of online discussions, yet other teachers expressed concerns relative to their ability to convey ideas online and noted that it took them much longer than it did on-ground.

The processes of interaction and learning in the online environment can be hindered by several factors. One important factor, supported both by this study and by others, is the class size: If class size is large, the number of postings can be overwhelming for the instructor, leading to poor information flow. If the class is very small, discussions may not go well (Brower, 2003). Hodgkinson and Holland (2002) also found that collaboration is more than simply exchanging information. At times, the students' online dialogue pertains to personal experiences and may not reflect well-supported reasoning (Angeli, Valanides, & Bonk, 2003). The cultural differences and their effect on learners' collaborative behaviors are also important and may hinder the interaction process if not taken into account; this is most important for the instructors who teach international students (K.-J. Kim & Bonk, 2002). The issue of student motivation as a personal formulation beyond the control of teachers (Ameigh, 2000) is also an important limitation—one, though, that can apply to both online, and on-ground environments.

Teachers are interested in discussing a wide range of topics with their peers. Access to a support group is welcomed by teachers and allows them to foster a sense of community where they can share their experiences, knowledge, and reflections (Babinski, Jones, & DeWert, 2001). Many of the teachers that I interviewed expressed a need for a peer-support system, of an increase of social interaction with other online teachers.

Learning

Various studies report different findings with regard to the subject of learning online, as compared to other modalities. Marold, Larsen, and Moreno (2002) found no significant differences in the grades between online and on-ground classes; nevertheless, a variation in student performance in examinations is documented, with teachers reporting higher, lower, or similar grades for their online students. Weems (2002) found a significant decrease of performance of online students across exams.

The process of learning in the online environment seems to be facilitated by the hybrid modality, which has been shown to have the potential to support deep learning (Garrisson & Kanuka, 2004). Also, most successful course outcomes have been seen in classes that are small in size and combine face-to-face with online instruction—a "Web-enhanced class" (Pallof & Pratt, 2001, p. 68). The study that is the basis of this book found that some teachers prefer a hybrid environment, because it allows them to take advantage of the temporal flexibility of the online environment while maintaining an on-ground classroom presence. Online learning may be difficult for some students, with student attrition rate exceeding 40% online (Parker, 2003). The profile of the online student is an important factor in the learning process: Students who do well online have been found to have low anxiety, high tolerance for ambiguity, field independence, and internal locus of control (M. D. Anderson, 2001). The teachers I interviewed found the online student attrition rate to be a significant concern, as it is higher than in on-ground classes. They also report that not every student does well online, an indication that personal traits and organizational skills are important when studying online.

Face-to-Face

As it has been established, the use of the online medium for teaching is special due to the lack of face-to-face interaction. This leads to an inherent complexity of the process of teaching online courses (Lo, 2002). Aggarwal and Bento (2002) report that Web-based education can simulate face-to-face teaching models successfully; however, adjustments are needed in terms of student assessment, faculty training and expectations, and student expectations and motivation. The balanced mix of asynchronous (Listserv) and synchronous (chat rooms) support in an online course can also ensure provision of a quality learning experience (Duin, 1998). The study conducted for this book found that teachers make adjustments when teaching online, mainly in how they package, structure, and deliver course materials. While some teachers report effective teaching in both environments, at least some teachers note a lack of synchronous communication in the online educational environment.

Faculty Development

With regard to the subject of faculty development, a general consensus exists between the results of this study and studies published by other authors, that this is an area that requires continued improvement. The faculty members interviewed report on factors that affect their use of Internet technologies in class: They do not know how to most effectively use it, they have design concerns, and they feel that they do not receive adequate prior training. Some of them even go as far as to question the usefulness of the Internet.

The rapid shift to online, resource-based learning is hampered by poor course design. In the presence of these difficulties, faculty members try to recreate the classroom experience via computer. Littlejohn (2002) found that teachers need training to help them move from passive, didactic forms of teaching toward incorporating new teaching methods. In the traditional form of education, the teachers handle everything (i.e., course design and development). Online, they also need to be the content expert, Web developer, multimedia designer, and system administrator. These expectations are unrealistic, and teachers should have access to support staff (Baker, Schihl, & Aggarwal, 2003). More so, faculty members need to receive education on the use of technology and support to develop instructional materials (Rockwell, Schauer, Fritz, & Marx, 2000).

Teaching Dimensions

The fourth category, *Teaching Dimensions,* groups factors that can be used to describe and explain the teaching experience. Among them are online presence, theatrical performance, and sense of community.

Presence

The concept of presence is applicable to virtual environments. Users can feel present in the artificial environment created by mediated information; online, presence is a subjective sensation characterized by several social richness connotations, such as realism, transportation, and immersion (T. Kim & Biocca, 1998). Teacher and students are equally social actors within the medium (Lombard & Ditton, 1997). Teaching presence can vary, depending on whether teachers use student modera-tors to reduce the number of teacher postings and to perform a substantial part of the teaching presence role. Teaching presence online is reflected in the number and content of teacher postings. These postings are affected by teaching style, subject taught, class size, and teacher's familiarity with the medium. As much as it is more structured, online teaching is not a "canned" lecture: The modality allows the teacher to modify content and learning activities throughout the progress of the course.

Teacher presence can also be enhanced through communication with the students by private e-mail, voice messages, or phone (T. Anderson, Rourke, Garrison, & Archer, 2001). The teachers interviewed for this study report using various means of communication yet feeling less effective in trying to connect, to bond with their online students. It seems the lack of visual cues continues to have a negative effect on their ability to bond with students.

In asynchronous environments, time becomes space on the screen (Robinson, 2000). The Internet, as our teachers say, and the technology used in online education separate teaching from location: The physical location of students and teacher is irrelevant as long as they can share in the educational experience hosted online. By making the location irrelevant, online education only preserves one other dimension, which is time. Online, time frames the classroom, for educator and learner equally.

Show/Theatrical Performance

Society and students have changed from what it used to be in the early beginnings. Nowadays, the students expect to be entertained most of the time, and learning must always be fun. In order to capture their students' interest and attention, the teachers try to adapt when teaching online. It has been found that teachers who use a friendly, honest, humorous style make students believe they will succeed. For this, online teaching requires commitment and appropriate interactivity (C. King & McSporran, 2002). There are differences in the teacher performance in the real vs. the virtual mode of teaching environments: While a classroom teacher may resemble a sage on a stage, the online teacher is more like a guide, on the side of the online classroom (Paris, 2000). The lack of classroom theatrics online may lead some teachers to miss the face-to-face teaching environment; others, say they can form stronger relationships online (Blair, 2002). Communication skills and enthusiasm enhance teaching effectiveness (Johnson & Roellke, 1999).

Communities

Successful learning outcomes hinge upon the capabilities of the existing and emergent social networks to form learning communities (Mohrman, Tenkasi, & Mohrman, 2003). These communities encourage problem-solving skills and increasing retention and success for students and faculty alike (Dodge & Kendall, 2004). Yet, effective online communities do not develop easily; learners must be helped to form online communities; otherwise, they will form them offline (Orey, Koenecke, & Crozier, 2002). From what teachers told me, oftentimes they notice students exchanging e-mails in an attempt to schedule telephone conferences, or in person meetings. This reveals an ongoing strive to bring more real-time, synchronous, and richer communication to the online mix.

Teaching With Technology

Teaching with Technology, the fifth category, associates constructs relevant to how teachers use technology in their teaching. It has many facets, ranging from frustrating to satisfactory, based on every teacher's personal experience. Teaching online is not for every educator; it is a different method of teaching, one in which the energy and the sounds of the real classroom are lost. Nevertheless, it is still an exciting one (Blair, 2002). The online environment is a simulated, virtual world, in which the social life develops across on- and off-line networks. Recognizing this, some of the concerns the teachers have with regard to the technical characteristics of technology pertain to interface features, collaborative tools, and hypertext structures. They see a need to change their communication style to accommodate the medium. The new modes of communication imposed by the replacement of the face-to-face interaction with the use of technology pose new challenges for understanding collaboration (Hinn, Leander, & Bruce, 2001).

Technology

The sixth category, *Technology,* refers to the use of information technology in education, in general.

The technology industry is still dictating the needs of education instead of education dictating the need for technology (Morinaka, 2003). There are concerns about how information and communication technologies (ICT) are incorporated into the on-ground environment. Teachers must reconsider the relationship of the physical setting to the students' learning experience: Students and staff need to be allowed to shape their places of teaching and learning just as they shape the curriculum (Jamieson, Fisher, Gilding, Taylor, & Trevitt, 2000). Yet, our teachers report they do not always have the ability to control the curriculum and to change their courses as they find it appropriate.

Universities are augmenting distance education with telecommunications media (Stadtlander, 1998). Web technology allows teachers to create multidimensional experiences that combine text, audio and video in a media-rich environment and engage the learners (Sensiper, 2000). The advantages offered by online (e.g., access to information, location, convenience) are reduced by drawbacks (e.g., time required for course design, faculty training). For many teachers, the use of technology is basic (e.g., e-mail, and dissemination of course materials), as per Vodanovich and Piotrowski (2001). In contrast, many of the current and future students are well immersed in technology.

Brown (2002) noted that today's students are always multiprocessing, and that ICT is a way of life for them. Some teachers note that it is difficult to teach students who are always on the computer, because their seemingly continuous multitasking changes the way they learn. The Web allows for two-way communication, much more so than the on-ground environment: What is discussed in the on-ground classroom is usually intended for the entire class. Not necessarily so online, where some communication are intended for a specific person.

The use of technology does not necessarily enhance the reaching out to students. The ability to connect emotionally with students makes for a "special" professor. Students have different communication needs than their teachers; this is especially true for the younger students, who prefer speed to face-to-face contact (Arnone, 2002).

Differences Among Modalities

The seventh category, *Differences Among Modalities,* pertains to differences among the online, hybrid, and on-ground classrooms.

Teachers report cognitive changes when teaching online, in the way that they shift to a deeper level of cognitive complexity (Walters Coppola, Hiltz, & Rotter, 2002). When teaching online, the instructional roles and teaching strategies are different from the point of view that a dramatic increase in demands on both teacher and students are noted. Inducing collaboration online requires a different design structure for activities, discussions, and assignments.

Online conversations are much more time-consuming. A significant challenge for teachers is how to create a supportive, stimulating, cognitive environment online. Teaching online is different, yet it does not require a completely new approach to teaching. For the online teacher, taking on a social moderator role is critical (Wiesenberg, 1999). Faculty members change their role when teaching online, with the focus shifting on facilitation and collaboration (Klassen & Vogel, 2003). With regard to classroom dynamics, for some teachers, they remain the same (Greenblatt, 2001). Other teachers feel that online, everything takes place at great speed; that it is a young person's medium. At times, teachers report a need to slow down the interaction in order to be able to control it (Hameroff, 2003). A great difference between the online and the on-ground environments is that the online classroom removes the need for the teacher. The student forms a relationship with the text, not with the professor. This requires a student-centered approach, appropriate for the nonlinear nature of the course (Knowlton, 2000).

Issues

The eighth category, *Issues,* pertains to factors that teachers identify in relation to online education.

Administrative

The administrative subject can be analyzed from both the teachers' and the school administrators' point of view. As an increasing number of colleges and universities offer online programs (Goral, 2001), distance education is moving into every industry, with online training being more pervasive than online education (Carnevale, 2003). Universities try to determine to what extent business decisions should drive their institutional policies (Wysocki, 2005). Tensions exist between the research and teaching components of the faculty role (Serow, 2000). Many faculty members in colleges and universities are embittered: They report feelings of regret, envy, frustration, betrayal, and isolation. This affects their attitudes toward work (Jensen, 1995). One study reports that 32% of the teachers would not volunteer to teach online, and 54% of them believed the quality of the course is lower online.

The increase in faculty resistance to technology is due in part to teachers' perception that it distorts the educational experience (Rayburn & Ramaprasad, 2002).Teachers who generally use little technology seem to be more likely to hold negative views about the online process. More from the point of view of faculty members, their perception is that there is a lack of appreciation for the teachers teaching online; they would also like to have better students (Magna Publications, 2004). Other issues the teachers have relate to inadequate access to appropriate ICT, excessive focus on business goals, and lack of support (Klobas & Renzi, 2003). As faculty is pressured by changes from education globalization and the potential of ICT to radically transform education delivery, there is more of a challenge for teachers who were formed under different circumstances (Clegg, Konrad, & Tan, 2000). In order to facilitate the education process, teachers need well-developed policies and guidelines for online education (Ershler, 2003). They need help in the development and delivery of course materials (Klassen & Vogel, 2003). A teacher is expected to teach, and to participate scholarly. Yet, building an online course may require 300 hours and $35,000 to $55,000 (Carnevale, 2004b). Despite all the difficulties, teachers who are interested in technology will eventually learn how to use it effectively for teaching (Speck, 2000).

As applies to school administrators, they focus on the fiscal implications of online education. As a result of this, the number of part-time faculty members is growing faster than that of full-time members (Feenberg, 1999). Teaching online seems cost effective (Greenblatt, 2001). Nationwide, in 2005 nearly half of all college faculty members are part-timer teachers, up from only 22% in 1970 (Hersh, Merrow, & Wolfe, 2005). Institutional administrators have to contend with various personnel issues: faculty skills, new personnel needed, faculty compensation, and resistance to technology. Faculty members' compensation includes money, tenure, release time, and course load. Current policies regarding personnel appear to be ad hoc.

Curriculum

There is very little experience in developing instruction for delivery online, and for teaching online. Teachers have to restructure much of what they have done routinely in the on-ground classroom, in order to become effective online (Meyen & Lian, 1997). There is a tendency to reformat course materials and learning strategies to fit the technology. Too much focus is on technology rather than education, and this compromises both students and the subject being taught online (Minasian-Batmanian, 2002). The design and delivery of courses that integrate new technologies is challenging. Technology may end up being used at a superficial level, and it may not have an impact on teaching practice (Torrisi & Davis, 2000). Information technology provides a challenge to teachers and course curriculum designers alike. For best success, developing online courses requires a team approach, because it is complicated and takes significant time (Chou & Tsai, 2002). For the course designers, it is advisable to avoid a cookie-cutter approach (Ershler, 2003) and to avoid technology limitations and design courses for maximum effect. Teaching, learning, and evaluation must reflect the differences between modalities (Ohler & Theall, 2004). Designing online instructional materials requires insight from instructional design, information design, interaction design, and graphic design (Shank & Sitze, 2004). Best practices in teaching are student-centered, collaborative and constructivist (Tomei, 2003).

Issues

Various issues arise with regard to the instructional process online and the increased use of technology in teaching in general. They arise from all the participants in the process, teachers, schools and students alike. Navarro (2000) was concerned that cyber-learning is a catalyst for replacing the teacher with "diploma mills." The Internet provides students with better access to information and educational resources. Yet, the Web-based instruction introduces new concerns and needs for the learners. There is a new need for the schools to help their online learners (Lowry, Thornam, & White, 2000).

Some teachers fear teaching online, as they feel it would erase their presence in the classroom (Banks, 1998). They find the expectations are exacerbated: Online students expect instantaneous service, and teachers need significant time to properly respond to students. Online teachers have no sick or personal days when teaching online. As long as the technology functions, the course is always on (Laird, 2003). Online faculty members spend significantly more time to develop Web courses (Cristianson, Tiene, & Luft, 2002). Teachers spend more time teaching online yet receive no additional compensation (National Educational Association, 2000).

Assessment is difficult, and the instructors would like to know more about their online students (Meyen & Lian, 1997). Online teachers have no way of knowing whether their students study all the course material, not just the material that is needed to complete the assignments (Bergstrom et al., 2004; Parikh, 2003). Internet abuse is more prevalent among Internet users taking online courses than those taking offline courses (Morahan-Martin, 2001). Online education is great for students who are mature, engaged, and well-organized (Seguin, 2002).

Online, there is a lack of spontaneous interaction and fewer stimuli in general (Carr, 2000a). As the teachers interviewed here indicate, online discussions seldom start spontaneously. They often have to do more probing, and to ask students to participate. Some of the online discussions are brief—certainly shorter than classroom-based discussions of the same issues.

Teachers are concerned with technical knowledge and technological access (Lauzon, Gallant, & Rimkus, 2000). Where teaching hands-on aspects of the course are important, computer simulation may be useful in replacing some lab activities (Carr,

2000b). Once again, the teachers I interviewed exhibit a preference for blending online and on-ground classes, where feasible, as a solution to the difficulties they encounter conveying some ideas online. In particular, on-ground sessions could be used for demonstrations that cannot easily be done online.

Adjustments

The ninth category, *Adjustments,* pertains to the modifications teachers make to their style, delivery, teaching, course materials, and philosophy when switching teaching modalities.

Ohler and Theall (2004) showed that teachers do not seem to have operationalized the differences between online and face-to-face instruction to adjust their teaching and assessment strategies. In contrast, this book reports that teachers make certain adjustments to how they teach in order to compensate for the differences among modalities.

Faculty members are influenced by intrinsic factors (e.g., convenience, comfort, common interests, future purposes) and extrinsic factors (e.g., external pressures). Some teachers are early adopters of distance education; others are reluctant to integrate technology into their instruction (Grant, 2004).

The literature shows that online education leads teachers to modify their approaches to teaching (Campbell, McGee, & Yates, 1997). The teachers interviewed for this book do indeed report they modify how they teach online. Yet, the academic culture is durable and resistant to change. While it is not difficult to change course materials, there are other decisions to make when adjusting to online teaching. Teachers who decide to teach online face decisions that will influence their teaching role and strategies. Naturally, these decisions are shaped by their beliefs, and the values they hold about teaching.

One study found that teachers who use video-conferencing adjust by being more entertaining, and theatrical (Grosse, 2004). They do so in response to seeing their faces on the screen, and to their increased awareness of how they look on the screen. While in the on-ground classroom, feedback comes from the students and not from seeing oneself in the mirror or screen. The teachers who participated in this study believe they used more theatrics in the on-ground classes, perhaps because they did not use video to teach live online.

Teachers become more conscious of their teaching, when combining face-to-face and online teaching (McShane, 2004). The data derived from our teacher interviews appear to indicate that when switching to a new teaching environment, teachers report increased awareness of how their teaching works (or does not work) in the new environment. They become more self-conscious and look for solutions to the issues they identify.

One study reports that teachers enjoy online discussion forums as the threaded discussions offer participants more choices, allow more diverse opinions, and can lead to deeper analysis (Li, 2003). Thus, they learn to focus more on interactivity and less on content and to give up some control (Pallof & Pratt, 2001). The opinions of the teachers who participated in the study that forms the foundation of this book vary in that not everyone agreed there was more quality in online discussions. While they recognized having difficulties at times controlling the flow of the online discussions, I did not find evidence that online teachers focus more on interactivity. If anything, interactivity is harder to attain online, given the asynchronous character of the media. Teachers do indicate that, at times, some degree of real-time interaction (i.e., interactivity), would be beneficial.

Gaining

Convenience, financial gains, and a feel of helping students better themselves in a way that on-ground teaching does not facilitate are just a few of the gains the teachers perceive when switching to the online method of teaching. Per Carnevale (2004a), when teaching online, teachers can teach more courses, for different schools, with less concern for institutional politics, and earn more money. For the teachers who teach both online, and on-ground modalities, they can supplement their on-ground instruction with technology from their online classes (Woods, Baker, & Hopper, 2004). More so, online courses prove to be convenient by meeting academic needs and helping students improve technological skills (Leonard & Guha, 2001).

Online, development of a deeper level of thinking has been documented, due to written communication; stronger relationships also seem to form (Smith et al., 2002). Web technology can also help students prepare for the social, academic, and personal challenges of higher education and offer a useful supplement to classroom instruction (Shafer, Davis, Lahner, Petrie, & Calderone, 2002).

Giving Up

Online teaching follows a steep learning curve, and online instruction requires regular contact between teacher and students. It is possible for online students to fall behind because they are "invisible." The loss of personal contact is a concern to teachers and students alike (Weiss, 2000). The online environment makes it difficult for the teacher to help students who are having problems with practical exercises (Bergstrom et al., 2004), while online discussions are difficult to establish and coordinate (Bonk, 2004). Knowledge is socially constructed. Isolation and lack of contact with faculty members may be a problem to developing effective learning communities (Grubb & Hines, 2000). Course materials require significant time to prepare, and everything must be prepared before the course starts, not just 1 week in advance (Kubala, 1998).

Choice

The tenth category, *Choice,* pertains to the choices made by teachers, to whether they choose to teach certain modalities or leave the profession altogether.

Many teachers leave the profession after a few years of teaching. They are frustrated by the emotional, physical, and psychological demands of the classroom (Darling-Hammond, 1990). Full-time faculty members are reluctant to go online (Carnevale, 2004a) and many teachers resist the effort to be forced into distance education. These teachers are concerned with institutional support, interaction, and education quality issues (Bower, 2001). Inadequate support can diminish teachers' enthusiasm, sense of purpose, and effort. Those who experience acute frustration may leave the profession (Baird, 1999). However, none of the participants I interviewed expressed this choice.

In one study, most teachers preferred online teaching to the traditional classroom (Cristianson et al., 2002). Some teachers preferred a hybrid model. Yet, there are still questions whether the hybrid modality can really support quality education (K. P. King, 2002).

This book reports that the majority of the teachers I interviewed have a preference for a hybrid model. They consider it to be the optimal teaching modality. However, the on-ground classroom still ranks high in their preferences.

A Theory of the Online Teaching Experience

The initial categories derived from interview data converge around 10 main categories: *Adjustments, Choice, Differences Among Modalities, Issues, Teacher Needs, Teaching, Teaching Demands, Teaching Dimensions Dimensions," Teaching With Technology,* and *Technology.* The triangulation of the core categories identified from interview data with the published literature proves the validity of the categories. This section discusses in detail their respective relationships.

Relationships

Relational statements that describe the interplay among categories are derived from data. Strauss and Corbin (1998) showed that relational statements can be woven into the narrative of the theory, as they are instrumental in showing how the categories are interrelated. As causal statements, relationships show how a change in one of the categories leads to a change in another category. Given the complexity of the model presented here, the findings are neither exhaustive nor do they explicate the entire web of relationships present in the model.

Teaching Demands has a direct effect on *Teaching*. The expectations set by the school administration affect *Teaching*. Class size is an important issue: Teachers prefer smaller classes and believe that larger classes make quality teaching more difficult. The quality of the students in the class is instrumental to improving teaching experience. Student assessment and feedback affect *Teaching*. So are the availability of office hours and the amount of effort required to plan and prepare for class.

Teaching Dimensions affect *Teacher Needs*. Teachers have their own views of the profession. For many of them, teaching is a vocation; yet for some teachers, teaching is a job. Teachers' own philosophies and views of teaching affect *Teacher Needs*, in terms of what they expect from the profession.

Teacher Needs affect *Teaching*. Teachers have multiple needs: rapport with their students, administrative aspects (e.g., administrative support, course design), faculty development, peer support, emotional involvement, and incentives, appreciation, and rewards. For some teachers, building rapport with their students is important; when they feel they cannot accomplish this, their *Teaching* is negatively affected. The level of administrative support available to teachers also affects their *Teaching* in the way that when teachers find administrative support to be inadequate, it negatively affects it. Teachers need help with course design; teachers who receive adequate support for course design feel that their teaching improves. Faculty development has a positive effect on *Teaching*. When adequate training is offered, teachers are more likely to accept online teaching assignments. For teachers who find that meeting their emotional needs is important, their teaching will be negatively affected when their emotional needs are not met. Teacher appreciation and compensation is very important to teachers. When adequate incentives and compensation are available, and their efforts are appreciated, teachers are more likely to accept new (online) teaching assignments. The availability of peer support groups also has a positive effect on *Teaching*.

Technology affects *Teaching With Technology*, and *Differences Among Modalities*. Technology availability, reliability, and ease of use are very important to teachers. They are more likely to use technology in their online teaching when they find that it meets their needs—that it is reliable and easy to use. When quality technical support is available, teachers are more likely to use technology in their online teaching. *Technology* may be used differently across modalities: Teachers who teach online rely on technology to a greater extent.

Teaching With Technology affects *Teaching*. Teachers have different needs: To some, synchronicity is more important than media richness. To others, the opposite is true.

When teachers believe that *Technology* is appropriate and can be used successfully to support online teaching, they will be more agreeable to accept online teaching assignments.

Teaching is affected by *Teaching Demands, Teacher Needs,* and *Teaching With Technology.* In an online class, teachers are less likely to improvise. There is more improvisation in an on-ground classroom. For some teachers, the interplay between *Teaching Demands* and *Teacher Needs* results in a show-like dimension of *Teaching.* Teachers who teach online are less likely to describe their *Teaching* in terms that describe a *Show/Theatrical Performance* than those who teach on-ground.

The category *Issues* is affected by *Differences Among Modalities* and by *Teaching.* The sum of the effects induced by *Differences Among Modalities* and *Teaching* affects teachers' satisfaction, their teaching effectiveness and efficiency and their communication style. In turn, *Issues* affects *Adjustments.* In response to the *Issues* they identify, teachers will make adjustments.

Adjustments affect *Choice.* The magnitude of the *Adjustments* required, combined with the relative importance of the *Issues,* leads teachers to make a *Choice.* They will also make a *Choice* depending on their teaching philosophy (*Teaching Dimensions*) and whether or not their *Teaching Needs* are satisfied. The *Choice* may be to stay in one teaching modality to avoid teaching online or to leave the teaching profession altogether.

A Theory of the Online Teaching Experience

The main outcome of the analysis was the emergence of 10 central categories: *Adjustments, Choice, Differences Among Modalities, Issues, Teacher Needs, Teaching, Teaching Demands, Teaching Dimensions, Teaching With Technology,* and *Technology.*

Teachers react to what they experience as teaching online. They may enjoy the experience and continue to teach online, or their frustration may lead them to avoid doing it. Teachers may decide to continue teaching in the on-ground classroom, or may decide to leave teaching altogether. The choice they make is the result of various factors. They react to the online environment, the technology, and to administrative and academic issues.

The categories derived from data were aggregated at a higher level of abstraction into 10 main categories, as stated earlier. The relationships among categories are depicted in Figure 1.

Figure 1. Main categories and relationships

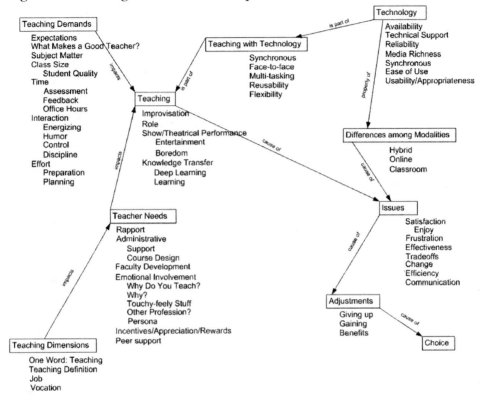

Teaching Dimensions

This category reflects the intrinsic factors (e.g., teacher philosophy, talent, interests) that drive teachers. Teachers are hard-working, dedicated individuals who care deeply about their profession. A teacher who views teaching as a vocation is more likely to be greatly concerned with the quality of teaching. When they perceive the quality of teaching is negatively affected by the online modality, they are less likely to teach online and may refuse to do it.

The overall impression is that very few faculty members refer to teaching in terms that describe a job. For most, teaching is a vocation. Adjunct faculty members are more likely to have strong opinions about teaching online and to avoid teaching online when they find that their needs are not being met. In contrast, academic faculty members more often describe their online teaching experiences as positive. Among adjunct faculty, there are several teachers who appear to be relatively unaffected by the differences between their on-ground and online teaching and are satisfied with the status quo. Those practitioner faculty teachers who taught at more than one school were more likely to report positive experiences teaching online.

Teacher Needs

Those teachers who value rapport with their students, and feel there is less potential for building rapport online, are more likely to avoid teaching online. A lower level of administrative support also reduces teachers' desire to teach online. Course design requires a great deal of faculty time and effort. For this reason, faculty members who do not feel they are provided with adequate resources, support, flexibility to make their own changes, and training to acquire skills that allows them to improve and/or optimize course content and delivery may avoid teaching these online courses.

Teachers need opportunities to improve their skills related to course design, class assessment techniques, and technology in general. When they feel that their skills are inadequate, teachers avoid teaching online. Adjunct faculty members would seemingly benefit from receiving more training. Such training should include technology and teaching-related topics.

Teachers' personal needs drive their expectations and lead to certain outcomes (i.e., satisfaction, personal growth and development). The technology just mediates the experience. Teachers have emotional needs. They need the interaction with students, and like to build rapport with their students. They enjoy receiving, and need the feedback they get in class. This helps them monitor the class, and the learning experience in general.

Teaching Demands

These are extrinsic factors that are controllable by school administrators. Teachers do not feel comfortable teaching every subject the same way. For teachers who would like to have access to different delivery mechanisms, it is important to offer them a variety of technologies to choose from (e.g., synchronous, real-time interaction; multimedia; simulations). When teachers do not feel they can effectively teach a course online, they may/will refuse to teach it online. Teachers who feel they are spending an excessive amount of time engaged in online teaching activities may determine that they are not fairly compensated for the extra effort, and consequently will avoid teaching online courses. An increase in time demands for the online teacher should be correlated with an increase in compensation, or other incentives and rewards. Otherwise, teachers may feel they are not adequately compensated and may avoid teaching online.

Teaching demands are predicated upon sets of expectations that come from teachers themselves, from their students, and from school administration. Academic dimensions relate to course and curriculum design. Subject matters have particular characteristics that translate into varying expectations. Teachers are concerned with student assessment issues, particularly in the online environment that offers fewer opportunities to assess the student. Teachers strive to meet expectations set by themselves, school administration, and students. While they react to administrators' and students' expectations, their personal expectations may appear to be the most important.

The quality and quantity of interaction taking place online is important to teachers. When they feel the interaction is inadequate, they are more likely to find they are less effective in their teaching and consequently more likely to avoid the online environment. For those teachers who thrive on the energy in the classroom, the online environment is not a desirable option.

Teachers find new and amplified problems in the online environment. They find it more difficult to address plagiarism, and to verify that their students are actually taking the examinations. Other demands are those related to time management and course organization. Schools that elect to rely on adjunct faculty (also called "instructor," "part-time," "practitioner," or "clinical" faculty) do so because they cost less. This is usually the case when courses are short (i.e., 5-6 weeks for a 3-unit course).

Teaching

When teaching, teachers engage in improvisation and informative entertainment, to some extent. For those teachers who consider teaching to be more like a theatrical performance ("the sage on the stage"), it is important to find this happens online. Should they not be able to replicate their showmanship online, they are less likely to teach online.

Teachers agree that teaching is not for everyone. Good teaching is about human interaction more than it is about technology. Technology is simply another tool used to augment and support teaching.

Learning does take place online, yet teachers do not agree on exactly *how much* learning. Some teachers feel that there is more learning, while others feel there is less learning online. At times, some teachers may feel they need to have more time with the students, as they are offloading a lot of material on them.

Technology

Teachers may avoid teaching online when they find the technology is not easy to use, unreliable, or just inappropriate for supporting quality teaching. Teachers who value real-time interaction are turned off by the lack of synchronous, real-time interaction in the online environment and are more likely to refuse to teach online.

The technology used in teaching poses specific concerns. First, the availability of technology varies. Second, teachers do not always have the necessary skills to use the technology they have available, or the one they would like to use. Third, the degree of usefulness of a given technology is subjectively determined by the users.

Teaching With Technology

Teachers use technology on a daily basis, irrespective of the education modality. They appreciate having access to technology that is easy to use, reliable, and offers adequate support for the subject matter being taught online. Teachers recognize the constraints set by technology and change accordingly. They change their teaching approach in terms of style, preparation of course materials, curriculum, and delivery method. Online, their lectures evolve into discussions.

Differences Among Modalities

Teachers note various differences among classroom, online, and hybrid modalities. Those of them who value face-to-face interaction are more likely to avoid teaching online. Teachers who put a significant value on the flexibility afforded by the online environment are more likely to teach online.

Issues

Teachers are sensitized to and identify various issues related to teaching modalities. The interplay between *Teaching Demands, Teacher Needs, Teaching, Teaching With Technology,* and *Differences Among Modalities* increases their awareness of the perceived advantages and disadvantages of each teaching modality.

Academic faculty members seem to have more consideration for, and awareness of, the online environment. Overall, teachers indicate that quality education may be achieved online. Yet, that is heavily dependent on technology, its availability and actual use, on careful selection of courses, faculty academic freedom, and student quality.

Teachers do not seem overly concerned with the possibility of building a two-tier educational system. Rather, a self-selection of students seems apparent, as the online education environment has more stringent requirements for self-discipline. This seems to be acceptable, in the end. Interaction is important to teachers, yet, some see more, and some see less interaction online.

Adjustments

Teachers respond to the issues they identify by making adjustments in their teaching, beliefs, and motivation. When teaching online, they adjust to the increased demand for structure by specifying more of the course upfront, and providing detailed instructions and guidance to their students. As their time management and organizational skills improve, these improvements transfer to their classroom teaching.

Choice

Teachers who place significant value on real-time, face-to-face interaction, as offered in a traditional classroom, are more likely to avoid teaching online. Also, teachers who are insecure about their potential effectiveness in the online environment are less likely to accept online teaching assignments when offered.

Those teachers who choose not to teach online do it for a variety of reasons. Yet, this is more prevalent among adjunct faculty. Whether online teaching is optional for all faculty members needs to be explored further.

A Grounded Theory of Teaching Online

The opinions expressed by the teachers interviewed reflect personal needs related to rapport, school administration, academic support, curriculum support, technology support, faculty development, and technology training. The theory presented here was developed and is consistent with the precepts of grounded theory research.

Teachers love to teach. To the majority of them, teaching is a vocation. To them, the real purpose of an education is not merely to transmit information but to transform people; to help students learn how to use that information as a source and means of self-inspiration; to foster self-development, self-transformation, and respect for themselves and others to improve the world in which we live. In this regard, education is about the moral development and character growth of students, not just preparing them to get a job. Yet, it seems the majority of these teachers are talking about knowledge, and information transfer. That is, they are not talking about education, but about transferring something (e.g., skills, knowledge). This seems different from the classical view of the teacher as an educator (Dreeben, 1970).

Teachers reflect on their *Teaching*. The explicit factors related to *Teaching Demands* and *Teaching Needs,* and the implicit ones associated with the *Teaching Dimensions* category, are at the core of their experience. They are exposed to *Teaching With Technology* as they use *Technology* inside and outside the classroom. Technology takes on a new dimension in online education. Consequently, they become sensitized and notice *Differences Among Modalities,* and this leads them to identify a number of *Issues* related their *Teaching.* In response to the perceived *Differences Among Modalities* and the *Issues* they identify, teachers make *Adjustments.* Teachers gain an increased awareness of how online teaching affects them, of what it means for their teaching. The magnitude of the *Adjustments* required, combined with the relative importance of the *Issues,* their teaching philosophy (i.e., *Teaching Dimensions*), and whether or not their *Teaching Needs* are satisfied, leads them to make a *Choice.*

The web of categories, interactions, and relationships described above forms the theory of the online teaching experience. The theory presented above in narrative form reflects the findings from the study. The constructs and relationships are grounded in data collected from interviews conducted with online teachers. Although the relatively large number of constructs may seem to lead to an overly complex theory, the diagrammatic representation and the subsequent detailed discussion should help visualize the constructs and their respective relationships.

Conclusion

Teachers react to the teaching environment in emotional and attitudinal terms. The qualitative nature of the study presented here poses certain limitations. Despite this, the findings may be relevant to teachers involved in online teaching and to administrators supporting online education. Variations in other institutions and online programs may exist, and subsequent operationalization of the study at different sites or with a different sample may lead to other results.

The study at the foundation of this book employed an exploratory, qualitative research paradigm. Consequently, generalization is expected to be limited, given the sample size involved and the procedures for informer selection. The data collection was conducted by means of interviewing, introducing the possibility that interview questions may have been misunderstood by participants. Furthermore, participant and researcher bias are common occurrences and can dramatically affect the results.

This theoretical model of the online teaching experience presented in this chapter applies specifically to the research participants. Ten constructs and their relationships are at the core of the theory that emerged from interview data. In the realm of institutional administrators involved in online education, the theory described in the study offers insight as to what variables can be manipulated and controlled in order to entice teachers to accept online teaching assignments, and to help improve the overall quality of the online education.

My research study relied on interview data to identify categories and relationships that eventually converged around 10 main categories: *Adjustments, Choice, Differences Among Modalities, Issues, Teacher Needs, Teaching, Teaching Demands, Teach-*

ing Dimensions, Teaching With Technology, and *Technology.* A grounded theory of the online teaching experience proposes that teachers make a choice relative to the teaching modality they prefer. Starting with the explicit factors related to *Teaching Demands* and *Teaching Needs,* and the implicit ones associated with the *Teaching Dimensions* category, teachers reflect on their *Teaching.* They are exposed to *Teaching With Technology* as they use *Technology* inside and outside the classroom. Consequently, they become sensitized and notice *Differences Among Modalities,* leading them to identify a number of *Issues* related to subsequent categories. In response to the perceived *Differences Among Modalities* and the *Issues* they identify, teachers make *Adjustments.* The magnitude of the *Adjustments* required, combined with the relative importance of the *Issues,* their teaching philosophy (*Teaching Dimensions*), and whether or not their *Teaching Needs* are satisfied, leads them to make a *Choice.* The *Choice* may be to stay in one teaching modality, to avoid teaching online, or to leave the teaching profession altogether. However, it is only fair to report that none of the participants I interviewed expressed this choice. Institutional administrators interested in online education have the ability to manipulate some of the variables that affect teacher choice, resulting in increased willingness to accept online teaching assignments and increased teaching quality. More research may be needed, as online teaching grows, to substantiate the findings presented here.

References

Aggarwal, A. K., & Bento, R. (2002). Web-based education. In M. Khosrow-Pour (Ed.), *Web-based instructional learning* (pp. 59-77). Hershey, PA: IRM Press.

Ameigh, M. S. (2000). On-line is on target for motivated learners. In R. A. Cole (Ed.), *Issues in Web-based pedagogy* (pp. 339-346). Westport, CT: Greenwood Press.

Anderson, M. D. (2001). Individual characteristics and Web-based courses. In C. Wolfe (Ed.), *Learning and teaching on the World Wide Web* (pp. 47-73). San Diego, CA: Academic Press.

Anderson, T., Rourke, L., Garrison, D. R., & Archer, W. (2001). Assessing teaching presence in a computer conferencing context. *Journal of Asynchronous Learning Networks, 5*(2), 1-17.

Angeli, C., Valanides, N., & Bonk, C. J. (2003). Communication in a Web-based conferencing system: The quality of computer-mediated interactions. *British Journal of Educational Technology, 34*(1), 31-43.

Arnone, M. (2002). Many students' favorite professors shun distance education. *Chronicle of Higher Education, 48*(35).

Babinski, L. M., Jones, B. D., & DeWert, M. H. (2001). The roles of facilitators and peers in an online support community for first-year teachers. *Journal of Educational and Psychological Consultation, 12*(2), 151-169.

Baird, J. R. (1999). A phenomenological exploration of teachers' views of science teaching. *Teachers and Teaching: Theory and Practice, 5*(1), 75-94.

Baker, J. D., Schihl, R. J., & Aggarwal, A. K. (2003). eLearning support systems. In A. K. Aggarwal (Ed.), *Web-based education: Learning from experience* (pp. 223-235). Hershey, PA: Information Science Publishing.

Bangert, A. W. (2004). The seven principles of good practice: A framework for evaluating on-line teaching. *Internet and Higher Education, 7*, 217-232.

Banks, I. (1998). Reliance on technology threatens the essence of teaching. *The Chronicle of Higher Education, 45*(8), B6.

Bergstrom, L., Grahn, K. J., Karlstrom, K., Pulkkis, G., & Astrom, P. (2004). Teaching network security in a virtual learning environment. *Journal of Information Technology Education, 3*, 189-217.

Blair, J. (2002). The virtual teaching life. *Education Week, 21*, 31-34.

Bonk, C. (2004). I should have known this was coming: Computer-mediated discussion in teacher education. *Journal of Research on Technology in Education, 36*(2), 95-102.

Bower, B. L. (2001). Distance education: Facing the faculty challenge. *Online Journal of Distance Learning Administration, 4*(2).

Boyd, D., & Arnold, M. L. (2000). Teachers' beliefs, antiracism and moral education: Problems of intersection. *Journal of Moral Education, 29*(1), 23-46.

Brower, H. H. (2003). On emulating classroom discussion in a distance-delivered OBHR course: Creating an on-line learning community. *Academy of Management Learning and Education, 2*(1), 22-36.

Brown, J. S. (2002). Learning in the digital age. In M. Devlin, R. Larson, & J. Meyerson (Eds.), *The Internet & the university: Forum 2001* (pp. 65-91). Forum for the Future of Higher Education and EDUCAUSE.

Cahn, P. S. (2003). Number crunching. *The Chronicle of Higher Education, 50*(16).

Campbell, N., McGee, C., & Yates, R. (1997). *"It is not out with the old and in with the new": The challenge to adapt to online teaching.* Retrieved April 11, 2005, from http://unisanet.unisa.edu.au/cccc/papers/non-refereed/campbell.htm

Carnevale, D. (2003). Learning online to teach online. *Chronicle of Higher Education, 50*(10).

Carnevale, D. (2004a). For online adjuncts, a seller's market. *Chronicle of Higher Education, 50*(34).

Carnevale, D. (2004b). More professors teach by using other colleges' online courses. *Chronicle of Higher Education, 51*(8).

Carr, S. (2000a). Even public speaking can be taught online. *The Chronicle of Higher Education, 46*(29).

Carr, S. (2000b). Science instructors ask: Can You teach students at a distance how to use microscopes? *The Chronicle of Higher Education, 46*(32).

Chang, C.-K. (2001). Refining collaborative learning strategies for reducing the technical requirements of Web-based classroom management. *Innovations in Education and Teaching International, 38*(2), 133-143.

Chou, C., & Tsai, C. C. (2002). Developing Web-based curricula: Issues and challenges. *Journal of Curriculum Studies, 34*(6), 623-636.

Clegg, S., Konrad, J., & Tan, J. (2000). Preparing academic staff to use ICTs in support of student learning. *The International Journal for Academic Development, 5*(2), 138-148.

Cristianson, L., Tiene, D., & Luft, P. (2002). Examining online instruction in undergraduate nursing education. *Distance Education, 23*(2), 213-229.

Darling-Hammond, L. (1990). *Teacher supply, demand and quality*. Washington, DC: National Board for Professional Teaching Standards.

Dodge, L., & Kendall, M. E. (2004). Learning communities. *College Teaching, 52*(4), 150-155.

Dreeben, R. (1970). *The nature of teaching: Schools and the work of teachers*. Glenview, IL: Scott Foresman and Company.

Duin, A. H. (1998). The culture of distance education: Implementing an online graduate level course in audience analysis. *Technical Communication Quarterly, 7*(4), 365-388.

Ershler, J. (2003). Policy development considerations for administrators and instructors of distance learning programs. *Journal of the United States Distance Learning Association, 17*(2), 1-3.

Feenberg, A. (1999). Distance learning: Promise or threat. *Crosstalk, Winter 1999*, 12-13.

Garrisson, D. R., & Kanuka, H. (2004). Blended learning: Uncovering its transformative potential in higher education. *Internet and Higher Education, 7*, 95-105.

Goral, T. (2001). Teaching old dogs new tricks. *Curriculum Administrator, 37*(2), 59-61.

Grant, M. M. (2004). Learning to teach on the Web: Factors influencing teacher education faculty. *Internet and Higher Education, 7*, 329-341.

Greenblatt, E. (2001). The more things change: Teaching in an online classroom. *Christian Science Monitor, 93,* 17.

Grosse, C. U. (2004). How distance learning changes faculty. *International Journal of Instructional Technology and Distance Learning, 1*(6).

Grubb, A., & Hines, M. (2000). Tearing down barriers and building communities: Pedagogical strategies for the Web-based environment. In R. A. Cole (Ed.), *Issues in Web-based pedagogy* (pp. 365-380). Westport, CT: Greenwood Press.

Hall, R. (2002). Aligning learning, teaching, and assessment using the Web: An evaluation of pedagogic approaches. *British Journal of Educational Technology, 33*(2), 149-158.

Hameroff, G. (2003). Keeping the education in online education. *Community College Week, 15*(20), 10-11.

Hersh, R. H., Merrow, J., & Wolfe, T. (2005). *Declining by degrees: Higher education at risk* [DVD]. New York and Washington, DC: Public Broadcasting Service.

Hinn, D. M., Leander, K., & Bruce, B. (2001). Case studies of a virtual school. *Journal of Adolescent & Adult Literacy, 45*(2), 156-165.

Hodgkinson, M., & Holland, J. (2002). Collaborating on the development of technology enabled distance learning: A case study. *Innovations in Education and Teaching International, 39*(2), 89-94.

Jamieson, P., Fisher, K., Gilding, T., Taylor, P. G., & Trevitt, A. C. F. (2000). Place and space in the design of new learning environments. *Higher Education Research and Development, 19*(2), 221-236.

Jensen, E. J. (1995). The bitter groves of academe. *Change, 27*(1), 8-11.

Johnson, S. D., & Roellke, C. F. (1999). Secondary teachers' and undergraduate education faculty members' perceptions of teaching-effectiveness criteria: A national survey. *Communication Education, 48,* 127-138.

Kim, K.-J., & Bonk, C. J. (2002). Cross-cultural comparisons of online collaboration. *Journal of Computer-Mediated Communication, 6*(1), 1-32.

Kim, T., & Biocca, F. (1998). Telepresence via television: Two dimensions of telepresence may have different connections to memory and persuasion. *Journal of Computer-Mediated Communication, 3*(2), 1-28.

King, C., & McSporran, M. (2002). *Online teaching demands hands-on commitment.* Paper presented at the 15th Annual NACCQ, Hamilton, New Zealand, July 2002.

King, K. P. (2002). Identifying success in online teacher education and professional development. *Internet and Higher Education, 5,* 231-246.

King, K. P., & Dunham, M. D. (2005). Finding our way: Better understanding the needs and motivations of teachers in online learning. *International Journal of Instructional Technology and Distance Learning, 2*(1).

Klassen, J., & Vogel, D. (2003). New issues arising from e-education. In A. K. Aggarwal (Ed.), *Web-based education: Learning from experience* (pp. 36-48). Hershey, PA: Information Science Publishing.

Klipowicz, S. W., & Laniak, T. (1999). Hebrew exegesis online: Using information technology to enhance biblical language study. *Teaching Technology and Religion, 2*(2), 109-115.

Klobas, J., & Renzi, S. (2003). Integrating online educational activities in traditional courses: University-wide lessons after three years. In A. K. Aggarwal (Ed.), *Web-based education: Learning from experience* (pp. 415-439). Hershey, PA: Information Science Publishing.

Knowlton, D. S. (2000). A theoretical framework for the online classroom: A defense and delineation of a student-centered pedagogy. In B. W. Speck (Ed.), *New directions for teaching and learning. Principles of effective teaching in the online classroom* (Vol. 84, pp. 5-22).

Kubala, T. (1998). Addressing student needs: Teaching on the Internet. *T H E Journal, 28*(5), 71-74.

Laird, E. (2003). I'm your teacher, not your Internet-service provider. *Chronicle of Higher Education, 49*(17), B5.

Lauzon, A. C., Gallant, T. B., & Rimkus, S. (2000). A hierarchy of access issues affecting on-line participation by community college students. In R. A. Cole (Ed.), *Issues in Web-based pedagogy* (pp. 317-337). Westport, CT: Greenwood Press.

Leonard, J., & Guha, S. (2001). Education at the crossroads: Online teaching and students' perspectives on distance learning. *Journal of Research on Technology in Education, 34*(1), 51-57.

Li, Q. (2003). Would we teach without technology? A professor's experience of teaching mathematics education incorporating the Internet. *Educational Research, 45*(1), 61-77.

Littlejohn, A. H. (2002). Improving continuing professional development in the use of ICT. *Journal of Computer Assisted Learning, 18*, 166-174.

Lo, Y.-H. G. (2002). Teaching behind the computer screen: An international graduate student's experiences in online education. *Reading Online, Nov. 2002*, 39-50.

Lombard, M., & Ditton, T. (1997). At the heart of it all: The concept of presence. *Journal of Computer-Mediated Communication, 3*(2).

Lowry, M., Thornam, C., & White, C. T. (2000). Preparing higher education learners for success on the Web. In R. A. Cole (Ed.), *Issues in Web-based pedagogy* (pp. 297-316). Westport, CT: Greenwood Press.

Magna Publications. (2004). *Gauging faculty attitudes about teaching online.* Retrieved May 11, 2005, from http://www.magnapubs.com/pub/magna-pubs_der/8_5/

Marold, K. A., Larsen, G., & Moreno, A. (2002). Web-based learning: Is it working? A comparison of student performance and achievement in Web-based courses and their in-classroom counterparts. In M. Khosrow-Pour (Ed.), *Web-based instructional learning* (pp. 179-189). Hershey, PA: IRM Press.

McShane, K. (2004). Integrating face-to-face and online teaching: Academics' role concept and teaching choices. *Teaching in Higher Education, 9*(1), 3-16.

Merrill, D. W., & Reid, R. H. (1981). *Personal styles and effective performance.* Radnor, PA: Chilton Book Company.

Meyen, E., L., & Lian, C. H. T. (1997). Teaching online courses. *Focus on Autism & Other Developmental Disabilities, 12*(3), 1-17.

Minasian-Batmanian, L. C. (2002). Guidelines for developing an online learning strategy for your subject. *Medical Teacher, 24*(6), 645-657.

Mohrman, S. A., Tenkasi, R. V., & Mohrman Jr., A. M. (2003). The role of networks in fundamental organizational change. *The Journal of Applied Behavioral Science, 39*(3), 301-323.

Morahan-Martin, J. (2001). Caught in the Web: Research and criticism of Internet abuse with application to college students. In C. Wolfe (Ed.), *Learning and teaching on the World Wide Web* (pp. 191-220). San Diego, CA: Academic Press.

Morinaka, B. S. (2003). Online education: Where should it be? *Journal of the United States Distance Learning Association, 17*(2), 83-84.

National Educational Association. (2000). *A survey of traditional and distance learning higher education members.* Washington, DC: National Educational Association.

Navarro, P. (2000). The Promise—and potential pitfalls—of cyberlearning. In R. A. Cole (Ed.), *Issues in Web-based pedagogy* (pp. 281-296). Westport, CT: Greenwood Press.

Nicol, D., Minty, I., & Sinclair, C. (2003). The social dimensions of online learning. *Innovations in Education and Teaching International, 40*(3), 270-280.

Ohler, S., & Theall, M. (2004). *An exploratory study of teacher opinions about teaching and learning on-line and face-to-face: the instructional choices of a sample of faculty in computer science.* Paper presented at the Instructional

Evaluation and Faculty Development Conference, San Diego, CA, April 12-13, 2004.

Orey, M., Koenecke, L., & Crozier, J. (2002). Learning communities via the Internet à la epic learning: You can lead the horses to water, but you cannot get them to drink. *Innovations in Education and Teaching International, 40*(3), 260-269.

Pallof, R. M., & Pratt, K. (1999). *Building learning communities in cyberspace: Effective strategies for the online classroom.* San Francisco: Jossey-Bass Publishers.

Pallof, R. M., & Pratt, K. (2001). *Lessons from the cyberspace classroom: The realities of online teaching.* San Francisco: Jossey-Bass.

Parikh, M. A. (2003). Beyond the Web: Leveraging multiple Internet technologies. In A. K. Aggarwal (Ed.), *Web-based education: Learning from experience* (pp. 120-130). Hershey, PA: Information Science Publishing.

Paris, D. C. (2000). Is there a professor in this class? In R. A. Cole (Ed.), *Issues in Web-based pedagogy* (pp. 95-110). Westport, CT: Greenwood Press.

Parker, A. (2003). Identifying predictors of academic persistence in distance education. *USDLA Journal, 17*(1).

Pike, R. (1989). *Creative training techniques handbook, tips, tactics and how-to's for delivering effective training.* Minneapolis, MN: Lakewood Books.

Rayburn, W. E., & Ramaprasad, A. (2002). Three strategies for the use of distance learning technology in higher education. In M. Khosrow-Pour (Ed.), *Web-based instructional learning* (pp. 27-42). Hershey, PA: IRM Press.

Robinson, P. (2000). Where is every-body? In R. A. Cole (Ed.), *Issues in Web-based pedagogy* (pp. 111-123). Westport, CT: Greenwood Press.

Rockwell, K., Schauer, J., Fritz, S. M., & Marx, D. B. (2000). Faculty education, assistance and support needed to deliver education via distance. *Online Journal of Distance Learning Administration, 3*(2).

Rosenberg, M. J. (2001). *E-learning: Strategies for delivering knowledge in the digital age.* New York: McGraw-Hill.

Schell, G. P. (2004). Universities marginalize online courses. *Communications of the ACM, 47*(11), 107-112.

SchWeber, C. (2000). The "time" factor in on-line teaching: Implications for faculty and their universities. In R. A. Cole (Ed.), *Issues in Web-based pedagogy* (pp. 227-236). Westport, CT: Greenwood Press.

Seguin, C. (2002). Games online students play: Building a firewall new instructors (and burned out 'old ones') can use. *TechTrends, 46*(4), 23-57.

Sengupta, S. (2001). Exchanging ideas with peers in network-based classrooms: An aid or a pain? *Language Learning & Technology, 5*(1), 103-134.

Sensiper, S. (2000). Making the case online. Harvard Business School multimedia. *Information, Communication and Society, 3*(4), 616-621.

Serow, R. C. (2000). Research and teaching at a research university. *Higher Education, 40,* 449-463.

Shafer, M. J., Davis, J. E., Lahner, J. M., Petrie, T. A., & Calderone, W. K. (2002). The use and effectiveness of a Web-based instructional supplement in a college student success program. *Journal of College Student Development, 43*(5), 751-757.

Shank, P., & Sitze, A. (2004). *Making sense of online learning: a guide for beginners and the truly skeptical.* San Francisco: Pfeiffer.

Shulman, L. S. (2000). Inventing the future. In P. Hutchings (Ed.), *Opening lines: Approaches to the scholarship of teaching and learning.* Menlo Park, CA: The Carnegie Foundation for the Advancement of Teaching.

Smith, G. G., Ferguson, D., & Caris, M. (2002). Teaching over the Web versus in the classroom: Differences in the instructor experience. *International Journal of Instructional Media, 29*(1), 61-67.

Speck, B. W. (2000). The academy, online classes, and the breach in ethics. In B. W. Speck (Ed.), *New directions for teaching and learning. Principles of effective teaching in the online classroom* (Vol. 84, pp. 73-82).

Stadtlander, L. M. (1998). Virtual instruction: Teaching an online graduate seminar. *Teaching of Psychology, 25*(2), 146-148.

Strauss, A., & Corbin, J. (1998). *Basics of qualitative research* (2nd ed.). Thousand Oaks, CA: Sage.

Sullivan, P. (2002). "It's easier to be yourself when you are invisible": Female college students discuss their online classroom experiences. *Innovative Higher Education, 27*(2), 129-144.

Tomei, L., A. (2003). *Challenges of teaching with technology across the curriculum: Issues and solutions.* Hershey, PA: Information Science Publishing.

Torrisi, G., & Davis, G. (2000). Online learning as a catalyst for reshaping practice—The experiences of some academics developing online learning materials. *The International Journal for Academic Development, 5*(2), 166-176.

Vodanovich, S. J., & Piotrowski, C. (2001). Internet-based instruction: A national survey of psychology faculty. *Journal of Instructional Psychology, 28*(4), 253-255.

Walters Coppola, N., Hiltz, S. R., & Rotter, N. G. (2002). Becoming a virtual professor: Pedagogical roles and asynchronous learning networks. *Journal of Management Information Systems, 18*(4), 69-89.

Weems, G. H. (2002). Comparison of beginning algebra taught onsite versus online. *Journal of Development Education, 26*(1), 10-19.

Weiss, R. E. (2000). Humanizing the online classroom. *New Directions for Teaching and Learning, 84*, 47-51.

Wiesenberg, F. (1999). Teaching on-line: One instructor's evolving 'theory-of-practice.' *Adult Basic Education, 9*(3), 1-10.

Woods, R., Baker, J. D., & Hopper, D. (2004). Hybrid structures: Faculty use and perception of Web-based courseware as supplement to face-to-face instruction. *Internet and Higher Education, 7*, 281-297.

Wysocki, B. (2005, February 23). How Dr. Papadakis runs a university like a company. *The Wall Street Journal, CCXLV,* A1.

Chapter XII

Conclusions and Recommendations

Introduction

This chapter concludes the discussion of the online teaching experience by making a few suggestions and offering advice presumably valuable to school administrators, online teachers, online curriculum and course developers as well as to educational technology professionals. It discusses ways to influence teachers to teach online—a direct application of the theory presented in the previous chapter. The intent of the chapter is to help these constituencies adjust to and be able to exert a positive effect on online education and online teaching in particular.

Background

In the previous chapters the views of the online teachers were reviewed and excerpts were presented from the stories they have shared in such an honest manner. The study that made this book possible relied on interview data to identify categories and relationships that eventually converged around 10 main categories: *Adjustments, Choice, Differences Among Modalities, Issues, Teacher Needs, Teaching, Teaching Demands, Teaching Dimensions, Teaching With Technology,* and *Technology.* It was found that these 10 categories were at the core of the online teaching experience. The categories and their respective relationship led to a theory of the online teaching experience, from the teachers' perspective.

A grounded theory of the online teaching experience proposes that teachers make a choice relative to the teaching modality they prefer. Starting with the explicit factors related to *Teaching Demands* and *Teaching Needs,* and the implicit ones associated with the *Teaching Dimensions* category, teachers reflect on their *Teaching.* They are exposed to *Teaching With Technology* as they use *Technology* inside and outside the classroom. Consequently, they become sensitized and notice *Differences Among Modalities,* leading them to identify a number of *Issues* related to subsequent categories. In response to the perceived *Differences Among Modalities* and the *Issues* they identify, teachers make *Adjustments.* The magnitude of the *Adjustments* required, combined with the relative importance of the *Issues,* their teaching philosophy (*Teaching Dimensions*), and whether or not their *Teaching Needs* are satisfied, leads them to make a *Choice.* The *Choice* may be to stay in one teaching modality, to avoid teaching online, or to leave the teaching profession altogether. Education institution administrators interested in online education have the ability to manipulate some of the variables that affect teacher's choice, resulting in increased willingness to accept online teaching assignments and increased quality of the overall educational process.

Several categories of people stand to benefit from the information contained in this book. Some of them are the teachers themselves; others are the course developers; the educational technology specialists; the school administrators; and last but not least, the students or anyone else interested and questioning this new area of development in the field of education. The teachers who are teaching online, or those considering doing it, would benefit from reading the findings of this report, because it is based on information shared by other teachers who have already experienced online teaching. In a similar manner, course developers could benefit from the insight provided by the online teachers to produce courses that take into account the shortcomings of the technology used for delivery. Educational technology specialists could stand to learn from the experiences of teaching online through better being able to identify new potential directions for research and technology development as well as for educational systems that are more user friendly, and that support rich media interfaces.

Implications and Recommendations

In the process of education, the online environment brings together teachers, students, and educational institutions staff such as school administrators, curriculum and course developers, technology specialists, and support staff. There is already ample published research that centers on the views, expectations, and performance of the online students. What makes this book special is that it focuses on the details of the process of teaching online through the eyes of the teachers. The following sections will focus on these constituencies and suggest possible implications that can be derived from the lived experiences shared by online teachers.

Implications for Educational Administrators

The theory presented in the previous chapter is of immediate interest to school administrators and institutions that offer online courses, because it can be used to explain, predict, and understand online teachers' reactions as well as help the teacher-selection process with the goal of reducing teacher turnover. A subset of the theory of the online teaching experience will be used as an example.

Schools and educational administrators are interested in outcomes related to online education; while the main desirable outcome may be financial, they need faculty to teach the online courses the school intends to offer. This translates into two desirable outcomes: *Online Teaching Workforce Adequacy* (having enough teachers with the right skills to offer the courses needed), and *Online Teaching Quality* (having teachers perform well enough that online courses are viewed by stakeholders as being good).

For *Online Teaching Workforce Adequacy*, immediate causes are the *Choice* made by teachers (i.e., their *Willingness to Accept Online Assignments*), and the *Teacher's Possession of Necessary Skills*. For *Online Teaching Quality*, immediate antecedents are *Adjustments, Teachers' Possession of Necessary Skills, Teacher/Assignment Fit*, and *Motivation to Teach*.

Choice is the result of the interplay among various categories in the model described earlier. The same can be stated for *Adjustments* (see Figure 1). They are affected by several variables. First, *Technology* (i.e., *Usability/Appropriateness*) and the availability of (better) technology will result in (a) an increased likelihood of teachers to accept online teaching assignments and (b) improved quality of the online teaching. These variables affect *Differences Among Modalities*, which in turn affects *Issues*. Second, *Teaching Needs* affects *Teaching* through two of its properties: (a) *Incentives, Appreciation, and Rewards* (teachers who believe they are adequately compensated and appreciated for their efforts are more likely to accept online teaching assignments), and (b) *Faculty Development* property (trained teachers are more likely to accept online teaching assignments). Third, *Teaching Demands* (i.e., *Subject Matter*) also affect *Teaching*: Teachers are more likely to accept an online teaching assignment when they believe they can effectively teach that particular subject online. In the theoretical model proposed by this book, *Teaching* is affected by *Teaching Needs* and *Teaching Demands*. *Issues* is affected by *Differences Among Modalities* and *Teaching*. In turn, *Issues* affects *Adjustments*, which affects *Choice*.

Adjustments also affects *Online Teaching Quality*. For example, *Technology* effects follow the same causal path (through *Differences Among Modalities, Issues,* and

Adjustments) to affect *Online Teaching Quality.* When teachers believe that *Technology* is appropriate, and can be used successfully to support online teaching, this increases the quality of their online teaching.

Teacher's Possession of Necessary Skills has a positive effect on *Online Teaching Workforce Adequacy,* on *Teacher/Assignment Fit,* and on *Online Teaching Quality.* It is directly affected by *Teaching Needs* (through its *Faculty Development* property). Faculty development and training results in improved teacher skills, and has a direct effect on *Teacher's Possession of Necessary Skills.* When teachers possess the necessary skills, the *Online Teaching Workforce Adequacy* is improved. Teachers who have the necessary skills tend to perform their online duties better, in effect improving *Online Teaching Quality.* In addition, this affects *Teacher/Assignment Fit.*

Teacher/Assignment Fit is affected by *Teacher's Possession of Necessary Skills* and *Teaching Demands* (through its *Subject Matter* property). In turn, it directly affects *Online Teaching Quality.* A good fit between teacher and teaching assignment improves the quality of the online teaching.

Motivation to Teach has a direct, positive effect on *Willingness to Accept Online Teaching Assignments* and on <u>Online Teaching Quality</u>. *Motivation to Teach* is directly affected by *Teaching Needs,* through its *Faculty Development* and *Incentives, Appreciation, and Rewards* properties. It is also affected by *Teaching Demands* (through its *Subject Matter* property).

Teaching Needs affects *Teacher's Possession of Necessary Skills* through its *Faculty Development* property. It also affects *Motivation to Teach* through its *Faculty Development,* and *Incentives, Appreciation, and Rewards* properties. *Teaching Demands,* through its *Subject Matter* property, affects *Teacher/Assignment Fit* and *Motivation to Teach.*

Therefore, the variables of critical interest to administrators are caused immediately by other variables. Among the variables described above, *Teaching Needs* (*Faculty Development* and *Incentives, Appreciation and Rewards*) and *Teaching Demands* (*Subject Matter*) can be manipulated by institutions and school administrators. *Technology* (*Usability/Appropriateness*) can also be manipulated and controlled by institutions in the sense of ensuring adequate technology support for the online environment. A graphical representation of the theory appears in Figure 1.

The theory presented here portrays the relational interplay among the variables of interest. It shows how the academic administrators can control some of the factors that affect the teachers' decisions of whether to teach online or not, inclining the balance towards the first one.

In order to respond to the teachers' need to teach every subject in a different way based on subject matter, the schools could research ways of how the presentation of the online course material could be individualized; the course structure, content, and delivery has to be fine tuned for each course. With regards to some teachers' need to have access to different delivery mechanisms, schools could offer a variety

Figure 1. Online teaching outcomes and antecedents

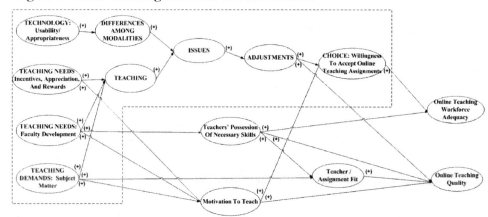

of technologies to choose from (e.g., synchronous, real-time interaction, multimedia, and simulations) to the extent this is possible. Educational institutions should invest in the appropriate technology, because too often, the technology available to teachers is a hindrance in itself.

Course design activities require a great deal of faculty time and effort. For this reason, faculty members who teach online need to be provided with adequate resources, support, flexibility to make their own changes, and training to acquire the skills that allow them to optimize course content and delivery. It is the up to the school administrators to make these resources available to their online teachers.

Another contention brought up during the research conducted for this book is that teachers must believe they can teach a course effectively online or they may refuse online teaching assignments. One way this can be addressed by educational administrators is by keeping the size of the online classes at a manageable level (e.g., 12 to 15 students) instead of 50 to 60 students, which is all to common. This would result in an improvement in the teachers' effectiveness when teaching online as well as their quality of life. The issue of student assessment ease in the online environment can be addressed through the deployment of appropriate technology by the schools, making it easier for teachers to assess and grade students online.

A great deal of attention has also to be given to faculty compensation: When teachers do not feel they are fairly compensated for their effort and for the increased amount of time that they spend engaged in online teaching activities, they may avoid teaching online courses. Any increase in time demands for the online teacher should be correlated with an increase in compensation or with other incentives and rewards. When they do an outstanding job online, teachers should be rewarded. At the present time, according to the teachers interviewed, the incentives, rewards and appreciation available to outstanding teachers seem to be lagging. To be put in unambiguous terms, more work should result in more pay.

Student quality is another factor that educational administrators can modify to ensure a successful online educational process and teacher attrition for teaching online. One suggestion may be that students should be taught how to use the technology that will be used online before enrolling in online education and should have to pass technology proficiency exams. In addition, the teachers themselves need to be offered training using modern technology, specifically the technology they will use online as well as other technology the school brings in to support future online courses. Teacher training should also cover modern classroom assessment techniques and class management.

As shown, there are a number of things that educational administrators can manipulate in support of online teachers. These include better technology choices, course design and curriculum development support, smaller online classes, improved teacher compensation and rewards, better student selection, and technology training for teachers. By addressing these issues, school administrators are able to impact the decision making process of the teachers contemplating online teaching and offer them an environment that is conducive for engaging in online teaching.

Implications for Online Teachers

Teachers who either teach online or are contemplating online teaching can prepare themselves to deal with the demands of the online environment by learning from the experiences of their colleagues, presented in this book. This subchapter presents a summary of the findings that the interviewed teachers report as both advantages and disadvantages when teaching online, based on the developed theory.

The theory presented in greater detail in Chapter XI shows that teachers reflect on their *Teaching*. They are sensitized to, and identify various issues related to teaching modalities. The interplay among *Teaching Demands* (e.g., *Expectations, Subject Matter, Class Size, Time, Interaction*, and *Effort*), *Teacher Needs* (e.g., *Rapport, Administrative, Faculty Development, Emotional Involvement*, and *Incentives/Appreciation*), *Teaching* (e.g., *Improvisation, Role, Show/Theatrical Performance*, and *Knowledge Transfer*), *Teaching with Technology* (e.g., *Synchronous, Face-to-Face, Multitasking, Reusability*, and *Flexibility*), and *Differences Among Modalities* (e.g., *Hybrid, Online*, and *Classroom*) increases their awareness of the perceived advantages and disadvantages of each teaching modality. Teachers gain an increased awareness of how online teaching affects them, of what it means for their *Teaching*. As a result of their exposure to the online environment teachers undergo changes: They make *Adjustments* in their teaching approaches, course preparation and structure, interaction style, and persona. Teachers react to the teaching environment in attitudinal terms, eventually making a *Choice*. When the *Choice* is to continue to teach, they accept and make *Adjustments* to their *Teaching* to accommodate the constraints associated with their chosen teaching modality.

There are benefits that transcend the educational modality: Face-to-face instruction can help the teacher become more sensitive to online learning, and online instruction can help the teacher to become more sensitive to mentoring students in a face-to-face situation. Another benefit is reusability, which was found to rank high with the teachers. Once they have their course materials online, it is much easier for teachers to reuse them in the on-ground classroom. Many a times, the things they learned that work online are transferred to the on-ground classroom, and vice versa.

Overall, teachers benefit from exposure to a different educational environment (e.g., online, on-ground, or hybrid) and gain additional skills and insight. They are quick to find that the online environment is quite different from the on-ground classroom. This affects them through behavioral changes, and changes in their communication style. The way they structure their courses may be different online. Some teachers do not feel they gain much from teaching online while others report a greater level of satisfaction associated with online teaching.

In general, the teachers who feel that they gain flexibility when teaching online report that there is less pressure online, in comparison to the on-ground classroom. Some teachers find the online environment as more forgiving, and more tolerant to error. Others report the opposite: a *less* forgiving environment—the result of having more structure online.

Disciplining online students is easier in these teachers' views in the sense that private communication is easier to attain when necessary. They perceive the interaction taking place online as superior, both in terms of quantity and quality. Yet, the lack of nonverbal communication cues subjects online communication to misinterpretation. Nevertheless, online, teachers report an improvement of their organization and time management skills, an increased awareness of what works online and what does not. They also report an improvement in their technology skills, and learning new ideas to try in the classroom.

One of the central issues brought up by the interviews is that teachers who teach online spend more time and effort developing materials for the online courses. They also report that time management is difficult online, where the class is open around the clock. A seeming time expansion is perceived as an advantage in the online classroom, because it results in more time for teaching. However, overall, what permeates from the interview data is that online teachers expend a greater amount of effort in their teaching, which is more time-consuming, and this affects their quality of life. Online, it just seems like time is not a factor. The teacher can cover a lot more in an online class, if the students want to. The online modality is a lot more flexible. It can be said that in the classroom, one only has the details of one book while in an online classroom, the book is the entire Internet. Time-wise, online it is a 24-hour class, so theoretically students may be afforded more time for assignments. In contrast, to other teachers, the experience of teaching online resembles *writing* a book, where there is a script to follow, one chapter at a time. The script allows for very little room for improvisation, and everything has to be scripted beforehand. Although class discussions may deviate a bit from this script and take on an unpredictable direction, they can still be tamed online.

When the interviewed educators reflect on the things they miss online, they most often refer to the emotional bond with the students. They feel that the emotional involvement is reduced online, leading to a lower quality of interaction. Other things some teachers report they feel they have to give up are teaching flexibility, personal time, sense of control, and feedback quality and quantity. In reaction to the online environment, teachers make adjustments, like changing the format of the course to adapt the materials to the different modality.

The teachers who teach "by example" may find that, online, the richness of the media is lacking. In their teaching process, they may have to repeat the same thing a couple of times, when the most efficient way would be to just be there in person, like in the on-ground classroom, where the teacher does not move on until he or she sees that the students had mastered or understood the steps. To be truly effective, the online teacher has to find a real substitute for being able to draw something on the blackboard and talk about it. He or she has to find a substitute for having people look at the information in real time and being able to get their reactions, their questions, and explain it. Teachers say that they are missing the visual portion when teaching online. A truly multimedia environment would correct this, helping people get involved a little bit more. However, the asynchronous communication tools in use today are somewhat of a constraint. Bridging the gap between the on-ground and the online classroom experience would help improve interaction significantly.

With regards to course subject, it has been determined that some subjects can be taught online extremely well (e.g., literature, languages, critical thinking) while others, like biology, chemistry, and sports, are difficult to teach online. The same may apply to programming, statistics, or math courses. In some respects, it all depends on the teacher, as anything that requires drawing on the board or working a problem on the board is difficult to accomplish online. It is more complicated to engage in "show and tell" when teaching online: While the entire solution or diagram can be provided to students up front, it does not seem to work out the same way it does in the on-ground classroom.

Those teachers who value rapport with their students are most likely to encounter difficulties online, where building relationships takes on a new dimension: There is less potential for building rapport online. The quality and quantity of the interaction taking place online is important to teachers. When they feel the interaction is inadequate, they are more likely to find they are less effective in their teaching and consequently more inclined to avoid the online environment. For those teachers who thrive on the energy in the classroom, the online environment is not a desirable option. They would find it very difficult to emulate the same level of energy they readily find in the on-ground classroom.

At times, some teachers engage in improvisation and informative entertainment. For those teachers who consider teaching to be more like a theatrical performance—the so-called sage on the stage described by Paris (2000)—they will find that is more difficult to perform online. Then, teaching online may feel strange at times for some teachers, because online students must be constantly reminded of deadlines and of the assignments that are due. The teacher has to keep on the students, and constantly pursue them, and remind them.

Online, there is an increased clarity in the course materials, and in class presentations. The amount of structure varies, from less to mainly more structure. The timing of the information preparation requires that all requirements are specified up front. Again, the scripted nature of the online course brings about more structure. In a way, the online course resembles a book; yet, a book is linear, and makes it difficult to accommodate different learning styles if the teacher follows the book strictly. Online, there are many more degrees of freedom, which can help accommodate different type of learners. Consequently, the online environment makes for added flexibility as well as complexity and increased difficulty. However, not all participants perceive this flexibility in the same way, as was discussed in previous chapters.

The environment commonly used for online education is asynchronous, and that is great in many respects, yet it does not work the same for everyone, students and teachers alike. There is a need for some level of synchronous communication (interaction) online. Often, online teachers talk about augmenting their online courses by using telephone conferences, instant messaging, Web cams, and scheduling online office hours.

A majority of online teachers seem to view a hybrid education modality as the ideal one. Teachers would like having technology tools that would allow them to move seamlessly back and forth between synchronous and asynchronous communication online. The use of interactivity, when designed properly, leads to a very rewarding learning opportunity: Human feedback is the element that makes or breaks a really successful online experience.

The online environment functions as a central archive where all course materials are stored, categorized, and are readily available to teachers. This repository of data and course materials makes it very easy for the teacher to reuse them in the on-ground classroom. On the other hand, this online archive may be perceived as a threat to privacy by some teachers.

Academic faculty members seem to be more aware of and to have more consideration for the online environment. Overall, teachers indicate that quality education may be achieved online. However, the outcome is heavily dependent on technology—on its availability and actual use, on careful course selection, faculty academic freedom, and student quality, among others.

All educators note the various differences among classroom, online, and hybrid modalities. Those who value face-to-face interaction are more likely to avoid teaching online, where they feel the interaction leaves a lot to be desired. Likewise, instructors who value the kind of flexibility afforded by the online environment are more likely to teach online.

Teachers' needs are a very important aspect of the process of teaching.   Their personal needs drive their expectations and lead to certain outcomes, such as satisfaction, personal growth, and development. The technology just mediates the teaching experience. With regard to the instructors' emotional needs, they need the interaction with students and seek to build rapport with their students. Teachers enjoy receiving and need the feedback they get in class. This helps them monitor the class and manage the learning experience in general. Online, as most teachers indicate, they have to work harder to attain a reasonable amount of feedback and be able to monitor student learning.

Good writing skills are very desirable and most valuable to a teacher who teaches online, because online education relies in large measure on written communication. Knowledge of the subject matter is also very important. So are communication skills and a caring personality, organization skills, training in teaching, an open mind, a genuine desire to help people, and being a people's person. Those teachers who do not have these qualities may find themselves unsatisfied by their online teaching experience.

The results of the study that led to this book warrant the suggestion that the educators who prepare to teach online are to acknowledge that differences exist, and flexibility will be needed. They need to hone their time-management and organization skills and improve their writing skills. They can expect to need more discipline, both for their own teaching as well as to keep their students on schedule. When designing their course materials, instructors should also have in mind that online education has the same ultimate goal as the traditional one, which is information/knowledge transfer; the difference is the change in the medium. For this, if the technology is lacking, a hybrid modality may be needed to compensate for the lack of face-to-face interaction, to ensure good teacher-student communication, and to ensure that teachers' needs are met, especially for the courses that are more difficult to be taught online.

Implications for Course Developers

Course developers strive to constantly improve the courses they design in order to facilitate the learning and teaching processes. This section tries to exemplify how some of the concerns and issues expressed by this study's participants can be addressed by course developer professionals, in order to improve the online educational process.

The theory presented in detail in Chapter XI shows that teachers reflect on their *Teaching*. Individualizing and applying the theory to show the connection to the course design and course developers, the following reasoning follows: The explicit factors related to *Teaching Demands* (e.g., *Subject Matter*, *Effort*, and *Time*) and *Teaching Needs* (e.g., *Course Design,* and *Faculty Development*), and the implicit ones associated with the *Teaching Dimensions* category are at the core of their experience. Teachers gain an increased awareness of how online teaching affects them, of what it means for their *Teaching*, and eventually will make a *Choice*. When the *Choice* is to continue to teach, they accept and make *Adjustments* (e.g., *Giving Up* and *Gaining*) to their *Teaching* in order to accommodate and compensate for, among others, course materials and course structure.

Offering greater support for course development through the inclusion of curriculum and course developers would answer one of the instructors' grievances that they are spending too much time and effort when they are alone in creating the materials for online courses. In this study, most interviewed participants indicated that they would like to receive greater support for developing the courses. These professionals, who are not only subject matter experts but have also been trained in the use of technology for online education, are ideally positioned to assist the teachers in the task. It is an added plus when these instructional designers are also educators, and not only technology experts.

With regard to the issue of the available technology not appropriately supporting teaching, a better fit between subject matter and the technology used to support online teaching would be very desirable and would solve the problem. This can be accomplished through careful analysis and screening of the courses and subject matters that are selected to be taught online.

While there is more time for teaching online, educators indicated difficulties managing time online, where the class is open around the clock. They also find they expend a greater amount of effort in teaching and that the online environment is more time-consuming, affecting their quality of life. Course developers must help find solutions to these problems faced by online teachers, because better formatted courses would lead to easier, less time consuming teaching, hence improve the teachers' quality of life.

Instructors are of the opinion that a course taught in different modalities needs to have its own testing strategies, fine tuned for the specific educational environment the course is being taught in. Student assessment, in particular, was found by our subjects to be more difficult to conduct online. One of the reasons was that there is less feedback online: A good teacher explores the communication cues present in voice and body language, and these only come out in real time, in the traditional form of classroom. The "glaze"—the facial expression that people have when they are confused—is not available online. Of course, meeting in person greatly enhances the opportunities for the student to know the instructor and vice versa, which is not exactly possible to accomplish online. Yet, even a limited amount of interactive communication between the instructor and students is viewed as beneficial. Course developers are in a position to design their courses so that they compensate for these shortcomings of the online environment.

Among other changes that online teachers would welcome are curriculum changes, access to more interactive courses, and quality homework assignments. Until technology that makes it easier for teachers to grade students becomes available, it may be possible that course developers can design student assignments that are easier to grade. Numerous online teachers indicate they would welcome this as a major improvement.

Another way course developers can improve the online teaching process is by taking advantage of the online phenomena referred to by some instructors as "collective brain." As explained by our subjects, as individuals take advantage of the group, they co-create knowledge. Yet somehow, this is still more effective to happen live. One can create groups online, but the technology has not advanced to a place where one can have more than four or five people in a group and still be effective. Online interaction needs also to be stimulated by using course materials and assignments that are appropriate, appealing to students and leading to interesting discussions, facilitating the "collective brain" effect.

There are instructors who thrive on the energy associated with the classroom and note its positive impact on participants: To what extent can this be replicated online? Again, should technology become available, course developers need to fine tune the course materials they develop to make the most of the technology that is available.

Online educators know better than to use humor in the online classroom, because more often than not, messages are misinterpreted. Yet, perhaps there are solutions to this issue. Through careful design and consideration, room can be made for some humor in the online classroom, in order to accommodate the teachers who desire a softer touch to their lectures while maintaining a nonthreatening and respectful environment for all.

There are privacy concerns regarding the course materials posted online. Perhaps course developers can find ways to address the issue of who has access to the course materials online—that would include discussion threads, e-mails, and any other course communications.

The inclusion of course developers in the process of teaching online is of utmost importance in order to ensure teacher satisfaction and a successful transfer of information to the ultimate recipient, the student. A hybrid education modality, which would allow instructors to move seamlessly back and forth between synchronous and asynchronous media, bridging the online environment to the traditional classroom, seems to be ideal. Interactivity, if designed properly, leads to a very rewarding learning opportunity: For many teachers, human feedback is the one element that makes for a successful online experience.

Implications for Educational Technology Specialists

As much as technological advances found their way in the classrooms progressively over the years, some teachers feel that technology cannot capture the essence of the physical presence in the classroom. Using technology in the online education process can be difficult. Some teachers believe that online classes are inefficient, and they view the technology available as helpless.

The theory that emerged from the study, which is presented in Chapter XI, shows that teachers are exposed to *Teaching with Technology* as they use *Technology* inside and outside the classroom. *Technology* (e.g., *Availability, Technical Support, Reliability, Media Richness, Synchronous, Ease of Use,* and *Usability/Appropriateness*) takes on a new dimension in online education. Consequently, they become sensitized and notice *Differences Among Modalities*. Teachers gain an increased awareness of how online teaching affects them, of what it means for their *Teaching,* and eventually will make a *Choice.* When the *Choice* is to continue to teach, they accept and make *Adjustments* to their *Teaching* in response, among several other factors, to the characteristics of the *Technology* available to support online teaching.

Not every subject can be taught well online: Anything that involves formulas, complex calculations, step-by-step explanations, and hands-on demonstrations prove difficult to perform online. Often, the technology available for course delivery online does not seem up to task, or that is what online teachers seem to believe. In teachers' view, some of the most difficult courses to teach are software development, software programming, and mathematics. In some respects, this puts an incredible burden on the teacher. Having access to technology that would allow them to draw things and work the problem step-by-step online or perhaps record them for on-demand video streaming would appeal to these teachers.

The teachers who were interviewed appear to agree that training for skills is doable online. To support this, there is some evidence that even subjects that develop motor skills can be taught online with some degree of success. For example, there were some attempts to teach violin online using multimedia (Scherer, 2004). Nevertheless, our respondents still believe that the desired outcomes for online education are different, and therefore harder to achieve; they remain of the view that the online environment is great for material that anyone can grasp on their own. Technology specialists can help ensure an optimal fit between course content and the technology used for delivery. By working together with course developers, they can select technology solutions that maximize the potential for delivery of course materials, for on-demand synchronous communication, multimedia, and support online teaching by means of a rich media environment.

Better technology for teaching might help instructors cope with the increased demands placed on them by the online environment. As teachers spend more time and effort developing online course materials for the online courses, they would welcome technology solutions that can help them spend less time on these tasks and would give them more time for teaching.

Back to the issue of student assessment, online teachers report spending a significant amount of time on tasks related to student assessment. Typically, students participate in online discussion by posting messages to a discussion thread. The teacher must monitor these postings to ensure they are pertinent, meaningful, and contribute materially to the discussion. Online discussions may result in a large number of messages, which is directly related to class size. Often, teachers have to read through thousands of messages posted online by their students. Under the circumstances, it should come as no surprise that the teachers report they have significant difficulties reviewing large numbers of messages and assessing the quality of the comments made by each of their students. Any type of technology that can automate this process would lighten teacher's workload and lead to a more appealing work environment for online teachers.

Online, there are many more degrees of freedom, which can help accommodate different type of learners. Consequently, the online environment adds complexity and makes teaching more difficult. The asynchronous educational environment is great in many respects, yet it does not work the same for everyone, students and teachers alike. Online, the richness of the media is lacking. When teaching "by example," the teacher may have to repeat the same thing a couple of times, and the most efficient way is just to be there and see: The teacher does not move forward until he or she sees that the students mastered or understood the steps. To be truly effective, the teacher has to find a real substitute for being able to draw something on the blackboard, and talk about it; for having people to look at in real time, and get their reactions, get their questions, and explain it. There is a need for some level of synchronous communication (interaction) online. Teachers talk about telephone conferences, instant messaging, online office hours, and Web cams. For example, they would like to know when a student is logged in online, and even have access to a Web camera so that they can actually see their students, and monitor them live. These are interesting suggestions that technology specialists may consider in their designs.

Teachers report difficulties in building rapport with their online students. Meeting in person offers a great opportunity for students and instructor to get to know each other. In this sense, even a limited amount of interactive communication between the instructor and students is seen as beneficial. Teachers feel that increasing the intensity of the communication may help them build rapport with their students. The online environment in its present form is not sufficiently conducive of communication.

Some educators note that the communication between teacher and students is improved when time is allotted for office hours. Online, for example, this could be accomplished by having students log in at a time that is scheduled in advance and to ask questions and receive live answers from their teacher. Some sort of a visual or audio signal, facilitated through improved technology setup, could indicate to the teacher that a student "walked in" and is requesting assistance; such an approach would allow the teacher to control and manage his or her time.

For many years now, pedagogical precepts prescribe that students should be assigned to study groups so that they learn from each other as well as benefit from the knowledge they create as a group. Teachers indicate that while it is easy to assign students to groups, the technology they have available to support group activities is not very effective in supporting groups of more than four or five students. Further research in Online Learning Support Systems (OLSS) would help address this issue.

Instructors expect to have some control over how the course is progressing, over the class interaction. The technology supporting online teaching should provide for an appropriate degree of control the teacher could exert. The more traditional, on-ground classroom used to be—and still is, to some extent—a teacher's unchallenged domain. Online, teachers feel they are less able to control access to the classroom. For one, other people (e.g., school administrators, other teachers, and practically anyone who is given access to the online class) can observe the course yet not have to identify their presence. This raises privacy concerns that can be addressed by employing technology solutions in conjunction with administrative policies and procedures.

The subjects interviewed are of the opinion that the ideal educational environment would support varying degrees of synchronicity. Teachers indicate the media richness to be relatively low online, and they say that they are missing the visual portion that is fundamental to the traditional form of teaching. A truly multimedia environment would help get people involved a little bit more. The asynchronous communication tools in use today are somewhat of a constraint. Bridging the gap between the on-ground and the online classroom experience would help improve interaction significantly.

Generally speaking, educators use technology on a daily basis, irrespective of the teaching modality. They appreciate having access to technology that is easy to use, reliable, and that offers adequate support for the subject matter being taught. With regard to this, the instructors recognize the constraints set by the actual technology in use and adjust accordingly, by changing their teaching approach in terms of style, preparation of course materials, curriculum, and delivery method. Not all of the changes are for the better: Too often the changes made are to compensate for the shortcomings of the technologies. Some of the teachers indicate that these shortcomings are significant.

One could argue that, in the end, it is not as much what teachers have access to in terms of technology as it is how they use the technology they have available. After all, teachers use some form of technology all the time: They use computers to prepare lectures and course slides, and to grade student assignments; they use e-mail and access the Internet for research. Still, some teachers find that the current technology that they have access to is, in many ways, too basic and are of the opinion that more extensive use of multimedia technology would improve their ability to teach online.

The technology used in teaching therefore poses specific concerns. First, the availability of technology varies. Educators are concerned with the fact that access to technology is uneven. Second, they do not always have the necessary skills to use the available technology or the one they would like to use. Third, the degree of usefulness of a given technology for teaching different subjects online varies widely, not all subjects being taught well online. Fourth, the quality of the technical support available to teachers is often inadequate.

To conclude, instructors may avoid teaching online when they find the technology is not easy to use, is unreliable, or just inappropriate for supporting quality teaching. Educators who value real-time interaction are turned off by the lack of synchronous real-time interaction in the online environment and are more likely to refuse to teach online. Educational technology specialists are in a position to help alleviate some of the teachers' technology concerns. Those teachers who thrive on the energy present in the on-ground classroom have a difficult time online where this energy is inexistent or hard to notice. To the extent that the technologies used to support online education can make this energy more evident, said teachers would find the online teaching environment more appealing. Consequently, they would be more inclined to accept online teaching assignments.

Based on the theory stated in Chapter XI and individualized to the educational technology specialists, course designers, and school administrators, there are many factors at interplay in the process of teaching. Depending on how the variables in the theoretical model are maneuvered, a different outcome will be yielded. The outcome will be on a continuum between either teacher satisfaction with the process of teaching online, or dissatisfaction and avoidance of this teaching modality, or anything in between. Since teachers are key elements in the process of teaching, and the ultimate goal of any educational institution is the successful delivery of information transfer in a profitable manner, this can offer insight into what variables can be addressed in order to achieve this goal.

What to do Next: Practical Advice

This section discusses some of the constructive steps needed to improve the teachers' online teaching experiences and to create a more effective teaching and learning environment. It provides concrete actions that each audience—from administrators to teachers to course developers to IT specialists—should consider taking. The advice stems from and is based on the results of this author's research.

A Sloan Consortium (2005) report shows that an increasing number of schools view online education as a critical component of their long-term strategies; they recognize that teaching online requires more time, and 64% of them believe that online students' self-discipline is a determinant of online learning success; furthermore, they are aware that faculty members continue to question the value and legitimacy of online courses, and online education. The report states that adjunct faculty members in general are more likely to teach online courses than on-ground (18% vs. 13%). However, for the time being, full time faculty members continue to teach more courses than the adjuncts: Full-time faculty at public schools reportedly taught 61% of the on-ground and 74% of the online courses, while adjunct faculty taught 8% and 9%, respectively. At private schools, the percentage of adjuncts teaching online courses is higher: overall, the private, for-profit schools report the largest percentage of adjunct faculty teaching online—37% (Sloan-C-Resources, 2005). Is this an indication of the for-profit schools being under pressure to maintain profitability? This is what the teachers interviewed for this book suspect.

With regard to teaching modality, most educational institutions appear to prefer online courses over blended courses (Sloan-C-Resources, 2007). For undergraduate education, the online and blended course penetration rates are 62% and 52%, respectively; for graduate education, the figures are 65% and 55%, respectively. It is no surprise then that only 38% of respondents participating in the Sloan (2007) study view blended courses as more promising than online courses. Where offered, blended courses are a valid, stand-alone modality and not just a stepping stone to offering online courses, used to transition to online (Sloan-C-Resources, 2007). In contrast, the teachers this author interviewed expressed a strong preference for the hybrid, or blended, modality.

The impetus toward online education is most evident, thus the natural concern for improving its quality and the quality of the associated teaching experience. Throughout this book, the teachers who were interviewed bring forth numerous issues relative to their online teaching experiences. They describe the kind of improvements they see as valuable and the changes they believe would lead to improving their online teaching. However, one must keep in mind there is a difference between the needs and wants that are expressed by these teachers.

For many of these teachers, the hybrid class is the preferred modality of teaching. In saying that, a number of questions still loom: How can we set up a hybrid class that meets their needs? How does one best handle students that are geographically far apart when setting up live meetings? Perhaps the solution is to allow them to use video conferencing and schedule these video-meetings periodically, while all along preserving the online environment's temporal flexibility yet allowing for some degree of synchronous interaction among teacher and students. The education institutions' administrators are the decisive force that can make these a reality, and bring needed improvement to online teaching.

Table 1. What teachers would like to change, and who can help

	Who can help		
Issue	**Administrators**	**Course developers**	**Technology specialists**
Syllabus; curriculum changes	X	X	
Train on how to use technology	X		X
Pay; rewards; other compensation	X		
Match subject matter to technology		X	X
Privacy	X	X	X
More work; time control	X	X	X
Interaction; feedback		X	X
Course development support	X	X	X
Unrealistic expectations	X		
Student quality; technology competency	X		
Class size	X		
Better technology			X
Video; multimedia; synchronicity; chat		X	X
Reliability			X
Manage growth better	X		
Grading/assessment tools; deadlines		X	X
More hybrid classes	X		
Training in teaching methods	X		
Greater institutional support	X		
Minimal technology requirements	X		
Entrance requirements	X		
Online office hours; videoconferences	X		X
Establish rapport			X
Online collaboration tools			X

As for suggesting that administrators pay attention and try to meet the teachers' needs, this, just like online teaching in general, is in many regards a trial-and-error process. As the online educational modality continues to evolve, the models used in decision making have to be constantly revised. For the teachers who were interviewed, there are many things that should be changed. When asked to identify aspects of online teaching that need improvement, these teachers listed a significant number of issues. The most important ones are presented in Table 1. Those who can help address them are the educational institution administrators, course and curriculum developers, and information technology (IT) specialists.

Advice for Educational Administrators

One element of interest to school administrators would be advice to help them choose online instructors. Educational institutions' administrators should focus on hiring the right teachers—those who have the potential to become great online teachers.

What are the qualities these teachers should have? How do we choose people to teach online? The ideal online teacher is one who is characterized by passion, and empathy for the students; knowledge of the subject matter; good communication skills, good writing skills, organizational skills, and time management skills; technology skills; patience and the ability to mentor students; and last but not least, having good students can make a world of difference.

In addition, such teachers would have a solid technical background, to the effect they can act as the first line of support for the students. Oftentimes, online courses are taught by whoever is available to teach them when in fact we should choose a teacher who has the necessary (teaching and technical) skills and appropriate training. A possible approach to selecting online teachers would rate them along several dimensions. In Table 2, there are five dimensions that are rated on a scale from 1 to 5. While the maximum score is 25, a potential hire should score at least a 3 in each of the five categories before further consideration is given.

Table 2. Online teacher selection tool

Skills / Traits	Score (1-5)
Passion; Empathy; Patience; Desire/ability to mentor	
Subject matter knowledge	
Communication skills; Writing skills	
Organizational skills; Time-management skills	
Technology skills	

Once selected for online teaching, these teachers must be offered training in modern teaching methods that are appropriate for the online environment and in online class assessment techniques. Other types of training offered should focus on using the existing course technology and on IT in general, as well as on organizational and time management skills.

Since online teachers spend more time teaching, they must be compensated accordingly. This involves money, rewards, recognition, sensible course load, and compensatory free time. Another important contribution administrators can make is to foster sense of community, of belonging for these online teachers by encouraging the formation of peer communities (online or offline). Such communities could provide resources to support less experienced online teachers by allowing them access to other online teachers, to mentors, to archived course materials, and to other resources that may help them. If nothing else, it would give them a place to vent off!

As for the online classes, it is important to keep them at a manageable level, somewhere between 12 and 15 students. In addition, all online students should pass technology competency tests and have to meet technology prerequisites. They should be screened to make sure they are in fact well equipped to thrive online: They are motivated, self-disciplined, and have good organizational and time management skills.

Last but not least, educational institutions administrators must manage everyone's expectations, including students and teachers. It is important to ensure the expectations are reasonable, are clearly communicated, and understood by the online education participants. Manage everyone's expectations; spell them out clearly, upfront. And remember, many teachers believe that the hybrid modality is better. Consider offering this type of courses.

Advice for Online Teachers

Online teachers or those considering teaching online are well advised to take into account the differences brought about by the different teaching modality. When teaching online, they have to contend with an increased degree of formality, a different type of interaction, various demands and expectations, and teaching approaches—all mediated by technology.

The increased level of formality that characterizes online education requires teachers to hone their communication skills. In particular, having good writing skills, and typing skills are most important. The reliance on written communication poses additional constraints in that everything has to be described in writing, even things teachers are used to demonstrate hands-on in on-ground classes. Nevertheless, as technology improves, there is hope for bringing in additional multimedia resources and synchronous communication that may help reduce the reliance on written communication.

In order to be able to deal with the different type of interaction present online, teachers must arm themselves with lots of patience. Not only do they have to be responsive to students' e-mails, they must also learn how to induce interaction, and to foster collaboration among their students. In addition, the time lag associated with the online interaction is a problem for some teachers. While there is also a perceived lack of control over the online learning experience of the students; in fact, regarding how the online course is progressing, the time delay issue is perhaps the most daunting. It is akin to driving a car: When steering the wheel to the left, the car will turn to the left. In contrast, control in the online environment arguably exhibits the characteristics of a really large ship: To steer it, one starts turning the wheel, yet it may take several minutes for the ship to start turning. Clearly, there will be some people who are better of driving the car, and not the ship, if they cannot handle the delay in steering the ship.

The online classroom can feel empty at times. Students and teachers alike can get very lonely online. It is very important that online teachers avoid being isolated from their peers; thus, the value of having a support mechanism that includes peer access and other resources. It also helps to develop partnerships with curriculum developers and education technology specialists, who can help address many of the concerns raised by teachers. Optimal design of an online course requires expertise in multiple areas, hence the value of a multidisciplinary team approach.

As for controlling the class interaction and the direction of the course, teachers must accept that, online, they often find themselves on the sidelines, no longer at the center of the class. In addition, they must learn how to become facilitators rather than continue to function as knowledge disseminators—as gatekeepers. Ultimately, they must learn to give up on some of the control they are used to exerting in the on-ground classroom.

Knowledge of the subject matter is, of course, very important. It is unlikely that two teachers will teach a course exactly the same way. However, it is important to determine whether the subject being taught is a good candidate for the online environment. Not every subject can be taught well online, as evidenced throughout this book. Nor will every teacher feel comfortable teaching online.

A creative use of the available course technology is strongly encouraged. Each teacher may have a different take on what it works online, and on possible work-arounds to their problems. Thus, training in the use of the technology that supports the online course is very valuable. One must keep in mind also that oftentimes the teacher is, nolens volens, the first line of technical support: Students often bring their technology-related complains to their teacher first, before contacting the regular help desk.

It also helps having good organizational and time-management skills. The materials used online must be prepared in detail ahead of time, and this requires a great deal of effort. It helps to be organized; to archive all course materials electronically, so that they are available for later use. As online teaching can be quite time consuming; contending with the numerous demands imposed on the online teacher is no trivial job. Maintaining a healthy balance between work and personal life can be challenging at times. Those teachers who arm themselves with a great deal of patience, have a genuine interest in helping others learn and succeed, and try to keep an open mind will find that online teaching can be a very rewarding experience. This being said, one must also understand that online teaching is not for everyone. Remember that not every teacher will be able to learn new things; not everyone will be successful online. Nevertheless, it could work—therefore you are encouraged to try it out. As long as you will continue to focus on the student, there is a good chance that your online teaching experience will have positive connotations.

Advice for Course Developers

Course and curriculum developers play an important role in the selection of courses, course materials, and course format and structure. Given that online everything is filtered through technology, it is very important that these subject-matter experts develop an appreciation of the issues associated with online teaching. They are instrumental in ensuring a proper fit between the subject matter and the technology that supports the online course, the structure and "flow" of the course, and the various student assessment, grading, and testing artifacts.

A course developer who is also trained as a teacher will have a better appreciation of the difficulties awaiting the online educator. As this book shows, there are numerous challenges that the online teacher has to contend with. Furthermore, training course developers on the various aspects of the technology used for online education gives them a better understanding of how the technology that is available to them can be used to optimally support a given online course. In this vein, they must ensure that the choice of teaching a subject matter online is appropriate and that the course objectives can be adequately addressed in an online delivery model. This means ensuring the technology fits the course and vice versa. Certain things can be taught better on-ground while other things are more suitable for online; therefore, we must teach on-ground those things that cannot be taught appropriately online. Hence the growing appeal of the hybrid course.

In developing the assessment components of the online course, course developers need to work with the online teachers to identify what works; teachers' workload can be dramatically reduced when the homework assignments (grading and testing included) are clearly defined and presented to students. To put it in layman's terms, the online courses need to have assignments that are easier to grade. Furthermore, teachers should be afforded a degree of flexibility in modifying the format and content of the student assignments. In many institutions, this relative freedom is limited.

The design of the online course materials must take into account the different type of interaction that takes place online. As students often build a relationship with a book rather than the instructor, it is important to develop and select course materials that will engage students. At the present time, much of the learning taking place online centers on student teamwork, on learning teams. For this reason, the course materials must be appropriate for group study and encourage student collaboration and knowledge discovery.

By some accounts, course developers should learn to be teachers first and course developers next. Whatever the case may be, they are an important group of stakeholders in online education. Where they are successful in their efforts to tame technology and manipulate the format and content of the online course materials, the result is a better learning experience for the students and a better teaching experience for the online teacher.

Advice for Educational Technology Specialists

The educational technology specialists are the experts who know all there is to know about what the technology deployed by the school can do and about how it works. It is only natural that they play an important role in improving the online teaching experience of the teachers. When these technologists are trained in teaching methods, they gain an appreciation of what teachers do; they have a better perspective on how technology and teaching intersect. In addition, they also need training in course development so that they can see first hand how the technology is or can be used.

The online teachers point to various things that have a negative effect on their teaching, and their effectiveness as teachers. One area where educational technology specialists shine is informing course developers, education institutions' administrators, and teachers, of the possibilities, as well as the limitations of the technology available to support an online course. They are the ones who can really fit technology to a course, and make the most of the tools available for online course delivery. Often, teachers call for having access to both asynchronous as well as synchronous communication mechanisms: The experts can help set up online chat, video streaming, messaging, and other multimedia solutions that can help increase the richness of the communication media in place.

One of the ongoing concerns related to online teaching pertain to student interaction, and collaboration: Teachers would appreciate having access to technology that supports collaboration, as they find it difficult to encourage and foster student interaction online. The technological solutions deployed should support Learner-to-Learner (L2L) collaboration; it should support study groups in their quest for knowledge. Equally important, the technology choices should take into account that online students tend to multitask. This is quite a common occurrence in the online classroom, and we are well advised to try and capitalize on this behavior.

By making available better grading and assessment tools (software) the teachers can use, technology specialist can help address some of the workload issues and time demands that frustrate online teachers. Often, the online teacher has to review thousands of messages and student postings. There is an obvious need for technology that can help evaluate both the quantity and quality of these communications, and help teachers assess student performance.

The goal shared by the constituencies identified in the beginning of this section is to improve the online teaching experience; to improve online education in general. This requires a collective effort to truly integrate communications technologies into education processes. Given the complexity of the components involved, a multidisciplinary approach is needed. This is predicated upon teamwork to ensure that the technology properly meshes with online teaching, and online education.

Future Trends

This book shows that teachers react to the teaching environment in emotional and attitudinal terms. As per the theory of the online teaching experience presented in Chapter XI, teachers make an educated decision whether to teach online. Administrators of educational institutions may consider better ways to allocate resources so that teachers improve their views of online teaching and become increasingly attracted to teaching online. Curriculum and course developers benefit from having a better understanding of what teachers experience teaching online. Last but not least, the technologies used to support online education can be improved. The ideas presented in the book can be further refined in subsequent studies.

Educational institutions are large organizations that foster their own organizational culture. One possible avenue for research would be to study the effect induced by the organizational culture on the online teacher. Other possible research directions would relate to decision-making and academic freedom, in the context of online education. Yet another avenue for research would be to expand the study to include a larger sample of faculty members from a larger number of educational institutions. Additional studies might help provide a better understanding of how teachers view online teaching, and of the adjustments they make in reaction to their online teaching experiences.

Conclusion

A good theory that explains online teaching helps modify the way teachers are placed in the online classroom. It also helps predict, control, and understand on-line educators' reactions. By improving the instructor selection process, it reduces turnover and assists the overall professional development process. A theory of the online teaching experience provides an improved understanding of how teachers might use online tools to enhance their teaching. It may provide an explanation of why some teachers do not teach online and how the technology used in education affects their teaching. In addition, it may help predict teachers' reactions relative to online teaching.

The contents of this book are the results of a rigorous study that employed an ex-ploratory, qualitative research paradigm. This study resulted in a theoretical model of the online teaching experience. The theory applies specifically to the research participants. Ten constructs and their relationships are at the core of the theory that emerged from interview data. In the realm of institutional administrators involved in online education, the theory described in this book offers insight as to what variables can be manipulated and controlled in order to entice teachers to accept online teaching assignments and to help improve the overall quality of the online education.

The findings may be relevant to teachers involved in online teaching and to admin-istrators supporting online education, to course developers, and educational tech-nology specialists. Variations in other institutions and online programs may exist, and subsequent operationalization of the study at different sites or with a different sample may lead to other results.

The material presented in this book offers a valuable view on what teachers think about online teaching. Whether one agrees or not, online education is here to stay. The more that is learned about the factors affecting online teaching, the more successful this activity can become. The conclusion of this book is that teaching online can be further enhanced and improved for the benefit of students, teachers, educational institutions, and society at large. One component that can help online education reach its full potential centers on the design, teaching, and technology support of the online courses. This requires a multidisciplinary approach and teamwork among teachers, course developers, technology specialists, and school administrators. Only by getting everyone involved will we be able to ensure an optimal fit between an online course and the technology that supports it.

Teaching "is a noble undertaking fraught with weighty responsibilities" (Berkowitz, 2007, p. A19). Teachers need all the help they can get in order to continue doing an excellent job. While at times the challenges may seem overwhelming, there is hope: Things are slated to get better as technology continues to improve and as we learn how to teach better online.

References

Berkowitz, P. (2007, October 8). Ethics 101. *The Wall Street Journal, CCL,* A19.

Paris, D. C. (2000). Is there a professor in this class? In R. A. Cole (Ed.), *Issues in Web-based pedagogy* (pp. 95-110). Westport, CT: Greenwood Press.

Scherer, B. L. (2004, December 30). Bowing to technology: Fiddling in cyberspace. *The Wall Street Journal, CCXLIV,* D8.

Sloan-C-Resources. (2005). *Growing by degrees: Online education in the United States, 2005.* Retrieved September 1, 2007, from http://www.sloan-c.org/publications/survey/pdf/growing_by_degrees.pdf

Sloan-C-Resources. (2007). *Blending in: The Extent and promise of blended education in the United States.* Retrieved September 1, 2007, from http://www.sloan-c.org/publications/survey/pdf/Blending_In.pdf

Appendix A

Grounded Theory:
Methodology

Introduction

Appendix A presents the methodology of the research used for this study. It includes the research design, sampling, data-collection methods and procedures, data analysis, and validity issues. The most important consideration in the design of the study was the author/researcher's interest in exploring the experience of teachers involved in online postsecondary education and his personal agreement with the qualitative paradigm of inquiry.

Background

This book builds on a study that set out to explore the teachers' experiences in the online environment, with a focus on the experience of teaching online. The research follows the qualitative inquiry paradigm and grounded theory methodology for answering the research questions posed.

The theoretical perspective is suited to explore the views of the participants and is therefore adequate for the purpose of this study. The researcher follows closely the principles and methods of grounded theory, from simultaneous data analysis and theory development to inductive analysis and constant comparison of the emerging theory across constructs derived from data (Strauss & Corbin, 1990, 1998).

The goal of grounded theory is to provide a framework used for theory generation. Grounded theory is concerned with generating theory following a meticulous, scientific approach. The goal is not to verify theory. Rather, it is to make sure the theory was generated following a methodological approach. As such, its purpose, procedures, sampling, and results are different.

Research Methodology

Grounded Theory

Grounded theory as a qualitative method involves theoretical sampling, constant comparison analysis, data coding (open, axial, selective), and memos. It is a method for building theory inductively, through a process of systematic coding and analysis. The theory is "grounded" in data, is integrated, consistent, and close to data (Charmaz, 1994; N. K. Denzin & Lincoln, 2000; B. G. Glaser & Strauss, 1967; Strauss & Corbin, 1998). A theory, in general, must explain something that is not well known. A formal theory is one that is developed for a formal conceptual area. In contrast, a substantive theory is one that is developed for a substantive area. It fits a certain reality and is relevant to a specific context (Barney G. Glaser & Strauss, 1995).

A good grounded theory is applicable to the substantive area of research; it provides an understanding that makes sense within the context of the study; it is abstract enough yet it includes sufficient variation so that it is applicable to other contexts related to the phenomenon; it aims at providing a degree of control over the phenomenon studied. Grounded theory is useful and appropriate for creating a substantive, mid-range theory that has explanatory utility (Strauss & Corbin, 1990).

In grounded theory research, data collection and analysis take place simultaneously. Data are coded into categories in a systematic, rigorous yet flexible approach. The researcher interprets the categories and evolves them into broader concepts. Through constant comparison, the concepts and categories are continually revised against the data. Characteristics of the data, category dimensions and relationships are (re)evaluated until no new meaning can be derived from the data. It is at that point that the study ends. The theory emerges from the research, at each of the steps (N. K. Denzin & Lincoln, 2000).

Grounded theory emphasizes inferences that result in a good explanation of the behavior observed. The rich details, well grounded in data, are useful in predicting human behavior. In an inductive manner, grounded theory arrives at hypotheses following an iterative, incremental approach that starts with collection of raw data, which is then coded qualitatively, to yield an initial theory. The major variables emerge from this preliminary coding, and lead to new questions; new data are collected and coded. Thus, theory generation involves a constant comparison with the new data collected. The theory matures with the integration of the data elements and the relationships identified.

Theoretical sampling is the term used to describe the data-collection process that involves collection, coding, and the analysis of data, with the researcher determining what data to collect next in order to develop a theory (Barney G. Glaser & Strauss, 1995). In Glaser's view, theoretical sampling is at the core of grounded theory research. Theoretical sampling is defined as:

the process of data collection for generating theory where the analyst jointly collects, codes and analyzes his data and decides what data to collect next and where to find them in order to develop the emerging theory, whether substantive or formal. The initial decisions for theoretical collection of data are based only on a general sociological perspective and on a general subject or problem area [...] The initial decisions are not based on a preconceived theoretical framework. (B. G. Glaser & Strauss, 1967, p.45)

While representative sampling seeks to gather accurate data on a sample representative of the larger population, theoretical sampling seeks to discover categories of the phenomenon studied and their relationships. The scope of theoretical sampling is determined by the researcher, based on what is needed to enrich the theory. At the point where no new categories or relationships emerge from data, the theoretical sample is "saturated." *Saturation* means the sampling is complete, and the generation of theoretical categories has been completed (B. G. Glaser, 1993).

Sampling

According to Robson (2002), sampling in grounded theory is purposive:

We do not seek a representative sample for its own sake... sampling of people to interview or events to observe is undertaken so that additional information can be obtained to help in generating conceptual categories ... the persons interviewed ... are chosen to help the researcher formulate theory. (Robson, 2002, p.193)

Purposive sampling allows for the selection of information-rich items that contribute to the overall quality of the investigation. The selection of the sample for a qualitative study typically involves small groups of people nested in their context and studied in depth. The samples are usually not pre-specified; rather, they evolve with the study. The sample should consist of respondents who are reasonably informed and knowledgeable of the phenomena being investigated. The initial choice of informers may change and lead to new and different ones (Miles & Huberman, 1994).

In grounded theory, theoretical sampling allows the researcher to choose respondents so that categories become saturated, in effect broadening the scope of the emerging theory.

According to Glaser and Strauss (1967), theoretical sampling involves the researcher engaging in data collection, coding, and analysis and deciding what data to collect next. Theoretical sampling helps maximize the opportunities to compare events and consolidate and saturate the categories (Strauss & Corbin, 1998).

For this study, the researcher used purposive sampling to achieve controlled comparison across an array of sub-contexts within the larger context of the online teaching experience. Accordingly, the primary sample involved instructors who teach both online and offline (traditional, classroom based) courses in postsecondary settings.

The population of interest for this study is teachers who teach online. Specifically, teachers that are teaching postsecondary education online, at the undergraduate or graduate level. No other specific constraints (e.g., subject matter, age, gender) were set. The only constraint was that the teachers had online experience and wanted to discus it. The population of interest was later enlarged to include teachers who taught traditional classroom-based courses yet may have either taught online, or considered teaching online. The intent was to establish a certain baseline to help evaluate and assess the online experience of the teachers.

An initial group of 57 teachers was identified, from which interview participants were selected. The researcher interviewed the teachers in person. The interviews allowed the researcher and respondents to co-research—collaborating and creating meaning together. While in quantitative research small sample sizes lead to difficulties in generalization and validation, the size of the sample is not that significant in qualitative research. The researcher engaged in qualitative research strives for balance and variety, while using his special knowledge when identifying the sample and selecting information-rich participants (Patton, 2002). The researcher's focus is on selecting a sample that is likely to produce the rich data necessary for theory development (Norman K. Denzin & Lincoln, 1998).

Procedures and Data Collection

The choice of the data-collection methods determines the type of data collected during the research. For this study, rich data were needed in order to produce a theory to explain how teachers experience online teaching. Interviews allowed for collecting the most suitable data.

Grounded theory is an emergent process that develops gradually, as the research unfolds. The researcher constantly moves among data collection, coding and analysis. Grounded in data, new categories develop and lead the researcher to ask new questions to test them. This involves an inductive process. The study proceeds in an iterative, incremental manner centered on a process of constant comparison between data and emerging constructs and theory.

The constant comparative analysis allows the researcher to identify gaps in the data. With coding and data analysis started shortly after data collection begins, the researcher strives to create a thick description of the phenomenon, highlighting meanings, motives, and processes revealed by respondents. The researcher returns to the field for follow-ups and more data collection to confirm the emerging theory and fill in the gaps found during the data analysis.

In grounded theory, the sampling process evolves during the research process. From the initial pool of potential subjects, the researcher reached out to include several more academic faculty members. The collection of data continued until all of the categories were fully developed, achieving data saturation. The sample size was not predetermined, according to the recommendations of several authors (Miles & Huberman, 1994; Patton, 2002; Strauss & Corbin, 1998). At times, a snowball approach may be used to help enlarge the sample, as the goal of the researcher is to obtain as differentiated a view as possible. Saturation occurred naturally during the progress of the study, once a specific number of interviews, 44 in this case, was reached.

Data Collection

Grounded theory relies on a process where data collection and analysis occur simultaneously. The researcher attempts to collect rich data through interaction with the respondents. Interviews allow respondents to offer their own views in an active manner (Holstein & Gubrium, 1995). Follow-up questions help clarify ideas and explain concepts identified during initial interviews. These additional questions formulated by the researcher and the subsequent interaction with the participants are instrumental in developing a theory about the phenomenon of interest (Maxwell, 1996; Patton, 1990, 2002; Strauss & Corbin, 1998).

Data-Collection Instruments

In this study the following data-collection instruments were used: interviews, field notes, and memos. Qualitative research interviews are appropriate in situations in which the focus of the study is on the meaning of a particular phenomenon, as construed by the participants (King, 1994). This was clearly the case with this study. An interview protocol was prepared and used for conducting each interview. The interviews were recorded using a digital audio recorder.

Interviews

Data were collected through in-depth, phenomenological interviews (Gubrium & Holstein, 2002; Van Manen, 1990). The interviews contain predetermined open-ended questions that have a defined wording and sequence. The questions were presented in the same order to all respondents (Patton, 2002). Strauss and Corbin (1998) suggest that the initial interview questions or area of investigation may be supported by literature. The literature review helped the researcher prepare the initial interview questions. Data were collected from the interviews using codification techniques. The informers were asked to talk about their online and offline experience—about their "in-situ" experience.

Before the interviews were conducted, confidentiality assurances were provided to respondents. All the interviews followed the same interview protocol. As suggested by Fowler (1995), the interview protocol was tested in a pilot allowing for its refinement and for increasing the researcher's sensitivity. The pilot involved interviews with four online teachers for the purpose of testing the interview protocol and refine the formulation of the interview questions. The interview pilot took place informally, as the researcher met other teachers at different occasions and sites during the fall of 2004.

Consistent with Seidman's (1998) model, each participant was to be interviewed several times. The intent of the first interview was to provide a context for understanding the participant's perspective. The interview focused on the participant's academic career, particularly on the online teaching experiences. The researcher focused on the concrete details of the participant's experience teaching online. The subsequent interviews were follow-ups to seek clarification of specific points brought up during prior interview(s).

The researcher relied on an interview protocol to ensure that the interviews followed a generic structure. The interview protocol helped the researcher stay focused on the issue he wanted to explore while allowing the freedom to explore, in depth, the thick descriptions provided by the respondents. Each interview was expected to last between 60 and 90 minutes in order to allow for establishing rapport between the researcher and the respondents and for detailed, intricate descriptions of the experience to emerge. The interviews started with nonthreatening questions that allowed the researcher to build rapport with the respondents. The use of open-ended questions allowed the participants to provide rich reports of their experiences. The researcher remained in control throughout the interview and followed through the interview protocol with rigor. Still, he adapted to each interview style and used follow-up questions to further probe for rich data. The ordering and wording of the questions were not changed from one interview to the next.

The interview questions were constructed based on the researcher's prior personal communications with online faculty members. What started as a vague inquiry into the online education realm led gradually to a set of themes that seemed to reoccur across the discussions. The questions were further refined to avoid any possible threatening formulation based on the findings from the interview pilot.

Field Notes

The researcher created handwritten yet copious field notes during the interviews. The field notes were used to record the account of the process. They include descriptions of settings, people, events, and activities together with personal comments, reflections, and ideas for further investigation. Mental notes made during interviews were written on paper immediately after each interview.

Memos

Memos written by the researcher during coding helped document germane views and ideas in the interviews. Memos allow the researcher to document the thinking about data and expand on the codes by providing descriptions, comparisons, and analyses. They help the researchers grasp the complexity of the data, refine categories and potential relationships, and highlight possible gaps that need further investigation (Charmaz, 1994). The very nature of the theoretical sample used in grounded theory requires the researcher to be sensitive to gaps in data. Data gaps require the researcher to return to the field to seek clarification. The memos offer an ideal format for documenting these travails.

After each interview, the researcher took the time to review the audio recording and began to reflect on what was discussed by the participants. He wrote memos describing his reflections and the emotions, reactions, and meaning that could be identified from the interview. Emerging concepts and themes, and possible relationships were documented in the memos.

Data Analysis

The researcher used word-processing software (Microsoft Word[1]) to transcribe the interviews, which were recorded on a digital recorder (Panasonic[2] RR-US360). The recordings were converted to Windows Audio files (.wav) using Panasonic Voice Studio 2.0 voice processing software. Speech recognition software (Dragon Naturally Speaking[3]) was used for several interview transcripts. However, the relatively large amount of data required the researcher to rely on several human transcribers to help transcribe the interviews.

As the interviews were transcribed and became available for analysis, interview data were analyzed for concepts and categories. Theoretical sampling guided the data collection. The preliminary analysis of the transcripts generated a number of concepts. Those with similar characteristics were grouped in categories. For each category, properties were identified by analyzing statements associated with that particular category, as per the transcripts. Similarly, dimensions were derived for each category. Categories were developed in a flexible manner, with the only goal being to reach saturation. Several concepts emerged from discussions with the respondents. Further examination followed in order to refine and revise the initial concepts and categories.

Data were coded from the interview transcripts and research field notes. The search for patterns involved building data categories, followed by a second analysis of the interviews and field notes. Records were kept of each category. The researcher sought similarities and differences across the interviews, and used pattern coding to identify common themes. Data analyses were conducted, together with brief descriptions of the participants. The common as well as the uncommon themes identified were illustrated using quotes from the interviews. It was determined that computer software was required for the data analysis and to help manipulate what was expected to be a large amount of data collected in the study. The researcher selected the ATLAS.ti[4] software (version 5) for analyzing the data obtained during the course of the study.

One important rule the researcher observed throughout the study was to be careful not to ignore or discard data that might run contrary to initial expectations. Consequently, when the researcher came across data that did not appear to fit comfortably in the emerging categories for analysis, the data were neither ignored nor discarded; rather, the emerging categories were revised, in deference to the constant comparison precepts at the core of grounded theory.

Coding

Data analysis was conducted according to the precepts of grounded theory. Codes emerged from the data through an interactive process where the researcher actively questioned and reviewed data. Codes and data were continuously revised to explore variations and achieve concept saturation. During the coding process, the researcher was concerned with developing an emerging theory, rather than testing it. In a creative, systematic manner, the researcher sought to identify, develop, and relate categories that became building blocks for the theory that was emerging from the data.

Grounded theory development involves three types of coding: open, axial, and selective (Strauss & Corbin, 1998). In grounded theory, coding begins immediately after the first interview, and continues in parallel with data collection.

Open Coding

During open coding, categories are identified from the data. Their dimensions are carefully evaluated, as they help establish and develop relationships. At this stage the researcher seeks to fully understand those data, through a process of constant comparisons. The researcher stays close to data. For each category, the researcher identifies properties and their respective dimensions (Strauss & Corbin, 1998).

Axial Coding

Axial coding involves assembling categories identified during open coding to allow for a more complete explanation of the phenomena to emerge. It helps to relate categories and detail their properties. It makes connections between categories and subcategories, presenting the data in new ways. At this stage categories continue to develop allowing the researcher to identify factors affecting the phenomena, contextual conditions, and outcomes, gradually evolving toward a more complex model (Strauss & Corbin, 1998).

Selective Coding

Selective coding involves selection of a number of categories that help integrate the categories and concepts. The researcher focuses on relating categories, validating relationships, and "filling in the categories that need further development and refinement" (Strauss & Corbin, 1998, p. 236). A central core category is eventually selected, which provides an explanation of the phenomenon in its entirety. Its related categories and subcategories form patterns as the analysis moves from description to conceptualization.

As concepts are validated against data, the emergent theory becomes grounded in the data. The theory is generated by linking categories, their properties and dimensions. The theory is validated against the data and presented in a narrative form that incorporates states of transition as well as intervening conditions (Brown, Stevens, Troiano, & Schneider, 2002).

Qualitative Issues and Trustworthiness of Data

The trustworthiness of findings from qualitative, flexible design research continues to be a subject of debate (Robson, 2002). Three broad categories of validity threats specific to qualitative research are reactivity, respondent biases, and researcher biases (Lincoln & Guba, 1985). Reactivity refers to the researcher's presence causing interference. Respondent bias and researcher bias refer to, among other things, assumptions and preconceptions (Robson, 2002). In order to minimize common threats to validity, certain steps were taken. First, the researcher minimized the potential for personal bias toward the subjects by seeking to interview individuals whom he had not met before. Second, the researcher considered, in detail, possible influences stemming from his life experiences. Third, by conducting multiple interviews over time and by employing multiple data-collection strategies, the researcher minimized the likelihood of any findings being due to chance.

In grounded theory, the theoretical sensitivity of the researcher, defined as the ability to recognize relevance in data and give it meaning, is important to the study. Theoretical sensitivity stems from the researcher being aware of the literature, from personal and professional experience, and through the interactions of the researcher with data throughout the study (Eason, 2000) The researcher brings theoretical sensitivity to this proposed study as follows: through an exhaustive literature review; through more than 5 years of teaching in postsecondary education; through his intimate involvement with the research study and data for the entire duration of the study.

The study includes detailed methods. The researcher verifies the accuracy of the account given. Rigorous data collection procedures are used. Data are adequately summarized and details are given about how data were collected (Robson, 2002). Grounded theorists advise that data collection must stop once no new information can be derived from the interviews. When things start to make sense, and meaning can be derived from collected data, at that point the theory is deemed to be acceptable.

Theory Development

The integration of the concepts identified during the coding phase was done by using a combined approach. The theory emerged as a storyline, vague at first, yet shaping up with each iteration. Emerging concepts were organized in a table and were continuously revised and reassessed in light of new data that was collected. The memos written by the researcher were reviewed and offered additional insight. The emerging theory was compared to the data to review internal consistency. The accuracy of the theory was ensured by the process of constant comparative analysis characteristic of grounded theory research. The emerging theory was continuously compared with the raw data. Once a suitable theory was identified, respondents were asked to confirm the theory as correct and point out possible discrepancies. This increased confirmability, and validity of the findings (Miles & Huberman, 1994).

Verification

Data saturation, where no new categories, relationships, or concepts emerge from coding, marks the point where the grounded theory has emerged. The constant comparative analysis at the core of the research design leads to a solid grounded theory (Strauss & Corbin, 1998). The researcher relies on field notes and memos to further increase the validity of the theory produced. A narrative form of the theory draws from across the multiple data-collection methods employed and is further validated with the respondents. If it makes sense, then it is a good theory. The grounded theory resulting from the study documented in this book explains teachers' experience teaching online.

Validity

Validity in the context of qualitative research centers on confirmability rather than reproducibility of the findings (Lincoln & Guba, 1985). *Confirmability* refers to validity that is associated with the particular data set. Given the same site, sample, data-collection method, and research protocol, the same findings (i.e., grounded theory) are produced. Validity increases when triangulation is used. Triangulation involves the use of multiple data-collection techniques in conjunction and leads to better findings and understandings. In this study, interview data were corroborated with field notes and memos to increase the validity of the study.

Transferability

The goal of researchers is to produce findings that are applicable to other situations that are similar to the one studied. While in general no theory will apply exactly to another context, other than the one it was originally developed for, the theory should still be broad enough to offer some applicability.

The specific data collection and analysis involved in this study ensure the study is confirmable and that a certain degree of transferability to other similar situations exists.

Strauss and Corbin (1998) emphasize the quality and quantity of the data used for creating the theory as well as the analysis involved:

If the data upon which [the research] is based are comprehensive and the interpretations conceptual and broad, then the theory should be abstract enough and include sufficient variations to make it applicable to a variety of contexts related to that phenomenon. (Strauss & Corbin, 1998, p. 23)

In order to ensure a degree of transferability, the results have to make sense to both those being studied and those practicing in the area (Lincoln & Guba, 1985).

Credibility and Dependability

According to Lincoln and Guba (1985), *credibility* refers to the description of the phenomena studied being accurate. Trustworthiness of a study is correlated with validity and transferability of the results. Furthermore, the study's settings, population of interest, sample, and theoretical framework have to be explained in detail for the study to gain credibility. Having study participants validate the findings helps lessen the chance for introducing researcher bias which is a common, significant threat.

Dependability is retained when the changes in the research design and overall conditions of the study are accounted for, and documented by the researcher. In grounded theory such dependability checks are built in by design. Namely, the constant-comparative analysis of data encourages the researcher to be responsive to the phenomenon studied. The explicit pursuit of thick descriptions pushes the researcher to review interview questions as needed and to revisit the research site and the ongoing dialogue with the theoretical sample involved (Charmaz, 1994; Strauss & Corbin, 1998).

Conclusion

The research questions explored for this book required a qualitative method. Grounded theory was selected, as it offers the means for building a substantive theory grounded in data. Data collection required interviews with participants in a theoretical sample. Coding (open, axial, selective) generated rich data, suitable for building theory. These steps are described in detail throughout this appendix. Validity, transferability, credibility, and dependability of the results of the study were discussed as appropriate.

The study that is at the foundation of this book established validity by connecting its results to the research literature. Generalizability was pursued through a number of different processes. This appendix highlights the rigorous research methodology as operationalized and the approach that was followed in order to ensure the trustworthiness of the results.

References

Brown, S. C., Stevens, R. A., Troiano, P. F., & Schneider, M. K. (2002). Exploring complex phenomena: Grounded theory in student affairs research. *Journal of College Student Development, 43*(2), 173-183.

Charmaz, K. (1994). Grounded theory: Objectivist and constructivist methods. In N. K. Denzin & Y. S. Lincoln (Eds.), *The handbook of qualitative research* (pp. 509-535). Thousand Oaks, CA: Sage.

Denzin, N. K., & Lincoln, Y. S. (1998). *Collecting and interpreting qualitative materials*. Newbury Park, CA: Sage.

Denzin, N. K., & Lincoln, Y. S. (2000). *Handbook of qualitative research*. Thousand Oaks, CA: Sage.

Eason, K. R. (2000). *A qualitative study of higher education faculty and their experiences training for, developing and teaching online courses*. Unpublished doctoral dissertation, University of Texas, Arlington, TX.

Fowler, F. J. (1995). *Improving survey questions. Design and evaluation*. Thousand Oaks, CA: Sage.

Glaser, B. G. (1993). *Examples of grounded theory: A reader*. Mill Valley, CA: Sociology Press.

Glaser, B. G., & Strauss, A. L. (1967). *The discovery of grounded theory: Strategies for qualitative research*. Chicago: Aldine.

Glaser, B. G., & Strauss, A. L. (1995). *Status passage: A formal theory*. Mills Valley, CA: Sociology Press.

Gubrium, J. F., & Holstein, J. A. (2002). *Handbook of interview research. Context and method*. Newbury Park, CA: Sage.

Holstein, J. A., & Gubrium, J. F. (1995). *The active interview*. Newbury Park, CA: Sage.

King, N. (1994). The qualitative research interview. In C. Cassell & G. Symon (Eds.), *Qualitative methods in organizational research*. London: Sage.

Lincoln, E. S., & Guba, E. G. (1985). *Naturalistic inquiry*. Beverly Hills, CA: Sage.

Maxwell, J. A. (1996). *Qualitative research design: An interactive approach*. Thousand Oaks, CA: Sage.

Miles, M. B., & Huberman, A. M. (1994). *Qualitative data analysis* (2nd ed.). Newbury Park, CA: Sage.

Patton, M. Q. (1990). *Qualitative evaluation and research methods* (2nd ed.). Newburry Park, CA: Sage.

Patton, M. Q. (2002). *Qualitative research and evaluation methods* (3rd ed.). Thousand Oaks, CA: Sage.

Robson, C. (2002). *Real world research* (2nd ed.). Malden, MA: Blackwell.

Seidman, I. (1998). *Interviewing as qualitative research* (2nd ed.). New York: Teachers College Press.

Strauss, A., & Corbin, J. (1990). *Basics of qualitative research. Grounded theory procedures and techniques*. Newburry Park, CA: Sage.

Strauss, A., & Corbin, J. (1998). *Basics of qualitative research* (2nd ed.). Thousand Oaks, CA: Sage.

Van Manen, M. (1990). *Researching lived experiences. Human science for an action sensitive pedagogy*. New York: State University of New York Press.

Endnotes

[1] Microsoft Office and Microsoft Word are U.S. registered trademarks of Microsoft Corporation.

[2] Panasonic is a registered trademark of Matsushita Electric Industrial Co., Ltd. All other product names, company names, or logos mentioned herein may be the (registered) trademark of, and are property of, their respective owners.

3   Dragon Naturally Speaking is a registered trademark of Nuance Communications, Inc.

4   The ATLAS.ti™ software is widely utilized by qualitative researchers for qualitative multi-media data analysis, document management and theory building. More information about the software is available on the Internet at http://www.atlasti.com.

Appendix B: Respondent Demographics

Respondent ID	01	02	03	04	05	06	07	08	09	10	11	12	13	14	15	16	17	18	19	20	21	22	23	24	25	26	27	28	29	30	31	32	33	34	35	36	37	38	39	40	41	42	43	44
Sex																																												
Female	X	X	X	X	X																															X		X		X	X		X	X
Male						X	X	X	X	X	X	X	X	X	X	X	X	X	X	X	X	X	X	X	X	X	X	X	X	X	X	X	X	X	X		X		X			X		
Modality																																												
All				X		X			X	X	X		X	X	X	X	X	X	X	X	X			X	X	X			X	X	X		X			X	X	X	X	X	X	X	X	X
Classroom	X						X				X					X						X									X	X				X	X							
Online			X					X															X				X		X			X		X		X								
Hybrid					X		X	X	X		X	X					X				X			X		X				X			X	X										
Age																																												
30-40							X	X	X	X	X						X										X			X					X		X							X
40-50			X		X				X							X												X			X	X	X	X				X		X	X	X		
50-60						X						X	X	X	X				X							X			X										X				X	
60+	X		X															X			X															X								
Degree																																												
Masters	X	X	X	X		X	X	X	X	X	X	X	X	X	X	X	X	X	X	X	X	X	X	X	X	X	X	X	X	X	X	X	X	X		X	X	X	X	X	X	X	X	X
Doctorate					X																														X									
Title																																												
Professor	X	X		X		X	X	X		X	X	X	X	X	X	X	X	X	X	X				X	X	X	X	X	X	X	X	X	X	X	X	X	X	X	X	X	X	X	X	X
Adjunct			X		X				X												X	X	X																					
Experience																																												
1-5						X	X	X		X	X	X	X	X																						X	X	X						
5-10	X	X							X							X	X												X						X					X				
10-15				X	X																									X	X	X									X			
15-20			X													X																X	X											
20-25																							X															X				X		
25-30																				X																		X						
30-35	X																																						X					

About the Author

Sorin Gudea lives in the Los Angeles area. An alumnus from Pepperdine University (MBA 1998) and from Claremont Graduate University (MSMIS 2004, PhD 2005), Sorin has worked in information systems for almost 20 years. At his current position with a large organization, he is involved with information technology projects.

At times, Sorin teaches technology courses in the undergraduate and graduate programs at the University of Phoenix, where he is a practitioner faculty in the College of Information Systems and Technology in the University of Phoenix's Southern California Campus.

Sorin's research interests gravitate around online education and training, information systems security economics, and knowledge management and organizational learning. He is an avid information systems researcher and has presented several papers at some of the major conferences in the field. Some of his work was published in the *International Journal of Electronic Business*, the *Journal of the AHIMA,* and *Perspectives of the AHIMA.*

Index